Women in America

FROM COLONIAL TIMES TO THE 20TH CENTURY

Women in America

FROM COLONIAL TIMES TO THE 20TH CENTURY

Advisory Editors
LEON STEIN
ANNETTE K. BAXTER

A Note About This Volume

Women played a key role in the social life of the Southern aristocracy. As this book shows in detail, they were the centers around which salons developed. They moved as gracefully in them as their French predecessors did a century earlier. They were arbiters of manners and taste, familiar with art and music, enthusiasts of fashion, practitioners of witty conversation and manipulators of plot and counterplot. This book chronicles the social conduct of Southern ruling families, lacing with gossip the accounts of courtships, romances, marriages and geneaologies in a society destined for collapse.

BELLES

BEAUX AND BRAINS

OF THE 60's

T[HOMAS] C. DE LEON

ARNO PRESS

A New York Times Company

NEW YORK – 1974

Reprint Edition 1974 by Arno Press Inc.

Reprinted from a copy in
  The University of Illinois Library

WOMEN IN AMERICA
From Colonial Times to the 20th Century
ISBN for complete set: 0-405-06070-X
See last pages of this volume for titles.

Manufactured in the United States of America

Library of Congress Cataloging in Publication Data

De Leon, Thomas Cooper, 1839-1914.
  Belles, beaux, and brains of the 60's.

  (Women in America: from colonial times to the 20th
century)
  Reprint of the ed. published by G. W. Dillingham Co.,
New York.
    1. Confederate States of America. 2. Southern
States--Social life and customs. I. Title. II. Series.
E487.D33 1974   917.5'03'3   74-3937
ISBN 0-405-06084-X

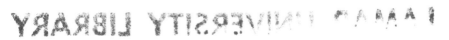

BELLES

BEAUX AND BRAINS

OF THE 60's

Faithfully yours
J. C. DeLeon

BELLES

BEAUX AND BRAINS

OF THE 60's

By T. C. DE LEON

In the land where we were dreaming.
DANIEL LUCAS

. . . . And with them Time
Slept, as he sleeps upon the silent face
Of a dark dial in a sunless place.
THOMAS HOOD

Illustrated with One Hundred and Sixty-six Portraits

G. W. DILLINGHAM COMPANY
PUBLISHERS   NEW YORK

*Belles Beaux
and Brains of the 60's.*

TO HIS
COUNTRYWOMEN
ON BOTH SIDES OF THE MYTHIC "LINE,"
WHO, IN TIME OF NEED, HAVE EVER PROVED THEMSELVES
WORTHY DAUGHTERS OF BRAVE SIRES,
THIS BOOK IS INSCRIBED BY
THE AUTHOR

IN PLACE OF PREFACE

My publishers ask for my preface. What readers I reach will thank me for having forgotten it.

It has been said that "a book without a preface is a salad without salt." Possibly: but a salad that carried with each plate a recipe for its every ingredient and condiment, might fail of digestion. The literary kitchen is not always appetizing, however dainty its perfected products may appear.

The preface is that defunct bore of Greek drama *Chorus* exhumed to interrupt the action. The book that needs that is apt to prove a pretty bad one; for the preface tells why a book is written and at what it aims. The latter is indubitably to instruct or entertain, and to sell. Should these motors be reversed?

The volume that does neither of these, without its own advice, will needs gather dust upon the trade shelves.

Decades ago when I wrote what James R. Randall named "the prose epic of the bloody Confederate drama" (Four Years in Rebel Capitals), Mr. E. L. Godkin began his *Nation* review of it with the words: "A participant's views are always the most interesting." Now I am hoping that he wore Cassandra's headgear.

In that book's preparation, thousands of names, incidents and deductions came up, which were not wholly consonant to its plan and scope. These, I have always felt, would group themselves some day; and most of my time for five years past has been given to arranging them into proper sequence and in boring thousands of old friends, for facts, dates, names—and especially for portraits, miniatures, photographs and tintypes of the blockaded-art epoch.

To these friends, one and all, a cordial acknowledgment is due for the invaluable aid given me. To list one tithe of them would be to print another volume. Suffice it to say that the faces and the facts are theirs. The comments, the statement and deductions, all my own.

Did I write a volume of preface, it would condense itself thus: I have written honestly and without fear, or favor, of people and events: and with as little of prejudice as is given to humanity.

Death and his precursor, Hymen, have been busy in very recent days, among notable people and dear old friends; causing halt for recasting many pages already typed.

"If this be treason, make the most of it!" If it be preface, forgive the solecism.

T. C. De LEON

Mobile, May 1st, 1909.

ILLUSTRATIONS

vii

ILLUSTRATIONS

ILLUSTRATIONS

ILLUSTRATIONS

CONTENTS

xi

CONTENTS

CONTENTS

CONTENTS

CONTENTS

Belles, Beaux and Brains of the Sixties

CHAPTER I

IN OLD VIRGINIA

YOUR *ante-bellum* Virginian was a rare old exclusive. His home was his altar and his family his fetich. He scarcely would have challenged the country postmaster, who refused him credit for a postage stamp, the latter not being his social equal, but he doubtless would have chastised him.

Before he was leavened by war and contact with the greater world the old Virginian may have been a trifle narrow. Friction against his fellows broadened him rarely, but at a cost that lost the world a type.

In his earliest form he was much like his contemporaneous South Carolinian, whom he "cottoned to" more cordially than to his other neighbors. Each, it was claimed by the envious, thought the sun rose behind his own proper east and set behind his western boundary line.

At this day, thanks to education away from home, travel and observation, both are citizens of a common country, properly prideful of the past, though really living in the present.

The strong red "Island Mastiff" blood of primogeniture still flows in the veins of both, but the planter's or professional life has left it perhaps less bubbling than when its ancestors came to these shores.

There was at one·time much popular clamor, rather needless

perhaps, about the overweening pride of the old Southerners. It was based on manner, in the main; the manner had reason-able origin.

LIEUT. CÓL. R. E. LEE, U. S. A., 1852.

The pride of the South had excuse in her record from Time. The Virginian and Caro-linian especially were of direct descent from the "rufflers" of Hastings and Templestowe, of Agincourt and Rochelle. They were kindred, too, in more than pride and sentiment, for the same English strain flowed in the veins of both, separating them from the Puritan English of the North, and warmed with the Huguenot flush and the dash of the Hibernian. The Washingtons, Lees, Taylors and Prestons, the Blands, Lewises, Byrds, Fairfaxes, Balls, Carters and Carys ("No mongrels, boy!" said Richelieu), had wedded "across the border," and both States had equal pride in their progress. Changed little by travel and new surroundings the Maryes, Maurys, Flournoys and Bondu-rants, the Micous, Latanés, Moncures and Maupins, were still French. They were as earnest in endeavor for the new land as later were the d'Iberville, de Bienville and Boisbriant planters of the Lilies in *La Louisiane*. The Egglestons, McGuires, Archers and Mayos proved fealty to new adherence on young soil, as had the knight of the Shamrock in the Crusades in France and in the Papal Guard. One and all, with the Cabells, Burwells, Amblers, and others living in history and song, later proved their loyalty to Virginia, as to the king they served so well across the seas.

"All Virginians are cousins," say outsiders. Marriages, cross marriages, intermarriages, mesh State pride in a tangle of consanguinity that no "Heraldry Harvey" might read. But every drop of that blood, English, Irish or French, throbs but for one spot of earth—Virginia. From the days of Smith and Jamestown, through those of Williamsburg as colony capital and seat of the oldest university, through the war that made the Colony a State and flooded her best names with a noonshine of glory, through the war that made her Richmond capital the goal of ambitious hate—through each and all the Old Dominion has been true to duty and to country. But blood is thicker than water, and she has been true to herself.

The *ante-bellum* Virginian was a great horseman. He rode to hounds as a matter of religion and was knight and courtier under gleam of my ladye's eyes. He was even more at home in the saddle than in the ballroom, and his love of horse aided other traits and circumstance to evolve later those terrifying "Black Horse" squadrons which made the names of Stuart, two Lees, Turner Ashby, John Mosby and their like as famous and feared as

MRS. W. H. CASKIE (MARY AMBLER)

was that of the Black Douglas on the Scottish border.

The Virginian was proud, but not arrogant; genial, but quick to offense. So he would pop over an antagonist from a sense of duty much as he did a turkey, or a "pa-atridge," from a sense of pleasure.

Much has been written as to his duelling habit in old times.

COLONEL JOHN S. MOSBY

The Virginian was no more addicted to that popular pastime than were his brethren of the South. From the Revolution to and through the Civil War personal honor was the religion of the Southern gentleman and the "Code" his creed.

This was herital. The English, French and Spanish who sired the incoming populations of all the colonies wore swords for other purposes than ornament. Often they had carved their fortunes with them and, on occasion, had found them handy to carve each other.

The courts were in their infancy in most sections and were wholly adult in few. Custom, too, had made a man what stern old Cedric the Saxon called "niddering," had he taken judical court-plaster for his bruised reputation: accepted money valuation for his wounded honor. The hand of a man affronted went naturally to his left hip for the hilt that hung ready for it. So, the duello of form, legalized by custom into more than written law, passed from the "meeting" of etiquette for a trodden foot or a chance brusquerie to the combat to the death for a grave and real wrong.

Just how distinct those gradations were would take much time to tell, nor would they interest those who persist that duels are a relic of barbarism. Yet they are a relic of chivalry as well.

He who would go about the world today with a metal pot upon his head, his family tree painted on his plate-covered breast and, with a pointed pole in his hand, "To ride abroad redressing human wrong," would be regarded as worse than a mild lunatic. Yet men and women still flush over the sentiment that made Launcelot and the Lion's Heart, Sydney and Alexander Hamilton, immortal. *Tempora mutantur!*

A wild outcry echoed through the land when one gallant youth fell dead in his tracks and another, maimed for his miserable remnant of life in that Richmond duel that ushered in a new era and made even a challenge a felony in Virginia.

Duelling was born in the McCarty blood. One of that poor boy's forebears had killed his own first cousin (a Mason) "in fair and honorable combat." But the duel personal was a child of the first trial by jury. We are all things of heredity.

As in duelling so have there been gross exaggerations of the old Virginian's thirst. Great are the miscomprehensions of the "gentlemanly dissipations" of those days. The "two-bottle man" of a century syne was probably not more thirsty than the familiar bibber of this day. He drank differently, however, and with far different surroundings. He

PAGE MCCARTY

made the glass the excuse for and the promoter of hospitality, sociality and good-fellowship. He never took a public pledge for its infraction in private, and he bade his fellow to stretch his legs beneath his private mahogany and sip Burgundy and rare Madeira, instead of leading him into the vulgar public bar to "hist in" doctored poison at "two for twenty-five."

Though the two-bottler sometimes succumbed, and slid gradually from his chair under the table, he may still have been "as good a man" as any millionaire clubman of the present who lurches from his club to his Brougham in the small hours of any metropolis today.

The South has never cavilled at the taste of her New England cousins, who drank and relished "Rumblullion," or "Will Devil," donated to the main land from the British sailors' "Rumbowling." This the traveler Josselyn calls in his writings: "That cursed liquor, Rhum, Rumbullion, or the Devil!"

This favorite drink of old time tavern and post house, is fully described in local chronicle, and embalmed in Miss Alice Earle's "Stage and Tavern Days." She states that this word did not signify Rum, but was the Gipsy adjective, "strong, or strenuous." Its components were rum or strong liquor; ale, or wine, egg and sugar, and this was the great New England tipple of Colonial days.

"Rumfstian" was another brain food made from 1½ pints of gin, yelks of 12 eggs, orange peel, nutmeg, spices and sugar. To these was added a quart of strong beer, and a pint of sherry, or other wine!!

And yet the Southerner was called a "two-bottle man!"

It has not been plainly demonstrated that polo, pinochle and draw poker have generated truer-hearted and more conservative men than did the tournaments for Love and Beauty, or the games of brag for "a bale ante and a nigger better."

Doubtless much fustian has been written about "the good old times," and still no proof is shown that the so-called progress of today has bettered them in all regards—if any. Methods and manners change with invention and surrounding, but the men and women they are used by are constant quantities. Only he whom Victor Hugo dared call "*Vieux Philosophe*" can truly differentiate the result of custom upon character.

In common with her sister planting states of the South the Old Dominion had no real middle class or even the substitute for it. Her planter, especially when he boasted direct colonial descent, was a closer counterpart of the landed gentry of the motherland than any other American. He was veritable lord of the soil: its judge, governor and dictator as well as its owner. The great "Virginia Plantations" of Elizabethan days had been subdivided into many and minor ones, all held literally, no less than legally, by these herital "English gentry."

The only other actual class was that of the hewers of wood and drawers of water, holding scarce closer relation to their masters, in any social or moral regard, than did those assistants in Scriptural days. His negro slaves the country gentleman held as

"Something better than his dog, a little dearer than his horse."

They were regarded more tenderly than his beasts of toil or pleasure, but as impossible of even hinted future equality.

The Southern owner of a blood-horse, or a bench pointer would scarcely cut off the feed, or scar and disfigure either by cruel or even careless treatment. The black chattel was merely a valuable asset. Never noted as a shrewd dealer, the Southern plantation owner was not so blind an idiot as to depreciate the worth of probably his most valuable possession. It were as logical to suppose that he might upon occasion have sown his cotton or tobacco fields with rock salt or burned his fences for winter fuel.

Thus only dementia or inborn ferocity could have caused modes of procedure ascribed to them by some too swift delineators of what they did not comprehend when seen or what more generally they "saw" from hearsay.

Fact often failed the purpose and fancy was drawn on to aid it. A twice told tale in point is that when Mrs. Stowe made her revision of her book she generalized her description of Southern cruelty and merely detailed it in but one character of her "Uncle Tom's Cabin." That detailed brutality was all committed by her Yankee overseer.

As lords of the soil the old Virginians lorded it easily, holding high their heads but never hardening their hearts. They were the gentry; below them a gap hard to measure in these days. Therein drudged the petty traders, the few white mechanics and laborers. The shopkeeper class, as I have noted, was an unknown quantity in the Virginian human equation.

In politics, then, as later in the war, the Virginian was an ultra. Whatever the "pa-aty" did was right, or at least right enough to uphold. This trait made him perhaps quite as useful a citizen in the main as had he wasted time and effort in trying to think for himself.

"There were giants in those days" nursing by the Mother of Presidents for their probable successors. These had brought the state to the fore in the teething struggles of the hobbledehoy nation; the men who "yaller dogged" at their heels were safe from being traded in droves, or from being sold at a cut price on the hoof. Men as well as measures were different in those days.

The soil that had given the first "Rebel" president, and three more in succession, had ever nurtured men who stood forth first for right through all the troublous councils of the Burgesses, the Revolution and the Union. The Hunters, Marshalls, Masons, Bococks, had stood side by side with Calhoun, McDuffie, Hampton, of the neighbor State, and Troup, Lamar, Yancy, Soulé, Davis and the men who made Secessia.

The Virginian was the cavalier class as compared with the colder Covenanter types of the Puritan and the Knickerbocker. There can be no question that the supposititious line of Mason and Dixon separated two people as dissimilar in thought and feeling, in habit and in need, as were the Saxons and the knights of the descent of Rollo the Norman.

Sift the innumerable theories of the cause of the war between the states and the whole residuum is the one of race. The Dred Scott decision, the crusades of the abolitionists, the contention of territorial slavery that killed Douglas and made Lincoln, these, one and all, were integers.

That much abused possibility, "the future Macaulay," will doubtless deduce

HON. JAMES M. MASON

that, had slavery not existed—and been transferred by rigor of climate alone from New England to the South—there still would have been division between the two wholly differing people that held the Union together by a tenuous thread of sentimental obligation, frayed and weakening each year. Absolute diversity of character and of habits of life, inborn sentiments and sectional prejudices growing more bitter each decade, simply from want of mutual comprehension, must have resulted in separation. The forcible separation of atoms means heat which in the human ones means blood-letting.

The vibration of preponderant power alone might have

stayed the torrent a while. Nullification on the one hand and the secession of Massachusetts on the other were symptoms of the body politic that showed fever.

However variant in tastes, habits and interests, Louisiana and South Carolina might have legislated for Maine and Michigan, Texas and Virginia for Pennsylvania and Wisconsin, had either understood the other. There was the rub.

The aristocratic Southerner looked down upon the crude young Westerner. He despised the keen, money-getting Yankee. He had the same contempt for the personality of these men as he had for their vocations. In return the Massachusetts man and the middle Western pioneer had equal contempt for the trans-Potomac upstart he pictured to himself. Prejudice in each did the grossest injustice to the other, and the masses on either side, mimetic as the monkey, took their tone from molders of opinion. It was mutual ignorance, converting into mutual hatred. Thus, to borrow from our axiomatic statesman, a condition, not a theory, confronted every effort of the thinkers to adjust a balance that had no standard for its scale.

No Southern thinker really believed that the South Atlantic aristocrat, or the blue blood Creole of the Gulf, was practically a better man than the earnest, if eager, denizen of the Eastern mart states, or of the prairie lands of the new West. No Northern politician, not a fanatic or a trickster, believed that men descended from the highest grades of almost identical stock were the slave-driving tyrants or the weak-kneed dawdlers popularly caricatured.

Yet all history proves that indurated error is quite as strong, while far more obdurate, as principle. There was but one way out of this centuried error; it was by the arbitrament of blood.

The war had to come. The North and South had to seek homogeneity, and they could be taught thorough understanding of each other only in the hideous clash that both felt was but deferred.

It was well that it came when it did, and for double reason. Delayed, it had been only a bloodier and costlier tug. Resulting sanity and mutual respect had brought interdependence at greater delay to that only foundation for the sturdy and respected nationalism of today—amalgamated Americanism.

But this is a social record, not a tract on politico-economics. The facts were there· their results are seen of all men. History, as ever, has repeated itself, and, as the wars of the Roses left the Saxon and the Norman only Englishmen, the Creole and the Yankee, the Carolinian and the Hoosier hold today one Nation, with one aim, one flag and one pride. Each has its memories and its glories; each feels the other's usefulness and respects him for it. Common interest is the one cement that holds the late dissevered parts in a concreted whole. So, disguised with hate and baptized with blood as it was, the war has proved itself a blessing. The cost was infinite; so are the results it purchased.

CHAPTER II

THAT pleasantry of courtesy, "This house and all it contains is yours," came nearer realization in Old Virginia than anywhere on the globe.

Her lords of the soil lorded it with expansive *bonhomie* and generous hand. Their broad acres and fat larders were shared with friends and strangers, and each was made to feel that he was a donor rather than a recipient.

The acme of entertainment is when the host sets forth for his guest the very best he has and then honestly enjoys it with him. Hospitality is like mercy as described by Portia:

"It blesses him that gives and him that takes."

And this the host of the rare Old Dominion knew and practiced.

To marriage and the church, in convertible ratio, their owners also devoted themselves. In almost every family we read of vestrymen who were made quite as useful as ornamental. They gave their time, means and enthusiasm to the advancement of the church and seemingly were as eager to be in the vestry as in the house of burgesses. There were members of almost all the notable families in the ministry, and, unlike the mother country, the selections were not always from the younger sons, but often from the heads of houses, who gave a living, instead of trying to make one. Bishop Meade's book is practically a roster of the well-descended who worked in and for the transplanted church, and his list includes almost every name that was, or now is, noted in Virginia.

Connubiality seems to have walked hand in hand with piety in the early colony. The sons and daughters of the great landed proprietors married early and devoted most of their time and all of their care to the direction of their own families' education, to their making suitable alliances and arranging proper settlements.

And these great family connections ramified into a meshed and interwoven consanguinity that held the interest of neighborhoods, and through them of all the Dominion, bound to common aspiration and to common interest. The unification of newer and less directly descended states has been a political or material advance; that of the Mother Virginia has been, time out of mind, one of pride and hereditament. Kentucky, Alabama,

SECRETARY GEORGE W. RANDOLPH

Tennessee and many of the later states owe their best blood to the colonial families of the Jamestown era. The Taylors, Raouls, Breckinridges, Maurys and Tylers, noted and useful in the upbuilding and publicism of the younger federated sisters, sprang from the lords of "the sacred soil."

It is hard to overestimate the influence of a great and strongly seated family connected with a dozen similar ones and all holding one common point of view and action. Take, as instance, the Randolphs. Their influence in their state has been direct and collateral.

William Randolph came over in 1674 and settled on vast

estates for which he had obtained patents, those on Turkey Island alone, where he made the family seat, reaching some 75,000 acres. He married Mary, daughter of Henry and Catherine Isham, of Bermuda Hundred, just across the James. Their seven sons and three daughters married into most of the families then founding social dynasties. William, of Turkey Island, married Miss Beverly, of Gloucester; Thomas, of Tuckahoe, Miss Flemming; Isham, of Dungeness, Miss Rojers, an English heiress; Richard, of Curls', Miss Bolling, a direct descendant of Pocahontas; and Sir John Randolph, the sixth son, Miss Beverly, the sister of William's wife; the last brother, Edward, wedding another English heiress. Two of the three sisters chose Reverend Yates's brothers, the third marrying William Stith. She became the mother of Reverend Dr. Stith who was the historian of Virginia and later president of William and Mary College. He married Miss Judith Randolph, of Tuckahoe, and his sister became the wife of Commissary Dawson. Another Stith sister married Rev. Mr. Keith, of Fauquier and was the ancestor of the famous John Marshall, Chief Justice. Still another sister married Anthony Walke, of Norfolk, and was mother of the Rev. Anthony Walke. Thus it will be seen that the family connection was as strong in the church as in the state. There was a Bishop Randolph in the close of the eighteenth century who was archdeacon of Jersey, then Bishop of Oxford and later of London. Thomas Randolph, the poet of England, was own uncle to Randolph of Turkey Island, and the colonist head of the great family himself had the poetic vein. All of the latter's sons, as noted above, made themselves name and position. William, the elder, was member of the council and treasurer of the colony; Isham was member of the house of burgesses, in 1740, from Goochland, and adjutant-general of the colony. Richard was, in the same year as his brother, member of burgesses, from Henrico; and succeeded him as treasurer. Sir John was speaker of burgesses and attorney-general.

A grandson, William, was clerk of the burgesses and succeeded his uncle as attorney-general. Peyton Randolph, son of Sir John, was speaker of the burgesses and became president of the first congress, held at Philadelphia.

The holding of high trusts descended steadily. Thomas Mann Randolph was a member of the Virginia convention of 1776 from Goochland; Beverly was a member of the assembly from Cumberland during the Revolution, and later governor of that state. Robert, son of Peter; Richard, grandson of Peter, and David Meade Randolph, grandson of the second Richard, of Curls', were all noted cavalry officers of the Revolution; David Meade was marshal of Virginia; and the famous congressman, John Randolph, of Roanoke, grandson of the first Richard, was also minister to Russia. His father was John Randolph, of Roanoke, who married the beauty, Frances Bland, daughter of Theodoric Bland, and thus a granddaughter of the Bollings. Her second husband was the first St. George Tucker; and thus she became the mother of another famous line.

Later members of the family were Edmund Randolph, secretary of state of the United States and governor of Virginia, and Thomas Mann Randolph, Jr., member of congress, of the legislature of Virginia, and governor of the state.

Nowhere does history show a more noted descent nor one that better upheld its traditions or better proved the training bestowed upon the early families. This one held seats that were household words and of which some names still exist, the owners, from their numbers,. being distinguished by their home affixes. On the James river stood Tuckahoe, Dungeness, Chattsworth, Wilton, Varina, Curls', Bremo, Turkey Island. As the race descended, so did the fame of the succeeding seats, as those of the Blands of Westover, the Harrisons of the James, the Cabells of Buckingham and Nelson, and others still existent or renewed as family memorials.

Next to entertaining his guest the old-timer took to sport with keenest zest.   Fox hunting came first in the love of all, and every manor home had its stud and its pack, blood stock

MRS. EVELYN CABELL ROBINSON,
OF COLLETON

of the best the old country could produce and hounds of lineage and high degree. The youth—and for the matter of that, the maid—who could not ride "anything that jumped" was recreant to race and custom, as was the knight who declined the tilt or the lady of the lists who wore no colors.

It is odd, therefore, that the first fox-hunting clubs were not formed at the South. The Glouster Hunt Club, of Pennsylvania, was doubtless the parent one of the Union. It was founded in 1776, a great and social affair, for the chase and entertaining.   Others may have arisen, but the second notable club was the Baltimore Hounds, founded in 1818; the parent of later organizations in Maryland and the District of Columbia.   Among these, today, are the Elkridge Fox Club, with Mr. E. A. Jackson as president, and W. Ross Whistler, secretary, and two hundred and forty members; the Green Spring Valley, seated in the most picturesque and fashionable of Baltimore outlyings, eighteen years ago, to hunt the wild fox exclusively, with its two hundred members.   The present vigorous heir of former attempt in the district is the Chevy Chase Hunt, founded on Thanksgiving day of twenty years syne. Its leading spirits are Messrs Clarence Moore, M.F.H., and Gist Blair, and its suburban club house is perhaps the seat of most diverse hospitality in the land.

Virginia now has four admirably organized and equipped clubs: the Deep Run, of Richmond, the Warrenton, the Cheswick (near Charlottesville) and the Piedmont, of Lynchburg. The Deep Run was organized just seventeen years ago, by Mr. S. H. Hancock and his sister-in-law, Miss Maude Blacker. They are English folk: and the lady one of the best riders and thorough horsewomen in the country. Her father, when he had reached eightysix, rode as straight to hounds as a youth and never missed a meet. Organized with only twenty-three members, it now has over two hundred and fifty. Notable men and some of the most charming women of the whole state follow its hounds: among its presidents and officers having been Philip Haxall, Joseph Bryan, Major Otway S. Allen, P. S. A.

CAPTAIN PHILIP HAXALL

Brine, and Dr. Jos. A. White, its longtime president and leading spirit. Among the ladies I recall Mrs. Thos. Nelson Carter, Mrs. Allen Potts (who was Gertrude Rives and had no cross-country superior), Mrs. Andrew Christian, Misses Skelton, Palmer, Sophie White, and the famous and beautiful Langhorne sisters, who seem to have been born to the saddle.

Shooting followed close in sport, for game was everywhere in those early clearings, big game and little. Crack shots laid the foundation of the marksmanship that won the colony wars, the Revolution and the War of 1812. Racing, too, was legitimate descendant of the hunt. The turf of the old days was led by Virginia stables and took its tone from Virginia gentlemen, the Randolphs, Doswells, Johnstons and many more familiar to younger ears.

Most familiar to them, likewise, are two ancient seats interwoven with the history and the courtliness of all our country, Arlington and Mount Vernon, literally household words today.

The first Custis we note is John, in 1640. He had six sons and one daughter. She married Colonel Argal Yeardley, son of Governor Yeardley. Her brothers in Virginia were John, William and Joseph; Thomas, in Baltimore (Ireland); Robert, in Rotterdam, and Edmund, in London. John, the eldest, took the family lead. He was what this day would have called a "hustler," a great salt maker, a trader, a churchman and a vestryman. In 1676, during Bacon's rebellion, he was appointed major-general. He was a favorite of Lord Arlington in Charles the Second's time, and after him was named the estate he received with his first wife. His second wife was Miss Scarborough, who bore him one son, named for him. The descendants of that son and of his uncle, William Custis, peopled the Eastern Shore with the Custis family and made the historical possibility of Washington's marriage. His son John, the fourth so named, returned from education in England, received from his grandfather the Arlington estate and married the daughter of Colonel Daniel Parke. It was the latter's son whose widow married George Washington. Daniel Parke's wife was a Miss Evelyn; their daughter married John Custis, of Arlington, who was the first noted Virginia ancestor of George Washington Parke Custis, whose grandmother was Mrs. Washington. The wife of Washington Custis was the daughter of William Fitzhugh, of Chatham; and his sister married Colonel Overton, of Westmoreland. These bits of brief biography antedate the later Arlington and the beautiful capital to which it is adjunct.

The owner of Mount Vernon was Lawrence Washington, elder brother to the general. He married the second daughter of William Fairfax, of Belvoir near Mount Vernon, whose mother was a Cary. This was the first of the five marriages between those notable families, which occurred within the course of a few years. The Carys, of Maryland, Virginia and Florida, all descend from that stock.

The Fairfax family dates back to the coming of the Conqueror, it being of Saxon stock and the name meaning "Fair Hair." The Herberts of both states also intermarried with the Carys and Fairfaxes.

Thomas was the first Lord Fairfax. His son Ferdinand was famed in the Parliamentary army, and his son Thomas was the celebrated Lord Fairfax who resigned the command of the army to Cromwell. William Fairfax had a fine seat at Belvoir, near Mount Vernon, and was father of the Rev. Brian Fairfax, as well as of Mrs. Washington. The second had two sons, Brian, a noted scholar and poet; his brother Henry was the fourth Lord Fairfax. Thomas, the son of this Lord Fairfax, succeeded to the title and married the daughter of Lord Colepepper. Their son Thomas was the first American Lord Fairfax. The Rev. Brian Fairfax, of the Episcopal church at Alexandria, was the first native lord of the name. The present Lord Fairfax is of Maryland birth and is first cousin to the Carys, who will figure later in this record.

The Fitzhughs, interesting in themselves and closely allied to the Washingtons, Lees and Herberts, were lords of

fine manors. William Fitzhugh, of Chatham, divided 60,000
acres between his five sons. His wife was a Miss Tucker and
his sons owned Eagle Nest and Ford, in King George, and
Belleaire and Boscobel, in Stafford. They married also into
the Mason and McCarty families. They were the parent stock
of the widespread Fitzhughs, of Maryland, New York, Virginia
and the newer states.

Another noted name is that of the Pages. The progenitor was Sir John, of Williamsburg. His son Matthew wedded
Mary Mann, of Timber Neck Bay, and left an immense estate
to his son Mann, who built beautiful Rosewell. *His* son Mann
married Judith Wormley, and later Judith Carter. The sole
daughter of the first marriage wedded Thomas Mann Randolph, of Tuckahoe. Three sons came of the Carter alliance:
Mann Page, of Rosewell, who married Alice Grymes, of Middle-
sex; John Page, of North End, who married Jane Byrd, of Westover, and Robert, of Hanover, who married Miss Sarah Walker.

The descendants of these brothers were great in number—
some of the families reaching the "baker's dozen," and they
in turn intermarried with the Carters, Burwells, Nelsons,
McCartys and Byrds.

This last is a family connected with the most interesting
growth of the state. To the second of the three noted in
the records is due the foundation of the "leaguered capital"
of our day. He inherited great tracts about Richmond and
surrounding his princely home of Westover. Colonel Byrd,
of Westover, was the author of the "Westover Papers" and
prominent in all public affairs. The third, and the last of
the name who owned Westover, was prominent in the Revolution and on Washington's staff when he encamped at Winchester in the early Indian wars. The descendants of this
family run in and out through the tangled skein of all early
Virginian intermarriage. To attempt enumeration would
produce a biographical dictionary. Even at that risk, there

is one more of the old liners peremptorily demanding notice because of the prominence in its impress upon its time.

Theodoric Bland settled at Westover in Charles City in 1654. His death seventeen years later left three sons, Theodoric, Richard and John. Richard, of Berkeley, married Miss Swann, and at her death married Elizabeth, daughter of William Randolph, of Turkey Island. He had three daughters who married Henry Lee, William Beverly and Robert Montford. His sons, Richard and Theodoric, lived at Jordon's, Prince George and Causon's, City Point. The elder married Miss Poythress and left the popular twelve children; the junior married Miss Bolling, of Pocahontas, and left one son, Theodoric, and five daughters. They married into the Bannister, Ruffin, Eaton, Haynes and Randolph of Roanoke families. This Mrs. Randolph is the one who later married St. George Tucker. Her brother, Theodoric, 2d, was lieutenant of the county and clerk of the house of burgesses, and the third Theodoric was a doctor in England. He returned, however, distinguished himself in the Revolution and became an intimate and favorite of Washington. Important in the family was also Giles Bland, gallant victor of Bacon's rebellion.

All memory of these stately old homes and of the men who made them gleams soft, but

MRS. ALFRED L. RIVES OF CASTLE HILL

warm, with the comeliness and courtliness of their dainty women.

Much of all that life has been reflected down the later years, through the *ante-bellum* country seats of wealthier planters on the James and the Rappahannock, Westover, Brandon, Castle Hill and others, known to the borders of the Union.

At these were entertained many distinguished guests from abroad as well as from our own side of the water. Their house parties at shooting season and Christmas, their rare welcome, rarer wines and rarest hospitality, have gone sounding down the aisles of sociality and gastronomy. Today many of the old homes have fallen into memories only.

Their home seats were replicas of those of the burgess days, where not the very houses—often scarce modernized out of that old-time grandeur and elegance that shone unimpaired up to the days when the sons of Light Horse Harry, of the Montfords, Latanés—changed pumps for riding-boots and threw their swords into the number-tipped scales of war, for country and for name.

It was heredity that spurred the Ashbys and Peytons and the Carters and Harrisons to the Potomac, marched the Valley meteor-like and held the Rappahannock, by the side of Lee and Johnston and Stonewall Jackson.

As with the men, so with the women, mothers of a line of gentlemen.

Who saw the women of the '60's at court, in camp or toiling in unaccustomed kitchen or fetid hospital, who sees them today "the favored guests at every bright and brilliant throng," and fails to see across the mists of time the forms and faces of those who presided at bounteous board, walked the minuet or romped in real Virginia reel, in those old manor houses of yore?

Every mention of Arlington conjures up the fair widow who wedded young Washington, walking a courtly measure in "baby waist and train"; or pretty Nellie Custis queening it merrily over congressional quadrilles at Philadelphia.

When the dashing Rives sisters, the Langhorne girls, the

Johnstons and the rest, witch the hunting world with peerless 'cross country riding, and doff habit for toilette to witch again the city rout or watering-place german, we recall that the Riveses were beautiful women ever since William, the grandfather of Minister William C. Rives, built Castle Hill; we recall that Mirador is no new seat, but of "the old Virginia way," which brings back the women of that Langhorne line who "danced with Washington."

One of the gravest of all the many errors cherished by the North as truth about the South, is that regarding the home education of its women. Differing as they do, in theory and practice of social life, from their more progressive—might I write aggressive?—sisters of the North, they have never been at all the pretty puppets described by overswift ignorance.

It has been accepted that the Southern girl, from pinafore to orange blossoms, was educated for a bride, but not for a wife. The theory of the uninformed has indurated by repetition that she was "incased in cedar and shut in a sacred gloom"; that she was held by her male kith and kin as "a toy too tender for the winds of heaven to visit too roughly," and that embroidery, twanging the guitar, plus a possible French novel and a *bonbonniere*, were her portion and Ultima Thule of educational variety.

The thoughtless forget in this picture the primal fact that most of these women, especially in Virginia and the Carolinas, were English in blood and bone. Their grandams were British born; themselves often colonists. They were almost invairably of high degree and of liberal education, scholastic and domestic. So, these women of colonial and Revolutionary days educated not only their daughters, but frequently large families of sons until they were of an age for the great university at Williamsburg. No person can really believe that the daughters of such mothers could be the dolls and playthings described by the myopic or the mendacious.

An hour spent in a library over the chronicles of the colony or in cursory reading of "Women of the Revolution" would preclude a folly which reflects only upon the intelligence of its believers.

The institution of slavery may have influenced the habits of the wealthier class of the Southerner in some sort, particularly in its plantation life, by excess of service. The little "nigger maid" was the appendage of every planter's daughter from the pinafore and candy stick age, and the white need never have tied her own slipper had she so willed. But the Southern girl then, as a rule, rode better and shot better than her Northern neighbor. And perhaps she danced better as well, but the taper hand that restrains the restive colt or drops the woodcock is not the one that belongs to the helpless woman.

The "Island Mastiff" strain ran in the veins of both sexes. What their early mothers had been in the colony, what their daughters were in the Revolution, that and more were the tenderest reared and most reticent women of the South, matrons and maidens, in that later struggle of the men of the same race.

Later in these pages I shall show that, as the flower of Southern youth threw down quill pen and billiard cue to take the sword, so their mothers and little sisters wrought in kitchen, sewing room and in the hideous hospital as only woman at her full stature and in her highest pride has ever wrought at trial.

CHAPTER III

AT THE "OLD WRECK"

Washington is today confessedly the show city of this continent and is one of the most picturesque in the world. All Americans—whatever their habitat or their sympathies—are proud of the national capital.

The Washingtonian of a half century ago recalls a wholly different place, and the returning parole bearer, who rubbed the smoke of a four-year battle from his eyes as he recrossed the Potomac, beheld with wonder and amaze the changes wrought by the Federal Aladdin. What was brought about in the brief space of the war had been solidified, broadened and burnished in as many intervening decades.

Yet, great as is the superficial transformation of a provincial village into a cosmopolitan center, it dwindles when compared with the change in the social confirmation of this literally central city.

Ante-bellum Washington was a mixture of Arlington grandeur, Jeffersonian simplicity, Dolly-Madisonism, Fillmore primness and the gracious chill of Miss Harriet Lane. Its society was a mosaic of elegance and pomp, of recklessness and parity, of culture and crudity. Its West End arrogated – and with some show of right divine—the *noblesse oblige* tone of the Faubourg St. Germain, but that outlying East, from the Treasury past Duddington, to the Navy Yard, had a decided smatter of the Latin Quarter.

It was a charming society and one much sought, that of Washington of the *mi-régime*. It ate its terrapin, not always

33

with a gold spoon, but with true gusto, and lacking red devils and electrics, it sought in cab, and even horse-car, balls as truly elegant and germans as delightful and as beauty-crowned as any of the present.

Those were the days of great leadership in both political

parties, and sectional estrangement had not spread from the corridors of the Capitol into the salons of society. This came later, with the swirl and heat of a consuming fire; but even one year previous to Beauregard's salute to "Old Bob" Anderson at Sumter, the mightiest men of the North sought eagerly the dark-eyed matrons and belles of the Southern coterie, while the Soulés, Slidells, Orrs, Breckinridges and Tuckers of coming war fame, danced stately measures with the

MISSES MATHILDE AND ROSINE SLIDELL

ladies of the Hales, Sewards, Pendletons and Pughs. Then, too, the gilded youth in pumps, the personal pride of german-dancing, were most often of the Southern sort.

In toning the society of the '60's, the South had the *pas.* This was doubtless due to the natural sociability and pleasure love of her daughters, but in part it was because the families of congressmen and government officials could not live in their plantation homes in summer, and, having once sipped Potomac water, *would* not in winter.

The leaders of society were largely Southerners. Cultured, gracious, or brilliant women there were from North, East and

West. Beautiful, attractive and quite progressive girls there were who rolled their "r's" roundly, and did a few other things that their Southern sisters had perhaps shied at. But these people all belonged to the caravan. They came in December when the congressional worry began; they left for distant homes after March 4, or for watering place and seaside in the swelter of the long session. They were in the society, and of it to a certain extent, but they were not it.

So this Southern resident put his impress upon the unwritten laws, and ruled with the little iron hand in the No 5 *gant Suède.*

We of that day remember beautiful Mrs. Pugh, wife of the Ohio senator. Double-gilded youth from everywhere fluttered about her as eagerly as about her handsome and popular sister, Miss Ada Chalfant. Miss Hale, daughter of New Hampshire's senator, was a favorite with old and young, and gay, graceful and audacious Mrs. John R. Thompson, "the senior senator from New Jersey," as Mrs. Phillips dubbed her, merely shifted her regnant belleship from Princeton juniors and Dons in the autumn to Washington solons in the winter. Stately Miss Marcy was ever sought and retained the friendship of all, and the Ledyard ladies of the Lewis Cass family were as geniune and hospitable as any in the set.

These are samples from great names; there were scores of others, but they were all birds of passage, nesting elsewhere and flying South only for the season. The home people were of another type and, nursing the society in the interregnum, they kept it warm with Southern temperaments and methods.

The winter before Sumter was the most lavish and brilliant that Washington had ever known. It was also the giddiest and most feverish. That was before the day of multi-millionaires and men were naught if not dollar stamped; before heiresses captured fledgling and penniless young army and navy men to build them cages on the Avenue. Women and men themselves counted for everything even in the maziest whirl of dinner and german.

I have said there were giants. So were there beautiful "princesses" whose fairy godmothers, Birth and Breeding, had dowered them in the cradle. What shaky old relic of that time, holding up memory's looking-glass, but fails to see Juno-like Miss Adèle Cutts, then not yet the wife of the "Little Giant," Stephen A. Douglas, or petite and graceful Henrietta Magruder, Miss Marion Ramsay, later Mrs. "Brock" Cutting, of New York, with her lovely childish face and baby waist, hiding that infinity of tact that made simplicity an art? Ah! Temptation to catalogue that time-reflected picture gallery is hard to withstand.

I have said that there were two distinct societies in the Washington of yesterday, nowise parallel, yet not always tangent. The general set included strangers in town of all shades and degrees, the congressional people and some in the departments. The resident set, salted with the diplomatic, met these on the neutral ground of card exchanging and crush receptions. But each had its own intimate and enjoyed circle, a closed one, in the main, on the part of the home set. Each naturally had its leaders and ambitions. Of one "Lady Ashley," as the flippants of the day styled Mrs. John J. Crittenden, was one-time queen; again Mrs. Clem Clay, of Alabama, mounted to the box and tooled a society coach that was full loaded with pretty and ancient-named Southern belles.

Of the resident homes remembered across the years are the Freemans, Clem Hills, William T. Carrolls, Countess Esterhazys, Emorys, Jesups, Aulicks, Gwins, Sliddels, and

"Each one bears a glass, to show me many more!"

Not too eclectic, "Us youth" who frequented the functions of both sets included young and promising army and navy men, many later major-generals and admirals like Captain

George B. McClellan, Ambrose E. Burnside, Lieutenant Gouverneur K. Warren, Fitzhugh Lee, John S. Saunders and such heel-celebrants as Renwick Smedberg and Alan Ramsay. Few of these dreamed then that four clicks of Time's watch would see them with stars on their straps, less legs than the average, or a memory gilded with a great deed. Civilians, later famous, were there too: George Eustis, who married philanthropist Corcoran's only child; William Porcher Miles, the bachelor of the Lower House who designed the first Confederate flag and, better, married the charming Miss Bettie Bierne, and many

another, not unloved even when unhonored and unsung.

Such were the components of Capital society in the winter of 1860-61, when dull clouds of doubt and suspense began to press low on the horizon. From East and West and North heavy, grumbling thunder rolled distant, but distinct. Through cumuli, black and threatening, red flashes threatened an early storm. Washington looked at the skies to the North, paused, hesitated; then went on waltzing and lobbying again. In society,

T. C. DE LEON AND COL. J. S. SAUNDERS

it whirled around in the german; at the Capitol in Buncombe and jobs; in both, with a speed dizzier than ever before. Still the horizon darkened and a few, timid or shrewd, began to take in sail and peer ahead for a port. Even the more reckless began to look from the horizon to each other's faces with unrest and suspicion. But two classes seemed ignorant of the signs: the people who came to spend money and the sharper ones who came to make it. The former had grasped at the outer circle, and having secured an insecure grip upon its rim away they went with a fizz and a spin, giddy, delighted, devil may care. The other class held those thousand who annually came to roll logs, pull wires and juggle through bills, in congenial and paying traffic, stuffed with terrapin and washed down with dry champagne. Who shall dive into and write the secrets of that marvelous committee of ways but no means and of its impartial preying upon government and client? This Caliban of governmental spawning was holding a very witches' Sabbath in the closing days of 1860.

On with the rush! Dinners, balls, suppers followed each other as unchecked as John Gilpin. Dress, jewels and equipage cost sums undreamed of heretofore. "This may be the last of it," was the answer unspoken, but acted out to the threat of the coming storm. Madame would not fold away her Worth gown and *parure* of diamonds, perchance bought with somebody else's money; madamoiselle must make one more exhibit of her velvety shoulders and of killing pace in the german and time for galoshes and umbrellas were coming fast. It would never do to miss opportunities now, for this might be "the end of the Old Wreck," as slang began to call the capital.

So the mad stream rushed on, and the old wheels, somewhat rusted, but unoiled, revolved as creakingly as ever. All the while that huge engine, the Lobby, pumped steadily on in the political basement.

Suddenly, a dull silence. A sullen reverberation across the Potomac. The long threatened deed had crystallized into fact. South Carolina had seceded and the first link had been rudely struck from the chain of states.

There was a little start; that was all. As for the Lobby pump, its piston grows white hot and all its valves fly wide open with the work it does.

Presently faces that were never long before lengthened visibly and thoughtful men wagged solemn heads as they passed one another, or paused to take important personages by the buttonhole. More frequent knots and earnest ones now discuss the status in hotel lobbies and the corridors of the departments. Prudent non-partisans with thick slices to butter on either side keep their lips tightly closed, and hot talk, *pro* or *con*, sometimes overrides the intended whisper.

At last the sleepy administration opened its eyes. Finding that effort too late, and not liking the looks of things, it shut them again. A little later came windy declarations and some feeble attempts at temporizing; but every sane man knew that the crisis had come and that nothing could avert it.

The earthquake that had so long rumbled in premonitory throes yawned in an ugly chasm that swallowed up the petty differences on both of its sides. North and South were at last openly aligned against each other.

One throb, and the little lines of party were roughly obliterated, while across the gulf that gaped between them men glared at each other with but one meaning in their eyes.

That solemn mummery, the Peace Congress, might have stayed temporarily the tide it was wholly powerless to dam, but the arch-seceder, Massachusetts, manipulated even that flim-flam of compromise. The weaker elements in that body were no match for the peaceful Puritan whom war might profit but could not injure. Peace was pelted from under her olive with splinters of Plymouth Rock, and New England poured upon the troubled waters oil—of vitriol.

When the Peace Commissioners from the Southern congress at Montgomery came to Washington all felt their presence only a mockery—however respectable a one, with

such names as John Forsyth, M. J. Crawford and A. B. Roman.
It was another verdict of that fatal "too late!" They came
only to demand what the government had then no power
to concede, even had the will not been lacking. Every line
they wrote to foes and friends was waste of ink, every word
they spoke a waste of breath.

Southern senators, representatives and even minor of-

ficials were leaving their long-
time seats by every train,
families of years' residence
were pulling down their
household gods and starting
on a pilgrimage to set them
up—where they knew not,
save that it must be in the
South. Even old friends
looked doubtfully at each
other and rumors were rife
of incursions across the Potomac by wild-haired riders
from Virginia. Even the
fungi of departmental desks
seemed suddenly imbued
with life, rose and threw
away their quills—and with
them the very bread for
their families—to "go South!"
It was the passage out of
Egypt in modern dress.

COLONEL JOHN FORSYTH

A dull, vague unrest brooded over Washington, as though
the city lay in the shadow of a great pall or was threatened
with a plague. Then, again, when it was too late, General
Scott virtually went into the cabinet.

"The General," as he was familiarly known, practically

filled the chair that Jefferson Davis had once held. Sagacious men foresaw no result from this, and all felt that the time had arrived when they must range themselves on one side or the other. The South had spoken and she seemed to mean what she said. All Washington was at last convinced that there might be war, that there must be separation.

Into this dull, leaden suspense, that a breath might lash into a seething maelstrom of passion, suddenly dropped Abraham Lincoln, unexpectedly and alone, in a Scotch cap and a long cloak.

The new president was a man of iron. His coming thus was not the escapade it has been dreamed by some. Far less was it the result of fear for himself. He had played a great game boldly for a great stake, and he was not disposed to risk his winnings, and perhaps his life, on some chance throw of a fanatic or a madman. Could any vague forecast of the doom hovering above him have whispered its half-heard warning: "Prudence!"

Certain it is that he was soon in conference with General Scott and the nominal secretary, Holt. Then unheard-of precautions were taken to safeguard the inauguration while seemingly devised to heighten its pomp and military glitter.

The night before that inauguration was a trying one to all Washington. The nervous heard a signal for bloody outbreak in every unfamiliar sound; thoughtful ones peered beyond the mists and saw the boiling of the mad breakers, where the surge of eight incensed and uncontrolled millions hurled against the granite foundations of the established government. Selfish heads tossed upon hot pillows, for the dawn would usher in a change boding ruin to many prospects, monetary or political. Even the butterflies of fashion felt an impending something, not defined, but suggestive of work instead of pleasure. So Washington arose, red-eyed, unrefreshed, expectant, on that famous fourth of March, 1861.

The ceremonial was planned to be grand and imposing beyond precedent. Visiting militia and civic organizations from every corner of North, East and West had been collecting for days, meeting loud receptions rather labored than spontaneous. The best bands were present in force and all available cavalry and artillery of the regular army had been hastily mobilized for the double purposes of spectacle and security. Notwithstanding, the public pulse was uncertain and fluttering and the military commanders were like unto it.

All night orderlies and cavalry platoons had dashed through the streets and guard detail had marched to all points of possible danger. Day dawn saw a light battery drawn up on G street, commanding New York avenue and the Treasury; others, with guns unlimbered and ready for action, were stationed at various points of "strategic" Washington, and infantry was massed at the Long Bridge, then the only approach from Virginia. All preparation looked to quick concentration should symptoms of a riot show head. All preparations seemed more fitting for the capital of Mexico than that of these United States. An augury were they for the peace and suasion of the administration thus ushered in. Happily, they were all needless.

In quiet that touched dismalness the day wore away. Studious precaution had drawn all the sweets from the elaborate feast prepared to catch the national taste. A dull veil seemed drawn over all glamour by the certainties of the close impending future. Street crowds wore an anxious air, all hilarity seeming forced, even from the young and thoughtless.

Many a lowering face looked down upon the procession to

the Capitol from windows, balconies and housetops, and some
of the residences along the route had shutters closed.

It was over at last. The new man had begun the new era
and I was ready for my start to Dixie. South Carolina's
secession had decided me to "go with my people."

Not all who did this were really convinced that leaving
the Union was surest accomplishment of claims made for
states' rights and Southern rights, under the Constitution.
Few of them, however, regarded the time-honored federation
as "the Old Wreck," as named by the hotheads and thoughtless. Yet almost every man of Southern birth—even when
reared and educated away from his state, as I had been—
felt a tug of sympathy and brotherhood at his heart-strings
that was resistless by reason or experience. If these two
moved him mentally, morally, it still was: "Right or wrong,
my country!"

I had waited to leave for days, despite curiosity to see the
end of the familiar old régime and the advent of the new man,
under request from the Peace Commission that I should carry
to Mr. Davis, at Montgomery, their report of the inauguration and its effect. Their despatch was to be ready for the
Aquia Creek mail boat that night. So I went to dinner at
Wormley's, with Wade Hampton, Jr., and a few others, to
say at least *au revoir* and to pick up the last news and gossip
for verbal despatch to the new "capital."

"Jim," as we then called that later imposing mulatto who
became the famous war-time caterer, had promised us a
dinner to remember *en route,* and a substantial lunch to
solidify memory. Toward the end of the former, Wormley
looked in with a face unusually grave and asked:

"Really going, gents? It's all jes' awful, an' no mistake!
The General's dining in the other room now an' he looks
worrit in his mind. He don't talk as usual, but he
eats, does 'the General'—he eats powerful!" Those

who remember General Scott will see the snap shot.

Soon we were in one of the night-liner hacks of the period, whose dusky Jehus knew Washington youth better than the directory. Jim bestowed the precious lunch tenderly upon the front seat and held the rickety cab door wide with the air of the Lord of the Ante-chamber. Several of the old set ran out for fare-wells, among them, of course, the three remaining members of what gay society knew as "the quartet," Renwick Smedberg, Frank Du Barry and Walter H. S. Taylor. The last was killed by a sharp-shooter while on engineer duty on the north side of the Potomac. Du Barry was buried at sea, in his gray uniform, as I may tell later, and "Old Smed" is now a

COLONEL W. R. SMEDBERG, U. S. A.

one-legged, bald old jollity of San Francisco, with a new generation or two around his board, and his bluecoat comrades giving him their highest honors in Legion and G.A.R.

"So you're really going? Sorry, but guess you had to!" "Never mind, old man, you'll be back in three months!" "Better not try it; you'll starve down there!" "Hope we won't meet, if it comes to a pinch, old boy!" were a few of the Parthian arrows flung at us as *obbligato* to cordial hand grip.

Then we were off. The wide level of the avenue was al-most deserted under the dismal drizzle that had set in. The dim lamps of that day reflected on the wet pavement, making the gloom more dim. The inauguration ball was about to begin and a 'bus passed us, gay with the red uniforms of the

Marine Band, under Louis Weber. Were we going where a
sudden turn might bring us face to face with old and dear
friends, where the hiss of the Minié would sing accompaniment instead of the latest galop that Louis had composed?

Beyond, a U. S. light battery was wending arsenalward
at slow trot. As our hack passed a better lighted corner
its officer drew rein to speak. He was Lieutenant John S.
Saunders, who had led the section at the Treasury corner
that day. He spoke anything but cheerily:

"So you fellows are off! Wish I were you. But today
settled it, and my resignation goes in tonight. I shan't wait
for Virginia. If I *have* to shoot at Americans, I'll do it from
the other side of the Potomac! Tell the boys down there
I'll be along soon. Good luck!"

He *was* down soon and did good enough work to embroider
two stars on his red collar. From him we verified the reports
that had already oozed through war office secrecy: that
the cannon in the day's pageant of Peace had been shotted
with canister; that the foot escort of the president, going
to take his oath of office, had ball cartridge in every musket;
that detectives in citizens' clothes were in every group on
the pavements.

Merely needed precautions? Possibly. But so far, there
had been not one overt act; the government was treating
still with the "new concern" at Montgomery; the peace
commissioners were still wasting breath at Washington.

CHAPTER IV

A NEW NATION'S NURSERY

The passage through Virginia was by night. The state was apparently in deep sleep and so she remained until that memorable seventeenth of April when her convention declared that the oldest, largest and most influential of the Southern sisterhood would cast her lot with the rest.

In the Carolinas and Georgia the hubbub began with the dawn and lasted continuously until our journey's end. The entire countryside was awake. At every station were aimless crowds, chewing tobacco, lounging in the sunshine and whittling sticks; some dull and listless, others wildly excited over some cause they did not understand. All wanted the latest news, and all were seemingly settled on one point: "Ther'll be wah, sholy!"

Plan, direction or information as to cause and conditions, there seemed to be none. That was all left to the leaders who carried the states out of the Union, and the limit of public knowledge seemed to be that *something* was about to happen.

The impression left was that the South was ready to fight, also that she was unprepared for it. This was my conclusion long before reaching the "Cradle of the Confederacy," as the Alabama capital had modestly rebaptized herself, and early information there more than confirmed it.

Though severed abruptly from her hope of becoming a Rome, the "Cradle" has a picturesque perch upon at least seven hills. As in most inland towns, "Main street," the artery of trade and activity, runs from river bluff "up town." This, in the present instance, is a high hill a full mile from the water. Here perched the Capitol, not a particularly imposing pile, either in size or architecture, yet it dominates the lesser structures as it stares down the sandy street with quite a Roman rigor.

The staff upon its dome bore the flag of the New Nation, run up there shortly after the congress met, by the hands of a noted daughter of Virginia. Miss Letitia Tyler was not only a representative of proud Old Dominion blood, but was also granddaughter of an ex-president of the United States, whose eldest son, Robert Tyler, lived at the new capi-

tal.   And   that   flag   had been designed by Hon. Wil- liam Porcher Miles, one of the brainiest of the younger statesmen   of   South   Caro- lina.

All Montgomery and her crowding visitors had flocked to Capitol Hill in gala attire, bells were rung and cannon boomed and the throng, head- ed by Jefferson Davis and all members of the government, stood bareheaded as the fair Virginian loosed its folds to the breeze.   Then   a   poet-

JEFFERSON DAVIS

priest, who later added the sword to the crozier, spoke a sol- emn benediction to the people, the cause and the flag.   The shout that answered him from every throat told that they meant to honor and to strive for it; if need come, to die for it.

Equidistant between river and Capitol and from each other

stood the two hotels of which the capital could boast. Montgomery Hall, of bitter memory and like the much-sung "Raven of Zurich," noted for uncleanliness of nest and length of bill, had been the resort of country merchants, horse and cattle men, but now the Solons of the hour dwelt therein with the possible heroes of many a field. The Exchange, with rather more pretension and decidedly more comfort, was then in the hands of a Northern firm. Political and military headquarters were there. The president and the cabinet resided there.

Montgomery seemed Washington over again, but on a smaller scale, and with the avidity and agility in pursuit of the spoils somewhat enhanced by freshness of scent.

Mr. Davis and his family would enter the long dining-room and take seats with only a stare of respectful curiosity from more recent arrivals. Even in the few weeks since I had seen him in Washington a great change had come over him. He looked worn and thinner, and the set expression on his somewhat stern face gave a grim hardness not natural to it.

On the night of my arrival, after an absent but not discourteous recognition of the general's salutation, he sat down to an untouched supper and was at once absorbed in conversation with General Samuel Cooper. This veteran had recently resigned the adjutant-generalship of the United States army and accepted a similar post and a brigadier's commission from the Confederacy.

A card to announce my presence brought an after-dinner interview with the president, to present the "very important documents" from one of the Peace Commission martyrs at Washington. They proved, seemingly, only a prolix report of the inauguration. Mr. Davis soon threw them aside to hear my verbal account; cross-examining me upon each minor detail of the effect of the show upon the populace.

He seemed especially interested in Mr. Lincoln's personal portrait and repeatedly asked if he showed any anxiety or uneasiness.

At this time the Southern chief was fifty-two years old, seemingly taller than he really was by reason of his thinness now worn to almost emaciation by mental and physical strain. The thin lips had a straighter line and a closer compression, the lower jaw, always firm and prominent in slope, set harder to its fellow. He had lost the sight of one eye many months previous, though that member scarcely showed the imperfection; but in the other burned a deep, steady glow. In conversation he had the habit of listening with eyes shaded by the lids, then suddenly shooting at the speaker a gleam from the stone-gray pupil which might have read his innermost thought.

Little form or ceremony hedged the incubating government and perfect simplicity marked every detail of its head. To all Mr. Davis's manner was unvarying in its quiet courtesy, drawing out all one had to tell and indicating by brief answer or criticism that he had extracted the pith from what was said. At that moment he was a very idol with the people; the grand embodiment of their grand cause. They were ready to applaud any move he might make. This was the morning; how the evening differed from it we shall see.

Closer acquaintance with the new capital impressed one still more with its likeness to Washington toward the close of a short session. Many features of that likeness were salient ones that had marred and debased the aspect of the older city. Endless posts of profit and honor were to be filled, and for each and every one was a rush of almost rabid claimants. The skeleton of the regular army had just been articulated by congress, but its bare bones would soon have reached hyper-Falstaffian proportions had one in every score of ardent aspirants been applied as muscle and matter.

The first "Gazette" was watched with straining eyes, but naturally left aching hearts; and disappointment here first sowed the dragon's teeth that were to spring into armed opponents of the unappreciative appointing power.

The entire nation was new. Everything had to be done, and who so capable—they being the referees—as that swarm of worn out lobbyists and "subterraneans" who, having thoroughly exploited "the Old Wreck," now gathered to gorge upon the new "concern." By the hundreds flocked in those unclean birds, blinking bleared eyes at any chance bit, whetting foul bills to peck at carrion from the departmental sewer.

Nightly the corridor of the Exchange Hotel was a pandemonium; its every flagstone a rostrum. Slowness of organization, the weakness of congress, secession of the border states personnel of the cabinet, and especially the latest army appointments, were canvassed with heat, equalled only by ignorance. Most incomprehensible of all was the diametric opposition of men from the same neighborhoods, in their views of any subject. Often this would be a vital one of policy or of doctrine, yet these neighbors would quarrel more bitterly than would men from opposite borders of the confederation.

Two ideas, however, seemed to pervade all classes. One was that keystone dogma of secession, "Cotton is king," the other that the war—did one come—could not last over three months. The man who ventured dissent from either idea, back it by what logic he might, was looked upon as an idiot if his disloyalty was not broadly hinted at.

I could comprehend these beliefs in the local mind of the South; but that the citizens of the world now congregated at Montgomery should hold them, puzzled those who paused to query if they really meant what they said.

Socially, as removed from this seething influx, Montgomery was a delightful city. Her leading families were those cotton planters and merchants, a few capitalists, and many noted professional men and a large class of railroad and steamboat managers. There was a trifle too much superiority in quarters directly connected with the state government; but that was now merged in the larger idea of nursing the national one. There had ever been much culture, more hospitality and still more ambition, both social and civic. Still, there was very much lacking of what the worldling expects of a metropolis. So it was natural that the choice as a capital should turn the whole social system somewhat topsy turvy. At the same time and possibly as a sort of escape valve for new sensations, the townspeople grumbled loudly and long. But the society proper plumed itself afresh and put on its best smile to greet the select of the newly arrived.

MRS. EMMET SIEBELS
(ANNE GOLDTHWAITE)

Very notable in Alabama history is the Goldthwaite family. Miss Anne, daughter of Judge George Goldthwaite, was one of Montgomery's most brilliant women. She married Emmet Siebels, of the South Carolina line, and is still a sprightly and vivacious woman. Her sister Mary married Judge Tom Arlington. Mrs. Charles B. Ball was the beautiful Mary Siebels, what the advance of today has called "a raging, howling belle."

The fresh, frank and fun-loving girls of the young set were

certainly creatures of beauty.   They were well educated, too, those inland and rather unripe belles of the early '60's, whether home taught or from Hamner Hill.   There was a spontaneity about them that was refreshing to the taste satiated with conventionality.

MRS. JOS. HODGSON (FLORENCE HOLT)

Reversing Time's operaglass upon that memory etching, many an old fellow still recalls "the girl I left behind me," at the first capital, and many another recollection survived the society campaigns of Richmond, Charleston and the West.   The "Ida Rice" columbiad spoke for one Montgomery beauty to the ironclads in Charleston harbor; gallant and reckless Calhoun Smith of Charleston, having so christened the gun after the well-remembered beauty who later married Henry Bethea.   In a snow-thatched shebang at Munson's Hill I heard reminder that the war gave no more lovely a bride than when Miss Knoxie Buford wore orange blossoms for Frank Lynch, of the famed old naval stock.   When Miss Alice Vivian came down from her country home she queened it with the triple royalty of Venus, Juno and Minerva.   Later she married General Quarles, whose social record proved him a judge of beauty.   Who does not recall the handsome and vivacious Holt sisters?   Miss Florence, as Mrs. Joseph Hodgson, is now one of the most popular of Mobile matrons whose equally popular daughter has just become Mrs. Julian Watters, of that city.   Mrs. L. C. Jurey, of New

Orleans, was Miss Mary Holt and her daughter is Mrs. Richard Weightman, so sought in the cultured circle of Washington. Miss Laura married William R. Pickett, grandson of the famed historian, and was as young, almost, at Miss Hodgson's wedding as her granddaughter, who was maid of honor, "pretty Florence" Davidson. Miss Eliza W. Pickett married Major Edwin A. Banks, and her daughter May married Frank B. Clark, of Mobile. Their children are now rising in the affairs and the "cloth" of their state. Mary Gindrat Pickett married Samuel S. Harris, later bishop of Michigan; her sister Martha married Major Mike L. Woods, the veteran writer and scholar of Montgomery. Corinne Pickett became Mrs. Edward Randolph, and Sallie, known to war belleship as "Tookie," married Carter Randolph.

Tradition tells the wide difference wrought by war, in these two Randolph weddings. At the first, the feminine interest was largely subordinated by the men. The war and its heroes were fresh and the uniforms were new. At the second ceremonial, the interior South was literally stripped of men at all suggestive of that name. At the church, attendants, ushers and all were girls; the groom and the aged

MRS. E. A. BANKS (ELIZA PICKETT)

father of the bride being the only males present, save the officiating priest.

A very popular girl of those days, Miss Rebecca Hails, married "Vince" Elmore; and Miss Mary Elmore became

Mrs. Warren Reese.   Then there was Miss Laura Snodgrass, later Mrs. Spencer C. Marks.   The Snodgrass sisters were great belles and beauties, as any old vet of today will testify. Miss Mary married William D. Tullis, of New Orleans.   Miss Clara Pollard, daughter of the railroad magnate, became

MRS. S. C. MARKS (LAURA SNODGRASS)

Mrs. William R. C. Cocke, her sister, Bettie, marrying Dr. Paul Lee.

And the rest? Alas! This list is not *Leporello's*.

She of the hundred tongues has used them all too freely in reporting the wild dissipations of Montgomery   in   the   nursery days.   Drinking there was general and sometimes deep, but somehow the constant excitement of the new life proved antidote for its bane.   I recall the rare cases when the habit produced any blameworthy conduct.   The stories of gambling, however, are almost wholly groundless.   All the South, and especially her westerly section, has been credited with love of reckless risks on the turf and at the card table.   Yet we never gambled to the million limit, until our Northern brethren set the example, though we did play rather recklessly.   I am quite ready to admit that any man who loses a five, by too much confidence in the virtue of three queens, is a gambler and should be haled from his club and punished by law—moral and statute.   I know, too, that the other fellow, who wins three millions on the rise of cotton which was never planted, or pork which was never pigged, is a Christian gentleman, and should have his deserved and well won villa, wife and automobile.

These Southern scamps in the '60's gambled as they fought, man to man, and with what they had in their hands. I fear I must admit that they did it often and recklessly. But that they gambled constantly at Montgomery is not founded on fact. I speak *ex cathedra*. I was there and chanced to be thrown in with the fastest of the fast set. There was, as I say, much drinking and much jockeying for place and favor, but the constant activity of the brain, the suspense, the keen contest and watch upon the foe crowding down to border and port, left no room for the real gambler. It was different at Richmond, with her larger and more mixed population, but whatever their other sins, the suckling paladins and statesmen at "the Nursery" had higher stakes to play for than those they found about the green cloth.

It was easy to distinguish the politician-by-trade from the rosy and uncomfortable novices. Secession was supposed to have been the result of aggressions and corruptions, which most of these legislators would have been utterly powerless to prevent, even had they not been active participants in them. Yet wornout politicians, who had years before been promoted from servants to "sovereigns," floated high upon the present surge and rank old Washington leaven threatened to permeate every pore of the new government.

Small wonder, then, that the action of such a congress was inadequate to the crisis.

If the time demanded anything, it was the prompt organization of an army, with an immediate basis of foreign credit to arm, equip and clothe it. Next to this was urgent need for a simple and readily managed machinery in the different departments of the government. Neither of these desiderata could be secured by their few earnest promoters, from those with whom the popular will of the new nation, or the want of that, had diluted her councils. Few indeed of the congressmen dared look the realities of the issue in the face and that minority was powerless to accomplish anything practical.

This was the Provisional Government, framed closely on the Washington model, with Jefferson Davis as President, Alexander H. Stephens, Vice-President, and this Cabinet: Secretary of State, Robert Toombs, of Georgia; Leroy Pope Walker of War; S. R. Mallory, of Florida, of the Navy; Charles G. Memminger, of South Carolina, of the Treasury; Judah P. Benjamin, of Louisiana, Attorney-General; John H. Reagan, of Texas, Postmaster-General. The public seemed content with the selections, in the main. The post-office and the department of justice looked to them nearly as useful as the state portfolio, at that junction; but to the war office every eye was turned and glanced askance at the man there. General Leroy Pope Walker was not widely known outside of Alabama, but those who did know him prophesied that he would soon stagger under the responsibilities that would weigh upon him in the event of war. Many declared that he was only a man of straw, set up by Mr. Davis simply that he might exercise his own well-known love for military matters.

Want of public trust in this vital branch was not strengthened by Mr. Walker's speech after the raising of the new flag. From the balcony of the Exchange Hotel I heard him pledge the excited crowd that he would raise it over "Faneuil Hall in the city of Boston!"

Such, briefly touched upon, were conditions at Montgomery when in early April, 1861, Governor Pickens, of South Carolina, wired that the Washington government had telegraphed the decision to resupply Fort Sumter "Peaceably if we can—forcibly, if we must!"

Deep and intense excitement held Montgomery in its grasp during those succeeding days, when news came that Beauregard had fired on the fort, on April 12. Business was suspended, all stores were closed and the people collected in groups in the streets and before the newspaper and government offices. Various and strange were the speculations as to the issue of the fight and its consequences; but the conviction came like a thunder clap, even to those most skeptical, that there *was* to be war!

Then, with rapid step, action distanced suspense. The swift following fall of Sumter solidified the South into a nation. Then came the adhesion of Virginia, the decision to accept her invitation to make her soil the battle ground and her capital the South's.

GENERAL P. G. T. BEAUREGARD

There was a grand parade and review of all the troops at Pensacola, by the President, aided by Generals Bragg and Beauregard. It left the country guessing as to which of the two would be commander-in-chief.

Immediately after it Mr. Davis moved his headquarters to Richmond: the government was boxed up and followed him, and the nursery of the New Nation was noiselessly deserted by its now growing occupant.

CHAPTER V

THE FIRST "ON TO RICHMOND!"

THE new capital of the Confederacy presented a very different appearance from Montgomery. The approach to the city of new hope was promising in its picturesqueness.

Threading the narrow span of high trestles, perched spindle-legged above the James, Richmond spread in pretty panorama. Green and tree-bordered, the May sun gilding white homes and tall spires, it receded to high red hills beyond the later famous heights of Chimborazo to the right and that historic City of the Silent, Hollywood, far away to left. Central gleamed the venerable seat of lawmaking.

> *Where looms the Capitol, antique and pure,*
> *The great "First Rebel" points the storied past.*
> *Around him grouped Virginia's great of yore,*
> *With Stonewall's statue, greatest and the last—*

had not then slipped from my pen. The statue of John Marshall, long delayed and missed, had not been placed to inspire Randolph's quaintly vigorous lines, beginning:

"We're glad to see you, John Marshall, my boy,
Along with the other old codgers."

Social Richmond was desiccated Virginia selectness, and only enforced acceptance of the war incursion could have rubbed the down from the peach. But for that, the lovely "village on the Jeems" had been of far slower growth into the cosmopolitan city of today.

At that day family first, with the concomitants of polish, education and "manner," were the sole "open sesame" to which the doors of the good old city would swing wide.

The learned professions were about the sole exceptions. "Law, physic, the church," and, as heretofore seen, the last especially, were permitted to condone the "new families."

Trade, progressive spirit and self-made personality were excluded from the plane of the elect, as though germiniferous. The "sacred soil" and the sacred social circle were paralleled in the minds of their possessors.

As his first introduction has shown, the Virginian of yesterday, particularly when he boasted high colonial descent, was still the nearest counterpart to the landed gentry of the motherland of any American soever. He combined many noble traits with the same old pride that so dominated them all.

In the country districts habit and condescension often overrode class barriers, but in the city, where class sometimes jostled privilege, the line of demarcation was so strongly drawn that its overstepping was dangerous.

When the news came that patriotism dictated the abandonment of inland Montgomery for border Richmond, a surprise that was not all pleasurable thrilled to the finger-tips of Richmond society. Its exponents felt much as the Roman patricians might have felt at impending advent of the leading families of the Goths. Her sacred fanes might possibly be desecrated by profane touch, her Vestal Virgins viewed by vulgar eyes.

At first blush of the new invasion it is assumable that older Richmond was ready to bolt the front door and lock the shutters. Younger Richmond perhaps was curious enough to peep between them. But the Commonwealth was heart and soul in the cause and the newcomers were of it. So, gradually, the first repulsion grew to sufferance, then that gave place to cordiality. There was still a lingering reserve in some quarters and a sense of an undefined something that might happen at any moment. But on the surface were urbanity and ease that are innate to the better Virginian. This was vindicated in most instances by the real worth and, frequently, the high grade of the social leaders of the influx.

It must be recalled that the very best elements of the old South began the war and went first to the front. In the army and, in degree, in every branch of the government were men of birth and breeding, women of culture, grace and social prestige. These soon segregated themselves from the dross of the incoming tide, and to them the jealous doors swung on spontaneous hinges. Later a common cause, common ambition and common sorrow drew all classes into a sympathy and contact that showed the best in each and all.

In the coarse butternut of the private soldier moved men of lineage as high, of attainment as fine, of social habit as elegant, as that under society's behest. Officer and man met on terms of perfect equality, off duty. The private of today might be the general of tomorrow, and the younger leaders in Richmond realized the fact, and early learned to judge their new beaux rather for themselves than for their rank marks.

All Virginia had long been noted throughout the South for a hospitality equal to her pride and for its lavish expression: and Richmond was concentrated Virginia.

This went out to all, only slightly differentiating, perhaps, those veritable *corps d'élites* from distant states: as the Louisianians.

These picked companies of peace comprised the "dearest and the best," the very flower of the highbred, or wealthy youth. Company F of Richmond, was one example, the Mobile Cadets another, in which many a man had refused proffered commission to "stay with the fellows," until merit and the demands of the service literally forced him upward. For such men as these the brightest eyes in all the land grew brighter, but Louisiana held her own.

In these early days of the war no section of the South had yet felt the strain upon its resources, and the entertainments at the new capital of the Confederacy were as elegant and as lavish as ever before. Later the gradual pressure upon pocket, as well as upon brain and heart, told first on the leaguered capital, but that wore away only the surface, leaving the social gold with all its pristine polish. Even when the "starvation parties" had replaced the lavish balls of gone yesterdays, as courtly nothings were spoken, and as cordial healths pledged in the substituted green tumbler of yellow "Jeems" river water, as had ever bubbled on the lip with congenial champagne. For these indeed were descendants of the Golden Horseshoe Knights; of the Huguenots of the Carolinas; of the Bienville-led Creoles; often of the oriole-crested followers of

CAPTAIN I. L. LYONS, 10TH LA. REG'T.

Lord Baltimore.   And they proved in later days —

> *"The kindliest of the kindly band*
> *Who rarely hated ease;"*

Later, when the crucial test had come, they proved themselves

> *"Those sons of noble sires,*
> *Whose foes had found enchanted ground*
> *But not one knight asleep!"*

And the fair women whom they toasted, fought for and loved proved themselves worthy of all three. So, while the fortunes and the larders lasted, the entertainments in Richmond were generous; when the direst constriction of the blockade crushed, the elegance remained, over the crust and the yellow water.

The thought of no habitué of Richmond society of that day can recur to it without being peopled with bright memories of men and women, since famous in the history and society of the Union. Whatever his tastes, business shadowed or pleasure tinted, they doubtless bear borrowed coloring from an era of storm and stress that left its impress deep on all natures, at a moment when most receptive by absorption in a common effort to one great end. The fate of a nation hung in the balance, but the hearts of its integers were hopeful, buoyant and sometimes giddy.

Dinners, dances, receptions and constant visiting followed the earlier arrival of the new government and its Joseph-coated following. There were drives and picnics for the young and, for aught I know to the contrary, much flirtation. The dizzy whirled in recurrent germans, and the buzz of the society bee was heard by the pinkest-tinted ears.

But besides the regular society routine at the capital, much like that in many another city, there was other sociality, quieter, but nowise less attractive to the incoming.

There were sewing circles, at which the assistants enjoyed the talk of brainy and refined women and cultured men; there music, improvisation and even dancing filled intervals of busy work.

As Dickens made his *Madame Defarge* "knit shrouds," before the greedy knife of the Terror, the sewing circles of Richmond stitched love and hope and sentiment into the rough seams and hems of nondescript garments they sent to the camps by bales. No lint was scraped for wounds to come that was not saturated with pity and tenderness; and the amateur cooks kneaded their hearts into the short piecrust and not always heavy biscuits for "those dear boys."

There were many, and some really excellent amateur concerts, charades and tableaux, by the most modest and sometimes most ambitious amateurs, all for the same good end. And through all of them passed the procession of stately forms and bright faces. On the joggling board of improvised stage, voices that had rung sonorous in the van of battle lisped the sugared nothings of society comedy to Chloes, who later gave the key to society in

GENERAL FITZ LEE
(IN 1863)

many a *post-bellum* city. Comic recitations were made by men who have since held listening senates, and verses were penned by women who have now impressed their names on the literature of a time.

Most of this was naturally in the *entr'acte* of war's red

drama, in the days of winter's enforced truce, from roads belt-deep in mire or frozen impassable. There were nights when hard-riding Fitz Lee was pressed to pose in a tableaux, or dashing "Jeb" Stuart took minor part in a small comedy, to brighten the eyes nearest but not the dearest, for that cause alone.

Of course the storm center of general society was about the presidential household and its actions.

In that dwelling the most weighty and eventful matters of the government had birth and were matured, and there the tireless worker, to himself the Confederacy incarnate, devoted all the days and most of the midnights, planning, considering, changing. The executive officers were elsewhere, but at that day Mr. Davis carried the government in his own brain, and that never slept.

His wildest admirer has never claimed that Jefferson Davis was a saint; his vilest vituperator has never proved him a devil. History shows no man who has faced such fierce and sweeping blasts of indictment, calumny and malice and so long stood erect: a mark inviting scrutiny, but not shrinking beneath it. It is simple truth that his name is today mentioned with respect, or praise, in the capital of every civilized country on the globe, save one, and there the cause of silence or of old-time iteration is more political than judical.

I am not planting seed for the future Macaulay, but it may be noted here that this absolute self-reliance was one cause of failure; he failed because he could not make the Confederacy Jefferson Davis. The *non sequitur* is often more logical than the epigram. When Sir Boyle Roche said: "No man can be in two places at once, barrin' he's a bird!" he was probably ignorant that he was double-barreled— talking nonsense and philosophy. He did not know that he was laying down a rule of procedure which, persistently deviated from, must result in disaster. That disaster followed was not Mr. Davis's fault. In an article of the *North American Review,* a dozen years ago, I showed that he was not only the president, but that he shouldered the responsibility for every member of his cabinet. He was the head almost of every distinct bureau, in each department of the government.

A tremendous national convulsion demanded that the executive should plan, distribute and order done the work in the various departments. Mr. Davis did this. He did not stop there; he attempted to do the work.

But it was not on governmental grounds that social Richmond felt uneasy as to the Davis family in these early days. There was no tinge of personality toward the inmates of the White House; only a nervousness as to that nebulous dweller on the threshold of legislative necessity. There was an undefined dread that the official head would be followed by a nameless, yet most distasteful, surrounding of politics and place seekers.

CHAPTER VI

WHITE HOUSE FOLK

FORTUNATELY, it chanced that Mrs. Varina Howell Davis was a woman of too much sound sense, tact and experience in great social affairs not to smile to herself at this rather provincial iciness.

MRS. JEFFERSON DAVIS

She put her native wit and all her fund of diplomatic resource to work; social cold storage rapidly raised its temperature and soon all about the Executive Mansion was broad sunshine, in which even the ultra exclusives early began to uncoil.

In her proper person, and not as the president's wife, Mrs. Davis was at home—informally and to everybody who chose to call—on all evenings of the week. On these occasions only tea and talk were proffered to her guests; but the latter seemed to evolve a finer aroma than the former, even before the blockade proclaimed its "substitute law."

It was her husband's invariable custom to give one hour of each day to unbending from the strain of public duty in the midst of his family circle. At these informal evenings the early caller was almost sure to meet the man of the hour; to shake his courteously proffered hand; to hear the voice upon the vibrations of which hung the fate of The Cause.

State dinners, save in very rare necessities as in case of some important foreign visitors, were not given, and the only other function was the fortnightly levee, after the Washington model. To these flocked "the world and his wife," in what holiday attire they possessed, in the earlier days marked by the dainty toilettes of really elegant women, the butternut of the private soldier, and the stars and yellow sashes of many a general, already world-famous.

The levee was social *jambalaya*, but it was also novelty. It proved appetizing enough to tickle the dieted palate of Richmond's exclusiveness.

Besides their novelty, these levees had their uses as an amalgamating medium, a social 'Change whereon the provincial bear met the city bull, nor found him deadly of horn. Most of all, they proved the ease with which the wife of the president of the Confederacy could hold her title of "The First Lady in the Land." She was politician and diplomatist in one, where necessity demanded, but long personal knowledge of her had already convinced the writer that Varina Howell Davis preferred the straight road to the tortuous bypath. She was naturally a frank though not a blunt woman, and her bent was to kindliness and charity. Sharp tongue she had, when set that way and the need came to use it; and her wide knowledge of people and things sometimes made that use dangerous to offenders. Mrs. Davis had a sense of humor painfully acute, and the unfitness of things provoked laughter with her rather than rage. That the silly tales of her sowing dissension in the cabinet and being behind the too frequent changes in the heads of the government are false, there seems small reason to doubt.

Surely, in social matters she moved steadily and not slowly, from at least coolness to the warm friendship of the best women of conservative Richmond and to the respect and admiration of all.

The Kemp-Howell family was of British stock: Scotch, Irish, English, Welch and Quaker in descent. Mrs. Davis's

father was William Burr Howell, a native of Trenton, N. J. He was son of Governor Richard Howell of that state; an ex-naval officer who had distinguished himself in the War of 1812.

Mrs. Davis's mother was Margaret Louise Kemp, a Virginian, born on her father's broad acres, over which the decisive charges of Bull Run were later made. The grandfather Kemp was a Dublin Irishman of means, a graduate of Trinity College and a

MRS. M. DE W. STOESS
(MARGARET HOWELL)

close friend of Robert Emmett. This brought him into political trouble and he was banished for alleged treason that seems never to have passed the stage of intent. The refugee sat down in Virginia, farming near Manassas, but later removing to Natchez, Miss., after a duel with a Virginian, which was fatal to the latter; although, at that day and date, such trivialities were merely *post* and not *propter hoc*. Margaret Louise Kemp was a small child, at the date of this migration. Later, the New Jersey Howell, touring in the South, met and won her, and himself became a Mississippian.

This pair became the parents of six children, all noted in the '60's. These were Varina, later Mrs. Davis; Margaret

Graham Howell, Jane Kemp Howell, and three brothers, Beckett, William Francis and Jefferson Davis Howell.

The third sister married William G. Waller, of Lynchburg, during the war, at St. Paul's Church, Richmond. She left a son and a daughter; the former dead, but the latter, Miss Elizabeth Tyler Waller, still residing in Savannah, Ga. Of the brothers, only one married. William Francis wedded the daughter of Rev. Dr. Leacock of Christ Church, New Orleans. This couple left three daughters, still living in the Cresent City, and two now married. These were the "little Howell girls," sometimes confounded in errant chronicle with Miss Maggie Howell and her sister, Jane Kemp, who was not very much in Richmond.

With Mrs. Davis, in matters social, moved her sister. Miss Margaret Howell was scarcely more than a débutante, but her adaptability replaced experience and she knew human nature by what surgery calls "the first intention." Her sense of humor was quite as keen and even more dominant than her elder's. Less restrained, she bubbled into *bon mot* and epigram that went from court to camp. Sometimes these were caustic enough to sting momentarily, but their aptitude and humor salved the prick of their point. It was stated that her comment did more to calm the tumult of "Pawnee Sunday" than all else. I am not posing as Miss Maggie Howell's Boswell, even in recalling the pleasant hours when we were "out together"; but the memory of all Richmond would indorse her naming as quite the most original and one of the most brilliant women in that bright and unique society. I recall that mention of her sallies one evening at Gustavus Myers's dinner table caused Mr. Benjamin to remark:

"Were this yesterday and did we live in Paris, she would be a de Staël!"

The young lady will be met again in these pages, and probably with the same spice of pleasure she gave in sudden *rencontres* in those days. That she will do this unwittingly is proved by her recent epigrammatic statement to the writer: "Had I known that my biscuits would be vended in public,

I should have kept my yeast in the pantry!"

Miss Howell's friends of yore will read with pleasure that she is still living. After the war she went abroad and married, in England, the Chevalier Charles William de Wechmar Stoess, then Bavarian consul at Liverpool. Her husband died some years ago, leaving her with a son and daughter nearly grown. These are the whole of life to the widow and

CHEVALIER C. DE W. STOESS

the trio made one of the happiest and most united families in Victoria, B. C. For a time they lived in Spokane, after Mr. Stoess' death. The son, Philip, is a mining engineer in Seattle, and his sister, Christine, paints well, and plays the violin.

Apart from distinction of parentage the little children of the White House had individuality of their own which made them notable to its habitués. They were three only when the move from Montgomery was made. One was killed in Richmond, and two others, the "Children of the Confederacy," were born at the new capital.

Mr. Davis, as noted, had been married twice. The second marriage was childless for years. Then, just as the father was called to the secretaryship of war by President Pierce, a son was born. Samuel Emory Davis survived but three years. He died in 1854.

A daughter came next, Margaret Howell Davis, named for her grandmother, and now the sole survivor of the family of six.

Jefferson Davis, Jr., was born in Jaunary, 1858, being the only son who reached adult age. He died of yellow fever at Memphis, in 1878, when within three months of his majority.

Joseph Evan Davis, the next son, was born in April, 1859, His was the tragedy that shadowed the White House beyond all else that brought sorrow through its portals. This second boy, gentle and lovable, fell from the balusters into the back court of the home and was almost instantly killed. The heart of a whole people went out to the stricken parents, and the sorrowing sympathy of Richmond was as real as universal; the little people had become familiar pets. But, as in the case of the first-born, the empty cradle was filled.

William Howell Davis was born in the White House in the first year of its occupancy. But three years old when his elder brother was killed, he lived to reach nearer to manhood than any of the boys save Jeff. He had perhaps the gentlest ways of any of the children; and they centered in him, as he gained in years, the love of mother and sisters that was beyond words. But

JEFFERSON DAVIS, JR.

"Billie's" death was almost as sudden as Joe's had been years before. He was seized with diphtheria at Natchez and died there in October, 1874. He was the elder of the "Children of the Confederacy." The cradle of little Joe had been filled by the other and more widely known one.

"Winnie" (Varina Anne) Davis was born on the 27th of

June, 1864, and her coming was accepted by the hopeful as a bright augury amid the gloom that shadowed her father's fortunes. Too familiar to the later generation to demand word of description, "The Daughter of the Confederacy," formally so named and adopted by the united camps of the Veterans, ended her promising career by sudden illness at Narragansett Pier, September 18, 1898.

In their latest trial it was not the heart of a section, but of a re-united nation,

"WINNIE" DAVIS

that went out to the aged widow and the stricken sister. Time had softened war-born asperities, and only the weakest and most brutal cherished the misbegotten falsities they bred. Men who had howled to "Hang Jeff Davis!" through the North had mellowed under second thought. It was genuine and heart-born warmth from every quarter that met the bereaved.

Again Time has worked his miracle. Today "Winnie" Davis lives again in the universal love of the South and the tender respect of the North.

She, like her brothers, had inherent traits, and strong ones. In her they had longer to develop into visible result. But the little fellows showed them early, and in "Billie" they were of sweet and tender promise. In Jeff they took expression and told strong truths at an age when those of most children are dumb.

Early in her Richmond life Mrs. Davis selected as teacher for her children the eldest of the daughters of Judge Raleigh T. Daniel, Misses Augusta, Lizzie and Charlotte. Highly educated and of studious bent, yet genial and popular socially, this lady became as devoted to her charge as she was fitted for it. After the lapse of years her memory of the Davis household, great and small, is as reminiscent as it is loyal and tender.

Margaret Howell Davis was her grandmother's namesake. She was more like her father than her mother.

In 1876 "Little Maggie," married Joel Addison Hayes, now of Colorado Springs. There she is refusing to grow old, although surrounded by a grown family and grandchildren.

The eldest son, named for his grandfather, died in infancy. Varina Howell Davis Hayes is now the wife of Dr. Gerald Bertram Webb. The second daughter, Lucy White, is two years younger. The eldest son of this family is Jefferson Hayes Davis, having taken his grandfather's surname.

The youngest child is "Billy"—William Davis Hayes.

"Little Maggie's" family have given two to the fourth generation of the living Davis descendants. Mrs. Varina Hayes Webb has a three-year-old daughter, who bears

MRS. J. A. HAYES

the name of Margaret Varina Hayes. Her boy, whom Mrs. Davis never saw, was born on December 17, 1906.

Mrs. Davis's brothers were rarely in Richmond. Beckett

and Jeff Davis Howell were both in the navy. Both died years ago and both will recur in these pages.

Such, in brief and imperfect retrospect, was the family about which most interest centered in the new Richmond. The greater portion of it was about Mr. Davis personally. Knowing him since my boyhood, intimate in his household then and in his office later, Senator and Secretary Davis ever seemed to me the grave, self-contained worker, rarely asking aid and never advice. His memory was marvelous, especially for names and faces. His grasp on a subject was as rapid as his decision was tenacious. He was of a nature slow to admire, but as loyal to friendship as he was inveterate on occasion. Being human, he was liable to error in either regard.

In private life, and notably in his own home, Mr. Davis was polished, affable and often cordial. He was easy of approach and patient to the woes of constituents and subordinates. He was a thoughtful, sound, and at times a free talker, and, strangely enough, he permitted others to express as well as to hold, their opinions. Thus Jefferson Davis appeared to the thinker in Richmond, thus he appears to this writer today. Such he is likely to appear to the future Macaulay.

This is no place to discuss the actions of the publicist or the motives whence they sprang. Neither does the time of which I write warrant introduction of the freshly mooted matter of his treatment after capture.

Philosophy, when she really comes to teach by example, will settle these for all time. So will she prick that poor invention of malicious mendacity that makes the simple capture of a great fugitive a farce incredible.

I truly believe that no man who is competent to comprehend the character of the Confederate chief, judged solely by its visible results, credits that silly figment of imagination.

No man who knows aught of human nature could believe Jefferson Davis capable of attempting denial of a fact, by a subsequent masquerade. Yet the portrait of him, in the clothes in which he was captured, is a certified and proved reproduction in every detail. That, without speech, confounds the patient and persistent liars.

The South resented the treatment of her most representative man just after the war, but it is doubtful whether much tenderness mingled with her wrath.

Gradually respect for the dead chief's great traits passes into mellowed feeling, and the sentiment of the vast majority of Southerners is doubtless voiced by an unknown poet's suggestion for his statue:

JEFFERSON DAVIS IN SUIT HE WORE AT THE TIME OF CAPTURE

Write on its base: "We loved him!" All these years,
Since that torn flag was folded, we've been true;
The love that bound us now revealed in tears,
Like webs, unseen till heavy with the dew.

It is so singular a fact that almost universal ignorance exists as to the lineage of the Confederate president. I have never been able to find an accurate published statement of either; and have at great pains, been able to present this brief summary:

Jefferson Davis, youngest of the ten children of Samuel

Davis and Jane Cook, was born in Christian county, Ky., on June 3rd, 1808. His ancestors were colonial and revolutionary; of sterling Welsh stock and "good people in the colony," though nowise of the gentry, or notable in its pre-revolutionary events. Their famous descendant had a contempt for genealogy; even his wife's biography of him giving but most meagre mention.

In earlier half of the eighteenth century, three Welsh brothers started for Pennsylvania, as settlers. One is believed to have been drowned on the voyage. At all events, he never reappears in anything I have been able to trace. The other two, Samuel and Evan, the youngest, settled near Philadelphia, presumably to farm, as they took up lands. Samuel is said to have removed to Virginia, but trace of him is lost, save in some old land transfer records. Evan Davis, grandfather of the President, drifted to Georgia, and there married a widow Williams, whose maiden name had been Emory. One son came to this couple, who was named Samuel, and was a youth in his teens at the outbreak of the Revolution. His half brothers, Williams, were in the rebel army, and the mother sent Samuel to their camp with clothing and home comforts. He caught the war fever, ran away, fought well and later raised a company and went to assist in lifting the seige of Savannah. Soon after the war, he married Miss Jane Cook, of Georgia; presumably his distant kinswoman, and doubtless connected with the later noted Hardins, of Kentucky. When he already had a grown family, he moved to Kentucky and established himself on a tobacco farm.

The eldest child of Samuel Davis and Jane Cook, was Joseph Emory Davis, born in Georgia but a lawyer and planter, residing at the "Hurricane" Plantation. Warren county, Mississippi. He married Miss Eliza van Benthysen. He was a great stay and aid to his father and, after his death, became its head and parent, rather than guardian, of the younger children. Little Jeff was devoted to him, and the later statesman never forgot to express his love and admiration of his elder. Joseph Davis rose to great influence and regard in his state and section; and acquired wealth.

Joseph Davis had a family of nine children, of whom six were daughters. These all died childless, except Mary, though Florida and Caroline also married. Mary married Dr. Mitchell and left one son and one daughter. The son, Captain Joseph Davis Mitchell, never married. His sister, Mary Elizabeth, married W. D. Hamer and has two children, William D. and Mary Lucy, now Mrs. J. G. Kelly.

The next brother was a doctor and planter: Dr. Benjamin Davis, of St. Francisville, La. He married Miss Aurelia Smith of that parish and died at an advanced age, after a quiet, respected and useful life. This couple died childless.

Samuel Davis, Jr. was the next in age. He was a planter and resided near Vicksburg, Miss. His wife was Miss Lucy Throckmorton and their only living child is Mrs. Helen Keary of Rapides Parish, La. There were four sons: Benjamin, Joseph, Samuel and Robert; the eldest of whom left six children at Boise City, Idaho. Robert, Samuel, Pauline and Ellen still live there.

Isaac Davis, the fourth son, was also a planter and resided at Canton, Miss. He married Miss Susan Guertly, and left one son, General Joseph E. Davis, of the Confederate army; and two granddaughters.

The fifth brother and youngest child was Jefferson Davis, the president.

Anna Davis, the eldest daughter, married Luther Smith of West Feliciana, and had a family of six, two of whom were daughters: Joseph, Luther, Gordon, Jedediah, Lucy and Amanda. She married Mr. Robert Smith and left one daughter, Anna Davis Smith.

Amanda, her next sister, married Mr. Bradford, of Madison Parish, La. Her living children are Jeff Davis Bradford, an engineer now stationed at Fort Moultrie in Charleston Harbor; Elizabeth Bradford White, widowed and residing at New Orleans in winter and Kentucky in summer, and Mrs. Lucy Bradford Mitchell, widow of Dr. C. R. Mitchell, of Vicksburg, Miss. Seven of this family died: David, Benjamin, Mary, Sarah, Anna, Laura, and a second David, born after the the death of his brother so named.

Lucinda Davis, the next sister, married Mr. William Stamps, of Woodville, Miss. Her three sons and two daughters all died and her grandchildren are Mrs. Edgar Farrar and Mrs. Mary Bateson, of New York, and Mrs. William Anderson; Hugh, Richard and Isaac Alexander, and one great grand-child, Miss Josie Alexander.

Matilda, the fourth sister, died in childhood; and the youngest and next in age to the later president, was his boy-hood's companion and delight, "Little Polly." She was Mary Ellen Davis, who married—without changing her name —Robert Davis of South Carolina; and left one daughter still living: Mrs. Mary Ellen Davis Anderson, of Ocean Springs, Miss.

It is another coincidence in the parallels of the lives of the two great leaders in the Civil War, that the Christian county birthplace of Jefferson Davis was in the adjoining one to Hardin county, in which Abraham Lincoln saw the light: a few miles only separating the spots and only eight months the arrival of those famous stars in the great dramas of poli-tics and war. Strange it is, too, that the two young men saw their first glimpses of war in the Black Hawk War; Davis as a lieutenant in the United States army, and Lincoln as the cap-tain of a company of volunteers he had raised and proffered, but which was never in actual conflict.

It might be an odd study for the psychologist ·to query

whether some innate characteristics of both men, acting upon circumstance—or acted upon by it—may not have led to similar aspirations: and whether they were not shadowed out in the strange, yet unmistakable, likeness in their faces. Looking at their portraits in manhood's prime, it needs no Lavater to read that similar early surroundings, education and pursuits might have softened the coarser lines of the one or hardened the more delicate tone of the other, into absolute similarity. And it is not least curious that the same causes drove the parents of one to the North and of the other to the South from similar points and at no long interval.

In 1811, when his youngest born was but three years old, Samuel Davis decided that Kentucky was not yielding him the returns hoped for when he left Georgia. He proposed to locate in Louisiana; but, finding the climate unhealthful for a young family, he decided upon Mississippi, and bought there his final family home. This was named "Poplar Grove" —from its splendid growth of those stately trees—was a picturesque and extensive site about a mile and a half from Woodville, in Wilkinson county, Miss. There most of the younger family were reared, the daughters were married and some of their children reared by their venerable grandmother, Mrs. Jane Cook Davis. Of these, was Ellen Mary, who never changed her name; and her early orphaned child and namesake, Mrs. Anderson, today recalls the delight of her life at the "Poplars."

It was with this sister "Polly," that the five-year-old Jefferson first went to school, at a log house a half mile away. Two years later, when not seven years old (in 1815) he was sent on a ride through virgin forests of nearly 900 miles, to attend the St. Thomas Academy at Washington Co., Ky. In three years more he was at Jefferson College, Adams county, Miss.; and in 1821, when but thirteen years old, was sent to Transylvania College, Lexington, Ky. He was an earnest and intelligent pupil; but gave little promise of the brilliance, acumen and erudition that illustrated his later career.

After their father's death, his brother, Joseph Davis, became the real head of the family; and it was he who gave special attention to the rearing of the youngest, and who directed his education. And by that time, Joseph Emory Davis had become a power in the law and politics of his section. So, in 1824, he obtained through Congressman Rankin, a West Point cadetship for his 16-year-old brother.

At the academy, the youth was esteemed as a careful, studious and dignified cadet, rather than an ambitious and dashing one; yet he missed no branch of useful acquirement and came out a fine rider, swordsman and tactician, as well as a courteous and dignified officer. He graduated 25 in a class of 33; going into the brevet lieutenancy in the Twenty-first Infantry, then under Colonel Zachary Taylor: afterwards general and president.

This was in 1828, and before his majority. At the Point, his intimates were Joseph E. Johnston, Robert E. Lee, Prof. Alex. Dallas Bache, Albert Sydney Johnston and others, with whom he held lifelong friendships, or—in rare cases— undying enmities.

Lieutenant Davis served with credit at Fort Crawford, in what is now Illinois; then at the lead mines near Galena, and at Fort Winnebago, in Wisconsin. He made his first campaign against the Indians in the closing of the Black Hawk War, in 1831-33.

Then, when service needs created more cavalry, the First Dragoons was organized and its adjutant was Jefferson Davis, now promoted to first lieutenant, in 1834. But he held the post only a few months; resigning in June of the next year.

For some reason, never explained, "Old Zach" Taylor had taken a strong dislike to his subaltern; but the latter was deeply and seriously in love with the fair young daughter of his chief, Miss Knox Taylor. To the surprise of every-one—and none more than her sire—Miss Taylor married the young soldier almost immediately on his resignation. Her father never forgave her; and he never saw her again. She went as a bride to the home of her sister-in-law, Mrs. Anna Davis at West Feliciana, La. Three months later, she was buried there, after a brief illness, and the shock broke down completely the health of the young husband, already under-mined by hard frontier service.

On his recovery, Mr. Davis made a tour of the West Indies; thence paid a long visit to his old friends in Washington and made many new and useful ones, who were loyal to him until the end. Then he settled in Mississippi; by his brother's advice becoming a planter in Warren county, but devoting really more attention to reading law and managing local politics. The latter proved the more congenial and success-ful. He was elected to the legislature in 1842; was elector for Polk and Dallas, two years later; and gained high repute as a debater, in a tilt with the famous Sergeant S. Prentiss. In February, 1845, he married Miss Varina Banks Howell.

In the autumn after his marriage, Mr. Davis was elected to congress by a handsome majority; promptly taking a prominent stand and gaining quick recognition for vigor and eloquence in championing the ultra pro-slavery and states' rights wing of the Democracy. Hearing his maiden speech in the house, John C. Calhoun said:

"Keep a watch on that young man: he will be heard from!"

In 1846, the Mexican War caused his resignation, to accept command of the regiment of Mississippi Rifles, soon attached to General Taylor's Army of the Rio Grande. There it gave such good account of itself and its commander as to warrant special mention in orders, for Monterey; and Davis' splendid charge at Buena Vista—in which he was severely wounded—brought another flattering report to Washington, whether, or not, his first father-in-law's personal feelings had changed.

In the session of 1847, Mr. Davis first took his seat as senator of the United States; having been appointed by Gov. Albert Gallatin Brown to succeed Hon. Jesse Speight, who died that year. The next session of the legislature elected him to fill the unexpired term. In 1851, he resigned to accept the nomination for governor of Mississippi, when he was defeated by that arch-manipulator, Henry S. Foote, who ran on the Union ticket. But he remained a power in politics and was especially active in the election of President Pierce, who made him secretary of war, in March, 1853. At the close of his term in the cabinet, he was again elected to the senate and again became the leader of the ultra Southern party. It was at this time that he made his famous Faneuil Hall speech on the rights of the states and the powers of the central government. Then, in January of 1861, Jefferson Davis made his farewell speech in the senate, withdrew from that body and went to Mississippi to carry his home people into the incubating Confederacy.

CHAPTER VII

CABINET TIMBER

THE head of the cabinet was, in constructive sense, Secretary of State Robert Toombs, of Georgia, but popular belief said it was really Mr. Benjamin, voicing Mr. Davis's views. Burly, rough, emphatic in his own opinions as his chief himself, the Georgian was a brainy and experienced politician and a born disputant. What he was not in remotest degree was a diplomat, and the early wonder grew why Mr. Davis had selected an ingrained aggressor, one whose method was to force a point rather than go around it, for the most delicate and possibly the most vital of all cabinet procedure. Mr. Toombs was, moreover, very strong in his prejudices, and they doubtless swayed his judgment, so it was asserted that he was unstable of tenet. Disputatious as Sydney Smith's missionary, who "disagreed with the cannibal that ate him," the secretary was not always of the same mind. A governmental wag once said: "Bob Toombs disagrees with himself between meals!"

Vigorous, able and well posted he certainly was, but perhaps his weakest point as a minister was his hyper-Southern underjudging of the men opposed to him in the North, men with whom he should have been familiar from long and close contact in the public service. At the moment of his selection the foreign policy of the Confederacy was unborn. The busy bureaux were those of war, finance and subsistence. Mr. Toombs had nothing to do but talk politics, tell stories and say some very clever things. Profane enough to have delighted Sterne's "Army in Flanders," he larded his jokes with things not in the church service, but they were usually to the point. In Montgomery I recall one retort, not new, but too characteristic to omit. A man of influence and loaded with recommendations applied to him on the street for a clerkship in his department. The secretary demurred; the man of influence insisted. Jerking off his well-worn Washington hat, the official held it up; pointed into it as he roared:

"Blankety blank, sir! *There* is the State Department of the Confederacy, by blankety blank! Jump in, sir!"

When the secretary resigned, avowedly to take a brigade in the field, there was little surprise among the initiated. There were however, varied rumors of ruptures between him and the President and other of his associates in council. None of these were probable, for General Toombs was restless under thwart of impracticable views, and he was doubtless sincere in preference for active service.

Secretary Toombs was succeeded, in July, 1861, by Robert Mercer Taliaferro Hunter. No Virginian of the older activities had been more prominent than he, and his experience had been earned in service as state legislator, congressman and United States senator. His unfinished term in the upper house would have ended, had he retained it, about the time when General Grant was arranging to accept the parole of Robert Lee. Mr. Hunter held the portfolio of state but a few months, resigning to take up the more congenial duties of Confederate senator from Virginia.   In February, 1862, his place was temporarily filled by Mr. Benjamin, who was already becoming the *Pooh-Bah* of the cabinet.

The social side of the cabinet was scarcely affected by Mr. Toombs's withdrawal. His only daughter, Miss Sallie Toombs, had long before married Dudley M. Du Bose, and had given up Washington belleship for domesticity. She died shortly after the war, in Virginia, leaving a son and daughter, Toombs Du Bose, of Athens, Ga., and Camille, Mrs. Henry Calley of Washington, Ga. An older daughter, Lula, had married Felix Alexander, but had died in 1855, leaving no children.

The Mallory household was an interesting one to all sorts of people, and from many aspects. General curiosity prevailed as to the naval future of the Confederacy, and that centered in the man who was to control at least its details.

Mr. Mallory was known to all as a tried publicist, who had headed the then infant effort of floating the starry flag triumphantly in long service as senator. Personally, he was little known on his arrival in Richmond; but his quick perception, decided cultivation, and especially his wit, genial nature and frank courtesy, soon placed him high in the estimate of even the severest critics of men in position.

STEPHEN R. MALLORY
(SECRETARY OF THE NAVY)

In two things Mr. Mallory took genuine pleasure: good cheer and a good joke. He was *gourmet*, while no whit *gourmand*, and one had but to note the twinkle in his eye and the placid curve of his full lips to know that the Irish blood in him had taken no yellow tinge from American rush. The color of his humor was not scarlet, but his quaint turning of an idea was often more effective than an epigram had been. The two salient sides of character noted were concreted in a brief love song he dedicated to "*Gumbo File*," the ambrosia of the Creole and the dietetic delight of the earnest Northern pilgrim. Brief, with a touch of genuine poetry, and as full flavored with humor as its delicate godmother *potage* with the bay leaf, the poem took at once. The press reprinted it; young ladies clipped it—often with but part conception of its quality—and it was sung frequently, and notably by Mrs. Mallory's brothers, Stephen and James Moreno. We may meet Mr. Mallory later, in his aspect as maker and manager of a navy on which opinions varied, as they did on all things governmental. But as a host there were no two views of the jovial secretary.

The Mallory home was not a very gay one, and there were no grown children to add the whirligig to its quiet, hospitable round. But the instincts of both husband and wife—for Mrs. Mallory's descent was pure Spanish—combined to make the crosser of their threshold at home immediately. There were rounds of informal droppings-in, where the intellect, wit and cultivation of the nervous and varied population could be found. Mr. Mallory brewed a punch as good as his stories and *mots*, and Mrs. Mallory knew tricks of Southern salads and of *daube à la Créole* that made many Northern eyes wink and mouths water. And almost always the little daughter of the house was allowed to sit out the stay of guests and often to aid in their entertainment.

Mrs. Mallory's long Washington experience as a senator's wife had quite Americanized her manner, but her pure Spanish taste lingered in the lady who had been Señorita Angela Silveria Moreno. Her family has many and influential ramifications in the Creole South, and notable members of it will be encountered by the patient one who follows these pages. The most familiar descendant was the late Senator S. R. Mallory, who filled his father's old chair in representing Florida until his death in 1907.

Little Ruby Mallory was about seven years old when the move to Richmond was made. She was one of the most intelligent and precocious children I ever knew, but there was nothing uncanny or irritant in her exceptional outstripping of her years. The darling of parents so informed, so careful, she absorbed and understood unusual things, and her magnetism was wonderful even at that age. Her natural elocution was the talk of Richmond and prophecies were freely hazarded that she would surely be a great actress some day. What she really did become, while still in her teens, was the facile queen of young society, in her native Pensacola, and her belleship continued until her marriage with Dr. T. S. Kennedy, of New Orleans. There the young wife had wider field for her tact, cleverness and inborn power to lead, all tempered and fused into general popularity by the warmth of a true woman's heart. She was long at the head of a gay and brilliant circle, but it is not of record that she ever wilfully misused her power or hurt the pride or the feelings of an associate, though she was absolutely fearless, a consist-

MRS. T. S. KENNEDY
(RUBY MALLORY)

ent hater of shams and prompt to spur to the rescue of a friend in distress.

With examples of this trait New Orleans drawing-rooms were rife. One of them I recall. Miss Lee was visiting the

city about carnival time. There was one especially fine
function among the many in honor of the great General's
daughter. When its main motif was satisfied the ladies sat
over coffee and—I had almost written cigarettes for—salted
almonds! Miss Lee drew off a quaint old ring, an heirloom
from the centuries, and probably worn by Martha Washington. It was eagerly seized and passed around, amid cho-
rused "How sweet!" and "Lovely!" and "So nice!" Then
family pride flared up, and one *mondaine* showed a ring left
by a triply great-ed grandmother, who had flirted with Bienville. Another trumped that centuried trick with the Court
of Charles the Bold, another still, straight from the Crusades.
Miss Lee sat smiling but slightly flushed. Mrs. Kennedy noted
the awkward situation of discounting the guest's social advance. Slowly drawing off a magnificent but most palpably
latest style ring, she said demurely.

"Here is a trifle of mine, ladies. That ring was presented
by Solomon to the Queen of Sheba!"

Then family pride went to roost again.

Mr. Mallory's eldest daughter, Margaret, had married early
in life Mr. Bishop, of Bridgeport, Conn., and her quieter life
left her less in public view than her little sister. This, and the
early maturity of the latter constantly made an absurd
"Buttercupping" of the two, and many bright sayings of
the younger were ascribed to the senior. Some grave actions
of the latter have been ascribed to Mrs. Kennedy while still a
child. Mrs. Bishop called on Andrew Johnson to protest
against her father's unjust imprisonment and demand his
release. Later I heard the statement, which has apparently
misguided some, that this visit was made the president "by
little Ruby Mallory!" At the date of its making *she* was
just twelve years old.

In 1901 a lecture engagement called me to New Orleans.
Looking to her for much of the pleasure of the visit, I wrote

her. The letter arrived just as the fiat incomprehensible had gone forth, and I met a sorrow, deep and universal, for her untimely death. Very vividly came back memories of that delightful, if not gay, Richmond home in which the Reaper had meantime been so busy.

The pleasantest houses of the "official set" were not always those of the cabinet. That body is somewhat Arabian. A secretary would fold his official tent, and steal away sandal-shod and in silence; sometimes, as one wag put it, "Ungloved, unborrowed and—unhung." But even were these changes explicable to the tyro in cabinet-making, this is not the proper place to seek their cause or their results. The retiring officials were rarely beaux or their families belles.

The most kaleidoscopic department was the war office. The first and provisional secretary was promptly replaced, on the regular formation of the government, but not before that Montgomery speech, in which he pledged to carry the new flag to Boston and plant it on Faneuil Hall. Leroy Pope Walker was scarcely permitted to "tote" it to the James. He was at that day the most prominent of four well-known Alabama brothers of whom the two least noted were the most popular. Hon. Percy Walker was perhaps the least so. A speech made to him by the learned and eccentric Judge Edmund Dargan was long-lived in the Gulf State. Returning with him from the convention in Montgomery, the old jurist noted that his junior was gloomy and wroth. Asked the cause, Walker cried:

"Why, judge, they threatened to hang me in effigy!"

The old man shifted his invariable quid, solemnly peered over his glasses and drawled: "*Which* party did, Percy?"

John J. Walker and "Billy" were not publicists, but stead-fast comrades and good soldiers. The latter was a "high roller, of the strictest sect."

Several successive shakes of the kaleidoscope, and the

peephole showed the "rearrangement" of Hon. James A. Seddon, with his thin, grave face and monkish skull-cap; General George Wythe Randolph, self-contained, decisive and ordained not to stay; General Braxton Bragg and Judge John A. Campbell, both as *ad interim* time-fillers; Mr. Benjamin temporarily acting as a "stop-gap," and General John C. Breckinridge finally withdrawn from more congenial field service to aid Mr. Davis's real control of that most vital department of the government.

Next in importance if not actual twin with the war office was the Confederate treasury. This was given into the trust of the Mother of Secession, its conduct being reposed in the hands of Hon. C. G. Memminger and George A. Trenholm, of South Carolina. This is not the place to consider its results. Later I may show what was claimed as the crucial error of Confederate finance, and how the non-acceptance of some foreign concessions and proffers left the South the first essayist in a "cheap" money experiment, and "demonetized" the true and potent "white money"—cotton. These may come under review later. Here it need only be noted that neither of these officials added much to the general social aspects of the capital. Courtly and cultured families in Richmond needed houses and chefs to make them notable.

Grim, grave and steadfast General John H. Reagan held the post-office portfolio with the same tenacity and quite the same satisfaction to his chief as did Mr. Mallory his secretaryship. Loyal, blunt and outspoken, he was the tried friend of Mr. Davis through good report and ill, and the latter trusted in his honesty even as he possibly overrated his judgment. To his recent death, which swept away the one remaining vestige of the Richmond cabinet, General Reagan was the quick and ardent champion of his dead chief, against every assault on plan or performance. Neither was the department of letters conducive to added sociality; but the head and family of the assistant postmaster-general were so in large measure, as will be seen.

Good men and true, doubtless, were all of these, but they scarcely counted in the sociality of the war, save one. General Randolph was a charming host, hospitable, frank and cultured. His wife was one of the most charming women of her day, graces of person, mind and heart blending in her to form a resistless personality. She had been Miss Mary Elizabeth Adams, of Mississippi, and had first married Mr. Pope, of Mobile. When still a brilliant young widow she married the noted Virginian. She was the soul of hospitality and an accomplished entertainer, so hers early became the most popular of official homes. She had the knack of making young and old, simple and high-placed alike, feel ownership. Mrs. Randolph was assisted by her niece, Miss Jennie Pollard; and the philosophic youth of war-time, knowing a good thing when they saw it, flocked to Mrs. Randolph's house as it had been a shrine curative of the blue devils. There reception, dance and theatricals followed in quick succession. In the last named the hostess promoted this writer to a post that has enabled him to rebuild from the débris of recollection a gilded structure, if it have some resemblance to the sand-projected palaces of Soliman the Magnificent.

One ubiquitous and most acceptable social factor of the official circle was that polished and smooth brevet bachelor, Hon. Judah P. Benjamin, attorney-general with the plus sign. There was no circle, official or otherwise, that missed his soft, purring presence, or had not regretted so doing. He was always expected, almost always found time to respond, and was invariably compensating. He moved into and through the most elegant or the simplest assemblage on natural rubber tires and well-oiled bearings, a smile of recognition for the mere acquaintance, a reminiscent word for the intimate, and a general diffusion of placid *bonhomie*. A Hebrew of Hebrews, for the map of the Holy City* was traced all over his small, refined face, the attorney-general was of the highest type of his race. Small and rotund, he was yet of easy grace in manner; and his soft voice was not only pleasant of sound, but always carried something worth hearing. That

JUDAH P. BENJAMIN

he was a great and successful lawyer all knew, and that he was an omnivorous devourer of books and of wonderful assimilative capacity. Astute and best informed, he was greatly regarded by Mr. Davis as an adviser. With his conduct of foreign affairs we may differ later, perhaps. He may have missed silver-lined opportunities in the overreach for impossible golden ones. He may have deceived himself and the people at once, in his optimistic utterances as to intervention by the Powers, and he may have played the Confederates' pawn abroad in a fool's "gambit." But socially the man was delightful and many-sided, and as popular with the young as with the older set about him. After the war Mr. Benjamin repeated the triumph of Disraeli, and by the same force of personality and brain. He achieved, alone and as the best known representative of a lost and a disaster-strewn Cause, the quickest advance to a barrister ever known to the most conservative legal system of the planet.

Hebrew in blood, English in tenacity of grasp and purpose,

*The Arabs call Jerusalem "El Khuds" (the Holy City).

Mr. Benjamin was French in taste, *jusque au bout des ongles.*
So were his family, and they never visited Richmond. Indeed, in a knowledge of him extending to a decade before the
war I recall but one visit made by them to this side of the
water. Mrs. Benjamin had been Mlle. de St. Martin and
she lived with her two grown daughters, permanently in Paris
where the girls married. But the secretary's brother-in-law,
Jules de St. Martin, was awhile in Richmond and later quite
a toast in Baltimore society. Very small, faultlessly groomed
and well equipped by travel and association, this gentleman
was very much of a man. He was suave and decided and an
expert in the code, as I chanced to learn.

The second Confederate attorney-general was a noted
Alabamian, though of Virginia-Georgia descent. His father,
Thomas Hughes Watts, of Fauquier county, Va., married in
1818, Miss Prudence Hill, of Clarke county, Ga., and immediately moved to Butler county, Ala., then the wild and lonely
home of the Creek Indians. There in the next year, was
born his son, Thomas Hill Watts.

In a log-hut school house with a puncheon floor, that received light and air through crevices of its sides and roof, the
youth got its first education. Thence, at fifteen years he
went to Airy Mount, in Dallas, and equipped for the University of Virginia, where he graduated with distinction in
1840. The next year he began practice of law in his home,
and in 1847 removed from Greenville to Montgomery.

Prior to the war he was an extensive plantation and slave
owner, and he was a staunch supporter of Harrison against
Van Buren, when a mere youth. Then, for three terms he
was in the legislature. In later years, he was both representative and senator from the Montgomery districts. In
1848, he was a Taylor elector at large; and eight years later
Know Nothing candidate for congress, but was defeated by
a narrow margin.

In the hot triangle of 1860, he labored for the Bell-Everett success. Vigorous in opposition, the election of Lincoln determined him to "go with his people."

With William L. Yancey, he represented Montgomery county in the Secession convention of January 7th, 1861; and, as chairman of its judiciary committee, did much toward taking his state out of the Union.

Showing his faith, as did many an "original Union man" the lawyer changed Chitty for Hardee, raised the 17th Alabama Infantry and became its colonel. While commanding it at Corinth, Mr. Davis chose Colonel Watts to succeed Mr. Benjamin as law chief of the permanent cabinet. He preferred the field to the office, but he accepted the duty offered.   In the following year, against his earnest protest, he was chosen governor of Alabama and held the office from 1863 to 1865—the most trying epoch of the war.

GOV. THOMAS H. WATTS

Post-bellum, Governor Watts returned to law practice; but, largely through assisting friends, soon found himself in debt for over $100,000.   Of white integrity and indomitable courage he bent every energy and every mastery of his profession to lifting the load; paying the debt in full before he died in 1892.

Governor Watts was twice married: first, in 1842, to Miss Eliza B. Allen, who died in 1873, leaving six children.   The second marriage was to the widow of J. F. Jackson, after two years of widowerhood; and she died in 1887.

The six children of Thos. Hill Watts and Eliza B. Allen were: Florence S., Kate P., John W., Thomas H., Jr., Alice and Minnie G. Watts.

The first married Col. Daniel S. Troy and left this family of five: Thos. W. Troy, married at Macon, Ga., and now resident in Honduras, C. A.; Florence Troy married Charles E. Hails, residing at Montgomery; Mary Troy, unmarried and residing at Philadelphia; Daniel W. Troy married Janie B. Watts and resides at Montgomery. Robert E. Troy married a Cuban lady named Trigi and lives at Honduras, C. A.

Kate P. Watts, the second daughter of the governor, married Robert M. Collins and left a family of six children: Robert M. Collins, a bachelor, of Montgomery; Lida B. Collins, living unmarried at Washington City; William H. Collins, of Montgomery, unmarried; James Collins, single, of Washington, D. C.; Florence Collins married Albert J. Pickett, and residing at Montgomery; as does her sister, Miss Catherine Collins.

Hon. John W. Watts, is today a leading member of the Montgomery bar and has a family of seven living children: Miss Gabriella Watts and Marion A. Watts, residing at Montgomery; Marghereta, who married Gaston Scott, also resides there, as do Sophia W., Annie Campbell and Flournoy S., all single and residing in Montgomery. John W. Watts, Jr., lives in Jacksonville, Fla., and is a bachelor.

Mrs. Johnness B. Watts (widow of Thos. Hill Watts, Jr.) has five children: John W. Watts, who married Miss Reid and lives in Birmingham; Ed. S. Watts, who married Miss Norwood and lives in Montgomery, as does his brother, Hugh K., who married Miss Pitcher; Troy Watts, a bachelor, and Janie B. Troy, wife of Daniel W. Troy.

The youngest sister, Alice B. Watts, married Hon. Alexander Troy, resides in Montgomery with her son, Gaston; Alexander Troy having married Miss Thames, of New York.

Even the most intense Virginian monopolizer will not hold that there are not families of Scriptural length in other states.

The third and last attorney-general of the Confederacy—the one who was the last of the cabinet to leave the flying president, in Georgia; and who survived him and the Cause until 1896—was another example of the force of Welsh blood in the arteries of the short-lived young government. In common with Jefferson Davis, G. T. Beauregard, and the President's brother-in-law, Robert Davis, the attorney-general was of good Welsh stock in paternal descent. On his mother's side he was English.

George Davis was born at Wilmington, N. C., his father being Thomas F. Davis, a well-respected citizen of that old city.

The young man was educated carefully and graduated, entering on the practice of law in his native town, when only twenty-one. He promptly made his way both in his profession and in politics, as an old-line Whig; gaining the confidence of all classes, and the respect of his political opponents. Yet, in a long life, he never sought a political office. He was a prominent member of the convention that took his state out of the Union, in 1861 and was elected senator from North Carolina to the provisional congress. Re-elected in 1862, he was serving his term when selected by the President to fill the seat in his cabinet, vacated by the election of Governor Watts to the head of Alabama's affairs. Conscientious, prudent and an excellent lawyer, he held the confidence of his chief until the very last gasp of the moribund government; accompanying the cabinet party in the evacuation of Richmond, with Breckinridge, Mallory, Benjamin and Clement C. Clay.

It was on his advice that the President acceded to the request of General Breckinridge, that the silver bullion should be saved capture by *pro rata* distribution among the soldiers of the escort. And, parenthetically, there was no wilder one of all the wild "yarns" of that rumoriferous moment, than that which placed the "Confederate treasure" high up in the millions. Including the security fund deposited in the treasury by the Richmond bank—and later returned to them by the government as private property—the gross amount of the bullion brought from Richmond by Treasurer Trenholm was not the quarter of a million. After the distribution to the soldiers and when the pressure of pursuit forced dispersion of the presidential party, Attorney-General Davis and the treasurer became custodians of the "treasure wagon," moving it toward Augusta.

Nominally for this participancy, but really in punishment for steadfast adherence to his cause, Mr. George Davis was later arrested as a "state prisoner" and held in durance at Fort Hamilton, New York.

After his release (on parole not to leave the State of North Carolina), the ex-official resumed the practice of his profession; prospering in it and regaining in part the losses from his adherence to public duty. He was general counsel for the several lines that consolidated in the Atlantic Coast Line; and then for that system. Then, in 1878, he was offered the chief-justiceship of his state, but was forced to decline for business reasons. His death, in his native city, in 1896, brought regret and sorrow to his whole state and section.

Judge Davis was twice married: first to Miss Adelaide Polk, of Holly Springs, Miss. Of this union came six children, of whom only two survive, the eldest Hon. Junius Davis, of Wilmington, and Meeta Alexander, who is now Mrs. George Rountree, of Wilmington, and has a family of four.

Junius Davis has himself illustrated the old Welsh name and "has done the state some service." He is a prominent citizen and lawyer, with a fine practice, in which he has his son as partner, and he finds leisure for literature and general study, being president of the State Historical and Literary Society. He has, like his father, been twice married: first, to Miss Mary Orme Walker, who died leaving eight children. His present wife is Mary W. Cowan, and they have three children.

The children of George Davis who died were Mary Eliza, Isabel Eagles, Emily Polk and Louis Poisson. The second Isabel, became Mrs. Spencer P. Shotter, now of Savannah, and has one child living. Emily Polk, the next sister, married John E. Crow, of Petersburg, Va., and left five childern to her husband, now of Wilmington.

The second wife of Hon. George Davis was of historic Virginia family, Miss Monimia Fairfax, of Richmond. Her two daughters are Mary Fairfax (now Mrs. M. F. H. Gouverneur, of Wilmington, and the mother of three children); and Cary Monimia (now Mrs. Donald Mac Rae, of Wilmington, and also the mother of three children).

These Davises have never seemed a self-illustrative family. but they have plainly borne their parts in the private and public life of their Southland.

CHAPTER VIII

THE homely saying that "it takes all sorts of people to make a world" finds especial verity at most national capitals. Naturally, its greater proof might be sought in the central city of a nascent republic, striving for life amidst the scattered members of an old one, and that one hated where not despised, by most members of its successor.

The *flotsam* and *jetsam* that had washed from Washington to Montgomery followed the hegira to Richmond. Echo from the "Cradle of the Confederacy" had penetrated to the banks of the James and, as has been stated, sent cold chills of apprehension down the sensitive Virginian spine. These soon wore away, but they early differentiated the personality of the leaders as the "official set."

The sobriquet included one and all engaged in making, or marring the young government. Early and better elements of this hodge-podge came to the top, by reason of better mind and better manners. The fittest not only survived the governmental evolution, but were so appreciated as to be much sought by the best home element, indeed to become an integral part of it.

Little may this change or its suddenness be wondered at on even casual glance at some components of the "official set."

Next to the actual and active head of the Confederacy

and his household, the vice-president ranked by virtue of his office. He had done so by other virtues, inherent and confessed.

Hon. Alexander H. Stephens was a tried and respected politician, far and away from both sides of the not then

clearly-marked line of Messrs. Mason and Dixon. He was idolized in the Cracker State, and the repeated expressions of her faith that had sent him to congress had begotten trust in the South and some fear in the North. Had the small South Carolina clique at Montgomery, headed by Lawrence M. Keitt, William W. Boyce and others, defeated the selection of Jefferson Davis for the presidency, their choice had probably been Hon. Howell Cobb, of Georgia. Possibly the North would have welcomed this

ALEXANDER H. STEPHENS

substitution and been saved a tough fighter by it. Later, had Colonel Louis T. Wigfall's reported comment to General Chesnut that "Jeff Davis ought to be hung in Richmond," resulted in a real and premature appletree, the North would have relished the vice-presidential succession very little.

Naturally, both suggestions were of "the stuff that dreams are made of." There was never more reality in the Montgomery than in the Richmond proposition, but they are noted to record the Northern view of the Sage of Liberty Hall. As in the South, Mr. Stephens was regarded as a keen, incisive

thinker, and essentially as a conservative. The North preferred Mr. Davis, not understanding him remotely. It regarded him as a "fire-eater," denied him statesmanship or
even judgment, and asserted that he would overleap himself
in his mad and blind rushes.

At the outset both sides to the war had an indurated belief,
in popular circles, in its brevity. Each side believed it would
whip the other in ninety days.

Having no family, Mr. Stephens did not keep house in
Richmond, but lived with those congenial friends, Judge and
Mrs. Semmes. Nowise fond of general society, from which
ill-health would have debarred him, he was ever a delightful
addition to any circle. Quick to grasp, thoroughly informed
and with quaint sub-acid in his dry humor, his talk was
equally educating and entertaining. Not so quick and bitter
—less "rifled," so to speak—he continually reminded me of
Randolph of Roanoke. After the war he retired to Liberty
Hall and preserved a reticence truly remarkable for such a
magazine of important facts There he wrote his able and not
divulgent book, contenting himself with doctoring and dis-
cussion, rather than directly stating new and important facts.
One most mooted point, of equal interest, North and South, he
did not settle, as he alone could have done. This was the
alleged remark of Mr. Lincoln when the Hampton Roads
conference broke up. The President, it was stated—and
without official denial at the time—pushed a sheet of blank
foolscap toward the Confederate vice-president and cried:

"Stephens, let me write 'Union' at the head of that paper,
and you may write anything you please under it!"

Later this statement was denied, but neither by Mr.
Stephens or Judge Campbell, the only direct witnesses possible. Both asserted that they had no option; that Mr.
Davis's ultimatum was, and naturally, independence, be the
other terms what they might. Lincoln's word "Union"

could never have headed that. Looking at the characters and at the hardened principles of the two presidents, the Hampton Roads conference may have been the grandstand play to the nations that some writers declare it; but it is still a pity that all who could really settle that point of it went to their graves with sealed lips. Mr. Stephens, like Judge Campbell, probably believed honestly, at that time, that the Confederacy had "died a-borning." He was indubitably ready to save further loss, strain and bloodshed, but he was powerless under that ultimatum. The speech of Mr. Lincoln is probable and I have no doubt that he made, and thought he meant it. Carrying it out had been another matter, especially in view of the mad Booth's pistol, but I know that it was reiterated in Mr. Stephens's presence, without denial.

Mr. Stephens died at Atlanta, in 1883, and was buried at Liberty Hall. His only surviving relatives are grandnephews and nieces; a notable one being Alex. W. Stephens of the Atlanta bar.

One department not officially nominated in the cabinet was of such importance and far-reaching influence on the strength of the army as to be classed with the regular portfolios. This was the commission for exchange of prisoners, under General Robert Ould. It demanded a man of mixed firmness and *bonhomie*, with widely extended acquaintance and tried knowledge of human nature. All these centered in "Bob" Ould, and he was probably as near "the right man in the right place" as it is given appointees to be.

Apparently the Federal officials did not wholly believe those wild "yarns" of the terror of Andersonville, the Libby and other prisons, upon which they fed full the horror-hungry maw of their public. Did they so believe they stand convicted of negligence and heartlessness in refusing urgent and continued appeals for regular and prompt exchanges.

For years Robert Ould had been one of the best known attorneys in Washington, popular in every club, cloak-room and café and influential by some occult process known only to the denizen in shadow of the dome.

In early life he married Miss Sarah Turpin, of a family noted for its handsome women, herself said to be the "beauty of the state in her time." The pair were popular in Washington circles, and regret was general when they "went South." They brought to Richmond with them a little daughter, who upheld the repute of her mother's side in the new generation.

MISS MATTIE OULD

Miss Mattie Ould did not enter her teens until the war was a year old. At its close and shortly thereafter she had made perhaps a wider reaching fame than any belle of the '60's. Forced into society when but a child, her striking and peculiar beauty had added to it a resistless manner and a wit that literally startled by its audacity and point. Men raved about her and women praised, although she was the cause of many a knight's recreancy. But dazzling as was her beauty, it was probably her mental originality and her indescribable magnetism that made this mere girl a marked figure among the noted women about her. But her early triumphs were not presage of a bright or happy future. She did not live to reach their full fruition.

Soon after the war and while still in her teens, she surprised her friends and set busybodies wondering by marrying Oliver Schoolcraft.

Almost without a honeymoon the gifted and beautiful young girl died. But young as she was, her beauty stands clear today on the memory of all who knew her, and Richmond men and women are still repeating her epigrams. Miss Sallie Ould, the second sister, married Mr. George Donaldson and resides at Charleston, W. Va., when not traveling abroad. The only brother, Jesse Bright Ould, named for the burly old senator from Indiana—now resides with his family at Unicoi, Tenn. The traditional beauty of the family is still evidenced at Mobile, in Mrs. J. Howard Wilson who was Miss Sallie Turpin, a first cousin.

Late in life General Ould made a second marriage, the lady being the well-known Widow Handy. The beauty and society fame of her daughter, Miss May Handy, had carried the name to the bounds of the Union ere the lady made a tardy choice and became the second wife of James Brown Potter, of New York.

It is a singular coincidence that the two most noted beauties of the Richmond of the recent past should have come from the same household.

In common with all who leave repute for wit, Miss Mattie Ould had had many things attributed to her which she not only did not say, but could not have said. Perhaps the most traveled one of these is that when found once with her head upon General Pierce M. B. Young's lapel, she only remarked coolly:

"There's nothing odd about it; it is only an old head upon Young shoulders!" The thing is not like Miss Ould in either of its aspects. Audacious as she was beautiful, the girl was no fool ever, and only such publish little affairs, if they have them. Moreover, Young himself, on the last meeting we had previous to his death, told me that there was not the least foundation for the story. He added in his blunt way, "I never knew Miss Ould very well and never had such luck as that!"

Young was reckless and essentially a "flirt," as the slang goes, but in a close intimacy covering years I never knew him to lie, and I do know of more than one case in which he went out of his way to see that justice was done to a woman's reputation.

Two examples of Miss Ould's quickness I can personally vouch for. Shortly before her marriage she was at a dinner in Richmond with several lawyers, one of whom was a noted Munchaüsen; he was also a desperate drinker and held long sessions. He was boasting of one case in which he had earned a $30,000 fee, and then spent it in a single spree. Her table neighbor asked Miss Ould if she credited the story. Her answer was prompt:

"I might doubt the storied earn, but he's all right for that animated bust!"

A bumptious young lady-slayer was insisting that the brilliant girl had been giving him some confessions. Someone cried: "He your father confessor!"

"Scarcely," she laughed. "He is only a gosling, and I am no such goose as to confess, except to the *proper gander!*"

Two homes directly opposite the White House were notable ones in the social as well as the official life of Richmond. These were occupied by the families of Senator Thomas J. Semmes, of Louisiana, and of Judge John Archibald Campbell, of the same state, assistant secretary of war. In the old government, no less than the new, this jurist had been a noted and potent factor. A native Georgian, he had moved to New Orleans in early professional life. There he made reputation so rapidly as to become head of a bar noteworthy for such advocates and orators as Semmes, Benjamin, Soulé and their peers.

Judge Campbell was the son of Duncan Greene Campbell and Mary Lawrence Williamson, and was born on the ancestral plantation in Wilkes county in 1811. Appointed to West Point by War Secretary John C. Calhoun, young Campbell was called home before graduation by the death of his father. This possibly lost the world a good soldier, but gave it a great jurist. He early moved to Alabama, and while scarce more than a youth married Anne Esther Goldthwaite. She was of English parentage and her brothers and cousins of Goldthwaite name have made the family notable in the subsequent professional life and in social matters in the Gulf State.

By this union there were six children, only one being a son, who was named for his grandfather. The five daughters have all helped to make social history in two capitals and many another city. Henrietta Goldthwaite, Katharine Rebecca, Mary Ellen, Anna and Clara.

Duncan Greene, the son, married Ella, daughter of Charles B. Calvert, of Riverdale, Md. He survived this wife, dying in 1888 and leaving four children to the care of his father and sisters.

Henrietta, the eldest sister, was a most popular and admired member of Washington society prior to the war, and esteemed as one of the most delightful women in its Richmond replica. She had married Captain George William Lay, later aide-de-camp and confidential secretary to General Winfield Scott. This high post, with his rank of colonel, Lay resigned, taking the same grade in the Confederate service, as Beauregard's inspector-general, in Virginia. Invalided after the Seven Days' fights, he was placed at the head of a special bureau of conscription with General John S. Preston, of South Carolina. A good soldier and true man, he died at New Orleans in 1867.

The second Campbell sister, Katherine, married General

V. D. Groner, of Norfolk, and the third, Mary Ellen, gallant and well-loved Arthur Pendleton Mason. The fourth is still Miss Anna Campbell and resides with her widowed sister, Mrs. Lay, in the Baltimore home left by their father. The fifth sister, the "baby of the family," was Clara, now the wife of Fred M. Colston, a prosperous and much esteemed banker of the Monumental City. But the Mason pair, young, gifted and with all to live for, passed away in New Orleans soon after peace was declared.

In war-time the Campbell home was much sought by the best of young and old in the new "capital." Mrs. Campbell was a gentle and delightful hostess and the attractiveness of her grown daughters—and of the exceptional men of her household—was a magnet for the grave as well as the gay.

There were no strained relations between that family and others of the government to which its head had made allegiance.

Judge Campbell, like General Lee and scores of great Confederates, was an "original Union man." He had practiced much in the supreme court at Washington, had been promoted to be one of its justices by President Pierce and was, naturally, saturated with national ideas. In the

JUDGE JOHN A. CAMPBELL

disruption of these he foresaw only suicide for Southern Rights, and he was outspoken of belief at the time of that so-called "Peace Commission," which the tergiversations of Mr. Buchanan made not only useless, but ridiculous.

When New Orleans became impossible as a field for his profession and Judge Campbell first moved his family to Richmond, he was offered several positions of importance. Differing from Mr. Davis as he did, the latter still respected his gifts and his loyalty. But the jurist declined, although when he had found "blood thicker than water" and had come to his people, it was for better or worse. At first he refused all proffers, but when his personal friend, George W. Randolph, importuned his assistance in the war department, the old jurist accepted the post and held it under all changes until the evacuation.

After the war he moved his family back to New Orleans, later devoted himself wholly to supreme court practice and returned to Washington. Changed conditions made that city no congenial home for the family and they went to Baltimore, where all the survivors reside, except Mrs. Groner, who lived in Virginia.

In the early war the Southern sentiment toward the so-called "Union men," however earnest and useful in the cause they had adopted on principle, "my country, right or wrong," was much that of the North toward "copperheads." Thoughtlessness, that could not differentiate free thought from grand action, overlooked the fact that Robert Edward Lee, Alexander Hamilton Stephens and their peers, if they had any, were, like John Archibald Campbell, "original Union men."

Of vital import at all times of war—and most of all in a young country just forming its army—is the adjutant-general. The secretary of war was helpless without a just, experienced and reliable guide to the fitness and records of new appointees.

The Confederacy was peculiarly fortunate in this regard. General Samuel Cooper was a veteran of two wars, thoroughly familiar with the personnel of both armies; clear-headed and without prejudice. A West Pointer of the class of 1815, he had served with Harney in Florida and on both the Scott and Taylor lines in Mexico. When he succeeded General Roger Jones as adjutant-general of the United States Army, he had already learned the men whom he was to handle later and those whom they were to meet, two points invaluable in assignments and field of duty. He resigned and was among the earliest to tender service at Montgomery, and there and in Richmond was a trusted and capable adviser to his chief to the bitter ending. General Cooper was a Northern man, having been born at Hackensack, N. J., June 12, 1798. He was the son of Samuel Cooper and Mary Horton, sterling people of the little state. In the early '30's he married Miss Sarah Maria Mason, grand-daughter of George Mason, of Gunston Hall. Naturally, when promoted to adjutant-general of the old army, the family removed to the national capital.

Mrs. Cooper was the daughter of a race noted for the strength, helpfulness and gentleness of its women. Prior to the war her quiet home in Washington had been a favorite resort of the best of official and society people, drawn thither by the beauties of person and char-

MRS. SAMUEL COOPER

acter of her young lady daughter, Maria. One of the prettiest and best remembered weddings of the capital was when this universally loved girl married dashing Lieutenant Frank Wheaton, and Fitzhugh Lee, then of the slender rank, was best man.

Eheu fugaces! The bride has been dead decades, but lives still in the memory of loyal friends and in her charming and tried daughter and her children. His native state, Rhode Island, has only lately reared a stately monument to Major-General Frank Wheaton and later still pæans and sobs

mingled about the bier of his lifelong friend, Fitz Lee. The only child of General Wheaton and his beautiful and universally lamented wife was a daughter, named for her mother. She married a young army officer, who gave his life for the old Flag at San Juan Hill—Captain Rowell.

His widow survives him, with a lovely family: Frank Ashley, Charles and Maria.

In Richmond the young lady of the house was Miss Jennie Cooper, a sunny-na-

MRS. NICHOLAS DAWSON
(JENNIE COOPER)

tured woman, bright, frank and of strong character. Never having had the society craze, she did not topple her home "into the swim," but free and genial hospitality met all who crossed its threshold and their name was legion. Captain Samuel Cooper was the only son, a quiet, easy-going fellow, always ready to do his duty, but not finding it, as a general thing, in the social rush of the early '60's. He and his sister were the sole survivors of the family. He never married and lived with her at "Cameron," where he died two years ago.

Popular with both sexes, Miss Cooper probably had more "reports" about her in war days and close thereafter than most women; many of them doubtless, with a basis. She married Nicholas Dawson, a merchant of Baltimore, but citizen of Virginia. The old family seat, "Cameron," near Alexandria, has been their home, the three children making the fourth generation its venerable walls have sheltered. Mrs. Dawson still resides there with her second son, Philip, of the Riggs National Bank, Washington. Cooper, the eldest child, recently married Miss Edna Horner, daughter of Major Horner, of the Confederate army. He has built a new home on the Cameron domain, to be near his mother; going into Alexandria for his business. The only daughter, Miss Maria Mason Dawson, still more recently married Rev. William Gibson Pendleton, grandnephew of General Pendleton of Confederate artillery fame. His father is Colonel William Nelson Pendleton, of the old and noted line.

So, in the midst of her children, the widow finds solace in their happiness.

CHAPTER IX

NEXT door to the Campbell residence, and differing from it in details of attractiveness, was another much sought and ever delightful home. Senator Thomas Joseph Semmes was the diametric opposite of his learned brother next door, in his secession views. He was an original of the advanced rank; had been a member of the convention that took Louisiana out of the Union, and his eloquence and ire in that body sent him to the Confederate upper house. A lawyer of high repute, Mr. Semmes had moved up the path to the head of the New Orleans bar steadily with Judge Campbell, but he believed that the South was safer out of the Union than in it.

In a delightful mention from his sister, Mrs. Ives, she tells that she was his guest in New Orleans when the fires of secession were being fast fanned into the lambent ones of war. Admiral Raphael Semmes, their cousin, chanced to be a guest under the same roof. He was fitting out the little *Sumter*, predecessor of the famous *Alabama*, and was deeply impressed with the spirit of the masses. Mrs. Ives tells graphically of the wild ardor of the torch-lit and yelling throng that came to tell her brother of his selection and to escort him to the convention hall. She also pictures the scene when the "Lone Star Flag," the Texan banner, sung by the minstrel Harry Macarthy, was first unfurled in the opera house.

The flag enthusiasm of that hour was epidemic. Maggie

112

Mitchell was at the Montgomery Theatre when I arrived and of course playing "Fanchon." The Texas flag reached the capital. That night, the canny little actress waved it, sang the refrain and danced a flag-dance, trampling the Stars and Stripes beneath her nimble feet, while the audience yelled itself speechless at her timely antics. The next time I met Miss Maggie was in Bulfinch street, Boston, but the war was over then, and she had quite "forgotten" her Montgomery engagement.

Mrs. Semmes was a queen among hostesses *ante-bellum.* As Miss Myra Eulalie Knox, of Montgomery, she had queened the bellehood of her own and other cities. When she married the rising and brilliant lawyer she held her conquests in New Orleans, the watering-places and in the capitals of the old and new federations. Gracious, quick-witted and diplomatic, she had been educated in the more solid as well as the showier accomplishments. She was a born actress and an admirable musician, playing the harp with especial grace and excellence. These gifts quickly and easily car-

MRS. T. J. SEMMES
(FROM A PORTRAIT BY HEALY)

ried her to social leadership in Richmond, and there her house was a center for the most distinguished of the men of the hour, and no less for that young set whom she entertained to their hearts' content, and used to that of her own.

In addition to the traits named, this matron had another

and a better one. She was a real and unaffected altruist long ere that word grew to be a fad. So there was no more open house than the one opposite the executive residence and it held a singularly notable "mess": Vice-President Stephens, her husband's colleagues, Senator Sparrow and Senator Garland, of Arkansas.   Another habitué of the Semmes household ánd almost a member of it was Hon. Pierre Soulé, of their state, former senator and minister to Spain.   This statesman, advocate and orator had a handsome face, introspective and rather priestly, that suggested little of the hot blood that would have spitted the Marquis de Tourgot, French ambassador to Spain, because the young Duke of Alva let a too glib tongue suggest an unpleasant likeness to Madame Soulé.   The *cause celebre* of that challenge and of the resulting and harmless duel of young Neville Soulé with the Duke of Alva was laughed out of becoming an international complication.   Great lawyer for the French, too, was Pierre Soulé, the fervor of his speech swaying the courts formerly conducted in that tongue at New Orleans. He was a widower in Richmond days, the gentle, motherly woman I recall so well in Washington having passed away. His son, I think, married a Mexican lady, daughter of a Revolutionary leader who, the legend runs, was captured and boiled in oil!

Full freighted with friendships and pleasant memories of Richmond, Mrs. Semmes returned to New Orleans after the war, her husband returning to the bar and rising to its head before his death.   There, at advanced age, she relives her life of good works, busied in church and general charities and seeing her youth again in her numerous grandchildren.

Her children are now Mrs. Sylvester P. Walmsley, Mrs. Albert Sidney Ranlett, Thomas J. Semmes, Francis Joseph Semmes and Charles Louis Semmes.

Mrs. Semmes's daughters have many children.   On one

occasion a waggish old friend visited her city and the proud grandmother told him that one of them had eleven and the other seven. He replied promptly:

"The youngest of each set should be named 'Craps,' of course." And when asked what he meant, repiled: "They 'come seven,' and 'come eleven!'"

Professor Alexander Dimitry was one of the most original and learned men ever put under the use of either government. Greek by descent he was a native Louisianian, being the son of Andrea Dimitry and Céleste Dracos, of New Orleans. He was born in that city in 1805 and died there in 1883. A natural student and devourer of languages, he was accredited with knowledge of no less than forty-one tongues and dialects. He graduated early at Georgetown College, returned to New Orleans and became the first English editor of *L'Abeille*, of that city. He was also professor or principal of several private schools, later at the head of more than one college in Mississippi and Louisiana, and under Buchanan became chief of the translators of the department of state. In 1859 President Buchanan made him minister to Nicaragua and Costa Rica, which position he resigned when his state seceded from the Union. Incidentally it is interesting to note that he succeeded in this post another notable scientist, Hon. E. George Squier, who followed Stevens's explorations into Central American antiquities and was also the first husband of the present Mrs. Frank Leslie.

Arriving in Richmond, Professor Dimitry was made assistant to General Reagan and the chief of the finance bureau of the post-office. The family was a noted one.

Mrs. Mary Powell Mills Dimitry was daughter of Robert Mills, of Charleston, her mother being daughter of General John Smith, of Hackwood, Frederick county, Va., where he was colonel in the army and county lieutenant during the Revolution, and later for sixteen terms member of the United

States congress. Robert Mills was grandson of the colonial governor of Carolina and cousin of General Monk, Duke of Albemarle, who restored Charles II after Cromwell's death. Robert Mills was an architect and civil engineer and was in the office of Benjamin H. Latrobe in Philadelphia. He was the first United States architect, appointed by Andrew Jackson and in thirty years' service built scores of public structures in all parts of the country, the Patent Office, Washington Monument and Treasury colonnade being among them, and he was all the while "capitol architect." The Washington Monument in Baltimore, Memorial church in Richmond, parts of the University of Virginia and Charleston Custom House are also credited to him.

The Dimitry family in Richmond included the Misses Eliza Virginia Dimitry (later Mrs. E. F. Ruth, deceased), Elizabeth Linn Dimitry (Mrs. C. M. Selph), deceased, Matilda T. Dimitry (Mrs. W. T. Miller), and five sons, John Bull Smith, Charles Patton and Alexander, were all in the army as privates, John being dangerously wounded in a charge at Shiloh. Robert, Andrea and Thomas Dabney were under possible fighting age. All these bright girls and gallant educated youths, who did so much to aid the higher intercourse of the younger set, are now across the shadowy border, except Charles Patton. Mrs. Miller died only two years since; leaving a son, Mr. Mills Miller, in New York. Charles Dimitry, after a brilliant and scholarly life in literature and journalism, is now the blind historian of Louisiana.

The capital held no household more thoroughly charming than that of Colonel and Mrs. Joseph C. Ives, of the president's staff. For a few years preceding the war they had been noted as the handsomest pair in Washington society. This was at a day when Burnside, McClellan, Crosby and Michler were young beaux and regnant beauties vied for the apple at every levée.

Young Ives graduated with distinction from West Point during General Lee's superintendence of that institution; went into the Engineer Corps and was early sent on the exploration of the Colorado river. On that expedition his work was so commended that he was ordered to Washington for duty under the chief engineer of the army. About that time he met the beauty of the Semmes family, of Georgetown, famed for its pretty women and noted men. Of course the handsome young soldier loved her—most men did. They were married but a short while when wedding chimes changed to war's alarums. Ives was of Northern family, but association made him Southern in sentiment, and he took his wife and young children to Richmond. There he was hailed as an acquisition and given position as chief engineer on General Lee's staff. This he held with credit until he was transferred, at the President's personal request, to his own staff as engineer aide-de-camp. Mr. Davis had known the Ives couple in Washington and assigned the husband to double duty, of which part devolved upon his wife. Besides discussing engineering problems and the defenses,

COLONEL JOSEPH C. IVES

Mr. Davis found the elegance of this couple such that he turned over to them the entertainment and care of distinguished foreigners whom interest or curiosity brought into the steel-walled capital. The soldiers of fortune, those of sympathy and the correspondents of the foreign press were met in Mrs.

Ives's home.   That it was not classed as a salon was probably due to its official character as a detached segment of the White House.

When the Marquis of Hartington, accompanied by Lord Edward St. Maur, made that semi-official visit to Richmond

CORA SEMMES IVES

which so disquieted the North for a space, the noblemen were placed in entire charge of Colonel and Mrs. Ives. That they were well content with the result is plain. When Mrs. Ives visited London, *post-bellum*, Hartington, then Duke of Devonshire, promptly found her out and offered her the courtesies of the peers' gallery of the House of Lords.

The Ives home was an open and much sought one, young and old alike admiring the handsome pair and their lovely sister, Mrs. Clara Semmes Fitzgerald.   This charming elder sister had married Lieutenant William B. Fitzgerald, of the old navy.   He promptly resigned, was made colonel in the army and given defense of the furthest advanced post on the Potomac.   The exposure broke him down and early widowed his devoted wife.   Both these ladies were convent reared, the elder being a splendid musician and one of the most delightful harpists I recall.   It is a coincidence that the wife of her brother, Senator Thomas J. Semmes, was the only other very noted performer upon Sappho's instrument in Richmond society of that day.

But besides her gifts as an entertainer Mrs. Ives was one

of the most industrious and resourceful workers for the soldiers and for the poor among that noble band of Richmond
women. She practiced what the flowery Oriental preaches,
and her house and all it contained was at the disposal of the
needy. There had been no let or stay to this in the beautiful
evening of her life. The two widowed sisters lived together,
Mrs. Fitzgerald broken in health and Mrs. Ives tending her
with the faithful gentleness of mother and sister combined.
The latter days of both passed in that deep content that only
love and religion can bring. Those of the younger sister have
been brightened by the fine maturity of three sons, but deeply
shadowed later by the loss of two. Captain Edward B. Ives,
chief of the Electrical Bureau, United States Army Signal
Corps, was laid at rest at
Arlington in the fulness of
a brilliant and useful career.
Major Frank J. Ives, who
was surgeon on Chaffee's staff
in China, was later in the
Philippines. He was men-
tioned in General Bates's
report of the Cuban cam-
paign; and years ago in
Indian wars won the title of
the "fighting doctor." Only
in November last, he was
laid to rest beside his elder
brother, at Arlington. The
youngest son, a lawyer, lives

MRS. CLARA SEMMES FITZ-GERALD
(FROM A PORTRAIT BY SULLY)

in Arizona. And so, amid soft lights and gentle shadows,
sunset was awaited by the tender twain.

It came first to the elder sister. Mrs. Clara Semmes Fitzgerald died at the Ives home, in Saratoga Springs, on September 7, 1906. In the supreme calm of her great faith her

sister now awaits the new meeting with the loved ones gone
before.

In all the mad rush of that *pre-bellum* winter in Washington, 1860-61, when grave heads shook ominously and light
heels danced over a powder magazine and recked little when
the fuse might reach, one handsome woman was constantly
in evidence. Colonel A. C. Myers, of the quartermaster-
general's department, had married the brilliant and picturesque daughter of old General David E. Twiggs, of Mexican
War fame. Grave and reticent as he was polished and accomplished, the husband was much older than his wife.
Moreover, he had as perfect a contempt for what he called
society as his wife held delight in it. No Othello in character,
Colonel Myers was willing to let the young beauty dance and
fritter the hours away at will. For several seasons prior to
the war she had been the reigning queen of Willard's and a
favored guest in every fashionable house. Her dancing was
perfect, her tact equal to it and her beauty even more exceptional. Two pretty little girls were not too much in
evidence, and the youthful mother enjoyed her freedom to
the full. So when the news floated through the snuffy corridors of the war department a little later that Myers had
resigned, the junior warriors doubtless felt vicarious regret
for the absence of his wife.

The colonel was an able and experienced soldier well
known to Mr. Davis and General Cooper, and was promptly
appointed quartermaster-general on reaching Montgomery.
Very valuable service he rendered, too, and the regular uniform adopted by the war department was, in larger part, of his
design. Toward the end, as was foreshadowed in that Montgomery board, the uniform was what any poor fellow could
get. At first however, the companies, battalions and sometimes whole regiments, poured in with nondescript clothing
that suggested ancient Joseph as their military tailor. Some-

times one company was frogged and laced in parade dress and
the next in homespun and home-made butternut. The
heads saw that for service as well as appearance there must
be uniformity so far as practicable.

A board was ordered to pass upon the preliminary design
for a service uniform. It consisted of Colonel Myers as president, Colonel George Deas, of the adjutant-general's department, my brother, Surgeon D. C. De Leon, acting surgeon-general, Colonel Tom Taylor, of Kentucky, another
volunteer, with Pierce M. B. Young, then fresh from West
Point and three years later a major-general, as recorder.
The French model for *Chasseurs-à-pied* was adopted and,
slightly changed, was used thereafter. There are as many
claimants for the Confederate uniform as there are for the
flag or the authorship of "Along the Potomac," or "Lines
on a Confederate Note." The above are the facts, four of
the board having been my mess-mates, and talked uniform
ad nauseam.

Mrs. Meyers was not permanently in Richmond, going
abroad, I think, to educate her children. When she was
there, however, her grace and beauty made the same impression as they had done in the older capital.

The two bright and pretty little girls of the Washington
days grew to pretty and popular society women, and both
have long been matrons. Miss Elizabeth Twiggs Myers
first married Algernon C. Chalmers, of Halifax county, Va.
There are three Chalmers children, Algernon C., Marion
Twiggs, now the wife of William Bryant, son of Captain
John Carlyle Herbert Bryant, of the Confederate army, of
Alexandria, and David Twiggs Chalmers. When widowed,
their mother married William C. Fendall, son of Townshend
Dade Fendall, of Alexandria, where the family now
resides.

Miss Marion Isabelle Myers first married Frederick Payne,

of the United States Navy, and later William Twombly, of the Paris-American colony, but now living in Florence.

There are two brothers, also; William Heyward Myers is now general superintendent of the Northern Central Railway, and the Philadelphia and Erie of the Pennsylvania system, and the younger is Major John Twiggs Myers, United States Marine Corps.

There is a little war reminiscence added to this historic family since the advent of peace. Three swords had been presented to General Twiggs at different times, for service in defence of the old flag. One was by resolution of congress, another by his native state of Georgia, and the third by the city of Augusta. These trophies were taken from the residence in New Orleans by General Butler. They were returned to the family after a suit in the supreme court of the United States, conducted by Hon. John Randolph Tucker.

Eighteen years ago General Myers died at Washington, and four years later, at Alexandria, his wife followed him.

CHAPTER X

In most cities of the "Old South," especially those that boasted colonial origin, as Creole Louisiana, Huguenot Carolina, or the "Virginia Plantations," society trended to a "four hundred." In the last, even from earliest days, as has here been shown, the landed gentry and learned professions held social vantage. The encroachments of the moneyed element were slower there than in the busier North.

Sometimes in Richmond the oldest families held aloof from the social swim, thereby abrogating no right to plunge into it at will. These formed a social reserve to the advance guard of gaiety and hospitality, but at the advent of the government the latter were marked enough, both in quality and quantity, to make that city a noted leader in Southern matters social.

One of the gayest of the Richmond homes, and one of the most elegant and luxurious, was the Macfarlands'. *Prebellum* it had been both, but with just a suspicion of frost in the atmosphere.

Mr. Macfarland was a gentleman of the old school, prim and with fixed ideas. In a land and era of reckless dressing, he was notable by his perfect grooming. Regularly as clockwork he passed to and from his mansion and the bank of which he had long been the head clad in immaculate broadcloth, gloves and silk hat, which no rigor of blockade seemed potent to avert. This produced something akin to awe in the verdant soldier, and did not always escape the flippant jokers of that day.

Mrs. Nancy Macfarland, a gentle and gracious matron of the old school, had ever been loved as much as respected by all who knew her. So, despite the flippant and perhaps the envious unbidden to it, the home was one of the most typical and much sought in Richmond at all times. During the early war days it was gladdened by as fair and charming a bevy of maidens as ever graced an old Southern home.

MRS. WILCOX BROWN
(TURNER MACFARLAND)

Miss Turner Macfarland was a débutante, bright, blooming and budlike enough to have almost justified the impertinence of Page McCarty's versed statement that

*"A   saint   his   lips   would
smack
On taking in the rosy charm
of tender Turner Mac!"*

Genuine, frank and womanly, this sole daughter of the house and heart of the old banker was permitted to fling wide the curtains and let the warmest sunshine of society and joyousness into the staid parlors. Popular and most attractive herself, she had ablest coadjutors in four sparkling and petite cousins, the Misses Bettie and Susie Bierne, Bierne Turner and Mrs. Breckinridge Parkman. All these were charming women. The Bierne sisters were heiresses of the famous Old Sweet Springs lands, and their conquest of belleship had been easy in Northern cities, at New Orleans carnival seasons and at the seaside resorts and the then peerless White Sulphur. So the once grave mansion bloomed as a social conservatory during some dark hours of the great struggle. But the dull shadow came there, too, as will be seen.

Brilliant and beautiful women graced all branches of two old families historic in Virginia. No parlors of the capital were sought more eagerly than those of Mrs. James West Pegram, who had been Miss Virginia Johnston, daughter of the famous "Turf King."

Her elder daughter was highly accomplished, a stately yet affable woman and the most noted conversationalist of her day. She was an experienced and loved teacher of girls, many a belle of the '60's owing much of her attraction to "Miss Mary's school." Admirable exponent of a school fast dying out, she inherited the courtly graces of the gentlest of mothers. The Pegram home was as much sought by the more mature society as by the best gilded of the youth, and it was especially popular with the foreign officers who had offered their swords to Lee.

One and all, these found double attraction in the bright and gracious younger members of the family. Miss Jennie Pegram, the younger sister, was a belle whose unsought reign had scarcely a compeer in war days. Dignified, gentle and quiet, she was never disparaged as a coquette, but there were rumors unceasing of serious beaux rising disconsolate from her feet. And in those happy parlors were cousins with the family traits, petite Miss Fanny and laughing Miss Mary Truxton Johnston—"Truxie" to half of the state; pretty and musical Miss Mattie Paul, and many another came and went—and conquered?

After the war Miss Pegram became the wife of General Joseph R. Anderson, whose Tredegar Works made the Hampton Roads tug of *Monitor* and *Merrimac* a possibility and aided in the long life of the struggling Confederacy.   Now widowed, after ten years of happy married life, Mrs. Anderson resides in the elegant Richmond home, where she dispenses old-time hospitality.

Miss Jennie also surrendered and to another good old Rebel. She married Colonel David Gregg McIntosh, of South Carolina, who from Sumter to Appomattox illustrated his state's high traits on red fields that brought his well-earned promotion.   In her long-time Baltimore home she repeats the gentle triumphs of her youth over the hearts of both sexes. No one would suspect her of being a grandmother. Her first daughter, named for and very like her, died unmarried.   The second, Margaret, is the wife of William Waller Morton, of Richmond, and has hosts of friends there and in Baltimore.   This marriage gives Mrs. McIntosh her double claim to play the venerable: her only son and youngest child recently married the popular Miss Charlotte Lowe Rieman, also of Baltimore.

MRS. DAVID GREGG M'INTOSH
(JENNIE PEGRAM)

Miss Fannie Johnston married an artist, Mr. Britton, and died after a brief married life.   Her children reside in South Orange, N. J., and her sister, Miss Truxton, is with them.   She has spent much of her later life abroad and is still unmarried.

One of the most noted families in recent Richmond, and

one that took on quite biblical proportions, was the Haxalls. All four of the pairs that headed it, save one, had many descendants and these married and intermarried into such other notable houses as the Wises, Masons, Tuckers and Tripletts, the Gordons and the Lees.

William H. Haxall, the exception in the family, had no children, living with his wife in the main street home so popular with their old-time friends.

Bolling Walker Haxall married Miss Anne Triplett, sister of William S. of that name, whose daughters, Misses Lizzie and Mary, were so noted in the younger war society. The eldest of this branch of the Haxalls was Miss Louisa Triplett, now Mrs. Charles K. Harrison, of Baltimore, lately widowed; whose family of nine sons and three daughters are her pride and solace and with good reason. The daughters are all married, but none of their brothers has yet followed that good example. Mrs. Harrison herself was one of the buds of Richmond society just before General Grant meddled seriously with it. She was a lovely girl, but always of rather an earnest turn, a result of surroundings, largely. In a recent letter she reminds me:

"In our house, as in many in Richmond, one large room was devoted to the sick and wounded soldiers. The cots were arranged as in a hospital, and filled again as soon as emptied. My father never bought one dollar in gold until the last week of the Confederacy; did not think it patriotic, and did not allow me to be dressed in anything brought through the blockade for the same reason. We sold our carriage to buy food when the Yankees took possession, having no United States money.

"My mother, as did many ladies, baked bread regularly twice a week for the Robinson Hospital, directly behind our house."

Thus it will be noted that this mother was one of those

bees who gave honeyed charity and love to the needy, and
that Bolling Haxall was loyal in the Covenanters' fashion.
The only daughter of his house was young in the trying days,
but took the color of her life from its sacrifices. Her three
brothers were still younger. William, the eldest boy, is
now a farmer and much of a town magnate at Bartonsville,
Orange county, Va. The next brother, Bolling W., also
makes the "sacred soil" yield him bread, farming in Loudon

MRS. ROBERT E. LEE, JR.
(CHARLOTTE HAXALL)

county. John Triplett Haxall, born during the war,
now resides in Baltimore.
He married the youngest
daughter of Douglas Gordon,
of Fredericksburg. They
have three daughters and
one son, Triplett, Jr. The
second brother, Bolling, married Miss Noland and has a
family of four, three of them
being girls.

The Barton Haxalls were
more in the social whirl,
there having been several
young ladies of that family,
and popular ones: Clara,
Lucy, Agnes, Hallie; May and

Charlotte having been only young girls at the war's close.
The last, Mrs. Robert E. Lee, Jr., is dead; as is Fannie,
another sister who grew up after the war and never married.
Rosalie, the youngest, is now Mrs. C. Powell Noland, the
mother of three daughters and four sons. Of them, Lloyd, Barton, Powell, Jr., Philip and Charlotte are all grown and are
lately described as "splendid young people, self-supporting,
all of them, including the daughter."

The eldest sister, Clara (Mrs. Grundy), was very popular in Richmond. She had two daughters, Mrs. Pue, now living in Baltimore county, Md., and Mrs. Leake, residing in Richmond. Barton Grundy married Miss Branch and also lives there.

Miss Lucy Haxall is now Mrs. Edward Lees Coffey, of New York City. She has a son, Barton, lately married, and a daughter, Lucy, who married Charles DeKay. They have several children.

The third of these sisters, Agnes, wedded one of the best loved and most courtly gentlemen of his day, Warrington Carter. She left one son, Shirley, who lives in Virginia.

Hallie Haxall, the next, married Henry A. Wise, Jr., a minister. They had numerous progeny who died young, and one married son; but his line is now extinct, except one female grandchild.

Mrs. Alexander Cameron, of Richmond (Mary Parke), is the mother of twelve sons and daughters. All of them live in the home city except one daughter who married in Harrisburg, Pa., and one son, a rising business man of that city.

Dr. Robert Haxall, the other of the senior four, died years ago. His widow removed from the old Grace street home they had built, to Washington. There she lived until her death, eight years since. And today there is but one of the old name still in Richmond, the junior Barton Haxall, whose brother Phil is now a bright memory only of days gone.

There are a number of fast vanishing pictures that stand out clearly against the misty background of memory. None of these better illustrates the good old times than the household of Colonel James Lyons. Seated about a mile from Richmond, Laburnum was a typical home of the gentry, having the English exclusiveness in delightful amalgam with

genuine American hospitality. There young and old of
the home set delighted to respond to frequent bidding,
and the number and the warmth of these increased with
the influx of accredited strangers.

At the outbreak of the war Mr. Lyons was a widower
with a grown family. About that time he married a beautiful Louisianian who had been educated in Richmond. Miss
Imogene Penn was regarded as one of the best posed, as
well as prettiest belles of the incoming decade, and her
gentleness, grace and thorough tact made her popular and
hold her in living remembrance. She had two younger
sisters, Misses Norma and Bertha Penn, just finishing their
education in Richmond when the war came; but they fled
southward and escaped the gods of war and love alike. Mrs.
Lyons died young and without children. Her husband
survived her some years, but the cloud over Laburnum that
her passing left was never lifted until its occupancy by
another noted Virginian, who died there lately, lamented by
all—Joseph Bryan.

During Mrs. Lyon's reign the very cream of war society
was found there, and today no habitué writes or speaks
of the giddy and long-guarded capital without mention of
the Lyons home.

The Misses Penn did not permanently escape by flight
from Richmond. Miss Bertha became Mrs. Krumbhaar,
of New Orleans, and is now the mother of six children, some
of whom are notable in all social functions. Miss Norma
married Mr. Conrad, and is now a childless widow residing
with her sister at the Penn Flats in that city.

Mr. Lyons was not only prominent in social matters, but
also in the graver one of the law. He was long a leading
member of the Richmond bar and a trusted and clear-headed
adviser in all affairs of private and public moment. Urbane as strong, dignified yet suave, he carried into serious

actions of life the same high methods that made him as much respected as liked in the pleasanter, if quite as difficult, field of social success. In his passing away another link was stricken from the shortening chain that holds the old school to the new.

Peter Lyons, his son by the first marriage, was heir to many of the traits that had made his father's popularity. He married in early life, and while the war was still in progress, the beautiful Miss Addie Abbott Deane, one of the pair of graceful and bright sisters who made the home of Dr. Francis H. and Mrs. Elizabeth Drew Deane so haunted by the best of the time's gilded youth. The three daughters of this union were the pride and solace of the lovely widow's heart. They had grown to womanhood and were all happily married: the eldest, Elizabeth Deane Lyons having wedded Hon. Claude H. Swanson, the noted and

MRS. DABNEY J. CARR
(ANNA MEAD DEANE)

popular governor of Virginia, in the outset of his successful career. Addie Heimingham became Mrs. Henry Bohmer. Lucy Lyons married Cunningham Hall.

It was just three years ago, that in the flush of health and happiness, Mrs. Lyons was suddenly taken from her sister and her children. On the very night of her son-in-law's nomination to the first office in the gift of his state, she dropped dead. So sudden was her taking that the blow stunned family and friends; and Mrs. Swanson recently wrote that she found an unfinished letter to me on her mother's desk, after her death.

The other sister, Anna Mead Deane, married Mr. Dabney Jefferson Carr and still resides in Richmond, surrounded by a family of five, and the friends and bright memories of happy youth. The Carr children are Dabney Jefferson, Wilson Cary Nicholas, Wallace Deane, Anna Deane and Cary Peyton Carr; all unmarried. In the third generation there is but one: Douglas Deane, the three-year-old son of Mrs. Cunningham Hall.

Another name that then sat pleasantly on every lip and has since lived in the kindliest memory of all who knew them, was that of the Allans: differentiated as the "Scotch" and "Irish" Allens.

Mrs. John Allen, in her picturesque old home, was the soul of gentle and genuine hospitality. Hers was the family that had befriended the erratic and immortal Poe.

Captain Willie Allen, the son of this lady, was deservedly one of the best loved and most respected of the younger set. Frank, generous and brave, he was as true as Mr. Hay's *Jim Bludso*, for seeing his duty,

> *"He went for it thar an' then!"*

Not essentially a society man in the *finesse* of the carpet knight, his truth and gentleness of personality won to him the reckless and the brilliant alike. Recently one of the greatest, yet most unspoiled, belles of that pleasant past wrote:

"One thing I do remember is that I danced my first german with you in Mrs. Enders' great parlor. My second I danced with Willie Allen. He did most of it on my insteps. Oh, he was a noble gentleman, but a cruel dancer!"

But there was not a girl in all Richmond who had not wet

with hot tears the lint she scraped, had that bad dancer stopped a live Minié ball.

William Allen, of Claremont—"Buck" Allen, or Willie "Irish" Allen, as known to his intimates, or to distinguish him from the "Scotch" Allens—did not actually belong to that family at all. He was a dashing young Irishman—indisputably of good blood and rearing, named William Orgain. Of superb physique, generous impulses and broad handed generosity and a constitution his entire life proved a marvelous one, he was universally popular with men and women.

Old William Allen, owner of the magnificent estates of Claremont, on the James, in Surry county, was a bachelor. He offered to leave them to young Orgain, if he would change his name, a proposition naturally accepted. The new master soon became as popular as his namesake; his genial hospitality and princely entertainments making his repute as a host a national one. He was a great horseman, hunter and sailor; had a craze for rare stock and pits, was unhappily overindulgent to his own tastes for the best of solids and fluids. He made money flow like water, and all bibulants flow like the money; and in the early days of the war his presence in Richmond with his yacht, "The Breeze," was ever an event for the home and visiting youth.

Allen married the beautiful Miss Catherine Jessup, of Canada; a high bred and gracious woman, whose native gentleness and courtesy made her a swift coadjutor in his hospitality. She was ever as helpful, with hand as well as purse, in the work of her less wealthy sisters in Richmond, as though she had been native there. After a time, the shadows came to her forehead and her clear eyes; but no other expression was ever given to any needs in her for sympathy or assistance, in her domestic life. The memories of the war-time are broidered with bright details of her pretty entertaining of young and old.

None of the original Allen name are now living, save in those pleasant traditions, out of which histories are builded. But the Orgain Allens had one son, Willie Allen, now a lawyer and referee in New York. He married the beautiful Miss Minnie Anderson, daughter of the noted Confederate general, and later mayor, of Savannah. They live in handsome style in the big city and have no children; but Mrs. Allen gained some vogue in literature, by her "Love Letters of a Liar," printed in "Town Topics," and later in book form. This couple never occupied Claremont.

William Allen, after the war, lived at Curls' or Claremont, in the old way; but his death was a pitiable one: alone, on the James, in his little sailboat.

There were a number of others, among the society centurions, well worthy of ampler note than space permits. Temptation is strong to linger among them, passing from door to door and rendering its meed to each.

There were the Warwicks, a popular household, shadowed by the early death in battle of its sons Bradfoote and Barksdale Warwick, loved by all who came within their contact. The then young lady of the name is now the widow of Captain Dick Poor, of Baltimore, but the little one, Imogen, who had posed for Washington's "Latané" died years ago.

Cheery and ubiquitous Judge and Mrs. Crump were always agreeable and always helpful. They passed the boundary years ago, but left a family of four, the two daughters of which are now Mrs. Lightfoot and Mrs. Tucker. Others, as the Enders, Cabells, Freelands and more, we shall meet elsewhere.

Ex uno disce omnes. It is given to no pen, however truthfully it try, to write all the truth. Where is the old-timer— facing the sunset, and watching his own shadow lengthen

and loom gigantesque—who does not feel, as he glances over
his shoulder, that—

> " *The mossy marbles rest*
> *On lips that he has prest*
> *In their bloom;*
> *And the names he loved to hear*
> *Have been carved for many a year*
> *On the tomb.*"

CHAPTER XI

THE TYRANNY OF THE 'TEENS

ONE time-honored custom, theretofore considered all essential, that the war almost wholly abrogated, was the demand for chaperonage.

In the good old times in the South and in Washington and Baltimore, which best voiced the proprieties of the South, the 'teens were dormant, if yet tyrannous. A young girl would as soon have thought of wearing a modern bathing costume or sporting divided skirts as of going alone to a ball, even with her very best young man. This was due, in Washington, to its early tinge of the cosmopolitan and to its whirl of gaiety and great admixture. For the Washington of the Fillmores and of Miss Lane was, on a miniature scale, as Joseph-coated and as polyglot as in the millionaire Mecca of today.

In the South the custom was lawful progeny of home education. There woman was regarded with a tender veneration that was a heritage from the days when the gentlemen donned metallic suits and mounted plated steeds to ride around the world at windmills, armed with a sharp stick and a dull sense of the difference betwixt *meum* and *tuum*. Young girls of the sunny section were reared so tenderly that the winds of heaven might not visit them too roughly, and they were ever chary of contact with the other sex, nor prodigal enough to do any unveiling to the man in the moon.

Neither were they made self-helpful in the necessity-born methods of today. They were, generally in the towns and invariably in the slave-crowded plantations, scarcely permitted to lace their own slippers or stays. That they were capable, however, was proved by the first and lasting response they all gave to the real demand the war made upon them. At its call these cherished darlings of Southern homes descended, as one woman, from the pedestals upon which the Quixotic chivalry had elevated them, and wrought to the bitter ending, and after it, in wholly unused methods and places, as though born to effort and to success. They sewed rough fabrics for rough men with their delicate hands, cooked wonderful messes for camp and hospital out of slenderly stocked pantries; they dressed wounds with never a tremor or a flush of false modesty.

Small wonder then that the true men of the South fought as well and as long as they did; it was for their true women.

But the belles of *ante-bellum* days were reticent with their beaux. Those were the days when the soda-fountain, the ice-cream saloon and the post opera restaurant were not the *prime media* of inter-communication between the young of the two sexes.

Then, to take Washington once more as exemplar, the chaperone was a constant if not always wakeful factor. And those old mothers were Trojan in their fear of the most Grecian of gift-bearing youth. A stiff bouquet, with a prim laced paper collar, or a very proper book was admissible; a too expansive use of confections was viewed askant, and gloves were tabooed. As for a buggy alone, perish the thought! Nor was it considered at all the thing for the escort to furnish the conveyance to a ball. If the family coach was non-existent, the harmless, necessary hack was provided by the mother of his belle, while he sought her shrine on foot, or in the horse-car of the period.

Richmond had early yielded her social queenship to the
tyranny of the 'teens. Many a stranger worldling wondered
at the absolute dominance of her unmarried element. There
was no city that had boasted more charming married women,
stately heads of handsome homes often, and many both

young and beautiful. These
were met at dinners and all
gustatory functions, but they
rarely attended the balls
and still more rarely
danced. The plain gold ring
seemed the badge of social
servitude to home and
nursery, as inexorable as the
welded collar of the feudal
serf.

Most of these fair young
tyrants are now grand-
mothers, where they have
not crossed the boundary
into the misty beyond. And
those then unmated charm-

MRS. THOMAS R. PRICE
(LIZZIE TRIPLETT)

ers, bright-eyed and daring in dance and flirtation, tender of
heart while firm of hand in hospital and sick-camp—alas!
some of *them* are grandmothers, too. Time whets the re-
lentless scythe for Beauty no less than the Beast.

> "*Where, where are the Anns and Elizas,*
>   *Loving and lovely, of yore?*
>   *Look in the columns of old advertisers—*
>   *Married and dead by the score!*"

Few society men from abroad failed to note this undisputed
supremacy of the unmated in all the gayer functions of Richmond. To me it constantly seemed that the young people
had seized society while their elders' heads were turned, and

had run away to play with it for a time, so I always looked to see some older ones come in, with reproof upon their brows, and take charge of it again. But I looked in vain, and one night at a dinner I remarked this to my neighbor, suggesting that it was only because of the war. She was one of the most charming women society could boast, scarcely out of her honeymoon, beautiful, accomplished and very gay.

"Visitors always remark that," she answered. "But it is not the result of the war or of the influx of strangers. Since I can remember, only unmarried people have been allowed to go to parties by the tyrants of seventeen, of whom I was one. We married folks do the requisite amount of visiting and tea-ing out. Sometimes we even rise in our wrath and come out to dinner. But a dance or a ball? No, as soon as a girl marries, she must make up her mind to pay her bridal visits, dance a few square dances upon sufferance, and then fold up her party dresses. However young, pleasant or pretty she may be, the Nemesis pursues her and she must succumb. The pleasant Indian idea of taking old people to the river-bank and leaving them for the crocodiles to eat is over-strictly carried out by our celibate Brahmins. Marriage is our Ganges. Don't you wonder how we ever dare the croco-diles?"

Who had not wondered? Though the French system of excluding mademoiselle from social intercourse and giving the patent of society to madame may be productive of more harm than good, its reverse seems equally dangerous.

Richmond may have been an exception to the rule. In those four unprecedented years she was to most rules.

In the South women marry much younger than in the colder states. So it haps often that the best and most attractive points of character do not mature until after the girl has gotten her establishment. The Southerner, more languid and emotional than her Northern sister and less self-dependent even when equally accomplished, is not apt to shine most at an early stage of her social career. Firmer foothold and more intimate knowledge of their intricacies are needful to her on the busy byways of fashion. Hence, many wondered that the better matured of its flowers should be so entirely superseded in the Richmond bouquet by the half-opened buds. The latter doubtless gave a charming promise of bloom and fragrance at their full, but too early they left an uneasy sense of crudity and unripeness with the unaccustomed visitor.

All the same, Richmond had inscribed over the portals of its dancing set: "Who enters here, no spouse must leave behind!" And that law was of the Medes and Persians so far as women were concerned.

The male element at all functions ranged from the passé beau to the boy with the down still on his cheek; ancient husbands and young bachelors alike had the *open sesame!* But if a married woman, however young in years of wifehood, passed the forbidden limits by intent or chance, *væ victis!* She was promptly and severely made to feel that the sphere of the mated was pantry or nursery, not the ballroom.

To the stranger dames, if young and lively, justice a little less stern was meted, but even they, after a few concessions, were shown how hard was the way of the transgressor.

But indubitably it spoke volumes for the pure and simple society that had gone on thus for years and that no chaperonage had ever seemed needful. But now the case was different. A large promiscuous element was injected into society and all felt that the primitive should give place to the conservative. The "Jeannette and Jeannot" stage was pretty. It told convincingly the whole story of truth and purity in men and women. But with the sudden influx, when the stray wolf might so readily borrow the skin of a lamb, a hedge of form need not in any manner have intimated a necessity for its erection.

Even in the youngest and giddiest assemblies the pilgrim to social Richmond found many people worth meeting as well as looking at. The most juvenile german was fringed often by those who would have danced and queened it in any other town, and the potent supposed-to-be grave and reverend molders of laws and makers of campaigns came to rest their eyes and brush the cobwebs from duty-dusted brains. Nor can I recall any assemblages of the last half-century where those *desiderata* could have been more comprehended. "The prettiest woman in the world!" is a fashion of speech so trite as to have lost all meaning. In Richmond, in the mid-war, it had taken on the simplicity of a dictum and the clearness of truism. Early in the novel social conditions, as I have tried to explain, the older and more dignified representatives of both home and visiting society did and accepted the entertaining.

This lasted only a little while. Then Richmond went back to the inexorable tyranny of the 'teens. As duties accumulated without their homes, as the problem of bare living became a producer of deep thought and, more still, as the suspense and strain, personal and patriotic alike, grew more dire on the older people, they gradually let the more emphasized of the gaiety slip back into the hands of the young and thoughtless. But in those starvation parties of the late war there were as beautiful young women to be seen as I have ever looked upon in any assemblages in any city, under any adventitious aid of costuming and lighting.

When the Grand Duke Alexis made that tour of America just after the war—the *entourage* of which was possibly more Oriental than Muscovite—I heard him say with seeming sincerity:

"The most beautiful woman in the world? Oh, I have seen her in your country." From the devotion of the Russian to at least two noted and rival belles from the East and West, he may have believed what he said. But had he happened in on starvation at Richmond a few years earlier, he might have been taken *au pied de la lettre*, with none to dissent.

MRS. WILLIAM M. FARRINGTON
(FLORENCE TOPP)
(FROM A STATUE OF HER)

The only difficulty, probably, had been to decide which one of the goddesses on that Virginian Olympus was entitled to the apple. In a society where Misses Hetty Cary, Mattie Paul, Leila Powers, Virginia Pegram, Evelyn Cabell and their peers were already assured belles, and herein were dropping each month new and startling beauties, judgment grew dazed and the critical were dumb. Nor were they all Richmond girls or even Virginian. Naturally the old city and state sent their best and prettiest to the meet of beauty, but the South and middle West and the far shore of the dividing river all had representation fully satisfying to pride.

In the early days of the war a sensation was made even in Richmond by the exceptional beauty of Miss Florence Topp. This Tennessee girl, only in her mid-teens, spelled young and old by her face and form and held them by her witchery of manner. Hers was a familiar face at the Stanards', Andersons', Lyons', and among her schoolmates were Misses Cornelia Rives, Evelyn Cabell, Ella Wimbish and Annis Alexander. She was the daughter of Robertson Topp and Elizabeth Little Vance, her grandsire being Roger Topp, who aided in founding Memphis and was a pioneer in Tennessee.

Returning to her home, Miss Topp was soon the undisputed belle of her section; leaders of the Southern armies, and later a Federal admiral seeking her hand, while the famous Albert Pike wrote poems at length in her praise.

At twenty-two the young lady surrendered to the seige, marrying William M. Farrington, a well-poised and wealthy bachelor of her city. There the pair still reside in the old homestead and with them two children. Miss Valerie Farrington adds to society charm a thorough knowledge of music and a magnificent voice, and William M. Farrington, Jr., has been a member of the Memphis bar for twelve years. The family has strong literary bent, Miss Farrington having written much for the current journals and having taken prizes for fiction.

Miss Florence Topp's only real rival for beauty and belleship of the West chanced to be her brilliant and famous cousin, Miss Betty Vance, daughter of William Little Vance and Letitia Hart Thompson, of Harrodsburg, Ky. There, in 1847, was born the beauty of the West, best known to Eastern society and resorts. Miss Vance queened it royally for a time, having been specially honored by the Grand Duke Alexis, whose

MRS. JOHN W. RUTHERFORD
(BETTY VANCE)

guest of honor she was when he visited New Orleans by river boat. After a phenomenal career Miss Vance followed her cousin-rival out of the lists. In 1874 she married John

W. Rutherford, of Scotland. She is still a young widow, residing in California, her daughter Marguerite remaining single, while Vance Rutherford married.

Four of Miss Vance's brothers are living: Messrs. George, William, Guy and Otey. One sister, Mrs. Thomas Martin, resides in Chicago, another, Mrs. De Pauer, resides at Mount Alberry, Md. Susan Shelby Vance married Dr. Vance, of South Carolina, dying soon thereafter.

MRS. JAMES FONTAINE HEUSTIS
(RACHEL LYONS)

Another marked type of Southern beauty was that of Miss Rachel Lyons, of South Carolina, who visited Richmond after the Seven Days' fights. She and her father were in search of a missing brother, Captain I. L. Lyons, of the Tenth Louisiana, who was reported captured and unhurt. Miss Lyons had already been a marked woman in Columbia society and her quick wit and sinuous grace at once attracted attention at the capital. She made many and enduring friends, but her stay was brief and was not repeated. Later she visited Mobile as the guest of her lifelong friend, Miss Augusta Evans, already noted as a novelist. On this visit Miss Lyons met a prominent young surgeon of Bragg's army, Dr. James Fontaine Heustis. He surrendered, and the pair married and settled in Mobile in the closing days of the war. Ever since, the Heustis family has been one of the most notable on the Gulfside, equally for the beauty, brilliance and the belleship of its women. The mother has ever been a remarkable conversationalist and her hospitality has been perennial. The eldest daughter, Miss Louise, studied art at home and abroad and several of her canvases have been in latter year exhibits. The second, Miss Mabel, had natural gifts in music and she is well appreciated in her own and other cities for her delicious alto voice. These two remain unmarried. The next, Rosalie, was one of Mobile's most noted belles, until she became Mrs. George Huntington Clarke, of Birmingham.

Mr. Liston Heustis, the only brother, is a prosperous banker of Belize, where he resides with a pretty young wife and very cherished baby.

Mesdames William Patterson and Joseph McPhillips, were until quite recently belles of the younger set of Mobile. Their mother is still a much-sought matron and the friendship between Mrs. E. A. Wilson and her is as fresh and strong as when it began in girlhood.

CHAPTER XII

THE "Three Graces, Junior," as Will Myers promptly named them, made *entree* into real society later in the war. If a prettier and more attractive trio ever turned the heads of male youth, I surely never beheld them. Misses Mary Triplett, Champe Conway and Lizzie Cabell were, speaking coldly and after the lapse of four decades, as pretty women as ever I saw. Differing in face, figure and expression, each foiled the other.

MRS. ALBERT RITCHIE
(LIZZIE CABELL)

In mentality and character they differed as much as in looks, and the attractiveness of the trio may have been enhanced by this variety.

Miss Cabell was of the gentlest and most dainty type of womanhood, conquering by simplicity combined with beauty. She reigned in the later days of the war, her subjects being her own sex as well as the opposite, but she never made the same resounding echoes as either of her girlhood's friends.

146

She is now a fair and placid reminiscence of that former time, as the well-preserved Mrs. Albert Ritchie, of Baltimore. Another of that trio, strangely enough, made her home in the Monumental City; Miss Champe Conway married Captain John Moncure Robinson, a Philadelphian, who served on Breckinridge's staff. Her children are familiar figures there and her own life has become part of the social history of the town. She died several years ago.

Miss Triplett's career was the most meteoric of the three. She was a veritable daughter of the gods, divinely fair and most divinely tall; a perfect blonde, classic-featured and wtith wondrous, expressive eyes. She was lithe and sinuous of motion and infinitely graceful. Mentally, she was receptive and brilliant, her natural wit running to repartee that stung sometimes beyond intent, and went abroad with wide reaching glare of the searchlight. Hers was a graceful audacity that ever stood her in good stead and bore her safely over many of society's quicksands, that might have engulfed a heavier natured woman. She was a belle from early girlhood, always sought and often feared by most ardent seekers. Less reticent than her rival beauties in "the Graces, Junior," she early began a series of conquests that gained celebrity, largely from the wondrous beauty of the girl, more, perhaps, because she was of clay too fine for common comprehension.

Indubitably without her intent and assuredly without her knowledge, that duel was fought that made most sensation in the last half-century and probably drove the code out of use in Virginia. It sent one respected and brilliant young man to speedy death, another, more brilliant still, to his end through a long and agonizing trail of the *descensus Averni*. Richmond lost no regard for the fair woman wronged by this wrangle. Years after, while still a brilliant and young favorite, she married an old-time friend and one of the best

loved men in his state, Philip Haxall.   Her beauty perhaps
gained as she grew older and more poised.   She mellowed
and love crept into the beautiful face, but her married life
had none of the thrill of her earlier days.   Previous to her
marriage, Miss Triplett visited the staid little city of Mobile.
Her brother John had won a fair and gentle débutante of the
previous season, daughter of an old and honored family of
Alabama.   Miss Sallie Ross was so popular as to make the
jeunesse doree feel the advent of the tasteful Virginian a per-

MRS. PHIL HAXALL
(MARY TRIPLETT)

sonal grievance, but they decided to solace themselves
with his dazzling sister.   Miss
Triplett, perhaps, was a trifle
blasée.   She hated boys in
dress coats and was at no
pains to conceal her views.
But despite her carelessness
to please, her beauty and her
wit conquered and the fame
of both echoed for years after
the present nieces were born.
Of the last, two are now
gracious young matrons of Mobile, two charming buds of
its society; Mrs. Dargan Ledyard and Mrs. Charles Hall, and
Misses Nannie and Helen Triplett.

The home of Mrs John Enders was perhaps the pivotal
point of gay and happy times for the younger set.   Spacious,
liberally kept up, and with doors that swung wide at a touch
the chief attraction was the lady at its head.   Mrs. Enders
was the friend of every boy who wore the gray and the confessor and adviser of about one-half of the Virginian army.
No fellow quarreled with his sweetheart or got in trouble
with his officer but he tramped to Richmond to tell this
trusted friend.   Rarely did he come in vain, for her goodness

and judgment were equal. The eldest daughter, Miss Sallie, was already in society when Beauregard saluted Anderson. The next sister, Miss Nannie, was not allowed to do more than take a peep. But she was pretty, jolly and bright, as natural as a fawn, though not so shy, and she said piquant things with a *naïveté* that tickled as it touched. The youngest, "Pidge" Enders, was quite a child when the war began, but one of its wonders was the quick maturity of young people. So, with warm welcome, good company and certain rations, the youth of war swarmed bee-like into the Enders home and found there honey galore. Saunders, Jim Fraser, Ridgley Goodwin, scores of gallant Maryland men, and the whole of the home youth, of course, felt that house their headquarters. There were more impromptu dances, picnics, rides and camp-parties at the Enders' than any house in town and—this in a whisper—more well-meant vows were there pledged and there re-cemented when cracked. But the daughters of the home held off siege and sortie alike until the war waned. It was only after General James Conner had a leg shot off that Miss Enders changed from flirtation and charades to a somewhat vivid Charleston matron. Miss Nannie was having too good a time to stop and think of marrying. If there was ever a popular woman, she broke that record. Loyal, original and great-hearted, the girls loved her, too. A rollicking trio were Misses Nannie Enders, Lillie Bailey and Truxie Johnston. They led every sport, from a fox-chase to a flirtation, and the old boys of that unforgotten yesterday find them ever in the first flush. When those girls rode or drove into a nearby camp, followed by a score of both sexes, there was more excitement than a raid had caused. They never came empty-handed, and unless discipline was drawn very tight, they rarely returned without fresh captures. Miss Baily has been dead many years, Miss Johnston lives far from her old state, and the jolly little "peeper" of the first war days has long admired the white beard of that good and persistent fellow who won her at last, Major Caskie Cabell, of Richmond.

Remembered members of the household are Winston, black butler, and Dan and Pinkey, who amused visitors with recitations and dances.

MRS. CASKIE CABELL (NANNIE ENDERS) AND LILLIE BAILEY

When Miss Lizzie Peyton Giles appeared suddenly in Richmond on July 4, 1863, there was a genuine sensation. It was quite doubled by the simultaneous arrival of another woman, equally beautiful and brilliant, Miss Josephine Chestney, of Washington City. Of both belles more will be seen, but it may be noted that the excitement was tripled by the array of seven trunks which Miss Giles had transferred to our exchange boat. With her mother Miss Giles had just returned from a trip abroad and, *on dit*, she had selected her rare trousseau.

Circumstantial evidence was the abnormality of war luggage and the nervous impatience of a noted, if not particularly handsome, brigade commander from the trans-Mississippi. General Quarles did not remain at the capital the full extent of his leave, nor was there any immediate wedding. After a time Miss Giles tired of society and conquests, but for the moment both she and Miss Chestney "just swung Richmond." General Quarles later married

Miss Alice Vivian, the world-famed beauty of Alabama, making another match after her death. Miss Giles is now the widow of a gallant and good fellow from Georgetown, Captain Sam Robinson, and Mrs. Butler, *née* Chestney, also lives at the capital.

The two other Giles girls with whom the beauty lived were of quieter tastes, but well known and popular. Miss Nannie did not marry and died young; and Miss Fannie became Mrs. Townes and was active in all social work for charity.

Dr. Herndon, C.S.N., had two pretty and gentle daughters in society, Misses Lucy and Molly. They were much in the Enders set and intimate with Miss Chestney. I remember calling with her when one of the sisters wore caps as a typhoid convalescent. She described the many things done for her, and how one lady bade her dress "her hair."

"Child!" retorted Miss Chestney solemnly, "you should read Mrs. Glass, and get your hare before you dress it."

Three charming girls in the younger circle were the Freeland sisters, Rosalie, Carter and Maria. Their home was a quietly elegant one and the trio had *chic*; talked and dressed well, and were admirable dancers; a necessity for any girl who had half an eye fixed on belleship. So the Freelands were a success with the inexorable autocrats of the german and at the later starvation parties of hungry memory. Miss Rosalie married Dr. Randolph Harrison and both are dead. leaving no issue. Miss Maria married Col. John R. C. Lewis; and their children were Maria Freeland and Lawrence. The latter married Miss Nicholas of Baltimore. Miss Carter Freeland married her brother-in-law, Daingerfield Lewis; and their family was large.

The Lewises were direct in descent from Fielding Lewis who married General Washington's favorite sister, Betty. "Daingy" Lewis was a splendid looking fellow and was on

General Lee's staff.   He was much in evidence in Richmond in the later war; and was a great favorite with men and women.   His brother John resigned from the United States Navy to come South.   Another brother, Ned Lewis, married the widow of Colonel Muscoe Russell Hunter Garnett.   She had been Mary Stevens, daughter of Mr. Stevens, of Castle Point.   She was South with her husband, and was a marked figure in society.

John Freeland, very soon after the peace, met and married Miss Mary Goldthwaite, of Mobile.   The wedding was notable, the bride's family being one of the oldest and most loved of the South and her personality winning her legions of friends. It was a grevious disappointment to these, and to the many new ones she won in her new home, that her married life was neither long nor happy.   Clouds arose to shut out the honeymoon, but the sympathy and respect her brief Richmond life won her, followed to her grave and linger lovingly about her memory.

There was probably no more widely known personality in all the Southland—and surely not more distinct against the background of mental and bodily activities—than that of Louis Trezevant Wigfall.

He had been successively state and United States senator from Texas; then her Confederate senator, though born on his father's plantation, near Edgefield, S. C., in 1816. He was also signer of the Confederate Constitution and commanded the First Texas brigade, as its general, in the field.

A man of brains, resource and untiring, restless energy, he was headstrong and dominant, and his opinion, once formed and firmly held to, was ever vigorously outspoken.

This possibly prevented his being entrusted with higher governmental posts, for his ability was conceded.   From his early mission, through a porthole, to prevent Major Anderson's fire-suicide at Sumter, down to the hegira of the government into the North Carolina finale, Wigfall was a conspicuous figure on the political stage. Naturally, he had some enemies and many friends, at the capital, where his representative duties held him and his family. But that family, which was one of the most pleasant of war-time Richmond, made only friends. Mrs. Wigfall had been Miss Charlotte Maria Cross, daughter of George Warren Cross, of Charleston, and was a congenial helpmate to her husband. Her Richmond home was made attractive to all by the presence in it of her two young daughters, Misses Louise Sophie and Mary Frances Wigfall; and, when his army duty permitted, of her son, Major Francis Halsey Wigfall. High mentality was a marked characteristic of the whole family, and so was exceptional frankness of its expression, both on public and social affairs. So the Wigfall sisters were attractive and sought in the Richmond whirl. Miss Mary Frances married Benjamin Jones Taylor, of Worcester county, Md., and is now a widow, residing in Baltimore. Miss Louise remained single until 1871, when she married a brilliant young Baltimore lawyer. Daniel Giraud Wright had enlisted as a private in the Confederate Army, was promoted to a lieutenancy in the Irish battalion, and served later with Mosby's corps. He is now associate judge of the supreme court of Maryland, and a popular and widely esteemed citizen of Baltimore.

In her life in that city Mrs. Wright has won hosts of friends in both the elder and younger strata of its sociality. Her Wigfall habit of thinking for herself, and the other of fluent and graceful diction, have lately combined in one of the pleasantest books upon the social South.

Judge and Mrs. Wright are the proud grandparents of De Courcy Eyre Wright, the son of their only child, W. H. De Courcy Wright, who married Miss Mary Eyre, daughter of that well-known Virginian, Severn Eyre.

Kingsley's great song has had innumerable settings, but there was never a more attractive version of *"Three Fishers"* than that pretty and popular trio: Misses Lucy, Mary and

MRS. HOWARD CRITTENDEN
(LOU FISHER)

Anne Fisher. The first two were sisters; daughters of Charles Fenton Mercer Fisher, of Richmond, and Anne Eskridge, of Mississippi. Young, graceful and vivacious, both were sought and admired by the choice fellows of the best set; but neither hauled down her particular flag of independence, until the more general surrender.

Then "Lou" Fisher took his parole from a capture from over the border. She married Howard Crittenden, a native of Kentucky but residing in California. They went to Texas and, scarcely a year after her marriage, the Richmond belle was run over at Galveston, by some vehicle, and died almost immediately. The fact of her death was unknown to most of her old friends, and it is doubtful if any of them know the details. The pressure of those times scattered the molecules of "the old set," and almost every one was absorbed in individual cares.

"Molly," as Miss Mary Fisher was ever known, was as much admired and widely popular as her sister Lucy. Very lately, an old time beau of hers wrote me, out of his multitudinous grandfatherhood: "She had little ways of her own, and was the best natured girl in all Virginia!" She married Mark Valentine, of Louisiana; the pair moved to Little Rock, Ark., and there resided long, with their one son, Mark Valentine, Jr.

The memories of these fair and gentle girls is still green; as is that of their beautiful cousin.

But second to none—not even to her cousins—in the race for the golden apple, was Miss Anne Fisher. She was the daughter of George Daniel Fisher, of Richmond, and Elizabeth Ganigues Higginbotham, of Albemarle. Mr. Fisher wrote the book on "the Descendants of Jacquelin Ambler." This pair had two sons and two daughters: Robert, Edward, Anne and Mary. The last is the sole survivor and is the widow of Col. Peyton Randolph, residing at Amherst, Va.

MRS. ROBERT CAMP
(ANNE FISHER)

Miss Anne Fisher married after the war Mr. Robert Camp, of Norfolk. Of this union came a boy and a girl, the latter named for her mother. She is now Mrs. John Cannon Hobson, of Pemberton, Va., having married the son of Captain Hobson, of Wise's brigade, whose wife was Miss Kitty Selden, of Westover. He is thus a nephew of Captain Plummer Hobson, who married Miss Annie Wise.

The Cannon Hobsons have two children: Bland Selden and Robert Camp Hobson.

Mrs. Anne Fisher Camp resided with Mrs. Hobson—who is said to resemble her mother strongly—during her widowhood, and died only in 1904.   I recall her as an exceptionally beautiful woman; and a friend wrote of her, at time of her death: "I think I can safely say of her, that she was one of the prettiest old ladies in Virginia."

CHAPTER XIII

"SOME AT THE BRIDAL AND SOME——"

SUNSHINE and shadow chased one another across the entire panorama of the war, as the cloud-scuds from mountain to crest mottle the bright valley beneath when they sail above it.

Hope ever seemed to tread the lighter just before the dull footfall of Despair numbed the heart upon which it fell.

Mrs. Chesnut tells the story of Hon. William Porcher Miles, confiding to her his real engagement to Miss Bettie Bierne. In those days confidences were cullenders, and next day burly and jovial Colonel George Deas and Bob Alston were sending the interesting gossip to society's four winds. Alston was no end of a talker. When captured with John Morgan, whose adjutant-general he was, the gallant little Georgian went to Richmond on parole to try and arrange the exchange of the raiders. We told him that

COLONEL ROBERT ALSTON
ADJT.-GENERAL MORGAN'S CAVALRY

157

the jailers had released him to have a much needed rest. By the way, he brought through the lines the first copy of General Lytle's "Antony and Cleopatra." Alston was a noble fellow and popular with all. His tragic murder, in his treasurer's office, shortly after the war was widely mourned.

The Miles-Bierne wedding at fashionable St. Paul's was the social event of the autumn of 1862, albeit one of the most limited in numbers, from recent mourning in the family. Scarcely over a score were present, the Davis, Preston, and A. C. Myers families and that of the bride only being admitted with the bridal party. There was an indefinable feeling of gloom thrown over a most auspicious event when the bride's youngest sister glided through a side door just before the processional.

Clad in deepest weeds, Mrs. Nannie Parkman tottered to a chancel pew, and threw herself prone upon the cushions, her slight frame racked with sobs.

Scarcely a year before, the wedding march had been played for her and a joyous throng saw her wedded to gallant Breck Parkman. Before another twelvemonth rolled around the groom was killed at the front. The bride, little recking that the guns that boomed diapason to her wedding march were ominous of personal woe, was one of the gayest and most attractive of society's war brides. She was as graceful as beautiful, and a much sought partner. One night I led a german with her, Willie Myers and I escorting the sisters home. At the Macfarlands' we spoke of the next night's dance; as we turned away, Myers said gravely: "Maybe Mr. Yank may keep some of us away from that, old man!" Was it telepathy? Before it came around the fatal summons had been bullet-sped to the young husband of scarce a year, and the joyous bride sat in the cold ashes of her desolation

The same elegant wedding dress she had worn was used

by Mrs. Miles; and Mrs. Myers, with a thrill of superstition—
or was that telepathy likewise?—whispered to Mrs. Chesnut:
"It was an evil omen. Those *point d'Alençon* laces make
me shudder!"

The second of the Bierne sisters, Miss Susie, yielded to
handsome and gentle-natured Captain Henry Robinson,
a Georgetown man, who had been popular in recent days
in the national capital's society. But she, too, held out
against Love's siege until the word "Surrender!" had begun
to grow familiar to Southern ears.

All these four have long since passed to the land that
knows neither marriage nor sorrow, but children of the beautiful and magnetic little belle of war-time Richmond and
her Carolina husband are still among the well-known and
honored Louisianians and Carolinians of today.

None of them live in Virginia, though both parents sleep
in the little cemetery at Union, Monroe county, where the
happy early days of their married life were spent. There
are five of the Miles sisters, of whom two are married, and
one brother, Dr. William Porcher Miles, who resides at the
Houmas, the family estates at Burnside, La., which he man-
ages. The eldest sister, Miss Sarah Bierne Miles, resides
there also most of the year. The second, Bettie Bierne
Miles, divides her time between there and Carolina. The
third sister, Miss Nannie, married William Gregg Chisholm;
was widowed and is now Mrs. E. W. Durant, Jr., and still
resides at Charleston. Miss Susan Warley Miles, the fourth
sister, resides in New York with the youngest sister, Margaret Melinda, now Mrs. Fred Pierson, Jr.

Mrs. Nannie Parkman went abroad after the war, and
there married a German nobleman, Baron von Ahlefeldt.
Again widowed, she spends most of her time in this country,
at the old homeseat, Union, W. Va.

Miss Turner Macfarland married Colonel Wilcox Brown,

of Baltimore, a true soldier and cultured gentleman, who was in charge of the artillery defenses of Richmond at the close of the war. Their eldest daughter is Mrs. John M. Glenn, both husband and wife being noted in the Monumental City for philanthropic work. The second daughter married H. Guy Corbett, an English gentleman who settled in Albemarle county, Va., a fruit-grower on a large scale and a perennial raiser of good words from his neighbors and his mother-in-law. Mrs. Brown passes much of her time with this pair, her only grandchildren being the two little Corbetts.

There is a third daughter of the Brown household, a charming girl of nineteen, still at school. But Elsham, at Afton, Va., does not monopolize all the time of the Richmond toast of yore, for a large circle of warm and admiring friends in the city attest that she is still very much alive.

John S. Saunders—the grave but sterling young Virginian lieutenant I have noted at Lincoln's inauguration, rose to a lieutenant-colonelcy. Then he found better promotion, for Miss Bierne Turner—the last of the quintet of cousins—married him in 1863. Their *post-bellum* home in Baltimore was an elegant and favorite resort of "the old set," for many a year; the husband last commanding the crack corps of National Guards, the Fifth Maryland. Three years ago he answered the last roll-call, and his wife is also dead.

The South Carolinians were notable during all the war, in the field, the council and in society. Tall elegant Jim Fraser and classic Sam Shannon divided the vote feminine for "the handsomest man in the army"; and cultured Frank Parker—adjutant-general to that unfortunate commander, Braxton Bragg—was no bad second. At dances and theatricals, as in the red sport of war, all three were in the front rank. All have passed across the border, the first two years ago, and Shannon is wasting intellect and elegance in a new home in the far West. Parker settled in Mobile, married

Miss Troost, of the old Battle family, and has grown children. One year ago all representative classes of his adopted city followed the bier of this true old cavalier.

It was Bernard Bee who christened Stonewall on Manassas field, just before his brave spirit went upward "in the arms of the white-winged Angels of Glory." And Wade Hampton? Wounded at Bull Run, and again severely on the retreat from Gettysburg, he was the same high-natured patriot in war and peace.

One battle sadly proved the mettle of that race. Both of the general's boys were in his legion. Wade, his first-born, and handsome, sunny-hearted Preston, his very Benjamin. The latter rushed recklessly into the hottest of the charge, far in advance of the line. The father called to Wade: "Bring the boy back!" The elder brother spurred to front, saw the other reel in saddle and caught

GENERAL WADE HAMPTON

him as he fell, mortally wounded. At the moment a bullet tore through his shoulder, and the father rode up to find one son dead and his bleeding brother supporting him.

The general took the body tenderly in his arms, kissed the white face, and handed it to Tom Taylor.

"Care for Wade's wound," he called. "Forward, men!" All through that long and bitter day the soldier fought with lead whirring by his ears and lead in his heart. It was not until the doubtful fight was ended that he knew that the other son still lived. Brutus of old was no more true than Hampton.

The women of the Prestons, the Chesnuts, and many another Carolina family, proved the truth of good old blood. One gentle old Carolina lady, calm and tender of heart, was

as heroic as Hampton. A veritable "mother in Israel," she was as Roman as he. What one in Judea or the seven-hilled city sent seven spears to victory for Joshua or David—for Scipio or Cæsar? Yet, this Christian mother of the South heard the thunder of hostile guns without one tremor, nursed her children, torn by their shells, without repining, but with perfect trust in the hand of the One Dispenser.

MRS. CHARLES THOMPSON HASKELL

Mrs. Charles Thompson Haskell (Sophia Langdon Cheves, daughter of Colonel Langdon Cheves) had seven sons in the army around Richmond when I met her at Mrs. Stanard's, in one of the several visits she made to tend their wounds. All of them had been privates in the army before the firing on Sumter. She was ever quiet, but genial; hiding what suspense and anguish held her; making unknowing, great history for her state and for all time.

The eldest son was Langdon Cheves Haskell, who served first on the staff of General Maxcy Gregg, later on that of General A. P. Hill, and surrendered at Appomattox as captain on the staff of "Fighting Dick" Anderson, of his own state. He married Miss Ella Wardlaw, of Abbeville, dying in 1886 and leaving three sons and one daughter, all adults.

Charles Thompson Haskell was the second son, a captain

in the First Carolina Regulars, and was killed on Morris Island when Gilmore landed to attack Charleston, in July, 1863. He, happily, left no widow.

The next was William Thompson Haskell. He was captain of Company H, First South Carolina Volunteers, and died at the charge of that corps at Gettysburg, while commanding a battalion of sharp-shooters under A. P. Hill.

Alexander Cheves Haskell lived through the day of Appomattox. He was colonel of the Seventh South Carolina Cavalry, of ruddy record, and still lives at Columbia. His first marriage was one of the most touching romances of the war. Miss Rebecca Singleton was a dainty and lovely, but high-spirited, daughter of that famed old name. In

CAPTAIN WILLIAM THOMPSON
HASKELL

the still hopeful June of 1861 Mrs. Singleton and her daughter were at the hospital at Charlottesville, crowded so that Mrs. Chesnut (as her diary tells) took the young girl for her roommate. "She was the worst in love girl I ever saw," that free chronicler records. Miss Singleton and Captain Haskell were engaged, and he wrote urgently for her consent to marry him at once. All was so uncertain in war, and he wished to have her all his own while he lived. He got leave, came up to the hospital, and the wedding took place amid bright anticipations and showers of April tears. There was no single vacant space in the house, so Mrs. Chesnut gave up her room to the bridal pair. Duty called; the groom hurried back to it the day after the wedding. That day one year later the husband was a widower, with only the news from his far-away baby girl to solace the solitude of his tent. After the war Colonel Haskell married Miss Alice Alexander, sister of General E. P. Alexander. She died after becoming the mother of ten children, six of whom are daughters.

A very marked favorite in society, and a gallant officer, was John Cheves Haskell, lieutenant-colonel of light artillery, when he surrendered with Lee. He married Miss Sallie Hampton, who died two decades ago, leaving one daughter and three sons, all now grown up. About seven years ago Colonel Haskell married Miss Lucy Hampton, daughter of Colonel Frank Hampton, who was killed at Brandy Station. They now live in Columbia.

CAPTAIN JOSEPH CHEVES HASKELL

Very much alive is the sixth brother, Joseph Cheves Haskell, now a resident of busy Atlanta and popular in his new home. When he gave up his sword at Appomattox he was captain and adjutant-general of the First Artillery Corps, on the staff of General E. P. Alexander. He married Miss Mary Elizabeth Cheves, and the pair have a grown family of three sons and a daughter.

Last in this remarkable family roster comes Lewis Wardlaw Haskell. He was but a youth when paroled with the remnant of the Army of Northern Virginia, having already served one year as a lieutenant of reserves on the South Carolina coast. This he gave up to go to the front and serve first as a private soldier and later as a courier to Colonel John C. Haskell.

Such were the exceptional septet of brothers, whose noble mother sent them to the field and hid her parting tears. The good old blood of the noted strains that course through the veins of all of her name made them stalwart, loyal and leal, and ready when duty called. They had but one sister, her mother's namesake. She is now Mrs. Langdon Cheves, of Charleston.

No home in Richmond welcomed its guests with more genuine and genial hospitality than that of the Gibsons. The noted and tireless chief of the historic Officers' Hospital was Dr. Charles Bell Gibson. He was a Marylander by birth, and son of Dr. William Gibson, who founded the Maryland University of Medicine, and was later dean of the University of Pennsylvania. The son, on early and high graduation, made his home in Richmond, rapidly acquiring reputation, popularity and a great practice, especially in surgery. When war came he was promptly used by the state and Confederate governments, and become head of the most important hospital, with Mrs. Lucy Mason Webb as his matron. In early life Dr. Gibson had married Miss Ellen Eyre, of Philadelphia. She swayed the war-time household with

> *The new school graces, grafted on those old*
> *That need no gilding, since they're purest gold.*

Able assistant in all social matters was her elder daughter, Miss Mary Elizabeth. This young lady, never seeking the rush and swirl of the giddier society became one of the most popular and most quoted of Richmond's women. Some of the cleverest *mots* that amused society originated with her; the keenest thrusts were so quickly and deftly given as rarely to cause pain.

At one german I chanced to be Miss Gibson's partner. A very swell staff officer had come in full uniform, including a pair of blind spurs. The lady, a graceful and tireless dancer, had evolved a stunning costume of mosquito netting, and it entangled with the cavalry insignia on the captain's boots. Stopping in mid-whirl, she tapped him on the shoulder and said sweetly: "May I trouble you to dismount, sir?"

After a bloody battle a boastful youth, who had been very slightly wounded, called on Miss Gibson. He spoke of the fight, when she demurely said, "Of course, you heard of General Lee's despatch to the President?" Then, while he wondered, she added, "He wrote, 'It was a glorious victory, but Lieutenant Blank was wounded.'" And, five minutes later, he was at the corner, telling every man he met of the honor the great chief had done him.

Little Annie of those days was the youngest of the family. She was a bright, pretty and graceful child, and Washington selected her as model for one of the children strewing flowers on the bier, in his Latané picture. She never married, and today resides in New York as the companion of her sister and the pet of her stalwart nephews.

Between the two sisters came four brothers, three in the army, though very young. William Eyre Gibson was in the artillery, and served in Texas. Beverly Tucker Gibson was on General Young's staff at fifteen years of age. All the boys have long since died.

Miss Gibson married, near the close of the war, Dr. Edwin S. Gaillard, a prominent surgeon. Of the old Carolina family, he had honored the name by duty nobly done, losing an arm on the firing line. After the war the pair moved to New York. Gaillard's *Medical Journal* was launched, and quickly became the leading one of the city. When the doctor died, his wife, with a large-and young family to rear, took prompt and full charge, held its old correspondents, gained new ones by the score; and the only medical magazine in America edited by a woman was easily kept in the lead for twelve years by this modest and resourceful Richmond girl. Then, when her idolized boys were educated and well placed, she took to her ease and to bridge.

There is object-lesson in this for swift decriers of Southern women's false education.

Even in her busiest days Mrs. Gaillard found time for altruistic work. She was the founder and first president of the New York Chapter of the Daughters of the Confederacy. She had the companionship of her gentle mother, as a member of her household, until her death at the age of seventy-two.

MRS. EDWIN S. GAILLARD
(MARY GIBSON)

The eldest of the Gaillard children is a daughter, Ellen, named for her grandmother. She married Dr. W. W. Ashhurst, of Philadelphia; but an alluring professional offer carried the pair to Chihuahua in Mexico. There the mother went and resided with them a year or two. She has now three granddaughters in the Ashhurst family.

There are five Gaillard brothers, of whom Edwin White Gaillard is the eldest. He is librarian and treasurer of the State Library Association and president of the City Library Club, of New York. He married Miss Clara Humphrey Sackett, of the same city. The second, Charles Bell Gaillard, is an underwriter in the Washington Assurance Company and he married Adèle, daughter of Rear-Admiral Erben. William Eyre Gibson Gaillard is vice-president of the Empire Trust Company of New York, and of the McVickar-Gaillard Realty Company. Only a year ago he married Mary Stamps, daughter of Mr. and Mrs. Charles Edward Bateson, of West Fifty-eighth street. This lady is the great-niece of Jefferson Davis, and granddaughter of Governor Humphreys,

MRS. JOHN PEGRAM
(HETTY CARY)

whose daughter Mary married Isaac Stamps.

The only unmarried brother is the fourth, Marion Hollingsworth, who is in the Trust Company with his brother. The youngest, Frank Paschal Gaillard, is in the Fifth avenue office, and recently married Miss Sara Stevenson Bradner, of New York.

Closely interlinked in the love and interests for the Pegrams was one of the most beautiful and most notable of all war belles, Miss Hetty Cary, of Baltimore.

Lee's Army knew no better soldiers, no truer gentlemen, than the three Pegram brothers. John, the eldest, had given his old army sword to his state, had risen through merit to his brigade and was recommended for promotion. He was rarely in Richmond—was "too busy with fighting for fooling," as reckless General Pierce Young phrased it—but he had met Miss Cary at his mother's home and later at the camps of Stuart and Fitz Lee. Like most other men, he loved her; like none other, he met return and they became engaged.

Ever at the front, the Pegrams seemed to bear charmed life. Willie, the second, was a cool but dashing artillerist with two stars on his collar at an age when most men were content with two bars. "Jimmy," the youngest—later noted as a wit and clever man of business, from New York down "t' Orleans"—had ridden scathless as the adjutant of "fighting old Dick" Ewell Mother and sisters at home began almost to trust in the luck of the Pegrams.

One bright spring afternoon near the end of the war as General Pegram felt it to be, he married Miss Cary at St. Paul's Church. Another Thursday, only two weeks later, the same throng stood in the same church as grief-crushed comrades bore up the aisle the flag-palled coffin that held the late bridegroom, stricken down at Hatches Run.

The happy spell was broken. In the next fight Willie Pegram also fell at the front.

CHAPTER XIV

MISUSED name! Society's *Via Sacra* is marginated with the graves of thy counterfeits.

Mimetic America has always coveted the *salon* on the French model. Since the famous home of Mistress Dolly Madison, on H street and President Square, many elegant drawing-rooms have so misnamed themselves, despite the fact that hers was no more one than their own. No one of the older cities of this Union, save, perhaps self-satisfied and conservative Boston, has failed its essay. *Ante-bellum* New York—like Beau Brummel's valet with his white cravats—might say: "We have had our failures!" Her better sociality, later, recalls the notable Sunday evenings of Mesdames Edward Cooper, John Sherwood, S. L. M. Barlow and others before its coaching by that strictly American imitation, Mr. Ward McAllister. Still a little later Mrs. Frank Leslie, that energy-saturated widow of two differently remarkable men, built a composite social structure on the *débris* of Madame Roland and Mrs. Leo Hunter. Mrs. Leslie, originally Minnie Follen, a New Orleans beauty was French in her instincts and education. Equally ambitious and lavish, she compounded an *olla podrida* and called it a *pâté*.

The society of Quaker Citydom had something near a salon in the parlors of a gifted and brilliant woman with a gifted and noted husband, in the days when Mrs. George

H. Boker queened it. Then Miss Emily Schomberg was its "immortelle" of bellehood; a truly wonderful woman who came out with every set of buds and seemed fresher than each.

Quite late in her reign Miss Emily Schomberg married Colonel Hughes-Hallett, of the English Army. She was his second wife, the first having been the daughter of Lord Selwyn. The union was less ideal than some inter-continental ones. The husband was forced out of the British parliament by some scandals. The American wife obtained separation and, childless and alone, spends the sunset of her days between Paris and Dinard.

If hurtling, whirling Chicago has ever attempted a similar imitation, it has died young enough to escape baptism. Possibly she has been too busied in "getting her growth"; and probably would not have liked it had she tried. Yet ample material would not seem lacking to any who recall the social swim of Mrs Potter Palmer—and the other of the handsome and accomplished Honoré sisters, Mrs. Frederick Dent Grant—there and in other cities. There is Mrs. Stone, too, who might have led the van in such an attempt, and the Chetlains, with others equally known.

One salon peculiar to itself was held at Smith's Inn, No. 65 Sibley street, at regular intervals, by that veteran soldier, mason and traveler, General John Corson Smith. Under his roof the most noted minds and brightest intelligence of old veterans in the three cults named, made new history, while his gentle and genial daughter, Miss Ruth Smith, was his efficient adjutant and comrade.

In her *pre-bellum* days Cincinnati held great pride in the birth, culture and elegance of her better class. She had a veritable old-school set of gracious women and men—as her own novelist has written—"who could put a dash of color even into evening dress!" And there was foundation in the pride in that old régime which made its impress at home and on any distant society it entered. For who there wanders about old residence streets and does not recall Mr. and Mrs. Charles Stetson, who held headquarters for all the literary; entertaining Emerson and Alcott and their peers. There reigned the beautiful and stately Miss Therese Chalfant, later so noted in Washington as the wife of Senator Pugh; and her handsome sister, Miss Ada. Then, those charming daughters of Dr. Rives, of Virginia, Mrs. Joseph Longworth and Mrs. Rufus King. The latter, a brilliant musician herself, made her home the centre for all of artistic taste. No old-timer but recalls Mrs. E. S. Haines, a potent leader in society and the aunt of General William H. Lytle, who wrote, "I am dying, Egypt—dying!" In Mrs. Alice Pendleton—daughter of Francis Scott Key—society had a brilliant and magnificent woman to represent it abroad, and her husband a help-mate and counsellor of value inestimable. Another who dazzled official circles, when her father was in congress, was Miss Olivia Groesbeck, afterward the wife of General Joseph Hooker, "Fighting Joe." An attractive and brilliant head of an old and typical Cincinnati house, still regnant in things social, was Mrs. Nicholas Anderson. Elegant entertainers in an elegant home, were Mrs. Robert W. Burnet and her two daughters, Miss Laura Wiggins and her sister, Mrs. Skinner, who were always as much sought in social functions for their personal charm, as in church and charity work for its even better expression. Queenly Mrs. John W. Coleman was also the centre of an admiring circle, and distinguished visitors from afar ever sought her society.

The city has nurtured not a few literati and journalists and some poets whose names are national. Witness Don Piatt and his brilliant wife and poetic brother; Murat Halstead, "Wash" McLean, and many a younger pen-driver who has forced a way in the East.

It is a grave error to suppose that trade absorbs all the interest of the new city. Her "Saturday Night Club" is a weekly congress of as bright and variously minded men as one might hope to meet anywhere. I recall vividly nights at that clubhouse when jest and educàting talk went flashing across the little tables, and when unrepentant Johnny Reb met his whilom victor, and was permitted to laugh at him from the improvised rostrum. Those, indeed, were veritably *Noctes Ambrosianæ*. And yet the prideful city of Ohio has no record of attempt at the French free-and-easy.

Indeed, nowhere in the Middle West has one seed of the French exotic wafted that lived long enough to shoot one noticeable sprout. St. Louis—with her Louisiana French contingent of population; Memphis, Louisville and Nashville, have all been noted for culture in their societies, famed for the beauty and charm of their women; for the gallantry and often the culture of their men.

Some of the former have been the regnant belles of exigent fashion on both sides of the ocean, as the names of the Gatys, Francises and Haywoods, the Vances and Johnsons, the fame of "Di Bullitt" and Mrs. Sallie Ward Hunt, the Bruces, Yandells and Craiks attest. Many of the latter have shone in legislation, affairs and war for all these years, but for all that none of the cities have followed the fad that has flourished but briefly along the Atlantic line. There may be some reason for this in climate and in hurry of life, or is it that the heads of some sections are harder and more "level" than the rest?

Baltimore, ever refined, eminently social, and with dazzling integers like Miss Lemmon, Mmes. Tiffany, Reed, Thomas and the rest, and wits like Teackle Wallis, and Tom Morris, never essayed the salon fad. Her nearest approach to it was the "view," or the soirée, of the Alston Club—not to be read, "the Maryland!" Probably Baltimore was too comfortable to copy anything.

Naturally, one might have looked to cosmopolitan Washington—with the brainy and handsome—to possess equally the elements and the need for such a foundation. But the capital—after the Madison régime, perhaps—was as reticent of essay as her Monumental neighbor; contenting herself with the East Room levee, as a social zoo; and absorbed in the struggle for the most elaborate dinners, the most crowded balls, and the smartest germans. Perhaps the society was too large and varied in taste, to an extent that forgot menticulture after once tasting it. Probably Washington of that day was too light-heeled—and headed.

CAPTAIN HENRY ROBINSON

The *ante-bellum* receptions, like those of Mrs. Slidell and Madame de Sartiges, of Mmes. Montgomery-Blair or Dahlgren, were nearer approaches to those of Roland and Adam than the country had yet seen. But that was, perhaps, because they neither attempted nor announced imitation. They bade clever, cultured and original people come and entertain themselves and each other. These are the *alpha* and *omega* of the true salon, not a political club or a conspiracy in fine linen and silken hosiery.

This basic fact the promoters of all American failures have forgotten. In the pronounced personalism and newness of our social superstructure on the lately dead century, in its crudity and rivalries—and most of all in its dollar domination—conversation became a lost art, replaced by the monologue; mentality and accomplishment being represented by X.

That elegance, culture and taste have—and ever have had —place in most American cities, is a self-demonstrated proposition. That they have been millionaired to the rear is another quite as plain.

Probably the most cogent reason of all for the non-existence of the salon has been the lack of need for its mask and dark lantern in our national system. The political battles of the Union have usually been fought in the open, or in the—prize ring. The official guillotine being the only one to dread, the stealthy tread, the veiled epigram, and the sugar-plummed conspiracy of the Quartier St. Germain found neither paternity nor cradle in cis-Atlantic society. A conglomerate people, the methods of the one race were antipathetic to the rest. Hence it happened that what was nearest approach to the Paris salon found birth and nurture more often in the South.

Madame de Sartiges, wife of the French minister to Miss Lane's court, was herself an American; one of the two Thorndike sisters from the ancient New England town Oliver Wendell Holmes called "Beverly-by-the-Depot." The Cape Cod poet once sang it as "Beautiful, baked-bean-loving Beverly!"

The second Miss Thorndike married Señor Banuelos, a pleasant and popular secretary of legation of long ago.

The real Parisian etiquette, however, prevailed at the Sartiges' Saturday evenings, on Georgetown Heights, and they were popular with all. There we met the *crême de legation* pleasantly diluted with the best of native sociality. There were no introductions. People who chose talked and danced together, and the refreshments never gave a headache. But the brightest people, as well as the best, went to these easy functions, sure of finding kindred spirits.

The wife of Senator Slidell (Mlle. Deslondes, of Louisiana) was Creole *au bout des ongles*. She had been educated and traveled much abroad, and brought the Parisian ideals to her Washington life. Her two pretty daughters, Mathilde and Rosine, were younger than the permissible age for "taking a peep" by the French girl. Still the two ventured an occasional one at these functions, much to the delectation of

MRS. PHILIP PHILLIPS

polyglot youth, for they were naive and sprightly.

Later, these girls became historic, when their whilom neighbor, Admiral Wilkes, reft Mason and Slidell from the protecting paws of the British Lion.

An all-around *casus belli* was barely escaped. The animated objection of the pretty young twain to return beneath the Old Flag was the sensation of the hour on both sides of the water. Later, Mlle. Mathilde married Baron Earlanger, the French banker, so familiar to still later American finance. Miss Rosine, caring less for money, married blood in the Quartier St. Germain.

Mrs. Eugenia Phillips, wife of the Alabama Congressman, came very near holding a salon, and quite without intent. This handsome and brilliant Southern woman had a national reputation long before General Ben Butler, of New Orleans and Bermuda Hundreds, gave her an international one.

Her arrest for alleged treason in laughing and chatting on her own porch while a military funeral passed, need not be rehearsed here. Time and decency have passed upon it. That was excuse for that inexplicable and unsoldierly "Order 28," which wrung from the impassive British premier the epithet "Infamous!" and sent the hero down the aisles of history ticketed with an unsavory sobriquet.

But in truth it was Mrs. Phillips's contempt of the general and her cool sarcasm that caused her imprisonment. Haled before him, she laughed equally at the charge and at his authority to war on women. When told that she would be sent to Ship Island, she blandly replied:

"It has one advantage over the city, sir; you will not be there!"

When told that it was a yellow fever station, she laughed:

"It is fortunate that neither the fever nor General Butler is contagious."

Robert Wood, younger brother of John Taylor, was likewise a born fighter—about their only common heritage. He was a reckless, sharp-tongued member of the young society, but his pride of descent from General Taylor was such that his actions paraphrased: "*Je n'y suis ni roi, ni prince: je suis* Taylor!"

At one of her receptions I heard him ask Mrs. Phillips: "Tell these ladies the best thing you know relating to me."

In a flash Ben Butler's later vanquisher—and his unintentional sponsor in sobriquet—responded:

"Your grandfather, Bob!"

Both the Wood brothers—sons of the elder sister of the first Mrs. Jefferson Davis—are dead. Robert, distinguished as a cavalry colonel in Wirt Adams's brigade, pursued various avocations in New Orleans, leaving a widow and family there. John Taylor, the elder, we shall see more of later.

Mrs. Phillips was not only one of the most picturesque personages in Confederate history, but a most potent and popular one in Washington society. With a strange infusion of sub-acid, she had great goodness of heart, and was ever loyal in her friendships. These included some of the most notable women, on both sides of then acrimonious thought, taking Mrs. Jefferson Davis and Mrs. William H. Emory as examples. She was Eugenia, the eldest of three handsome and brilliant daughters of Jacob Clavius Levy and Fanny Yates, of Charleston; the latter an Englishwoman, who was a marvel of sprightliness when I knew her in Washington, close *ante-bellum*, when she was in her late eighties.

The second sister, Phoebe, now the widow of Thomas Pember, of Boston, we shall meet frequently in these pages. Miss Martha, a gifted and popular woman, survived the war and died unmarried. The fourth of the sisters, Emma, married Prioleau Hamilton, of South Carolina.

The three Phillips girls were heritors of their mother's beauty and graces, but not of her satiric turn. As they came "out" successively, Misses Fannie, Caroline and Emma became and remained popular belles in the home and foreign sets, and were all conceded beauties in a society where plain women were exceptional. Miss Fannie had a long and romantic engagement with dashing Charley Hill, nephew of the millionaire banker, W. W. Corcoran. Hill went South, and will be seen again, and when he came home and entered the state department, after winning his majority for gallantry on General Forrest's staff, the pair were married. The widow is still a remarkably preserved woman, residing in Pittsburg with three grown sons and the wife of the eldest—Charles Philip Hill—who was the popular Miss Catherine Montague, of Baltimore. Yet, this "pretty young woman" as some one lately wrote me of her, is four times a grandmother. Her handsome daughter, Mrs. Benney, who lives only one block away, has four children.

Miss "Lina," the next sister, is now Mrs. Frederick Meyers, of Savannah; head of a family, but retaining the delicate beauty of feature which made artistic Walter Taylor name her "the Cameo." Miss Emma Phillips married Walter Carrington, of Virginia, and also boasts a grown son and daughter at her Long Island home.

The boys of the family were notable, too, for manly beauty and traits; and two of them—Clavius and John Walker Phillips—were in the army. The former married Miss Georgina Cohen, of Savannah; the latter Miss Nellie Jonas, of New Orleans. The only other living son is P. Lee Phillips, of the Congressional Library, who—with an exceptionally beautiful young wife—resides in Washington. Eugene, an elder brother who served in the Confederate navy, and Willie, the youngest, are dead.

The Phillips family were little in Richmond during the war, but sometime "refugeed" at La Grange. In both, the brilliance of the

MRS. CHARLES A. LARENDON
(LAURE V. BEAUREGARD)

mother and the marked beauty of her daughters made them even more noticeable than did the Butler episode.

All of these were not the real salon. Its first planting on American soil was almost coeval with that of the Lilies in *La Louisiane*; and it flourished—somewhat with the luxuriance of a wild growth—in the Law-built second capital on the Mississippi. Then the exclusiveness of the Creole régime —the Villerés, Lallandes, Zacharies and the rest—cloistered itself behind the *portes cocheres* of old French Town; leaving New Orleans to barter, building and growth. Today the unique and rapidly merging society of the Crescent City has known no salon.   It finds ample occupation in the usual home routine, its Opera and races and its pre-eminent carnival functions.

CHAPTER XV

WHEN old General Desha moved with his second wife from North Alabama to Cottage Hill, near Mobile, he brought the three daughters of his first marriage—Misses Phoebe Ann, Caroline and Julia Desha. The eldest married Murray Smith, a young Virginian who had drifted to the city by the Gulf, little dreaming that Fate had marked him for grand-father-in-law of a Duke of Marlborough. The second sister, Carrie, married Mr. Barney, and, when widowed, Lloyd Abbott, of lower Fifth avenue, then the most fashionable residential quarter of New York. She was fond of society, but had a veritable craze for private theatricals. This culminated in two disasters: it put her protégée, Miss Cora Urquhart, of New Orleans, at large upon the real stage as Mrs. James Brown Potter and it sent Mrs. Abbott into the same profession. New York has not forgotten her unfortunate début at Daly's theatre in "The Duchess," and her death followed soon after that ill-advised experiment. Miss Julia Desha, handsome, clever and ambitious, married in France and did not return.

Mrs. Murray Smith was socially ambitious beyond the family limit, and very lavish of means to attain the desired result. She took a handsome city residence, issued invitations for unremitting entertainments, and served the guests with all that market and *chef* could produce. Somehow, these could not command success, however they may have deserved it. The functions were costly, but not popular; the social usufruct did not come, and Mrs. Smith found Mobile too rooted in old ways to comprehend a salon after the mode of the one she longed to sway.

This ambitious lady had four daughters: Misses Armide, Alva, Virginia, and Mimi. She planned a final and still more elaborate function; larger, more costly and all-embracing. She certainly studied the injunction to Sempronius, but success again refused to crown deserving persistence. Some people ate Mrs. Smith's suppers; many did not. There was needless and ungracious comment, and one swift writer pasquinaded her social ambitions in a pamphlet for "private" circulation. Then the lady concluded that Mobile was as unripe for conquest as for introduction of the salon. She carried her daughters and her advanced tastes to New York, where the field was broader for deserving effort; including *Mr.* Smith's business ones. Results, in one sense at least, justified the move. She lived, despite failing health, in a whirl of society, and died in it.

Her second daughter, Alva, married W. K. Vanderbilt, and after divorce O. H. P. Belmont; and her granddaughter was the mistress of Blenheim.

Miss Virginia married Fernando Yznaga, brother of the dowager Duchess of Manchester, the first Consuelo; and, on legal separation from him, became Mrs. William G. Tiffany. Miss Armide never married. She seemed to inherit none of the family taste for smart society, and devoted herself to charitable works for her sex. She died in New York in April of last year. Miss Mimi, I believe, followed her aunt Julia's example of marrying and dying abroad.

Mrs. Octavia Walton Le Vert was the daughter of Colonel John B. Walton—so well known to the clubs of Washington, New York and a dozen other cities—and the wife of a well-known doctor of Mobile. She was a pretty and plump blonde, and fond of society and dress. In her husband's easy circumstances, the eager little lady gave full rein to her natural tastes; went abroad, came back, and tried to entertain in quite foreign and all-embracing fashion.

"M. D.," as Mrs. Le Vert was wont to call her spouse, in place of his baptismal Henry Strachey, was not a devotee of society by any means, but a skillful and popular surgeon and cultured gentleman. His profession gave him ample means, and he was complaisant enough not to balk his wife's desire to entertain all of society, including the most pronounced freaks that clung to its periphery. To be a novelty in fact or reputed, was sufficient to secure *entrée* into the salon of this *mondaine.* Her house was large and her heart larger; and no end of good things that she did still stand to her credit on the Great Ledger.

MRS. HENRY STRACHEY LE VERT
AND DAUGHTER "DIDDIE"

Mrs. Le Vert's evenings were eagerly sought by all classes in the amusement hungry city. They were wholly unceremonious, the exclusives herding together and the others intermingling as best they could. Everybody was welcome. A sort of staff collected around the entertainer, its chief being gallant and reckless Major Harry Maury. This stalwart and witty cousin of the little but able General Dabney H. Maury, some time in command at Mobile, was an original in all regards. It was he who asked that famous "Lazarus conundrum," repetition of which by Bishop Wilmer, in New York, set the sensitive North agog.

ADMIRAL FRANKLIN BUCHANAN
(COMMANDER OF THE MERRIMAC)

Maury was a privileged character in Mobile, and especially at Mrs. Le Vert's. It was there, as reported, that he vented the now ancient reason for declining egg-nogg. Coming in one night, when already laved internally, the hostess proffered the foaming yellow mixture. Maury said: "Thank you, none for me. I prefer my eggs poached; I take my milk and sugar in my coffee, and I'm man enough to take my whiskey straight!"

With diametrically opposite intent, Mrs. Le Vert was alert as any spider with invitations into her parlor. No stranger with name or record could escape. When Kossuth came to this country, she seized and exhibited him, making more ado over him than over the sturdy old commodore, Duncan N. Ingraham, who had rescued the Hungarian under the guns of the Austrian frigate *Hussar*. At her house were met the generals of the armies within reach of Mobile, whenever they had duty in the city. There also came Admiral Franklin Buchanan, naval chief of the station, and with him his daughter, Mrs. Scriven, of Georgia, one of the lovely twin sisters who had been such belles at the Washington Navy Yard, and then in her early married life.

Randall, of "Maryland," was an habitué, and on rare

occasions the pale, worn face of Henry Timrod was seen in their quieter corners. Poor Timrod! Oversensitive, unarmored for the *mêlée* of life's tourney, he died for sheer want of bread, and, all too late, his state gave him a stone.

Dashing Tom Ochiltree, the arch romancer of the war: Nathan Bedford Forrest—ready to run away from the battery of bright, admiring eyes—all sensational fish, big and little, came to Mrs. Le Vert's net and made a social *jambalaya* not possible to match in all Dixie. There, too, were musical and dramatic people galore, for the fair hostess was patron of art, no less than leader of the mode. John T. Raymond was then at the Mobile Theatre, a tyro player who did not dream "There's millions in it!" Burly, big-voiced Theodore Hamilton, who sometimes did actor stunts at the soirées which perhaps helped him to some reputation thereafter. There was an old auctioneer in Mobile who had several pretty daughters. One of these Phillips girls married Hamilton and went on the stage until invalided. A second was a royal beauty. As Marie Gordon she became Raymond's first wife. She won repute for good acting, especially as blind *Bertha* to her husband, Jefferson, and John Owens, as *Caleb*

MRS. WILLIAM BECKER
(MRS. LAURA FORSYTH)

Plummer. But it was not altogether by her acting that she dazzled all of one continent and parts of another.

"Johnny" Chatterton—later Signor Perugini and one

of the numerous husbands of Lillian Russell—was a pupil of Madame Kowalewski-Portz, and sang at her Christ church choir and at Mrs. Le Vert's.

The women met at Mrs. Le Vert's are tempting, but dangerous themes to touch. There were the dashing Oliver sisters, known to every camp; the beautiful bride, Mrs. Laura Forsyth, already famed in the A. N. V. She is now Mrs. William Becker, of Milwaukee, and the last direct descendant of Jackson's secretary of state and grandson of the great editor is her son, Charles Forsyth. He also lives there.

Fascinating Mrs. Dan E. Huger was another of Mrs. Le Vert's war brides. As Miss Hattie Withers she had won triumphs in a Washington winter. She left two charming daughters, Mrs. Cleland Smith, of Memphis, and Mrs. Robert Wilkie, of New Orleans. Their daughters, in turn, wondered to the day of her recent and lamented death, whether that young and sprightly lady was really their mama's mother.

Mrs. Le Vert has gone, long years. "M. D.," her husband, went before. Gone too, are her daughters, Octavia, and Henrietta. The former, whom intimate friends knew as "Diddie," was the aide-de-camp of her mother's lavish social days, the stay of her less happy ones, when the declining sun was no longer worshipped by inconstant devotees.

One drawing-room of *ante-bellum* Mobile—much sought and ever compensating—was that of Mrs. Fearn, wife of Dr. Richard Lee Fearn, a very noted surgeon who died in the late '60's. Mrs. Fearn had been Miss Mary Walker, sister of the four brothers of that name elsewhere noted.

There were met such notables as Governor John Anthony Winston, full of acumen and satire; Dr. Claude H. Mastin, the noted surgeon, with his keen wit and blunt speech, but using sub-acid where his brilliant son now applies the triple oil of gracious courtesy; brilliant young Theodore O'Hara, who wrote "The Bivouac of the Dead," and scores of other home people then and later in national repute. Distinguished visitors from abroad were ever introduced at Mrs. Fearn's, and though the maltreated French word was not whispered of her receptions, they held its sponsorial essence.

Dr. and Mrs. Fearn had one son, Walker Fearn, already a courtly, gifted and accomplished man, who gave earnest of that later high acquirement which made him a marked type of the Southern gentleman and diplomatist. He died a decade ago. Walker Fearn married Miss Fannie Hewitt, of New Orleans, in the early flush of her belleship after she had been the first queen of the carnival. He went to that city to practice law, but was sent as secretary of legation to Spain in Buchanan's time. When the war came he returned to enter the army, but was ordered to Paris as secretary to the Mason-Slidell embassy to the sentiment of the unsentimental powers, who heeded not the wooing of Mr. Benjamin, as there lisped by his chosen messengers. After the war, Mr. Fearn returned to the Crescent City and resumed his practice in partnership with Captain Edward M. Hudson, a cultivated Virginian who had returned from his German university to serve on General Elzey's staff; and who still resides there with his accomplished wife, formerly Miss Fannie Ledyard. But Mr. Fearn's diplomatic taste and experience again carried him abroad as minister to Greece, under Mr. Cleveland. Later he was named as American judge of the international court established by the Khedive in Cairo. On his return to America, he was chief of foreign installation at the Chicago World's Fair. He died soon after, leaving a widow and one daughter, now Mrs. Seth Barton French, of New York. There was another girl, Clarisse, who died abroad, and one son, Hewitt, also dead.

Percy Leroy Fearn married Eva Onderdonk and the family live on Long Island. Mrs. Walker Fearn now resides with Mrs. French, devoting her energy and experience to lecturing in aid of the blind. She frequently visits her old New Orleans home, where her cousins and she made a brilliant trio in years gone, and where they still remain. They were Minnie and Clara Norton, now Mrs. Newton Buckner and Mrs. Arthur Lee Stuart. Mrs. Stuart's elder daughter is wife of the Rev. Norman Guthrie, priest and poet, and the piquante Miss Minnie is yet with her mother.

The four handsome and brilliant daughters of Mrs. Newton Buckner are Katie, Mrs. Daniel Asery; Minnie (who was Mrs. William Barkley, and died only last year); Edith, Mrs. Harry Howard; and Frances, Mrs. James Bush. As girls this quartette were popular and much quoted and their marrying has not changed those conditions. Norton Buckner, their brother, is married and lives in New York.

After the death of Walker Fearn's mother, Dr. Lee Fearn married Miss Elizabeth Spear, of Mobile. There are three children of the second family: R. Lee Fearn, Jr., chief of the *Tribune* bureau at Washington, and almost as widely known as secretary and president of the irrepressible Gridiron Club. He married Miss Egerton, of Baltimore, and resides at the capital with their young son and daughter, Miss Mildred who has just made her *entrée* in Washington society. Miss Sallie Fearn was one of the sweetest and most lovable girls that Mobile has relinquished to a distant state. She is now Mrs. H. M. Manley, of New Jersey, and the mother of a family of three. Dr. Thomas S. Fearn, the youngest, never married.

In the Fearn home often was met a representative of the old French family of de Vendel de Genance, noted in the first French revolution and before. Madame Adelaide de Vendel Chaudron, however, carried her own patent of mental nobility. She was the wife of Paul Simon Léopold Chaudron; and during her half-century life in Mobile was leader in the twin arts of literature and music. She was a great linguist, a close student and an omnivorous reader. It was she who translated the Louise Mühlbach stories of royalty, and many other works. The only extant copy, of which I know, is kept under glass by her son, Louis de Vendel Chaudron, who still resides in Mobile.

Madame Chaudron died a decade since, at the age of eighty-one.

There were four de Vendel sisters besides Madame Chaudron. Louise never married and died years ago. Angèle married Henry Hull and both are dead, and their son, Edgar Hull—who lost a leg in the Civil War—died very recently at Pascagoula, Miss. The next sister, Josephine, is the widow of Augustus Sellers, and resides in New York; and the last, Pauline, is the widow of

MRS. MARY KETCHUM IRWIN
(FROM AN AMATEUR PLAY)

George J. White and lives in Mobile.

Here came Dr. George A. Ketchum and his then young bride, Sue Burton, of Quaker Philadelphia, who celebrated their golden wedding a decade ere they both passed away, leaving but one child, Mrs. Georgia Ketchum Stratton of Mobile. The last, not then born, has later proved one of the most popular and gracious of hostesses; and her friends are found in many a city far away from the noted old homestead she still graces. She is also one of the most versatile and "fetching" of society amateurs. This gift she has in common with her cousin, Mary Ketchum, the then girlish daughter of Col. Charles Ketchum. One of the most beautiful and gifted women of her day, she sometimes joined her uncle and aunt at Mrs. Fearn's. She married the elder of the gallant Irwin brothers; was the acknowledged beauty of her set and an accomplished woman in many ways; notably in high comedy. Only three years ago she died, universally regretted; and her home at picturesque "Oakleigh," is presided over by her only daughter, Mrs. Daisy Irwin Clisby with her three "boys": her stately old father and her own sons. There, were seen the Clark brothers, Francis B. and Willis Gaylord; the former the first president of directors of the Mobile & Ohio Railroad when only twenty-six years old, and now a well-preserved resident of Birmingham, at nearly ninety years of age. Willis Gaylord Clark died ten years ago, leaving no children.

At Mrs. Fearn's Mr. and Mrs. Henry A. Schroeder, precise but suave; Jurist Peter Hamilton and his cordial wife, and the Ledyard family were frequent guests.

Mrs. William J. Ledyard was the eldest of those six brilliant Erwin sisters, whose culture and force did for Tennessee what the "Wicklyffes" did for Kentucky. She was Laura Erwin, a woman of golden heart and mind. Much of her nature showed in her children, the eldest of whom has just been mentioned, Mrs. E. M. Hudson; William Ledyard, who fell before Richmond; Erwin, who carried the colors at Malvern Hill and bore to his still green grave the scars for it; and gentle Miss Leila, now also passed away.

Jane Erwin, later Mrs. Goff, was the second sister; and Amelia, Mrs. Yeatman, and Mrs. Hillman, Marie Louise, all of Nashville, were the third and fifth. All are dead, as is the beautiful and gentle Caroline, "the baby sister," who married Willis Clark. It was her son by her first marriage, Ledyard Scott, who was the second husband of the authoress, the present Mrs. Fenellosa.

The only living sister of the Erwin name is Ellen, Mrs. George A. Hayward, of St. Louis. For years hers has been a familiar name in society and literature in the river metropolis. She has had in later years the aid of three popular daughters. The eldest of these, Miss Florence Hayward, has made her own name notable on both sides of the water. She was the woman commissioner of the Louisiana Purchase Exposition, whose work in London and Rome did so much for the foreign exhibit; and to whom especial credit is due for its famous history section. Foreign recognition of her work has been exceptional. The French Academy made her an honorary associate, she being the only American woman so named and one of the only five or six in the world. The exposition authorities gave her the only special gold medal for service rendered, presented to any officer. Her next sister, Miss Fanita Hayward, married George Niedringhaus. She was an ever popular girl at home and in the distant cities she constantly visited. The youngest sister, Erwin, was a bright and regal type of woman, with a fad that she would not marry: so she is now— Mrs. Higginbotham, of Canada. The Hayward boys, both married, but not before St. Louis society had made them *enfans gâtés* for a number of years.

The Ledyard-Erwin-Hayward connection is too Virginian in extent for detailing here. William Ledyard's brother had a large family; one of the daughters, Anne Ledyard, being one of the most popular women in the South. She married Fulwar Skipwith, of Clarkesville, Va., grandson of Sir Grey Skipwith. Her sister Laura was one of the most beautiful women of her day, and brilliant too.   She became Mrs. Marion Vaughan, of Columbus, Miss.   William Ledyard married Miss Adelaide Dargan, daughter of the great lawyer, Edmund Dargan; and it is their son who married the daughter of John Triplett, as before noted.

Mrs. Fanny Ledyard Hudson's three sons have families in Louisiana. William Alexander, the eldest, married Miss Anna Dontey, of Rapides Parish, and early died a hero's death, to save the lives of passengers on his railway train.   Wallace and Leigh married sisters, Misses Luckett, of Rapides.   So the old stock will not be forgotten in the old South or the young West.

CHAPTER XVI

HIGH-HEADED, refined and historic Charleston has not been without her sensations. She has been the seat of one great seismic convulsion and of several political ones. She was the cradle of nullification and of Civil War. There was held the conven-
tion that sent the triple democratic Horatii to hold the bridge against Lincoln, and laid them, slaughtered, at his feet. There was the glory of the palmetto-logged Moultrie, the theatrical one of Sumter, when gallant men with silk hats, and red sash-es binding swords to their frock coats, marched away from weeping wives, to dress on Beauregard. Not a few of these must have smiled, in quick-succeeding scenes of field and hospital, at the

GENERAL JOHN CHESNUT

dramatic terrors of that undress rehearsal: "Mr. Chesnut somewhere on that black harbor in an open boat!"—a noble

old dame wiring her blessing to her grandson for shooting
away the flagstaff, and Wigfall crawling through a rear
porthole and praying grim old Robert Anderson, in the name
of humanity, not to commit fiery *felo de se.*

Charleston and the whole state of South Carolina have
given famous men and noble women to the councils and
the wars—to the matronage and the society—of the Union
ever since the Rattlesnake flag.

Rarely an imitator, she transplanted the indigenous Boston fad and fostered it into secession. She has had her
social sensations, indubitably, while never vaunting them,
but Charleston never took the salon infection. Her one
case was mild and sporadic.

James L. Pettigrew was the most noted lawyer and the
most quoted wit of his day in the city of the battery. He
had two daughters, Mrs. King and Mrs. Carson. "Sue King,"
as her intimates called the elder, was audacious and original.
At odds with society, she attempted a salon in the hope
of getting even with the feminine contingent. Scarcely
any woman could have made one popular, with all its needful
unconventionality. Mrs. King assuredly did not. Her
evenings were conspicuous for masculine crowds and feminine
absences. She dropped them, as soon as the men stopped
attending. "Busy Moments of an Idle Woman," which
was largely read in the boudoir and boarding-school, came
from the pen of Mrs. King, who was as quick-witted and
as pointed in epigram as Mrs. Andrew Simonds—the second
of that noted name—who recently married Barker Gummere,
Mrs. Simonds was Miss Daisy Breaux. She came to New
Orleans from Georgetown's Visitation convent, and shortly after acted in Atlanta as the bridesmaid of Miss Emma
Mims. As Mrs. Simonds she founded the "Villa Margher-
ita" in Charleston. It is to her that a clever retort to President
Roosevelt is credited. She had entertained him in Charles-

ton at the time of the Exposition. Later, at Washington, when the appointment of a negro postmaster was agitating the city, it is said that Mr. Roosevelt asked Mrs. Simonds:

"Tell me frankly what your people think of me now."

"We think we have cast our bread upon the waters, and after a few days it has come back in a little brown Crum!"

One of Mrs. King's best remembered witticisms was the introduction of the two elegant Rhett brothers, Alfred and Edmund, in the oft plagiarized words:

"The Lilies! They toil not, neither do they spin; yet Solomon in all his glory is not so arrayed!"

MRS. JAMES W. CONNER
(SALLIE ENDERS)

Yet, Charleston never had her salon, despite her having Mmes. King and Simonds and James Conner, whom she borrowed from her twin state.

With its many comings and goings, Richmond offered opportunity for American imitation of a salon, but the social leaders were not so inclined. The receptions at the White House, at Mrs. Robert Stanard's, Mrs. Semmes's, Mrs. Macfarland's, Mrs. Ives's and, in their quieter way, at Mrs. Virginia Pegram's, were the perfect mixture of easy elegance and brains in evening dress. But, at the executive mansion, the "every evenings" of Mrs. Davis took on this likeness rather than those public—and necessarily mixed levees which contemporaneous error insisted upon misnaming her salon. They are well worthy of a passing retrospect, for they were the most remarkable aggregations of distinction and commonplace.

Gradually, as she melted the social frost about her, Mrs. Davis collected the more important of Richmond's society leaders, making of them, unawares, a sort of informal staff. These were always present, after the first few "Washington imitations"—as the bi-monthlies were at first called.   They proved very attractive to the better posed and more distin-

guished visitors, and were most useful in letting the President and his wife devote more attention to the plainer people.

A military band was always in attendance, generally dispensing popular music, but sometimes classic.   Cabinet ministers, congressmen, heads of bureaus and departments, new generals and old admirals, fresh-faced young recruits and distinctively foreign types from the coast South, all mingled to-

LT.-COL. JOHN CHEVES HASKELL

gether.   There was more variety than in the East Room levee at Washington, and more action and eagerness.   We were then not making history very rapidly, but many of those present later filled whole pages.

Here was seen the red beard of Ambrose P. Hill; Beauregard would sometimes glide through the rooms with his staff.   Dashing Pierce Young attended and gallants from Maryland, soft-voiced Carolinians and sturdy estrays from Kentucky and Missouri, mingled with the home set and the dainty débutantes and belles.

These assemblages were great amalgamaters, and brought together people who had never met elsewhere. No doubt many moves in politics—not always friendly to the head of the house—were begun or discussed there; and that campaigns of a tenderer nature were also carried on, goes without saying.

Mrs. Davis received every comer with pleasant, if not wholly genial, welcome. She never differentiated, and all were made to feel that they were present by right and not on sufferance. Here, as in all social matters, Mrs. Davis found able assistance in her young sister, Miss Howell, a great favorite with the official set, and she relieved the dulness of many a group.

The President himself unbent more at these levees—though they assuredly bored him—than anywhere else. He had that marvelous memory which locates instantly a man not seen for years, and his familiar inquiries so pleased the visitors that they were not aware that the handshake was none too warm and that he was gently but speedily passed along. Miss Howell said he "helped them as though they were sandwiches at a charity picnic."

Years ago, writing to me of something I had said of these receptions, sturdy, brave General Brad Johnson said:

"The photograph you give of Mrs. Davis's drawing-room is exquisite. I never was there but once, just after second Manassas, when I marched in—booted and dirty and straight from the train—with a letter from Jackson to the President. I never quite knew whether he liked my soldierly unconventionality, for he may have thought I should have presented myself in better guise to the commander-in-chief. But I had been trained to believe that promptness was the highest military virtue, so I lost no moment in doing what I was sent to do. There was no doubt to the battle-stained soldier as to what *she* thought and felt. She was glad to see me, and I believe that night I promised to capture a Yankee flag for her; and she then and there captured my heart. I sent her the flag in '64, as she records in her memoirs.

> "Your obliged comrade,
>
> "BRADLEY T. JOHNSON."

What came nearest to a salon in Richmond—and, as far as I know in all America—was held at Mrs. Robert C. Stanard's. Her home early became noted for hospitality as lavish as it was elegant. She was a widow of ample means, and had been Miss Martha Pierce, of Louisville. She courted social success, had traveled extensively, and made many and distinguished friends.

When stress of war mobilized an army of these in Richmond, Mrs. Stanard's doors swung wide and early for their reception and refection. She was one of the very first to break that thin layer of ice over the home society which formed at first hint of the white frost of social invasion, and for a moment threatened to chill the dreaded unknown.

It has been shown how the natural warmth of Virginian hospitality soon dissipated this premature film; and how the natural sunniness of Richmond nature returned and rose to higher degree than normal. This disideratum was due to practical people like Mrs. Stanard, who had known some of the incoming and were ready to take the whole crop, as the cotton buyer does, "by sample." Those who met the best of the influx at such houses, early "went in and bulled the foreign market."

At her frequent dinners, receptions and evenings, Mrs. Stanard collected most that was brilliant and brainiest in government, army, congress and the few families who followed either, apparently because they could afford to.

There, one met statesmen like Lamar, Benjamin, Soulé

and their peers; jurists like John A. Campbell and Thomas J. Semmes; fighters like Johnson, Hampton and Gordon; and the most polished and promising of the youth of war, as gallant and classic Kyd Douglas, handsome John B. Castleman, Lord King and a host more, not to name all of whom seems invidious. And with these came the best of her own sex that the tact and experience of the hostess could select.

Bref, at Mrs. Stanard's one met people already noted for something—or were sure to be ere long. Her house was one unremittent salon, in the regard of variety; and with the difference that the comers were entertained as well as entertaining.

A statement has recently found it way into print— doubtless unintentionally— that she boasted "that she never read a book." If she made the boast, in jest, it is certain that she read men and women, and that very thoroughly. Her personality

COMMODORE BARRON, C. S. N.

outside of her rôle as entertainer, was delightful and magnetic; and she attracted and held to her such strong men as Alexander H. Stephens, Pierre Soulé and grand and gentle Commodore Samuel Barron, Charles L. Scott— " '49-er," congressman and diplomatist. She was a "woman's woman," too, her most ardent admirers being of her own sex and the regret for her untimely death lingering sweetly with them still. Her motherhood was deep, tender and unadvertised. Her only son, Hugh L. Stanard, was her idol, and his early death left a shadow that never lifted from her life.

Mrs. Stanard has been called "Madame Le Vert of Richmond." The misnomer must be patent to all who have seen the receptions of both. They were diametric opposites in almost all regards; hospitality seeming their only common trait. The Mobilienne threw wide her doors and bade all enter, with the prodigal hospitality of the scriptural wedding. The Virginian chose her guests studiously for what was in them; and quite as much for their adaptability to each other. Hence the two noted houses of war sociality were equally wide apart in theory and in practice. If the two go down in history as parallels, it must be because they are tangent at no point.

CHAPTER XVII

WHAT was known as the "Quiet Set" to the giddier ones was possibly the best and most compensating portion of Richmond society. It gravitated sedately around such households as the Daniels, Grattans, Munfords, Brookeses, Gays, Wallers and a dozen more. These made small pretense of entertaining in the lavish old way, but Hospitality sat on their front steps and invited the proper passer within. Their quiet homelike little dinners and those unspeakable little teas of later and more trying days—ah! but these last are ever green in the memory of us ancients, veritable oases in the desert of privation.

If some good housekeeper fell heir to a large jug of sorghum, had a present of some real flour or acquired a tiny sack of "true-and-true" coffee, then and there went forth the summons. And it came to "the boys from camp," refreshing as the dew on Hermon. Then, with the gloaming, came that crown of patient but earnest anticipation, a home supper; what Page McCarty was wont to call "a muffin match," or Eugene Baylor baptized "a waffle worry."

It was in these unique evenings that was found the origin and home of the famous Mosaic Club—as it came to be called, *sans* godfather or sponsor.

This club was like none other before or since; legitimate progeny of abnormal social conditions. It had no descendants. Neither had it any officers, rules or specified objects, and especially had it no treasurer. It might have taken for motto *elevere antiquum Henricum*, but it needed none. It was simply the clashing of bright minds in hospitable and cultured homes under stimulus of rare good cheer and rarer good coffee.

Such pianists as Miss Mattie Paul performed the works of the masters or accompanied the not always tuneful wandering

MRS. W. R. MEYERS
(MATTIE PAUL)

minstrels from camp. Miss Paul was an accomplished player and was perhaps the moving center of things musical in Richmond. Literally she was the *enfan gate* of the Mosaic, as popular with women as with men. Mrs. Gustavus Myers might well have quoted, when her son married:

> "*No sweeter woman e'er drew breath*
> *Than my son's wife.*"

Probably no war-time wedding was prettier or more picturesque—surely none more "showered" with golden wishes—than that of Miss Paul to the popular Willie Myers, Breckinridge's adjutant-general.

Myers survived the war but a few years. In her Virginia home his widow has seen the youth she seems never to have lost, renewed in daughters as fair as she was in war-time. Lelia, the elder, is wife of John Hill Morgan, a member of the New York bar, residing in Brooklyn. The other, Adela, is now the wife of Dr. Richard Frothingham O'Neil, of Boston, a son of the admiral of that name. She is the mother of one child.

At these informal Mosaic Club evenings rare "Ran" Tucker forgot dusty tomes and legal lore to tell his inimitable stories.

The poets and authors were familiar at the Mosaic. John R. Thompson—already famous as longtime editor of the *Southern Literary Messenger* and accepted as the best poet of the war—was an earnest member, and more than one of his immortal poems was there read first and discussed with a frankness that sometimes made the hypersensitive little poet stare. The current and coming features of the only Confederate magazine were there frankly discussed and anticipated, and if memory does not trick me, the beautiful poem, "The Battle Rainbow," was first read to the "old Mosaics." Poor Thompson! tender and too true—victim of his own sensitiveness and of a time of stress it might not withstand—died in the mid-rush of *post-bellum* New York. His mission took him to London to edit that useless organ of Confederate thought, the *Index*, to a people that did not take the trouble to think of us at all. This paper—and along with it the entire system of Confederate diplomacy abroad—was one of the direst mistakes made in the whole management of the great effort. Returning broken in health and fortune, Thompson met sympathetic friends in New York. Richard Henry Stoddard and his wife, and especially William Cullen Bryant, whom his true poetic temperament had long attracted, befriended him. On the latter's *Evening Post* he found work that was congenial; work that was rather made for him than useful to the paper. We lodged at the same substitute for a home, and I saw that disappointment and uncongenial surroundings were killing the tender poet. He did not die precisely as poor Henry Timrod did, but his ambition none the less starved him to death as literally as pride and poverty starved his Carolina brother. But now he sleeps in native soil. In his own words:

> "*Gently fall, ye Summer showers.*
> *Birds and bees, among the flowers,*
> *Make the gloom seem gay!*"

John Esten Cooke, poet, romancer and the Walter Scott of our Southern "Tales of the Border," dropped in on the Mo-

JOHN R. THOMPSON

saics when the activity of Stuart, whose aide he was, permitted flying visits to Richmond, even in winter. Cooke was rarely reticent as to his literary ventures, imparting portions of them to any chance listeners. Sometimes he was accompanied by his brilliant and boy-hearted chief, and those were indeed memorable nights when a Richmond soirée heard his manly voice troll out—merrily, if none too correctly—the camp ditty linked with his name, as to "Jining the cavalry" and the warmest of abodes:

"*If you want to catch the Devil, just 'jine the cavalry.'*"

It was not unfrequently that one met lights of cabinet and congress, or those of science and law, at these informal gatherings. The burly form of famous Professor A. T. Bled-

soe rolled in more than once, and his sledge-hammer disputa-
tion contrasted humorously with the quaint, easy argument
of Judge Raleigh Travers Daniel. Wide indeed was the range
of subjects that came up spontaneously at the informal meets
of the Mosaics. Wild, too, sometimes, were the vagaries
into which its members lapsed under the stimulus of contact
and unwonted rations. Some of these are tradition, yet
probably unfamiliar to most of my readers.

At one time a hat was passed around containing the most
absurd questions and another with unusual words. The
members drawing both were to link them in a speech, poem,
brief tale or song, in some sort of logical sequence. As example, that facile wit, Innes Randolph, once drew the question: " What sort of shoe was made on the last of the Mo-
hicans?" and with it the word, "Daddy Longlegs." Naturally
there was jubilation, for the aim of all his friends—and one
never attained—was to pose this wag. Almost immediately
he wrote and recited this glib impromptu:

"Old Daddy Longlegs was a sinner hoary,
    And was punished for his wickedness, according to the
        story.
    Between him and the Indian shoe this difference doth
        come in—
    One made a mock o' virtue and one a moccasin."

The applause had not ceased when the poet interrupted it
with:

"Corollary One: Because the old sinner stole the Indian
shoe to keep his foot warm, was no reason he should steal
his house to keeep his wig warm!"

In mid laughter and wonder at this addendum, Randolph
raised his hand and cried:

"Corollary Second: Because the Indian's shoe wouldn't
fit ary Mohawk is no reason that it wouldn't fit Nary-gansett!"

And so he ran on for a dozen ready quips that brought roars.

Music, as has been noted, was a strong factor in the cohesion of the Mosaic Club. No mention of it must omit Miss Evelyn Cabell, now Mrs. Russell Robinson, of Colleton, the ancient Cabell seat, in Nelson county. A schoolgirl at Miss Pegram's when war began, this beautiful and gifted girl became a popular belle. She was the daughter of Dr. Clifford Cabell, of Fernley, in Buckingham, coming of that good old-country stock, that manor house life, that to foreigners suggested country gentry and republican simplicity combined. With assured position and the numberless cousins, that are ever herital appurtenances of the well-born Virginia girl, Miss Cabell had a personality that left its impress on all she met.

After an all too short reign Miss Cabell threw away her sceptre, and one of the best remembered of all war receptions was that at the residence of Mrs. Wirt Robinson, when her son Russell brought the belle as his bride from the Fernley seat. In her new realm she has queened it ever since. Today, although widowed and several times a grandmother, she is young in spirits and as popular as ever in society, in and beyond Virginia. She is active in the best of women's associations and is honorary life regent of the Colonial Dames.

Colleton, the first of the six colonial seats of the Cabell family, has passed into her hands, and with her there, in her new widowhood, resides her second son and her granddaughter and namesake. Cabell Robinson is far over six feet tall, an engineer by profession and a widower, residing with his mother. His elder brother, Major Wirt Robinson, is a noted artillery officer of the regular army. He is an accomplished linguist and inherits his mother's gift as a vocalist. He married Miss Alice Henderson and has two children.

Two sisters followed pretty Eva Cabell into Richmond society, but later in the war when depletion and suspense had changed it greatly. Misses Mary and Alice Cabell were gifted and attractive girls, and gained a popularity that their maturity has broadened and deepened. The elder is now Mrs. John Cabell Early of Lynchburg, and is the mother of two soldier sons. Clifton Cabell Early was a feature of the West Point riding school, one of his feats being to ride two horses, with one foot upon the bare back of each. The younger son, Jubal A. Early, was the Annapolis midshipman whose appearance in the inaugural parade of President Roosevelt, with another descended from the Toutant-Beauregards, made pleasant comment in the Northern press. Both brothers are now lieutenants in the 25th U. S. Infantry. Mrs. Early also has two daughters, Evelyn Russell and Henrian. The elder has traveled much abroad with her godmother and aunt.

MRS. JOHN CABELL EARLY
(MARY WASHINGTON CABELL)

Miss Alice Cabell, the last sister to exchange Miss Pegram's school for war-time belleship, has long been a matron and head of the Richmond home of Charles Turner Palmer. Only one of her three lovely daughters is now left to her.

These three sisters are linked with memories of the Mosaics, as is the family name with all the most pleasant sociality of Richmond, as elsewhere shown. They were cousins of Colonel Coalter Cabell, of the artillery, who married Miss Alston. The belle and heiress was also a famous beauty, and her social triumphs are deeply impressed upon that day.

So are those of another cousin's wife, Miss Crittenden, of Kentucky, who married Colonel Carrington Cabell. Still other cousins, if not so near, were the beautiful Miss Lizzie Cabell and her gallant and popular brother, Caskie Cabell, who made his best siege and happiest capture when he surrendered to Miss Nannie Enders, *post-bellum.*

The Mosaic boasted instrumental and vocal experts whose performance had taken rank in the amateur circles of any city. All of these lent their gifts freely to the charities, but while the make-believe actors essayed ambitious comedies, no attempt at opera is recalled. Among the favorites were Madame Ruhl, a noted soprano singer and teacher, who was also in the choir of St. Paul's church.

Miss Nannie Robinson, who married her cousin, Ed. Robinson, later, was a finished and obliging pianiste. Her aid is recorded in many of the plays and charades that made amateur art notable. Misses Nannie Brooke, Alcinda Morgan and Annie Palmer were able aids to musical successes, and lent their gifts from time to time to the club symposia. Mrs. Thomas J. Semmes and Mrs. Clara Fitzgerald have already been noted at length, their favorite instrument being the harp. Washington, the artist, had a pretty taste and a sweet, light tenor, well used in German ballads and college songs. He whistled admirably, too, as did Willie Myers, and their duets ranged from "Peanuts" to "Norma." General John Pegram, though not an educated musician, or performer on any instrument, was a delightful and artistic whistler. The rare occasions when devotion to duty let him leave camp were pleasant ones to the Mosaics, many of them being his lifelong friends.

The comic singers *par excellence* were Innes and John Randolph—the latter with his undying "Grasshopper" and his saucy "Good Old Rebel" ditties—and "Ran" Tucker, of "Noble Skewball" and "Mr. Johnsing" recitative. Wonderful was that refrain—and the action that accompanied it—when the great jurist sang of the immortal racehorse! Gray Latham trolled his "Eveline" with great effect, but his hearers could not readily accommodate themselves to the ingrain wag's dropping into sentiment, as *Mr. Wegg* was wont to do into poetry.

The pretty and gracious Macmurdo sisters, Saidie and Hennie, lent their good soprano and alto to music of that day, and Hector Eaches —the gifted young painter with the sunshine face— would sometimes run up from camp in his private's jacket, a new sketch in his pocket, an old song in his clear, strong throat and a huge appetite a few inches below it.

The gayest of the Haxall homes of that day was that of the Barton Haxalls. Its daughter, Miss Lucy, was among the most sought

MRS. EDWARD L. COFFEY
(LUCY HAXALL)

of the younger set of society women. Handsome, stylish and with mingled geniality and *savoir faire*, she made friends and held them. Not a prominent musician herself, Miss Haxall loved music and was promoter of many concerts and other affairs combining music and charity. It was at her house that the "Musical Club" met most frequently. This grew out of the self-collected material of the Mosaic. Washington, Myers and Randolph were its originators, and it grew rapidly. It was an equally original club, and if memory serves me, was likewise without organization, and had no officers. It collected the best musical material, quite in the same fashion that the Mosaic did the mental and the humorous. Yet, some of its most useful members were not Mosaics. One instance was Professor Thilow, a fine performer on the violoncello; another, James Grant, whose virile basso was a real feature, until the act of his own hand put him beyond the pale.

This club was the origin of many an improvised orchestra for charity functions. Its real object was to furnish mutual entertainment and education to its own coterie, but it searched out musical merit and removed any secreting bushel from its light. Possibly exclusiveness crept in, to the sometime detriment of good result. I recall one occasion when a new soprano —not even on the boundaries of "*the* set"—was discovered by an ardent male seeker. He waxed enthusiastic over her voice, and urged her prompt introduction into this sacred circle of Calliope. But that shook haughty head and murmured, "Nay! Nay!"

One stately and gifted girl was the most emphatic dissenter. Shortly after, she was led to the piano, she cast one glance at the music rack and turned red to the furrows at the sight she beheld. Some graceless wag had placed upon the music a large card, upon which were plainly written some verses. Needless to say, the "Mrs. Grundy" referred to in them, was the pseudo-type for society gossip, not the charming and popular Richmond lady of that name, who had been Miss Haxall before changing her title.

The disturbing lines ran:

> "*In the old days of faith, with a beauteous accord,*
> *The people united with hearts that were one;*
> *And mingling meekly, accepted the Word*
> *And sat at the feet of the Carpenter's Son.*

> *" But it much exercises the monde of today*
> *To know—if defiant of custom—they ought to*
> *Neglect the sharp things 'Mrs. Grundy' would say,*
> *And admit to their music—the carpenter's daughter!"*

No record of this unique "club" can approach completeness that omits Misses Sally and Lucy Grattan. They were the closest friends of the Daniel sisters early named; and from those two hospitable homes, warmest and most frequent welcome went out to the "members." Brainy women were all of them; and as womanly and genial as they were brilliant.

MRS. OTHO G. KEAN
(SALLIE GRATTAN)

Miss Sally Grattan married Otho G. Kean, a prominent young lawyer of Richmond, who left her widowed long before the fullest ripening of his life. He left besides the precious heritage of a name never spoken, even at this day, without the mingling of regret and praise. She still resides in Richmond and has one son, William Grattan Kean.

Miss Lucy Grattan married Major W. F. Alexander, of Washington, Ga. He died but two years ago. Their daughter, Elvira, is now the wife of Edmund Byrd Baxter, of Augusta.

The Grattans of war-time were children of Peachy Ridgway Grattan and Jane Elwin; the husband having been reporter of the court of appeals for over thirty years. Of his eleven children, only Mrs. Kean and her sister Elizabeth survive.   George Grattan was killed at Gettysburg.

Rare, dry " Trav " Daniel; clever and comic " Jimmie " Pegram—who won gentle Lizzie Daniel for wife, only to lose her next year; Olivera Andrews and——.

Great the temptation—even though all the Mosaics were not Solomons—to exclaim with her of Sheba: "And behold, the one half of the greatness of thy wisdom was not told me." But even memory must draw reins, though spurred by thought of men and women who represented the Brain of Dixie, while yet its beaux and belles.

CHAPTER XVIII

" All the world's a stage,
    And all the men and women merely players"

is a never-trite truism of Shakespeare.

The whole South was one great stage. From opening overture at Sumter to final curtain at Appomattox, the men and women played in endless tragedy of battlefield and hospital, or in comedies of statecraft, intrigue and love-making. And there were plays within plays. Richmond was to the rest of the South what the Comédie Francaise was to the world of art.

Never before—not when the maidens gave their hair for bowstrings—had womanhood been so unanimous to fulfil the mandate of the poet:

"Fold away all your bright tinted dresses,
    Turn the key on your jewels today
And the wealth of your tendril-like tresses
    Braid back in a serious way.
No more delicate gowns—no more laces;
    No more loit'ring in boudoir or bower;
But come—with your souls in your faces—
    To meet the stern needs of the hour."

But it was not alone in a serious way that the women at the

Southern capital won the necessary dollars to aid their rougher work. All the labor of love was not in the Village of Dumdrudge, and those who had gifts of beauty and brain and silvery tongue turned them to vantage—

> *"To do for those dear ones what woman*
> *Alone in her pity might do."*

Not one old boy who even peeped into Richmond society, will fail to recall the piquant face and gentle manner that combined in the charm that made Lillie Booker two household words, "at camp and court." With never one visible effort at capture, she perhaps had more scalps to dangle at her girdle than any girl of her set; but she hid them under the meekness of the real *ingenue.* This may have been inborn pity, it may have been the tact that told her that trophies are also a warning. Her triumphs were lasting ones, too; and very lately an old fellow wrote me from the farthest West,

MRS. ROBERT. F JENNINGS
(LILLIE BOOKER)

that her photograph was the prized decoration of his snowed-in cabin.

Elizabeth Taylor Booker was the daughter of George Tabb Booker and Caroline Richardson; and was one of six children, of whom the only survivors are Thomas Booker, of Richmond, and Mrs. R. D. Roller, of Charleston, W. Va.

At the close of the war, Lillie Booker married Robert

Frank Jennings, son of Robert Garland Jennings and Elizabeth Edmunds, of Halifax county.   After a long life devoted
to her children's rearing—first in Halifax and later in Danville, she died in 1891, leaving a son and two daughters.

George Booker Jennings married Miss Eva Lawson, of
Danville, and now resides in Richmond with two daughters.
With him lives the unmarried sister, Lillie Taylor Jennings.
Ellen also resides in Richmond: being the wife of William
Freeman Dance, formerly of Powhatan county.   They have
two sons and two daughters; so the old friends of the war
belle may be assured that her memory is kept green in the
field of her old triumphs.

Fresh from the sickening and heartrending scenes at fever
cot and operating room, the stately dames of a dozen states
came gravely in nurse's dress or simplest of attire, and *presto!*
an hour later the charity grub had fluttered into the society
butterfly.   But these were nowise Hydaspean; not

> "*Born to live one brief and brilliant day, and die,*"

as on the Indian stream.   These live sempiternal in the hearts
of gallant men they flirted with, lived for—aye, died for.

Clad anew in the best bravery of the past—in the rummage
of trunk and closet since days when grandma danced with
Mister Washington—they strode behind the tallow dip foot-
lights, and the *Polonius* of Venus's court mumbled: "My
lord, the players have come!"   Never, perhaps, was drama
more earnestly done or had actors won more genuine and
often merited *bravas!*   Nowhere have I seen results more
conscientious, more satisfying, in view of scanty resources
and amid such strain on brain and heart and body.

Behind that Chinese wall of floating fortresses and bayonet-
bristling border, from first to last, even when the wolf was at
the door of the rich and the diapason of near cannon was the
dread bass to improvised orchestra, there were musicales,

charades, tableaux and even dramas that had been applauded in the perfumed capitals of plenty.

The male actors in most of these shows, and invariably in the impromptu ones, were mere "supers" to the woman-interest. They were—like the husband prayed for by the rural spinster—"Any, good Lord!" They were conscripted by the provost-managers out of the "males of any condition," who happed at hand. Often they were as "physically impaired" or as "mentally incapable" as the results of another and sterner conscription. When a play was to the fore, and Mrs. Semmes, Miss Cary, or another, needed a cast, any man in Richmond for a night was impressed. Generals, privates—at least once a chaplain—did a turn at the word of "She who must be obeyed." As will be seen, extempore art was no respecter of persons, and it is possible that in dire strait Mr. Davis himself might have been asked to do a stunt. The audiences, too, were as conglomerate as the casts. Highest and lowest sat side by side before the extemporized stages, erected in the best mansions in the capital.

MRS. CHARLES T. PALMER
(ALICE WINSLOW CABELL)

Mrs. Davis and the members of her household were almost always present, for the Cause and for example. The broad, quizzical face of Mr. Mallory and the smiling placidity of Mr. Benjamin, or the flutter of Mrs. Stanard, the dignified port of Mrs. Preston, or the fresh beauty of some budding belle like Alice Cabell varied the view from the stage.

Often elegant old Colonel George Deas—society man by instinct and *viveur* by habit of half a century—would escort a débutante, or John R. Thompson, the editor-poet, might flutter from bud to mature bloom, contemplating a stanza in every glance. So, the auditorium was as interesting as the performance it came to applaud.

Almost always there was sympathetic, helpful, intent Mrs. James Chesnut. And ever by her side was her true knight, her energetic and many-sided lover-husband—recalling gone days of another rebellious congress, at Philadelphia, when his sire made laws and made wild love to pretty Nellie Custis at the same time.

As already noted, there had been desultory movements to raise funds for soldiers' relief through musicales, tackey parties, sewing bees and minor methods. In the winter of 1862–63 the twin wolves, War and Want, showed their ugly fangs closer to camp and court; and that year some more elaborate and attractive entertainments were devised by energetic and capable householders for the good work of raising money.

The first of these was the charade reception at the hospitable home of the wife of Senator Semmes, opposite the White House. It was one which has lived long in the memories of spectators and participants, for it comprehended all that was prettiest, most cultured and distinguished in the capital's sociality.

Four charades were given, each demanding a complete scene for each syllable, and another for the whole word. The acting was in pantomime, a tactful resource that prevented stage fright of untried players and reduced the labors of the stage manager. Those labors rested mainly in the practiced hands of Mrs. Semmes, even if recently she had made futile though generous effort to shift most of the credit to the un-

deserving shoulders of this narrator. She wrote me, with a
wonderful store of facts and details:

"Your lovely sister, Agnes De Leon, had recently returned
from the East and loaned me her experience and her Oriental
trinkets and scarfs. Mrs. Davis turned over the entire
wardrobe of her household, and you were my trusted adjutant and actor."

The latter was my only claim to notice, and that because
my scenes were with Mrs. Semmes—one of the very best
amateurs I ever saw. .Her resource was exhaustless, and
her quickness in emergency simply marvelous. Both—in
addition to her easy grace as a hostess—she proved that
evening to an audience as large and as brilliantly representative as ever assembled, for any cause, in those four years
of "fighting and fooling."

The well-arranged stage, at the end of the great parlors,
first revealed its attractions in the charade word "Industrial." The first syllable was a simple tavern, at the moment
of the stage arriving: guests bustling, and horse-boy (Captain
Page McCarty) and boots (Captain Salle Watkins) stumbling
over their own elbows. The house bore the sign: "Entertainment for Man and——"; the missing final word replaced
by a capital likeness of the obliquity who had recently captured New Orleans and Mrs. Phillips. This, I am reminded,
was the handiwork of Major Willie Caskie. *Si non evero*, it
bore his hall-mark, though unsigned. The guests were the
beaux and statesmen best known in town; and the hostess
and assistant housekeeper drowned the applause that greeted
each new arrival. That popular pair were Mrs. Lucy Mason
Webb and Miss Saidie Macmurdo. Mrs Webb, as pretty Lucy
Mason, had captured hosts of friends who clung to her through
life, warming its desolation when she dedicated her widowhood to the care of the suffering, in charge of the Officers'
Hospital. Miss Macmurdo, now Mrs. Alfred L. Rives, of

Castle Hill, was one of the most deservedly popular of Richmond beauties. She and her sister Helen were noted as singers in war-time concerts, and both have carried through their married lives the gentle graces that won for them the love of old and young. Miss Helen is now the wife of that typical Virginian of yesterday, Colonel Walter Harrison. Mrs. Rives has reared three daughters who have been as widely known as any ever born in the bounds of the Old Dominion, Amélie, Princess Troubetzkoy, the authoress; Gertrude, now Mrs. Allen Potts, confessedly the best 'cross-country rider in Virginia; and Landon, now Miss Rives, who has defied all comers of the frequently softer sex.

The second syllable of "Industrial" revealed a bevy of pretty young girls, each with a feather broom, or mop, and apron, the latter to hide, perchance, the scalps each had hanging at her girdle. Misses Hetty and Constance Cary, Mattie Paul, Sallie and Nannie Enders (now Mesdames James W. Conner, of Charleston, and Caskie Cabell, of Richmond); Lou Fisher and Hennie Hill, daughter of the great Georgian; Evelyn Cabell, Bettie Brander (as popular in her widowhood as Mrs. Edward Mayo as she then was)—these and possibly others whom I do not recall mopped, brushed and blew, as though dust were more dangerous than the blue foe at the gate.

Then came the trial scene, with it the first demand for acting, and it was answered in well-won applause. The stage was transformed into a court, with judge (General Robert Ould, Commissioner of Exchange of Prisoners), sheriff, jurors and crier. In a recent letter Mrs. Semmes writes:

"You were the prisoner, my husband, on trial for some great crime and in the dock, loaded down with cable chains (not very ethical, yet perhaps realistic). I rushed in, just as sentence was pronounced; threw myself at the judge's feet, and tried to scream in gesture: 'Mercy! Mercy!' Then I swooned in pantomime, exactly how I do not recall. But I do recall the kindly applause; and I must have done some acting, for my little adopted daughter had to be brought into the dressing-room, dissolved in tears, before she could be convinced that I was not dead."

The whole word showed a parlor, the same bevy of pretty girls—I think reinforced—all doing something useful, looking

in mirrors, sewing, kneading dough, scraping lint or indulging in animated flirtation with such good-looking fellows as Shirley Carter, Stewart Symington, Tom Price, Tom Ferguson and their partners in that fine art. A veracious chronicler reminds me that the word was not guessed, but had to be announced—of course the fault of audience, not of actors.

"Harum-scarum," the second word, changed to lush

ROBERT A. DOBBIN

Orientalism. Its first scene showed Miss Enders as a gorgeous Sultana. Around her grouped the recent dusters, transformed to odalisques, their recent swains still handsomer in turbans and bags. Irrepressible Miss "Buck" Preston tried to look demure severity as the duenna, and maidens and slaves played the zither or danced in Jenness-Miller integuments before their mistress.

The second word touched on horrors, a weird and sheet-clad spectre (General P. M. B. Young) affrighting lasses and laddies as he stalks "unrevenged among us." The whole word, guessed by several "in front," showed romping girls and giddy youths, all in the fullest enjoyment of tricks upon one another, skipping rope and indulging in similar innocent recklessness.

Presto! The stage has changed to a street. Mrs. Ives, as a thin woman, and Robert Dobbin, as a fat man, meet a quack. His pills, per placard, cure fat and make the lean obese. Purchase is made, and the next scene shows the reduced Dobbin prancing airily and Mrs. Ives puffing under great access of flesh.

The same street suffices for second syllable. Here a rich and acrid *Gradgrind* is importuned by a wretched woman. Her pantomime tells clearly that she is starving; she points piteously to the little boy, tugging for release from her firm grip, his real tears running down his face. But the rich man frowns, glowers and strides away, the woman eloquently beseeching the boy not to weep. The beggar (Mrs. Semmes), called to the scene, saw little Frank Ives at the entrance. Sudden inspiration of effect! She seized and rushed him on, all unrehearsed; and his weeping brought down the house.

For the last syllable John Anderson (Captain Ed. M. Alfriend, with cotton wig and his fierce mustache chalked) listens to "the auld, auld story," from the auld, auld wife, to low strains of the song.

Rittenhouse's orchestra, which, hidden behind a covert of palms and potted plants, had discoursed *entr'acte* music throughout the evening, in this scene played softly the air of the undying old ditty.

Then came the whole word: a magnificent picture. The stage became a shrine, draped and flower strewn, the Cross surmounting it. Toward it slowly moved pilgrims from every age and clime, entering from opposite sides and walking in pairs. Peasant, priest, knight, Imaun, beggar and emperor, all approached, kneeling to lay their offerings upon the Cross.

Then they separated once more, grouping on either side in brilliant contrast. A little pause. The band struck up "See! the conquering hero comes." Forth strode grand "Jeb" Stuart, in full uniform, his stainless sword unsheathed, his noble face luminous with inward fire. Ignoring the audience and its welcome, he advanced, his eyes fixed on the shrine until he laid the blade, so famous, upon it. Then he moved to a group, and never raised his eyes from the floor as he stood with folded arms.

MRS. LEIGH R. PAGE
(PAGE WALLER)

Next came Mrs. Ives and Mrs. Leigh Page garbed as nuns, passing to the shrine to bless the sword laid there as votive offering to country: no breath now breaking the hush upon the audience. Last, handsome Tom Symington, of Baltimore, and myself, in green turbans and robes of the Mecca pilgrims, entered, salaaming to each other, then to the shrine as we approached it. There we two touched the sword, prostrating ourselves before the shrine.

The music had softened to a sweet pianissimo as the sword was laid upon the altar. Now it swelled out into a solemn strain, and the Franciscans, the Paulists, the Capuchins and the nuns in the pilgrimages stood forth and chanted the "Miserere," as the refrain softly closed.

A wedding in the halls of Lammermoor to sign the bridal contract was the first syllable of the next word. "Lucy Ashton," represented by Miss Lelia Powers, holds the pen, only to dash it down on the appearance of the "Master of Ravenswood" (Captain Sam Shannon, of Carolina). "Henry," her irate brother (Page McCarty), rushes on the intruder with drawn sword, only restrained by the "Priest" (W. D. Washington) and the "Laird of Bucklaw" (James Denegre). The scene was effective in pantomime and costume.

In the second syllable an older and happier courtship showed. Mrs. Semmes, magnificently dressed as "Rebecca," stood by the well and heard the tender words of "Isaac," proxied by Eleazer (Burton Norvell Harrison, secretary to Mr. Davis). The pair were admirable in their pantomime, and the hostess radiant in the Eastern silks and gems, in which she later received her guests.

In the final scene of that final word this writer once more disported his congenial chains in a cell of Bridewell Prison, and doubtless all present thought his acting well merited the situation. Then came the social part, of which Mrs. Semmes writes me:

"I never saw my supper-table until I went in with my guests. Mrs. Campbell, Mrs. Crump, Mrs. Lucy Webb, Mrs. Grant and Mrs. Cane prepared it for me. Although the ice-cream was sweetened with brown sugar, it was good; and everything the markets of Richmond then supplied, from the farms around, was fine and fresh. I can never forget those friends in need."

CHAPTER XIX

"RIVALS" AND FOLLOWERS

THE success of this entertainment urged the willing workers to fresh effort and the actors to new laurel-reaping.

Mrs. Ives offered her handsome home and her abilities to another ambitious attempt at fund-raising, with Sheridan's famous comedy, "The Rivals." Of this occasion, Mrs. Chesnut tells a good story in her diary:

Big, blond-bearded and gentle-hearted Hood was present when the prince of comedians, Frank Ward, played *Bob Acres*. So true to life was the terror of the country gentleman, in his "very pretty quarrel" with *Sir Lucius*, that Hood, fidgeting in his chair awhile, at length blurted out: "I do believe that fellow Acres is a coward!"

Catching Mrs. Chesnut's attention, General Breckinridge whispered:

"Hood is better than the play and that is all good from *Sir Anthony* to *Fag!*" And, omitting the small grain of critical salt, the great Kentuckian was right.

The cast was made from the best talent of the town; the costumes put all society's wardrobe under contribution, and the spacious drawing-rooms, crowded with the beauty and culture of the capital, made an auditorium that would defy competition in metropolitan peace times.

Sir Anthony Absolute was played by John Randolph, one of the three exceptional brothers of that family, a clever actor,

224

a humorist and a musician, and he had used his gifts un-
stintingly for his co-actors at rehearsals. He played the
trying rôle with discretion and original conception, in thorough
sympathy with the author. But nowise second to him was
Paymaster L. M. Tucker, C.S.N., in the cleverly played rôle
of *Jack Absolute.* This was a clear-cut and manly performance, full of quiet humor and overdone in no detail of stage
business. Mr. Tucker was a popular member of war's gilded
youth, a reader and a writer
of neat prose and verse.
The eldest of three hand-
some Mississippi brothers,
also in the army, he was
the only one who did not
later go into the church.
The late Dr. Louis J. Tucker,
of Baton Rouge, La., and
Dean Gardiner C. Tucker, of
St. John's, Mobile, being the
others. Their sons have, in
turn, followed parental example. Indeed, the time when
there has not been a Tucker
writing poetry and reading
divinity at the Seminary of St.

JOHN RANDOLPH
(SIR ANTHONY ABSOLUTE)

Luke, Sewanee, runneth not to the contrary in man's memory.
Louis, Jr., Gardiner and Royal, are today proof spirits of the
fact, from as many Louisiana pulpits. But the sailor-actor
and eldest brother proved the family rule by exception.
When the last Confederate ship went up in home-made flame,
Lee M. Tucker changed his Confederate bonds for a gold
dollar, and took to assuring lives that were merely mortal.
He became the leading insurance manager of Mississippi;
found the field too small and moved to Atlanta. There he

throve until ill health and partial blindness forced him to change. He is now in California.

Fag was very unctuously played that night. No one who met Clarence Cary at the Bar Association in New York, or is permitted to read his study-born translations of the great Latin poets, would have suspected the early comic instinct that brought roars when he played *Jack Absolute's* valet.

CAPTAIN L. M. TUCKER
(JACK ABSOLUTE)

David and *Coachman*, respectively, fell into the hands—and right capable ones they proved—of George Robinson, of the artillery, and Robert A. Dobbin, of Baltimore, now "most potent, grave and reverend 'senior' " of the Monumental bar. He is that also of an adult family, whose homes are so close about him that grandchildren clamber all over him at will. The exception is his daughter, Ellen Swan Dobbin, who was made an especial paragraph of by the leading young journalist, Frederick Hoppin Howland, of Providence *Journal,* and is now a popular young matron of that town. When he retired from the stage Mr. Dobbin played the lover's part so successfully as to bring him very close to the "old flag," and with no desire to rebel forevermore. He married Miss Lizzie Key, the fair and lovable daughter of Philip Barton Key, the handsome, popular and lamented district attorney of older Washington days, and *his* father was Francis Scott Key, who wrote "The Star Spangled Banner." Mrs.

Dobbin was doubtless proud of that anthem; but she had even better reason to be proud of the praiseful prose she heard of her sons the elder, Dr. George W. Dobbin, being at the head of his surgical branch in Baltimore; and his brother Robert winning golden opinions as secretary of that city's United Sureties. But, at the closing of the last year, pride was replaced by mourning in all these homes; the tender, helpful mother having been called from them; leaving her husband lone and desolate.

I am chatting of "The Rivals" with the glibness of senility, but it was one of the greatest social successes of its time, and a dramatic one, in real view. Some of the characters must needs be touched upon more briefly, in view of recent and detailed description by a pen too trained and facile for mine to cross. And when its keenness of Saladin's scimitar is wielded by one of the players herself the mace of any would-be Richard must make dullest thud indeed.

Mrs. Malaprop in the mouth of Mrs. Clem Clay, now the brilliant and still young-hearted widow of Judge David Clopton, could have evoked but one comment. I only dare to add that it was as congenial and as true to her conception of it as was her other congenial one, when I saw her as *Mrs. Partington*, at the Gwin costume ball, at Washington. She has herself written minutiæ of the great and star-sought rôle, which were impossible to any other not so intimate with them. Mrs. Clopton has told us, too, of the rollicking and funny part Major R. W. Brown, a gallant North Carolinian on General Winder's staff, made of *Sir Lucius O'Trigger*, the rôle that stands as unmossed epitaph for Sothern, rare John Brougham and "Dolly" Davenport. And "tenderer far to tell," she has recorded the real triumph of that then conquering belle and perennial many-sided *mondaine*, Miss Constance Cary.

Dainty, pretty and piquante were the minor parts of

saucy *Lucy* and sentiment sought Julia, intrusted to Mrs. Lawson Clay and Miss Lucy Herndon; one as much sought in her new wedded life as when pretty Lestia Comer; the other, one of the two popular and modest daughters of Dr. Herndon, of the navy.

Major Frank X. Ward scarcely played the great part of this great play: he realized it. In a make-believe managerial experience from college days and later vented on half a dozen helpless cities, I recall no better acting by a nonprofessional.

The war over, Ward returned, was admitted to the Baltimore bar, and practiced there awhile. Later he married Miss Topham Evans. Subsequently he removed to Germantown, Pa., where two of his sons, Frank and Topham, were engaged in electrical work. His only daughter, Miss Nora, was also married there.

The eldest son, Johnson, went to the Cuban war, and was the only Democrat from Maryland who received one of the regular army commissions. He is now in the Philippines, but with all the rest of his family about him, the veteran "star" now, like *Cawdor*, "lives a prosperous gentleman."

A delightful addition to the plays was the *entr'acte* music. Mrs. Fitzgerald played rare selections on the harp rarely well, and Miss Nannie Robinson, always reliable and facile excelled herself in the accompaniment.

"Bombastes Furioso" Rhodes' classic burlesque of "Orlando" was the afterpiece of the evening. John Randolph was *Bombastes*, singing and acting the part in his family style. Mr. Robinson, who had so cleverly done *David* in "The Rivals," was intrusted the harder rôle of *King Artaxaminous of Utopia*, and scored a great hit. So did Mr. Dobbin, promoted from *Coachman* to play *Fusbus*, the statesman, As captain of the army, Captain Frank Ward was inimitably droll. "He was ineffably funny," says Mrs. Ives, "in marshaling his troops, consisting of a half-dozen lame, blind and wretched ragamuffins, I can recall nothing more droll, and he brought roars of laughter, as did Mr. Randolph, in his scenes with me, and his admirable comedy in singing."

And of that lady herself too much cannot be said. She lent the fairest of forms and faces to the part of *Distaffina*, "bought from *Bombastes's* love, for half a crown," and she added the seriousness of *Lady Macbeth*, a point too frequently missed in make-believe playing. Non-comparable as are the two, the burlesque was probably quite as well played as was the ambitious comedy, and assuredly it brought more laughter and applause than any bit of amateur work done in Richmond, "eenjurin' ov de wah."

"The sincerest flattery" followed these two successes. Practical welldoers had found what society wanted, and gave it to her freely. Until the fangs of the wolf and the cry of Rachel took away the men and the means, sock and buskin were the only wear for Charity. To list even one tithe of the shows would demand a volume, but a few brilliant ones show clear against their background of gloom.

During that winter Mrs. George W. Randolph gave a charade reception with added picture gallery. One of the words acted was Penitent. In its first syllable Miss Josephine Chestney, of Washington, was a far too pretty, but extremely clever *Fanny Squeers*, perched on a high stool, and sharpening quills viciously for the master of Dotheboys Hall—Captain W. Gordon McCabe.

Laurence Sterne's daintiest and most cunning conception furnished the second syllable. In a cozy room cute *Widow Wadman* and my *Uncle Toby* enacted the searching scene from "Tristram Shandy" with great effect. The act itself was cleverly done, but the importance of the players outweighed all else with the beholders. The widow was Mrs. Phoebe Pember, sister of Mrs. Phillips, and quite as brilliant a woman in a different way. A belle and early a widow, she made herself loved in the army camps by that good work of her Chimborazo Hospital, at which a later glance will be taken. And past the recent cypress we see the then young major-general, dashing, reckless and jovial, the

man of reliance in an international crisis, later the choice of an opposing party, to command his own old foes in the re-cemented Union— Fitzhugh Lee.

The last of the word was an *al fresco* scene in the Orient realizing one in Byron's "Corsair."

Miss Evelyn Cabell enhanced the perfect fitness of her beauty by a rich and correct costume, again terminating in divided skirts of shrimpest pink satin. About her grouped a most enticing

MRS. THOMAS PEMBER
(PHOEBE IEVY)

array of harem beauties, the strict adherence to Eastern ethics inhibiting the presence of man, even when clad likewise in bags.

Over the whirr of great peacock fans, the coiled pipe-tubes and the graceful dancing-girls and coffee-bearers, spread the folds of a great tent; a pretty picture and easily guessed. Then, for the whole word, Miss Lizzie Giles veiled some of her beauties under the severe dress of the novice; most of her other—and perhaps more dangerous attraction, beneath a demure and devotional cast of face that was irresistible.

There were other charades, but there is a trifle of sameness even in too much of the beautiful. One, however, was acted by Mrs. Pember alone and in one scene that meant the four separated syllables and the whole word. Clad entirely in the beloved gray of "her boys," with gloves, bonnet and shoes of same, she put her graceful head through the port- ieres of an empty room, then opened them, stepped nimbly in and closed them behind her as she advanced; looked triumphantly around and gave a sigh of content. Then she produced from one pocket an army hardtack, from the other a piece of camp bacon and began eating them ravenously. Rushing out she reappeared, eating more hungrily than before. This she repeated three times; the announce- ments showing: "First sylla- ble"—"Second"—"Third"— "Fourth" —and "Whole word!" The charade was not guessed and had to be an- nounced: "Ingratiate!"

Then, when all the cha- rades were done, really beau- tiful pictures were shown, the special effort to se- cure beauiful women being voted the success of the evening. Miss Hettie Cary was a perfect "Simplicity," decked with that seductive grain in realization of "Comin' thro' the Rye." That there was

MRS. JOHN MONCURE ROBINSON
(CHAMPE CONWAY)

no "laddie" in the scene made sundry gallant fellows wretch- ed. Miss Mattie Paul was a Guido-like "Venetian Lady," in rich costume to which she lent charm. Genial Salle Wat- kins and that jolly tar, Lieutenant Walter Butt, with pow- dered arms and paper wings realized Raphael's "Cherubs."

Then Miss Champe Conway posed as the "Mignon" of Goethe, later linked to pretty music by Thomas; and Miss Josephine Chestney, as a "Syrian Girl," gazed with unwonted pensiveness from her high lattice upon her lover below, who twanged a zither. That enviable serenader was Captain "Jimmy" Denegre.

Next comedy came: "The Flower of the Family," shown as an empty flour barrel. The laughter that greeted this was dry with reminiscence, until it quickly changed to affirming applause as the pretty, plump shoulders and laughing lips and eyes of popular Miss Bettie Brander emerged from it.

A long-remembered picture was Miss Constance Cary as the *Hermione* of "The Winter's Tale," in profile statue. Perhaps, however, the most entertaining feature of this show was the descriptive program, written in dainty and humorous verse by John R. Thompson and recited by Miss Mary Preston in the graceful drapery of the Muse of Poetry. Mrs. Randolph bade me act as her prompter, call-boy and utility man on this occasion, and the onerous duties were shared by her charming niece, Miss Jennie Pollard, youngest sister of that family. She married Dr. Wm. Nichols. Her sisters, Mdes. Smith (Ellen) and Edward Swain (Mary) live in San Francisco and New York.

There were many and notable offerings for charity and amusement in that last of the gay winters in Richmond. Even were there general features not too similar to detail, their *dramatis personæ* were too nearly the same to make report a special novelty. Among them may be noted the palpable hit of tasteful Mrs. Fanny Townes, *née* Giles, in "An Artist's Studio Party." There were three lovely pictures in frames: Murillo's "Madonna," by Miss Lizzie Giles, "Mary Stuart," Miss Mattie Paul, and "Beatrice Cenci," Miss Champe Conway. As offset to the color, statuary showed "Hermione," by Miss Constance Cary; bust,

"Spring," Fannie Giles; the "Magdelen Lectans," Miss Nannie Giles, and "The Maid of Saragossa," Miss Lizzie Giles.

In the same season, Mrs. Tardy had a novelty in the shape of a tableau reception, where "Paradise and the Peri" was illustrated by the prettiest of the younger set of girls. Aspiring male youth naturally was excluded from this Eden. Miss Addie Deane, later Mrs. Peter Lyons, was the *Peri* and among the angels were Misses Nannie Enders, Mary Cabell, Champe Conway, Lizzie Cabell, Lelia and Rosalie Bell and many another. As the scene succeeded, brave, eloquent and inveterate John Mitchell, the Irish patriot, read the poem.

MRS. SAMUEL ROBINSON
(LIZZIE PEYTON GILES)

Such, in insufficient glance, was the dramatic side of Richmond's society charities: a side that lights the leaden gloom that slowly began to weigh upon the spirits of even the most hopeful: that lightened the labors of hospital and diet-kitchen drudgery, that made the furlough red-lettered with memories of bright faces, sweet voices and airy forms that had made its holder long for the next bullet, had he been a believer in the Koran.

CHAPTER XX

TEARING down an old established government and up-rearing a new one upon its ruins necessarily brought into the South all sorts and conditions of men—and women.

In all Virginian history the Tucker family has borne its part, and borne it well. Coming from colonial stock in days when men hewed their fortunes with their swords or molded them with their brains, when women ruled by graces of heart and head, which they bequeathed to their daughters, this family stands picturesque in the annals of its state.

Colonel Beverley Tucker was early a conspicuous figure at Richmond, as he had long been in the social and political life of Washington.

With massive frame, keen eye and a prodigality of tawny beard, he had a stomach as strong as his brain. Mr. Davis and all other members of the government knew him well, and often called upon his varied experience of men and events.

In 1771, young St. George Tucker came from the island of Bermuda to Williamsburg to finish his education at William and Mary He went home, but was so impressed with the colony that he returned and settled in Williamsburg to practice law. There he married the beautiful Widow Randolph, who had been Miss Frances Bland; prospered, and became noted in the land of his adoption. The fair

234

widow, as heretofore noted, had two children, Richard and John, the later famous Randolph of Roanoke. Her marriage with St. George Tucker brought two other sons, Henry St. George and Beverley. It is with the former that this narration has most to do.

Henry St. George Tucker married Evelyna Hunter, and their family numbered thirteen children; eight reached adult age. Eldest of these, Dr. David Tucker, was long a popular and respected physician in Richmond, but was too old and feeble at the outbreak of the war to take any active part in it. He married Miss Lizzie Dallas, niece of the vice-president and minister to England.

Beverley was next adult brother. He was educated as civil engineer, and was a while a merchant. He established the *Sentinel* newspaper at the capital in 1853, where he had already laid the basis for that phenomenal acquaintance he had with men all over the world. He

HON. BEVERLEY TUCKER
("THE SUSPECT")

certainly aided greatly in the election of President Pierce, and was made printer to the senate and in the same year, consul to Manchester.

At that time Roger A. Pryor, member of congress from Virginia, later Confederate brigadier and now retired judge of the New York supreme court, was rival editor to my brother and guardian, Hon. Edwin De Leon, who had been called from his Columbia paper, *The Telegraph*, to establish the

Washington organ of the Southern Senators, *The Southern Press*, in conjunction with Elwood Fisher.   Activity in the Pierce campaign sent him to Egypt as consul-general and diplomatic agent.

When the Democracy committed harikari at Charleston in 1860, and Abraham Lincoln took charge of the tripartite corpse, both men tendered him their resignations.   By strange coincidence, both were kept abroad by Mr. Davis as commissioners to the press and public opinion of Europe; a mission wholly different from the "diplomatic" one of Messrs. Mason and Slidell.   It was equally—well, to put it politely, unsuccessful.

In 1864 he was sent to Canada on a secret business mission entirely different from the nature ascribed to it by the terror, or worse, of the Great President's successor.

Mr. Tucker was in Canada when Wilkes Booth fired the fatal bullet that made a great martyr of a great statesman and echoed as Hope's death knell in the heart of every Southern thinker.   But Andrew Johnson proclaimed jovial, chivalrous Bev Tucker as an accomplice of the crazed assassin, after Boston Corbett's too ready bullet had closed the only lips that could have spoken the truth, and set a price·upon his head.

With Tucker the charge coupled George N. Sanders, an old Washington lobbyist and also a Canadian supply agent of the Confederacy.   Both men promptly offered themselves up for trial by jury, but the offer was refused and the crazed press of the moment continued to hold them up to a world's obloquy.   Then Mr. Tucker tried his presidential accuser before the world's bar.   That promptly acquitted *him*, whether or not it convicted his culprit.

His denunciation of Johnson, broadsheeted to the world and still extant, is terribly lively reading, even after this lapse of time.   *Rem acu tetigit.*   He broached the president upon his once congenial weapon, but he made it a darning needle and its point was Damascene.

Acquitted without the world's jury leaving the box, Mr. Tucker went to England in search of work. He was accompanied by that lovely and devoted wife, ever at his side in the trials of a varied life and by his gentle and charming daughter, Margaret. Some of the soldier sons were delving at breadwinning in Virginia and two of the younger at school in Canada.

In England an offer came to go to Mexico for lucrative control of an immense ranch property, the details of which in Mrs. Tucker's letters read like a fairy-tale. The Maximilian failure there forced the errant seeker to a new home in Canada once more, and he took a hotel at St. Catherine's Wells, which his great hospitality kept so full of old friends and comrades as to leave no room for paying guests. The home was a delight, but the business side was a failure, and in his age and in failing health the great-hearted Virginia gentleman laid him down to die, his face still to the foe—poverty. All that remains is a stainless and picturesque record and a love undying in the hearts of his descendants and of a host of friends.

In the January of 1841 Beverley Tucker had married Miss Jane Shelton Ellis, of that notable Virginia family, and their children were Miss Margaret, who never married and resides still in Richmond; James Ellis, the next adult, was color-bearer of the Second Virginia Cavalry, married, has two sons and lives in California; Beverley D. was a private in the Otey battery, enlisted in the church *post-bellum* and is now coadjutor bishop of Southern Virginia. He married Miss Maria Washington, of Mt. Vernon, and their family numbers thirteen. Henry St. George, their first-born, is president of St. John's College, Tokio, Japan. Eleanor S. came next, and Jane B. married Rev. Luke White. Lila,

Maria W. and Augustine W. are medical missionaries at Shanghai. The others are John Randolph, Richard B., Herbert M., Laurence F., Ellis M., and Francis Bland.

JOHN RANDOLPH TUCKER
(JURIST, TEACHER AND WIT)

The next son of Beverley Tucker, John Randolph, married Miss Crump and died in 1880, leaving two sons, Beverley Randolph and William Crump Tucker.

Charles Ellis Tucker married Mabelle Morrison, of Memphis, the eldest of their three children, Margaret T., being the wife of William Carroll, of that city, and the other two being William Morrison and Elizabeth M. Tucker.

The children of Dr. David Tucker and Elizabeth Dallas were six: Henry St. George died in the army; Virginia B. never married; Dallas is an Episcopal minister who has one daughter; John Randolph, a lawyer and unmarried; Cassie B. married Thompson Brown and has six children—four sons and two daughters; and Emma Beverley married Forrest Brown and has one son.

John Randolph Tucker, fifth son of St. George Tucker and Evelyna Hunter, has been met elsewhere in this *causerie*. Scholar, poet, wit and attorney-general of Virginia, he was also congressman for twelve years and law professor at her university schools. He married Miss Laura Powell and laid down his useful life, at Winchester in 1873. Of their children, Evelyna H. married William Shields, of Natchez, Miss.; died and left two sons: John Randolph and Benoit Shields.

Nannie Tucker, her sister, married Dr. William McGuire, of Winchester, and they have six children. The third sister, Virginia Tucker, married William Carmichael and is the mother of four children.

The youngest sister is Mrs. Morgan Pendleton, of Lexington, and has several children.

Their brother is Hon. Harry St. George Tucker, formerly member of congress and later president of the Jamestown tercentenary. He married Hennie, daughter of Colonel William Preston Johnston, who died leaving six children. His present wife was Miss Martha Sharpe, of Pennsylvania.

The great jurist's fourth daughter, Gertrude, was the gentle light of his age in his Lexington home, and was exceptionally popular with townspeople and students, as well as family connections. She married John Lee Logan; thus intermeshing another notable family with the great connection. Since her widowhood, in 1900, she has remained a marked figure before the eye of society.

John Lee Logan was the second son and fifth of the thirteen children of James W. Logan, of "Dungeness," Goochland county, Va., and Sarah Strother, of Culpepper county. Mr. Logan was son of Rev. Joseph D. Logan and Jean Butler Dandridge. Her

MRS. JOHN LEE LOGAN
(GERTRUDE TUCKER)

father, William Dandridge, married Anne Bolling and he was grandson of Governor Alexander Spottswood and fifth in descent from Pocahontas. This makes the Logans of the present generation sixth in line from Governor Spottswood and eighth from the Indian bride of John Rolfe.

James W. Logan, of "Dungeness," was born in Goochland, but adopted by his great aunt, Mrs. George Woodson Payne; and from her he inherited the estate, formerly owned by Thomas Isham Randolph. There the planter reared his family of thirteen; but after the war they moved to Salem, Va., for the cultivation of the younger branches of the spreading family tree. There the parents died, leaving as the actual head of the family Mrs. Anna Clayton Logan. She was now the eldest, Mary Louise having died in 1862. In 1871 Anna Clayton married her cousin, Colonel Robert H. Logan, who had left West Point when Virginia seceded and made a fine war record. After peace, he studied and practiced law; leaving his widow with five children. Of them the three daughters are living; the brilliant son, John Lee (2nd), died in Norfolk, in 1906, just at the threshold of a promising career. His sisters are Mary Louise, who married Prof. W.

MRS. ANNA LOGAN

Paul C. Nugent, of New Orleans, now in the civil engineering chair of Syracuse University, New York. They have two children. Elsie Addison married her cousin, Joseph Clayton Logan, a Columbia A.M. and LL.B., now secretary of Associated charities, of Atlanta. The third, Sarah Strother, married Dr. Stephen Russell Mallory Kennedy, of Pensacola, son of the brilliant and beautiful Mrs. Ruby Mallory Kennedy, already met in these pages. They have one son.

Mrs. Anna Logan divides her time with her daughters in their northern and southern homes.

Of the thirteen children of James W. Logan and Sarah Strother, seven are still living. George Woodson, the eldest brother, and fourth child, is a planter, at Salem, Va. He has married twice: first to Miss Grant, of Atlanta, and later Miss Kate Burks, of Bedford county, Va., a daughter of Colonel Jesse Burks of C. S. A. They had ten children.

Joseph D. Logan married Miss Georgine Willis, a niece of Catherine Murat. They have seven children; and Mr. Logan is a practising lawyer.

The next brother is Dr. Mercer Patton Logan, rector of St. Ann's Episcopal Church, at Nashville. He married Miss Elizabeth Kent Caldwell, of Wytheville, Va., and they have a family of six, all grown. Elizabeth Kent, who married John Reeves Jackson, of Nashville, Tenn; Ellen Claire, Josephine Dandridge, Sydney Strother, Anne Gordon and Dorothea Spottswood.

A sister, Edith Erskine, married Thomas L. Hart, of Nottoway county, and their family is of three children.

Of the brothers of this immediate family who died, all gave great promise or had done good work. John Lee Logan, taught school with Virginius Dabney and, at the same time studied law with John Randolph Tucker. He went to New York, where he entered the law office of Pryor, Lord, Day and Lord, at request of Judge Roger A. Pryor. He was getting a good practice, a little later, when his health broke down and he was ordered to Idaho. Cleveland made him associate justice; but he died there in 1900. He and his elder brother were both in the army with Fitz Lee's cavalry. George Woodson was at Point Lookout as a prisoner, but was exchanged and went in for the rest of the war. John Lee was with Colonel R. V. Boston, but was so young he saw but eight months' service. Both boys went in at seventeen.

The youngest brother, Sydney Strother, was a brilliant member of the *Journal of Commerce* staff, and an all-round journalist. He died in New York when only thirty-one.

Next of kin in blood to the Tuckers of the Ellis stock—and even nearer in the mutual love of a generation—are the noted Munford family, straight descended from the Huguenot colonist Montforts of my

COL. GEORGE WYTHE MUNFORD
(SECRETARY OF COMMONWEALTH)

second chapter. Colonel George Wythe Munford, of Richmond, secretary of the Commonwealth, married Miss Elizabeth Thoroughgood Ellis, whose sister was wife of Beverley Tucker. All the men of the name were noted in the war, one son, Charles Ellis Munford, giving his life for his state at Malvern Hill. General Thomas T. Munford commanded a cavalry brigade with distinguished dash and credit all through the war. He is still living in Lynchburg. He married Etta, daughter of George P. Tayloe, of Roanoke. They had four children and a Virginian wealth of third generation. These were George T., with several children; Emma, who married William Boyd and has three children; William, unmarried exception and living in Alabama, and Wythe, married and the father of several children. By his second marriage with Miss Emma Tayloe, of Richmond, there are three sons, all unmarried.

Colonel William Munford commanded the First Virginia, as stated heretofore. After the war he married and went into the Episcopal ministry in Mississippi and the West. He was a magnificently handsome man and a gifted one, and died only five years ago. A much younger brother, Robert, married and lives in Macon, Ga. There were nine Munford sisters of the secretary's household, but the younger members were not all very active society belles in the war-time.

One of its brightest and most charming women was Miss Sallie R. Munford, now Mrs. Charles H. Talbot, and the mother of four children. The other sisters are Margaret N,. Lizzie E., Jane Beverley, Lucy T., Fannie E., Caroline F., Etta and Annie B., who married William S. Robertson, and lives in Richmond as do all the others.

CHAPTER XXI

ONE name recurs often in these pages, a name broidered deep through the joy and sorrow, the sweet and the bitter that make up the Lost Cause. The Cary name is not only one of the oldest, but the worth of its men and the character and beauty of its women have made it integral with American history.

I have shown that the Fairfaxes date beyond the Norman conquest of their Saxon forbears of "Fair Hair," and trend westward would seem to have left no laggards of their blood. Of that blood are the Carys by intermarriage in early colonial days.

Two Maryland branches of the Cary family were active in the war. What they did has been touched upon briefly; who they are can be told.

Archibald Cary, of Carysbrook, Fluvanna county, married Monimia Fairfax, daughter of Thomas, ninth Lord Fairfax, Baron of Cameron, in the Scotch peerage, and of Vaucluse, in Fairfax county. There were three children of this union, Constance, Clarence and Falkland. The last died in 1857, while in his teens, but the other son and the daughter passed the hurly-burly of war and became notable residents of New York.

Miss Constance Cary, already familiar to my readers as a beautiful and gifted war belle, and to readers of two conti-

nents as prominent in later literature, married Colonel Burton
Norvell Harrison, a young Mississipian who was Mr. Davis's
secretary from the Richmond advent to the collapse of the
Confederacy. He was professor of a university of his state.
when Colonel L. Q. C. Lamar urged Mr. Davis to appoint him
to the responsible post of confidential assistant. Harrison
yielded his desire to enter the army, accepted and served
with infinite credit to himself and advantage to his chief.
After the war he moved to New York, practicing law in connection with his brother-in-law, Clarence Cary, while his
wife rapidly won fame with her pen. Five years ago, while
in Washington on legal business, he died suddenly, in full
fruition of his early promise. He was a grave, dignified,
man, but of high nature.

There were four children of this marriage: Fairfax, Francis
Burton, Archibald Cary and Ethel. The daughter died in
infancy. The eldest son married his cousin Hetty, daughter
of John Bonne Cary, of Baltimore. He is assistant to the
president, and solicitor of the Southern Railway.

The second son, Hon. Francis Burton Harrison, M. C., has
made too recent a mark in politics and social life to need
recital. He married Mary, daughter of the noted Mr. Crocker,
of San Francisco. The later romance of his life has no connection with belles so remote as mine. By some strange
mistake of the Denver Democratic Convention, Mr. Harrison
was saved the enactment of *Aaron* to the *Moses* of Colonel
W. J. Bryan.

Archibald Cary Harrison married Helena Walley, and
all the brothers make the metropolis their home when not
abroad with their mother.

Since the sudden and stunning shock of her widowhood
Mrs. Harrison has been much abroad and her facile pen has
been at rest, but she has returned, and her work, it is to be
hoped, will be resumed regularly.

Clarence, former midshipman, C. S. N., married Elizabeth, daughter of the late Howard Potter, of Brown Brothers
& Co., and niece of Bishop Potter. Their sons were Guy
Fairfax Cary, who became a member of the New York bar
four years ago, and Howard, then a senior at Harvard.

Clarence Cary himself did some very clever acting during
the war on the amateur stage and on the naval war boards.
In his sailor rôle he served on the blockade runner, *Nashville*,
on the *Palmetto State* ironclad, off the Carolina coast and
on the James river fleet, proving himself a good officer.
After the war he studied law and practiced in New York,
where he has since resided and found leisure for extended
Oriental and other travel, and to make some admirable
translations of the classic poets, especially Horace. His
cousins are the Baltimore Carys.

Wilson Miles Cary, head of that branch, was brother to
Archibald Cary and closely related to the Fairfax family
by intermarriages in early years. He married Jane Margaret Carr, daughter of Dabney Carr and Hetty Smith,
moving to Baltimore where he reared a family of six—
Hetty, already noted here, Jenny, Mrs. J. Howard McHenry,
John Bonne, Wilson Mildes and Sidney C. Cary.

Mrs. Hetty Pegram married Henry Newell Martin, dying
in 1892, when her husband returned to England and survived her several years.

Wilson Cary never married. He has long been a member
of the Baltimore bar, but an expert and enthusiast in genealogy. He is now in London with Miss Cary and is pur-
suing his loved work there.

John Bonne Cary, the popular young soldier at Richmond
and equally popular Baltimore business man of today,
married Miss Frances E. Daniel. They have a family
of six, all adults, with eleven grandchildren. Four of the
five sisters married and the only son, Wilson M. Cary, Jr.,

married Miss Helen Snowden Lanahan and has two children. One of the daughters married Fairfax Harrison, son of Burton N. Harrison and Constance Cary. This was Miss Hetty Cary, godchild of her beautiful aunt.

John Cary's twelfth grandchild is a "Philipino," born at Manila to his daughter who married O. K. Gilman, a Johns Hopkins man, now professor in the U. S. Medical School, at that Province.

The Carys are not quite so numerous a family as some in Virginia history, yet they have enough to give their genealogical member something to think about.

A figure that attracted swift attention whenever duty brought him to Richmond, was Frederick Gustavus Skinner, colonel of that fine regiment, the First Virginia, which August, Munford and Williams had before commanded. Immensely tall, great-boned and of

COL. FREDERICK G. SKINNER
(1ST. VIRGINIA)

tremendous strength, his grave, intellectual face swept by a drooping gray mustache, this soldier was a marked man in any throng. Cadet of an old Virginia family, he was still a thorough Frenchman in many regards. His father, John S. Skinner, was a prominent man and a noted writer on agricultural and sporting subjects. He started the first farm paper ever printed in the Union, *The Plow, Loom and Anvil*. Later he owned and edited the *Country Gentleman* magazine. He was once acting postmaster-general of the United States and held the Baltimore post-office at the time of his death. He was with Francis Scott Key on the schooner when he wrote "The Star Spangled Banner." He married Elizabeth Glenn Davies of the old Baltimore family.

John Skinner was a warm and lifelong friend of the Marquis de Lafayette, and that hero took his son to Paris, educating him in his own family and at the famous military school of St. Cyr. He remained there ten years, and when the revolution came and Lafayette went to the palace to save the king from the mob, he found that young Skinner—who had escaped from school by a window—was at his side in the thick of the fray. After Paris, the youth passed through West Point and very soon was sent as attaché to the court of Louis Philippe.

In command of his regiment Colonel Skinner was distinguished for gallantry, and bore to his grave its guerdon in the shape of a hideous and unhealed shell wound. Of this his daughter wrote me:

"The hand-to-hand fight you describe in 'Crag Nest,'as *Ravanel's*, was very like father's charge at Manassas, where he killed three men with his sword, after receiving the bullet of each. He was so magnanimous that one night when I thought him dying, and I was feeling such bitter resentment, as though in response to my thoughts he opened his eyes and said: 'I hated to kill those brave men. How splendidly they stood by their guns.' "

Strange combination of reckless courage, of bluntness and urbanity, Skinner was. French in his tastes, universal in his acquaintance—and a *gourmet* by instinct and education, he was true Virginian, too. He chewed tobacco like a sailor in his camp; in the *salon* approached a lady like a prince, and never did man describe with such unction and such rolled, fat R's, *filet de truite à la sauce Tartare.*

Later, when I tried to make the old Valley homestead

the real hero of my romance of Sheridan's ride, the strong personality of this veteran—and that huge sword no other arm could sweep from scabbard—dominated "Crag Nest," and made him the centre of interest. Charles King, that fairest weigher of Blue and Gray equally, wrote me: "You have pictured the grandest old lion of all Rebeldom, in your Virginian *Colonel Newcome.*"

Colonel Skinner's wife was of notable descent, direct from Mildred, daughter of Colonel Francis Thorton, who married Colonel Charles Washington, younger brother of George Washington She was Miss Martha Stuart Thorton, of Montpelier, Rappahannock county.

COLONEL SKINNER AT 16
(MINIATURE OWNED BY LAFAYETTE)

Of this marriage there came to the young couple a son, Thorton, and a daughter, Elise. Constant to the old soldier as his shadow was this girl, who made even strangers friends by the frank and sunny nature that combined daughter, nurse and comrade in one. When he was stricken down this grand girl took him from the field, watched every fluttering phase of the long struggle 'twixt life and death, and literally brought him back from the border. Hear her own words:

"I cannot understand how you got such a likeness. Had you ever heard of our terrible ride, when we were taking him from the battlefield and were more afraid of a hemorrhage from the artery than of the Yankees, who were going from house to house, near Manassas, making prisoners of wounded officers? 'From that we were fleeing.' "

When partial peace came and with it partial recovery for the father, the daughter married a young Alabama soldier,

MRS. ISOBEL GREENE PECKHAM
(LONDON EXHIBITION PORTRAIT)

Thomas Tileston Greene. She had two children and removed to New York, where she educated them and a number of young ladies now notable in the great city's society. At this period Colonel Skinner lived with his daughter, having gone into journalism in his father's way. He was writing agricultural and sporting notes for the press when he died. Popular and beloved by old and young, the press published a memoir of him, and N. P. Willis wrote in the *Home Journal* the story of his Paris life at the court of Louis Philippe.

Mrs. Greene had good cause to be proud of her two children. The son, Frederick Stuart Greene, is a graduate of the V. M. I., and is now a civil engineer in New York. The daughter, Isobel, was a noted beauty, even in the metropolis, her popularity being gained not by her face alone. Before her mother's death she married Frederick Peckham. They now reside in London, and the fame of the American girl's beauty has crossed the ocean with her. The Peckhams have friends in the most fashionable circles of the world's metropolis. Mrs. Peckham has been presented at Court and made the staid dowagers stare, and her miniature is exhibited at the Academy views.

Only within a few years Mrs. Greene laid down her useful and eventful life, leaving genuine sorrow in a large circle of friends and a memory that will live. She went through many trying and strange adventures, the least of them being that she was the last person who spoke to Wilkes Booth, before Boston Corbett's silly bullet sealed his mystery forever. Miss Skinner was visiting her cousin, Dr. Richard Stuart, on the lower Potomac. None on the place knew that Lincoln had been assassinated, but about eight in the evening the doctor was summoned to attend a man who had sprained his ankle. Later the man hobbled into the dining-room, using a boat oar for a crutch. Dr. Stuart dressed the limb hastily while Miss Skinner got food for the half-famished patient, the servants having deen dismissed for the night. Within a few hours the man met his death and only then they learned that he was the assassin of Abraham Lincoln.

A very notable personality of the Richmond war-time, and later for many years on the streets of Mobile, was that of William Washington Augustin Spottswood, once surgeon-general, C. S. Navy. Towering high above average men, with muscular and vigorous frame, he walked with the roll of the veteran sailor;

MRS. T. TILESTON GREENE
(ELISE SKINNER)

his long white beard bannered to the breeze. He was archetype of the days ere "the men behind the guns" changed to the scientists in the conning tower. He was in the eldest line of the fifth descent from that famed Governor Spottswood, whose self and descendants are interwoven in all the wars and policies of colonial, Revolutionary and "Rebel" Virginia. The family was Saxon in origin and the name was Spottiswode; and its blood is allied to that flowing from the veins of Rolfe and his Indian princess wife. Today, its branches have rooted in every state that Virginia has foster-mothered.

In the early '40's Young Surgeon Spotswood wedded the beautiful and much sought Miss Mary Eastin, daughter of Mr. Thomas Eastin of Mount Vernon, Ala. This was one of the four weddings within as many years, that added to the fame of the great and hospitable mansion on the Mobile river; and it connected two families equally notable in Virginia and the Carolinas. The other weddings were those of three of Mrs. Spotswood's sisters: Matilda to Captain Alex. Montgomery, Lucinda Gayle to Dr. W. T. Rossell, and Fannie to Lieut. W. H. Tyler, all of the U. S. Army. The fifth daughter preferred civil to military life: marrying Col. R. P. Pulliam, of Fort Smith, Ark., an eminent lawyer.

The Eastins were likewise distinguished and well-descended. Lucinda Gayle, mother of Mrs. Dr. Spotswood, was a daughter of Matthew Gayle of Charleston, South Carolina, and was born there in 1798; developing into one of the most brilliant and great-brained women of the South. The head of the family was English and came over to the Virginia Plantations in the early days of the 17th century, with John Smith's expedition. His son, Matthew Gayle, migrated to South Carolina prior to the Revolution, where he married Mary Reese, a planter's daughter, on the "High Hills of Santee." His family went to Alabama, where Miss Lucinda was an ornament of the executive mansion of her brother, Governor John Gayle. The Gayle family fled to Mobile during the Indian wars and there Thomas Eastin met and won his noted wife. In 1823 they were married, and until her death at Mobile in 1872, she was one of the most virile thinkers, and most outspoken women of her day. Like many another strong-brained Southerner, she was opposed to secession from the first. She pointed out the hopelessness of a decision by the sword and warned of the future with the foresight of Cassandra. Later, however, when her prophecies had been verified, she was the bitter foe of reconstruction and lashed its creators and abettors mercilessly, with tongue and pen.

Of their nine children, only two are living, Mrs. Pulliam, of Eureka, Ark., and Mrs. Fannie Wait, of Little Rock.

Thomas Eastin, father of Mrs. Spottswood, was born at Lexington, Ky., in 1788, and youngest of a very large family, he was self educated. He moved to Tennessee and became known to Andrew Jackson: a close friendship springing up. He was colonel and quartermaster on General Jackson's staff, in the Seminole and Creek wars of 1812-17.

Then, camping with the general on the fine U. S. reservation, at Mount Vernon, Eastin was so delighted with its site that he later built there the famous home, burned in 1859. Singular coincidence it was that his grandson, Dr. Dillon J. Spotswood, of Mobile, saw his first service under the U. S. at the same spot, where his ancestor camped, with Jackson in the Indian wars.

Thos. Eastin was the pioneer printer and publisher of Alabama. He issued the "Halcyon" at St Stephens. Unfortunately, all its files and early records were lost in the burning of his Mount Vernon home. He died at the residence of his daughter, Mrs. Mary Eastin Spotswood, Monroe county, in 1865.

The living children of Doctor and Mrs. Spotswood are Thomas Eastin, Montgomery B., William Chase and Dillon J. Spotswood. George and Eastin were in the Confederate

Army, entering at eighteen and fifteen years respectively. Both won praise as good soldiers; and the younger was in prison at Camp Chase. He was married to Miss Caroline Mann, who left three children: Leo Dandridge, Curran Lamar and Manning W. Spottswood. The second wife, Miss Ella Hermann, has four children: T. Eastin, Jr., Ella Marion and Robert Lee.

George Washington, the eldest of these brothers, died at Mobile at the age of sixty-six, only while this page was going to press. The brother next him in age, Gayle Spotswood, died years ago, both he and George being bachelors.

Montgomery Barclay married Miss Josephine Otteson, of New Orleans, and is a timber merchant of Biloxi. This family is Malcolm Barclay, Winona L., Anita, Julian and Audrey.

Chase Spotswood married thrice. His first wife, Anna Thornton, left these: Anna Mary, Wm. Chase, Jr., and Harry Ingraham (recently dead). The first of these is now Mrs. Benjamin Toomer. The second wife, Adelaide Demouy, left two children: Marie Adelaide and Demouy. Of the present marriage to Miss Claudia Shields, there is one son, James Ellis.

Dr. Dillon J. Spotswood, following the example of his eldest brother, is a bachelor and practices in Mobile.

A very notable and equally picturesque factor of those days was Major Livingston Mims, of Georgia. Young, handsome and of elegant address, he was unique in an era of bustle and strenuous rush. He affected, even then, somewhat of the euphemism of the gallants of good Queen Bess' court.

I recall him as a young and well groomed captain on Gen. Joseph E. Johnston's staff. Not a generally popular man, at first touch, he was one that grew on better knowing. His comrade on the same staff, Major A. D. Banks, held that attribute in common with him; and both were notable men, in and out of military life. Mims was on quartermaster duty and Banks in the commissary. Banks was a popular fellow with his comrades and in later life was prominent in politics and made many warm and lasting friends. It is coincidental that Banks' wife—who was great granddaughter of Patrick Henry —was the school friend and roommate of Emma Mims' own mother.

Mims got deserved promotion on Gen. J. E. Johnston's staff, and the typical figure of latter-day Atlanta was "the Major," who was at one time its mayor, at most times president of its elegant Capital City Club and for many years *doyen* of its life insurance guild.

Rotund, always urbane, courtly and careful of the comforts and feelings of all, Mims was more regretted at his death than many a more famous publicist had been. He passed away

MAJOR LIVINGSTON MIMS

three years ago, well in his 80's, but never confessing any age. Had he lived in their day, the Major would have ranged with Mr. Brummell and Mr. Nash, their equal in *chic* and lacking their pettiness. He had brains and knowledge of men, was a reader of books as well, and what he himself called a "compensating" companion. Withal, he was elegantly profane enough to have served with "our army in

Flanders," but it was with a grace and deep feeling that lent the unction of knighthood to an oath.

He married a beautiful woman, who was gracious and pleasant in general society, of which the couple seemed equally fond. As wealth grew, they moved to the later well-known residence near Ponce de Leon circle. Then, and especially after the début of their daughter, Mrs. Mims entertained home people and strangers, but she suddenly dropped society as though it had been red-hot, and took to science—Christian of that ilk. She has gone to the length of the ism, has preached at home and abroad and been one of the most active and advanced agents of the much-berated sect. Her daughter—the magnificent, stately and universally known "Em" Mims, had never taken to the fad and, certes, my cheery and chivalrous old friend, her father, was seemingly no more scientific than religious. Yet his death left a great gap in Atlanta society and clubdom.

After leaving Georgetown Visitation convent, Miss Emma Mims entered society with *verve*; winning friends easily by her fund of grace and quickness, losing them sometimes by too much *sauce Tartare* upon her tongue.

Her wedding to Colonel Joseph Thompson collected society girls of her convent classmates from several cities, among them Misses Margaret Demoville, of Nashville, now Mrs. Herman Justi of Chicago; Daisy Irwin, of Mobile, now Mrs. Clisby, and Daisy Breaux, of New Orleans, elsewhere noted as the brilliant Mrs. Andrew Simonds, of Charleston, and now the wife of Barker Gummeré, of Trenton, N. J. Her life since has been known to all society; and her leaving it—suddenly, if not wholly unexpectedly—has renewed memory of her better traits. She has left one child only, the pride of her life, Livingston Mims Thompson, of New York.

CHAPTER XXII

WITH LAUGH AND SONG AND SATIRE

"AND there is a time to laugh," was the dictum of the wisest king in sacred history. Yet he also said there is a time to weep.

There was no home-leaving of Southern youth for the front, no whitewashed wall in the roughest hospital, no blackened smolder of barn and mill and home but wrote its epic of heroism and self-forgetfulness.

When the half-starved and march-worn shivered around smoky brush fires the moisture in their eyes too often had other cause. When Famine kept them grim companionship by the camp fireside and Fever stalked noisome and gaunt through their best defended lines; when news came from outraged homes far away, the men of the South dipped their pens in their hearts and wrote.

When the battle-flag forged to the front in fight or flaunted gaily in pursuit, their rifles rang in songs of hope and triumph as they laughed in the "Rebel yell." And ever and anon, through darkest midnight of their cause, from hospital and prison camp and high over the charging victory, rang out the broad guffaw or the cheery laughter of natural ring and wonderful digestion.

Yet the facile prince of war wits was Innes Randolph, engineer captain on the staff of that brilliant trooper, who himself laughed as he charged fiercest and sang as he rode back victorious, not a pæan of joy, but a rollicking soldier ditty—"Jeb" Stuart.

There were three of the Randolph brothers, of this branch of the name, in the Army of Northern Virginia—Innes, the oldest; John, captain of infantry, and Wilton, the youngest, and *post-bellum* secretary of the Southern Society of New York. All three had a peculiar strain of humor and a natural gift for music and poetry.

When the black days of '63 were upon us, and Mr. Davis issued a Thanksgiving Day proclamation, he set forth the best side of the dark theme. Promptly Innes Randolph put the state paper into burlesque rhyme, detailing point by point. I recall but one complete verse, that on Bragg's defeat:

> "*And Bragg did well, for who can tell—*
> *What merely human mind could augur—*
> *That they would run from Lookout Mount,*
> *Who fought so well at Chickamauga?*"

Randolph's serious poetry, while less known, was superior to his comic work. It had strength and delicacy welded, and his "Torchwork: A Tale of the Shenandoah," written at my request when I essayed the *Cosmopolite* magazine, of fleet memory, at Baltimore in 1866, is the best tale in verse of all the war-time.

One story of this wag cannot be omitted. On a "wild night"—in both senses—a rollicking party was led by him in a "round" that defied patrol and provost guard. Doorplates and signs were interchanged; and jumping at one of the latter, the joker's hand caught in the iron brace, hanging him suspended and in great pain. He called lustily, but cheerily for help: "Take me down! Quick! A wicked and a stiff-necked generation, searching after a sign!"

What this multi-sided genius did in art is elsewhere told.

What he did *not* do, and do well, is not recorded on memory's tablet.

He was eldest son of John Innes Randolph, of Virginia, who moved to Washington and was long a well-known resident of that city and Georgetown. Innes married Miss Anna King of the latter city, who survives and resides in Baltimore. They had four children, all inheriting much of the paternal gifts. But the eldest son died childless. Harold, the second, lives in Baltimore, being a skilled and popular musician and composer and long the musical director of the Peabody. The eldest daughter, Clare, married Thomas, son of Major Stuart Symington, and they have two children, Thomas and Catharine. These are the only direct descendants of the poet-wit. The other daughter, Miss Maude Randolph, is unmarried and lives with her mother in Baltimore.

CAPTAIN INNES RANDOLPH

Very lately a story has gone the rounds of the press, which *à la Buttercup*, "has mixed them children up." It stated that General Felix Agnus, of the Baltimore *American*, when a dashing captain of volunteers, was desperately wounded in the Seven Days battles before Richmond. Waking from his faint, he felt something heavy lying on him, which proved to be a badly wounded Confederate, moaning for water. Agnus recalled a canteen of cold coffee, reached for it and handed it to the man on him. The latter drank thirstily, sighed and returned it with the words: "Thank you, Yank—damn you!"

Years later, the story goes, General Agnus was telling the facts at a press convention in Philadelphia, when a fine look-ing delegate stepped forward and said he was the Confederate and his name was Major Innes Randolph. The story is a good one; would be great, indeed, were it correct. In truth, Innes Randolph was never a major, never was on Jackson's staff and never was wounded before Richmond. He was a captain on engineer duty under Stuart. John Randolph was in the battles of the Seven Days, and was badly wounded in the thigh at Cold Harbor, though no one recalls his having related the story, which such a joker would have done in convalescence or later.

In a late letter to me, General Agnus vouches for the facts of the story, but Innes Randolph's family confirm my view that it must have been John Randolph, his next brother, as the latter only was shot before Richmond. Further con-firmation of this odd mix-up comes from Mrs. Clem Clay Clopton. Her book quotes letters from her brother, Colonel H. L. Clay, and his wife (Celestia Comer), written just after the fights. Colonel Clay writes:

"Mr. Randolph, the *Sir Anthony Absolute* of your play, was wounded yesterday in the shoulder and thigh, and will lose the limb today."

He did not, however; but he was wounded only in the thigh—another proof of the way history was making itself.

John Randolph the second of the brothers, left two sons and a daughter. Wilton, who was the baby-soldier brother in Richmond days, left two sons and two daughters. The eldest boy died in Cuba, fighting to uphold the flag his father had fought against.

After the war Innes Randolph went into journalism, winning high praise for critical and editorial work on the Richmond *Examiner*. This secured him a position on the

Baltimore *American*, which he held with credit until his last illness.

Fighting, fun and fancy, in equal potencies, chemically compounded jolly and gallant Gray Latham, of the famed "Latham's Battery" in the A. N. V. He was wit, wag and poet, no danger of joke being too serious for him to laugh at and half the stories that went the round of court and camp began: "As Gray says." He sang sweetly, as "Eveline" proved; and his own "Castles in the Air" had dainty thought and neat verse, rounded with a chuckle, in none too restrained form. The *non sequitur* was his force, a dryness of absurdity unequalled save perhaps by Tom August and Ham Chamberlayne, but he lacked the acidity of both. One of his oddest pranks was when a party of officers, without leave of absence, "took the town" one night. The provost guard halted them. There were quick, steady-witted men in the crowd, but none had retort when the green provost asked for papers. But, with lordly sweep of his big arm, the artillerist answered suavely:

"Papers, sir! Why, we are all left-handed men!" and we passed the open-mouth guardian of discipline without let. And it was he who defined the duties of a quartermaster, to a lady seeking information:

"The quartermaster, madame, has three duties, all performed regularly. The first is to make himself comfortable; the second, to make everybody else uncomfortable; the third, to make himself *blamed* comfortable!"

To him, justly or not, were ascribed two stories on Mr. Macfarland's crisp dignity and perfect elegance of dress and manner. *Non e vero*, doubtless both, but who shall deny the *ben trovato?*

When Magruder's army fell back from the Peninsula on Lee's new base at Richmond it passed a line of gaunt, begrimed and wretched-looking men, hobbling and half-starved up Main street from Rockett's. The men eyed the smart banker curiously, as he stood on the bank's low porch, genuine pity in his face, but with no word that could aid them, *en masse.* Suddenly one "hero without a name" side-stepped to the pavement, halted and came to a "carry" as he whined:

"Sa-a-ay, mistur, kin we 'uns sleep in Reechmon' ternight?"

The other application was equally apocryphal.

In mid-war, a blockade dinner was tendered some important strangers. The host's trusted butler fell ill suddenly, but the best *restaurateur* in town supplied his place. All went well with the much-recommended substitute, save a rather unusual flourish, until the meats came on. One of these was a ham of princely size, wine dressed and flanked by a rare salad. These were to be helped from a side table.

Conversation in polite murmur was punctuating mastication. Suddenly clashed into it the wild click of steel on knife, that mocked a hand-to-hand fight with sabres. Then came the stentorian and repeated yell:

"Ha-a-ammm! an' sallud on th' side table! Gents, pass up yer plates fer ha-a-ammm an' sallud!"

Captain Woodie Latham, handsome, brave and true, had a wit of his own, but it withered in the light of his elder brother's. Both men are gone. After life's fitful fever they sleep well; while it lasted they did most things well.

Brilliant, misdirected Page McCarty was a veritable wit, in those sunny days of the early war, before the piquant subacid in him fermented into gall. Later, his X-ray showed clear through tissue; but it blistered.

McCarty, Will Myers, Innes Randolph and I had a habit of occasional letters in jingle, when at separate points, which gave the town topics of that day. They passed from one recipient to the next nearest, a sort of endless chain of mild gossip. One of Page's headings, yellow and smoke-stained, I found only a few years ago. It was written from near

Mason's Hill, when he and Hampden Chamberlayne were "blanketing together" in outdoor winter, and its caption read: "Off Chamberlayne's Cape (also his overcoat)."

It is sad to recall the promise of McCarty's young career, for he was brave, joyous and loyal to friends, and compare it with his after years, as he hobbled along to a neglected grave, with Remorse and Defiance on either side.   And the change was wholly wrought by his own hand.

MAJOR WM. B. MYERS

Will Myers was witty and full of quaint satire, but rarely bitter. On one occasion he described to General Breckinridge the details of a fight, in which the brigade of a rather slow commander had crumbled before the enemy. He ended his report: "And there tottered old . . . like a mud wall."

Thereafter, in that army, he was ever known as "Old Mudwall."

Myers saw a judge-advocate, who was a famous romancer, lead the other members of his court to a bar-room and tell them wild yarns. He told me: "He lied like a warrior taking his rest with his court-martial around him!"

Some crude rhymester whose swift zeal gave him corns on his prosodical feet, indited an ode to the great French general of the A. N. V. This Myers sent me, with his amended version, four decades having obliterated all save this;

"Oh! the North was evil-starred, when she met thee, Beau-
regard!
For you fought her very hard with cannon and petard, Beau-
regard!
Beau canon, Beauregard! Beau soldat, Beauregard!
Beau sabreur! beau frappeur! Beauregard! Beauregard!"

That was the "poet". Myers wrote it thus:

"Yes! the North was scarred and barred, and she took it very
hard
When we trumped her winning card, Beauregard!
Beau blagueur, Beauregard! Beau blesseur, Beauregard!
Beau Brummell, Beau Nash, Beau Hickman! Beauregard!"

A good and reliable soldier, as proved by his advancement
under the immediate ken of a leader like Breckinridge, Will
Myers was a man of delicate and refined culture and of innate
critical tact. His sense of humor spurred but never dominated
his judgment of men and affairs; and his broad, sunshiny
nature made men love him as well as many women thought
they did, and one noble one proved. He was the idol of a
cultured father and mother and in his visits to Richmond
added much to the bright society of their elegant and hospitable home.

A noted joker of that and of later time was General Zeb-
ulon B. Vance, of North Carolina. By turns congressman,
Confederate brigadier, senator and governor of his state
"Zeb" Vance's jests and epigrams were so quoted as to have
almost a "chestnutty" flavor, yet like that abused favorite,
they held their own peculiar aroma. The most repeated of them
all, owing possibly to its place of birth, but more to its touch
of nature, was his address to the buck rabbit. His brigade
lay in the woods at Malvern Hill, the well-timed shells show-
ering branches and twigs upon them from treetops overhead.
Dead stillness awaited the expected order to go in. Suddenly

a great white rabbit broke down the woods trail, at top speed toward the rear. From the tree that screened him General Vance yelled cheerily after him:

"Go it, stumptail! If I followed my impulse, I'd be with you!"

But wit was only the condiment that seasoned the strong meat of the North Carolinian's character and mentality.

CHAPTER XXIII

ALL the colonels of the great First Virginia were noteworthy men, but none was more widely known than Thomas P. August. He was a wag and a punster by nature and he talked in quips as naturally as though all men expected them. They went far and wide in repetition until he was really, as McCarty expressed it, "the most traveled by-tongue fellow in the army!" He was the real father of the over familiar retort, chestnutted by frequent misapplication. When the convention that carried Virginia out of the Union was debating that vital point someone said to August: "Well, colonel, I suppose your voice is still for war?"

"Yes, damn still!" was the quick reply that ended this conversation.

Just before the final evacuation of Richmond, rumors of that move were rife and every act of the departments was watched and reported. Colonel August was hobbling downtown on his crutches, when a friend called across: "Tom, the surgeon-general is removing all the medical stores!"

"Glad of it," he called back. "We'll get rid of all this blue mass!"

One very early morning, while on sick furlough, the officer limped into Ed Robinson's popular drug-store for needed seltzer water. Taking him for the proprietor, a mild old lady asked: "Can I buy a little hippo?"

"No, madame," the joker replied; "we give it away to cure the general chondria."

Major Willie Caskie, the quaint artist and joker of Mosaic memory, had a close kinsman who was so badly crippled by rheumatism that he could walk only with assistance from his negro body servant. Answering a comment on the fact, Willie Caskie said: "Yes, he reverses Noah of old"; adding in explanation: "Noah was an upright man and walked with God: Jim is downright crooked and walks with Ham!"

The inveterate major married pretty and gentle Miss Mary Ambler, of the old Huguenot colonials, who survives him.

He was equally apt as wit and draughtsman as he was as fighter. In capping verse and parody, he was as quick as Randolph. It was he who

MAJOR WILLIAM CASKIE

twisted the stirring lines "You can never win them back, Never, never!" from their patriotic to their Pharoaic sense, thus:

> *You can never win them back,*
> > *Never, never!*
> *And you'd better quit the track,*
> > *Now, forever!*
> *Though you cut and deal the pack*
> *And copper every Jack,*
> > *You'll lose stack after stack,*
> > > *Till you sever!*

A strong mentality and vast store of information was the asset of Colonel William M. Burwell, editor of *De Bow's Review.* As social interest, he extended lavishly the small coin of humor, minted at will. An able disputant and vigorous essayist, he dropped puns and epigrams like the fabled maid who scattered pearls with speech. Someone spoke of Mr. Davis's habitual gravity, when the editor retorted:

"Yet he is devoted to Benjamin, who is surely a Jew *d'esprit!*"

It was he who commented on the secretary of state's disputatious habit:

"All the cabinet expects Toombs to disagree with himself between meals!" Nor was it a surprise when his name was pinned to the cleverest, perhaps, of all the "Confederate Mother Goose."

That rollicking but most indicative string of satires had accidental birth. George Bagby's simple sanctum, with its "cartridge-paper tablecloth," was the "Wills' coffee house" of the war wits, lacking the coffee, but replacing it with frequent pipes and unhappily infrequent "nips," when appreciation sent a bottle their way. One night, during what Bagby called the "mire truce" of winter, Randolph, Myers, McCarty, Colonel Burwell, Will Washington, myself and a few others dropped into the den editorial. Soon the room was cloudy with smoke, but sunny with speech. Someone picked up the short but inspiring stub of George Bagby's editorial pencilholder and scribbled a verse on the paper tablecloth. Another read it, laughed, took the stub and scribbled in turn. The first one read was on that bold invader who dated despatches from "Headquarters in the saddle." It ran:

> *Little Be-Pope, he lost his hope,*
> *Jackson, the Rebel, to find him;*

> *But he found him at last, and he ran very fast,*
> *With his bully invaders behind him!*

The second took theme from that general most respected by his Southern opponents as a tactician and a man:

> *Little McClellan sat eating a mellon,*
> *The Chickahominy by*
> *He stuck in a spade; and a long time delayed,*
> *Then cried: "What a great general am I!"*

Next, the arch-enemy of all woman-respecting men had his turn:

> *Hey! diddle Sutler, the dastard Ben Butler,*
> *Fought women, morn, evening and noon;*
> *And old Satan laughed, as hot brimstone he quaffed,*
> *When the Beast ran away with the Spoon!*

The next was reminiscence of Barton Key's murder at Washington some years before:

> *Yankee Sickles came to fight, and Dan was just a Dandy;*
> *Quite quick to shoot when 'tother man had nary pistol*
> *handy!*

The "Cæsar of the Peninsula," as Lord King named McClellan, got this:

> *Henceforth, when a fellow is kicked out of doors,*
> *He need never resent the disgrace,*
> *But exclaim: "My dear sir, I'm eternally yours,*
> *For assisting in changing my base!"*

"Fighting Joe" Hooker had taught us to respect him, but he was hit too:

> *Joe Hooker had a nice tin sword;*
> *Jack bent it up one day.*
> *When Halleck heard, at Washington,*
> *He wrote: "Come home and stay!"*

Others on Pope and Butler ran thus:

> *Trickery, dickery, slickery Ben—*
> *Eluding and dodging the fighting men—*
> *Was never afraid of a matron or maid,*
> *But cent for no cotton, or silver, he paid!*

And, finally:

> *John Pope came down to*
> *Dixie town, and thought*
> *it very wise*
> *To sit down in a 'skeeter*
> *swamp and start at telling*
> *lies.*
> *But when he found his lies*
> *were out, with all his might*
> *and main,*
> *He changed his base to another*
> *place, and began to—lie*
> *again!*

Probably the most sur-
prised men of all who heard,
were the writers of these

MAJOR J. W. PEGRAM

skits when they were read from print, at a subsequent
meeting of the Mosaic Club. The authors had forgotten
them in intervening rush of graver matters and someone,
most probably Bagby, had joked the jokers by tacking the
name to each of the squibs.

One irrepressible wag, who never wrote a line or even
knew he was a wit, won a later width of fame as great as
any of his elders. "Jimmie" was the youngest of the three
gallant Pegram brothers and the only one who survived the
war, though he followed through it as grim and foremost
a fighter as Gen. R. S. Ewell. Pegram rose to major's rank,

despite his youth, as Ewell's adjutant-general. In camp, in society—at the sick-bedside, the retreat, or the hot pursuit he was full of original humor that had infection in it. A born mimic, he was a raconteur equal to Ran Tucker; a gift that gained him representation of a New York house, *post-bellum;* and aided his genial, manly nature to make him one of the most popular men—in society, trade and the clubs—that ever was sent "on the road" by the war. He lost his lovely wife, as noted before, after brief married life and never married again. But girls, as well as matrons and men, loved "Major Jimmie"; retold his jokes and spoiled his stories in a dozen states; while they later mourned his untimely death. He was a loyal friend, with all the courage of his race and the courtesy of the Old Virginia gentleman.

But it was not only in stirring if trying scenes, or in the cheery ones of the "mire truce," not only in the free or freezing air, that Rebel humor asserted supremacy. Even the half-spectres of hospital recuperation laughed over what they called their "lush." In one sick mess of the trying days, toward the end, a long, skinny Georgian was charging on a piece of stubbornly resisting neckbeef. His yellow face wrinkled in a grin as he drawled: "Say, fellers, didn't them fellers ez died las' spring jest *git* ther commissary, though?"

And even in the fetid starvation pens of prison camps, the unexchanged martyrs drowned the sigh of hope deferred in the jest at their own misery. One familiar example was the clever versed letter, sent from the grim walls on "Fort Delaware, Del.," as the prisoners' song called it. That was written by Thomas F. Roche, of Baltimore, to his mother, in close imitation of General Lytle's "I am Dying, Egypt, Dying"; and was a mock heroic plaint for a check to be sent the prison sutler. Too long to quote, its opening and final plea will show its humor under trying conditions:

> "*I am busted, Mother—busted:*
> *Gone th' last unhappy check;*
> *And th' infernal sutler's prices*
> *Leave my pocketbook a wreck!*"

And it ended with this human paraphrase:

> "*Ah, once more, among the lucky,*
> *Let thy hopeful buy and swell:*
> *Bankers and rich brokers aid thee—*
> *Shell, gentle mother mine—oh, shell!*"

Another satire, though grimmer, while of higher grade than Roche's, slipped through the portholes of Fort Warren. There Severn Teackle Wallis, the polished acidity of the Baltimore bar of yesterday, was long a political prisoner. On one Thanksgiving Day, when the "loyal" pulpits of Baltimore were expected to flame with patriotic fire over several Federal victories, a printed note sheet was mysteriously found in the prayer-seats of fashion. It had come, "underground," from Wallis's cell, at Warren. Only its opening and a few sample lines can find room here:

> "*O God of Battles, once again, with banner, trump and drum,*
> *And garments in Thy wine press dyed, to give Thee thanks*
> *we come!*
> *No goats nor bullocks garlanded to Thine red altars go:*
> *With brothers' blood, by brothers shed, our glad libations flow!*
> .   .   .   .
> *We give Thee praise that Thou hast lit the torch and fanned*
> *the flame—*
> *That Lust and Rapine hunt their prey, kind Father, in Thy*
> *name!*
> .   .   .   .

Where'er we tread may deserts spread, 'till none are left to
    slay;
And, when the last red drop is shed, we'll kneel again and—
    pray!"

An irrepressible war wag was that correspondent from
the Atlantic lines who hid his light under the pen-name of
"Solitary John." The real one I have never been able to
find, but his quaint letters helped to make the starving
fighters "laugh and grow fat." One of them began:

"Old Sherman, like Old John Brown's soul, 'is a marching
on,' and double-quicking. When Tecumseh was born,
his dad said to the nurse: 'This is a nipping and an eager
heir,' and proved himself prophet, to our loss. Billy is
making Johnny as mad as a March hare by marching here
and there. Yesterday we were ordered to cook, *and eat*,
ten days' rations immediately; and for the next ten, nothing
could be heard but

    The rhyming and the chiming of the rammer and
      the hammer,
    Keeping time, time, time, in a hungry sort of rhyme."

This "Johnny" laughed off suspense and starvation in
the free air and with broad sunshine about him. But even
in the smoke-thickened atmosphere of Vicksburg, with
ceaseless burst of shells, dwindling ranks and absolute starvation wasting the men who burrowed like rats to catch rare
sleep: there in that worse than Valley Forge of later war
for opinion's sake, joke and jest leavened the heavy strain.
Endless stories of the "pounded city" are sworn to.

One stifling noon a Mexican veteran colonel crept out of
the guard casemate to hunt a scarce possible bottle. A
whoo and a whiz, then a small earthquake, as a ten-inch
shell dropped just before him. A wild yell and a clatter
of swift-running boots brought the query: "What's that?"

Peering from the earth-thatched casemate, Major Tom Reed answered: "Nothing but the kernel breaking from the shell!"

When the bombardment grew hot and more accurate, a wooden house on a hill was deserted. Some wag charcoaled on it: "For Rent: Inquire of Davis & Pemberton." That night a mortar shell tore a great hole through the building and soon the crayon had marked out the spared sign and improved it: "Rented, by Grant and McPherson!"

When the torn and splintered city was surrendered after sufferings and horrors unparalleled, a scrawled card was found pinned to the posts supporting a subterranean mess room. It was a *menu* showing the varied modes of mule cooking, dated from the "Hotel de Vicksburg, Jeff Davis Co., proprietors." Broadly humorous, it listed: "Soup: Mule tail. Boiled: Mule bacon, with Polk greens. Roast: Saddle of Mule à *la* teamster. *Entrees:* Mule head stuffed, Reb fashion; Mule beef, jerke à *la* Yankee; Mule liver, hashed à *l'explosion*. Dessert: Cotton-berry pie, *en* Ironclad, China-berry tart. Liquors: Mississippi water, vintage 1492, very inferior, $3. Limestone water, late importation, very fine. Extra (black seal) Vicksburg bottled-up—$4. Meals at Few Hours, Gentlemen to wait upon themselves. Any inattention in service to be promptly reported at the office. Jeff & Comp., Props."

This was only one more proof that strong arms and strong stomachs went to aid the barefoot boys to make their strong arms uphold so long the tottered fabric, built upon their hopes and painted with their blood, still standing in its ruins as their monument.

CHAPTER XXIV

ART AND ARTISTS IN DIXIE

WHILE the art of war was the consuming study in the capital, with old and young, man and woman, the gentler arts were not allowed to fall wholly into disuse. The sentiments and the scenes of the day were suggestive ones, and souls that had once been touched by the sacred fire were wont to glow afresh and sometimes spring ablaze.

Men had busier and more needed avocations, it is true; materials were hard to get at first and later were impossible to obtain. But the painted record of the war was so valuable a one and was made under such trial and discouragements that it is the more remarkable that its conservation was not more looked to and that examples extant are so rare and hard to find.

VIRGINIA MOURNING HER DEAD.
(SIR MOSES EZEKIEL.)

Most pictures that won note, and probably all that remain

275

today, were what may be classed as incident pictures. They were conceived in the very throes of action of some great event, perfected in discouragement and often danger.

There were a number of pictures produced in Richmond during the war, and probably in other sections of the South, that were good artistically, and some that had real intrinsic art-value wholly dissevered from historic use.

Nearly equal to Washington in the number of his paintings, and quite his equal in popularity, was John A. Elder. This gifted and manly painter was the son of a Fredericksburg bootmaker, and with common school education. He had, however, real genius and great ambition and with them he coupled industry and genial nature. While a soldier in the ranks he proved a rapid and faithful reproducer of the men and movements around him. Old John Miner of his native town, took deep interest in the youth and proposed to send him to Europe, and this was done by several gentlemen advancing fifty dollars each. This, Elder only took on agreement to pay it back—a pledge he later fulfilled to the last dollar.

His first success was "The Scout's Prize." A medium canvas shows two horses at top speed through a wintry Virginia forest. One, ridden by the ill-clad "Reb," with slouch hat drawn down upon his speed-lowered head, was bony, sorry and jaded; his rough coat flecked with the foam of plucky effort and his red-veined eyes walled backward to the unceasing thud of close-pursuing feet. These were from hoofs of a splendid troop-horse, accoutred for a general's mount, his sleek coat and high head telling the tale of provender-bred mettle.

Admirable in drawing, artistic in contrast and with Meissonier-like fidelity to detail, the brutes told the story of plenty and privation that opposed each other through four long years. And the constancy that drew out their weary length, that made each capture an era rather than an episode, was seen in the gleam that lit the half-shadowed face bent above the neck of the ridden horse, as the trooper tugged at the resisted bit of the led one.

"The Crater" told the details of that hand-to-hand slaughter before Petersburg when the Federal mine under the near-lying Confederate centre was countermined and exploded. Its scene was in mid-fight. Under dense, low-hung masses of smoke, lurid jets of flame shot high, and on them rose the torn limbs and trunkless heads of the victims of War's devilish delight. Writhing, or stark upon what ground was visible, stretched the forms in blue and gray, mixed in "dizziest dance of death." This picture was sold for a good price just after the war to a British member of parliament. Elder reproduced it, somewhat enlarged, and the copy was purchased by General Mahone. His widow sold it to the Westmoreland Club of Richmond, where it now hangs. "Appomattox," the most suggestive and reminiscent of Elder's works, was the valued possession of Joseph Bryan, at his beautiful and historic home, Laburnum. The conception and figure-drawing, are admirable. Of his pictures, Mr. Bryan wrote me in a personal letter, which I make bold to quote, that he saw the canvas in the window at Tyler's, shortly after the war:

"I was struck by the picture, and went in to ask the price, which was only $50; but that was a large sum to me then and I took time to consider. I did, however, after a day, buy the picture at the price. I was gratified to learn that its removal from the window caused many inquiries. It had attracted much attention, but the population were not able to gratify their appreciation by even inquiring the price. . . . As to 'The Scout's Prize,' to which you refer, I have a copy of that which I particularly prize, because I had almost that identical experience myself, while with Colonel Mosby, in the winter of '65."

What became of Elder later I am not sure, but I think he died before his early promise, amid discouraging surroundings, fruited fully into the success it seemed to warrant.

Another artist, one who seemed to find a specialty in sea views, was Lieutenant John R. Key, of the engineer corps. Tall, boyish-looking, bright-witted and a trifle eccentric, he was "the grandson of The Star Spangled Banner," as Myers put it. Sumter seemed to grow chronic with him, for, with really excellent taste for landscape and a perseverance and pluck that overcame difficulties, he spent all his spare time and more than all his spare change, on the crude but costly materials for his bombardment stretches of sea view, punctuated by puffy cannon smoke.

But the pictures won attention and commendation, for they were faithful to their not exciting theme. Perseverance, however, found material reward in several *post-bellum* sales of the Sumter canvases, but he did better work then.

We went together, the summer succeeding the surrender, to spend months along the slopes of Cheat Mountain and fish in the river of that name, he sketching and I scribbling on the pioneer volume of Southern song. Some very clever bits he did then of mountain scenery, and later of that in California and its coast, found ready sale. Some of them were the pioneer of picturesque railroad advertising and specimens were in the old Corcoran Gallery and other collections. But Key was practical beyond the wont of artists. He exhibited four of his Sumter canvases in Washington and New York, selling two of them later to Admiral Dahlgren, and the others to a London M. P.

In 1869 Key made studies through California, and in the next year went to Paris and there painted "The Golden Gate." This he sent to the Centennial at Philadelphia, and it received the first-class medal. His most important later work was illustration of the World's Fair at Chicago. Of that he painted four large pictures (10x20 feet). These were taken by the state of Illinois and were made important parts of its exhibit at the first Omaha Exposition; a separate gallery being built for them. At the second Omaha, Key was made art director. Since, he has produced many pictures of the Buffalo and St. Louis Expositions; fourteen of the former now being the property of the Buffalo Historical Society.

Recently he returned to the home of his youth and took a studio in the Corcoran Gallery. There he is busy making studies for an elaborate suite of Washington views, which are to form, on completion, the scenic history of the capital.

A gifted young Virginian also painted in Charleston harbor. Conrad Wise Chapman (named for David H. Conrad and Governor Wise) was son of John G. Chapman who painted "The Marriage of Pocahontas," for the rotunda at Washington. He had been a V. M. I. cadet but was in Rome with his father; ran the blockade and joined a Kentucky regiment and was badly wounded at Shiloh. General Wise had the youth transferred to his brigade as ordnance officer to Tabb's 59th Virginia, where he won fame in the attack on Williamsburg. Later, at Charleston, Beauregard detailed him for engineer work. In 1864 he was secretary to Bishop Lynch, on his noted mission to Rome; and was en route home when he read of Appomattox. He fled to Mexico, thence back to Italy, and lost his mind temporarily. He had painted many and varied sketches of battle scenes, mainly of Kentucky troops in action; and his father etched them at Rome and gained them much favor. The artist recovered his mind, married in Mexico; and now resides in New York in hermit like fashion.

William Ludwell Sheppard was another Richmond boy

whose work even then gave decided promise. He essayed nothing very pretentious and his later results have been made popular in *Harper's* and other New York magazines and journals. In 1861 he was at the Academy of Design, New York, but promptly came South and volunteered in the Richmond Howitzers, serving all the war and winning his lieutenancy. *Post-bellum* he painted one work which became notable—"Virginia in 1864," an artillery duel. This was much copied and is still very popular with the "boys." He also did some clever and effective sculpture, especially "Johnny Reb," a statuette of the Rogers school. Equally effective were his typical Confederates, representing infantryman, artillerist and trooper. He also did the Soldiers' and Sailors' monument, that for the Howitzers', and for General A. P. Hill. He has drawn considerably for New York publications and still resides in Richmond.

Innes Randolph, that Briareus in accomplishments, sketched almost as cleverly as he wrote, improvised and sang. He was a lightning illustrator and ever in demand for the unceasing "shows" of those dear women who never wearied in well-doing. Sometimes Randolph's programs in poetry and picture were better worth the entrance fee than the entertainment they explained. Unhappily, not one of them is now in existence or at least traceable by diligent search. He was a natural but untaught sculptor; several death masks and a bust of himself being especially fine.

In some important instances the chisel replaced the brush in Richmond. Alexander M. Galt was a notable example. This Norfolk man showed early promise that had already given result in fine and classic marbles of Thomas Jefferson, President Davis and General Jackson. Then, while arranging for new works in every hour to be spared in those trying days, his career was cut short abruptly. Galt was seized with smallpox in Richmond, and despite skill and care of loving friends, died there in 1863.

Sir Moses Ezekiel was another Richmond boy who turned to art in early life. He was a student of the V. M. I., at Newmarket. Later, he went abroad, perfected himself in sculpture and has been a facile and industrious worker. He designed a handsome allegorical fountain for Cincinnati, and the fine figure of "Virginia Mourning Her Dead" in the campus at Lexington, at the entrance of Jackson Memorial Hall, was donated by him, in 1903, to his *alma mater*. Years ago he was made a Chevalier by the Italian government, and he now resides at Acme, in the land of flowers, art and spaghetti.

CHEVALIER MOSES EZEKIEL

In the June of 1907, there were pleasant observances at the University of Virginia, to receive another great work of Chevalier Ezekiel. This is a fine Homeric group, in heroic bronze, donated by Mr. J. W. Simpson, of New York, and the sculptor. Hon. Robt. L. Harrison, of New York, and Dr. Edward N. Calisch, of Richmond, presented it for the donors. It was received by President Alderman; and Dr. Thomas Nelson Page spoke of the sculptor and his growth in art, as well as of his patriotism.

The Homeric group presents the blind Homer, resting on a stone by the wayside; the graceful young Egyptian guide recumbent at his knee.

Coincident with his work upon the Homer, Ezekiel, made the heroic Jefferson, for the city of Louisville, in commemoration of the great founder of the University of Virginia. He is now perfecting, at his studio in the Baths of Dioclesian, a new heroic statue of Stonewall Jackson.

Some unique contributions to art emanated from Major William H. Caskie, of the artillery. A born joker, he was as reckless in his fun as he was in his fighting and other trifles of life—and death. His bump of veneration was never visible to the amateur phrenologist. Like Randolph, his sketches were often the extreme of caricature and took original expression. He would catch an admirable likeness of some civil, military or religious notability, but always with a twist of face and form. These heads topped figures cut from the proper cloth and decorated with rank insignia or other hall-mark. These pasquinades were always recognized and appreciated. The completed result was always a joy to the sinner, but anything rather than contentment to the subject. Caskie's little men were great prizes in society and in the distant camps to which they traveled, until illegible from dingy thumb marks.

Last, but nowise least, Willie Myers comes up dainty and correct in his drawing and painting, as he was in every regard of life. He had seen much good painting and was a fair enough critic to be merciless to the bad, even when that of a near friend. A neat executant himself, he had no patience with sloppiness in any department of art. So his judgment was much sought, though known to be flattering in rare instances.

Myers left a number of clever sketches and a few things more important. These, if they have withstood the touch of time, have a better value than that of mere reminiscence.

It is pleasant to recall that my first essay in the novel, "Cross Purposes," was illustrated by him in 1865.

The art photographic, if not precisely in its infancy in war-times, was scarcely out of skirts. Alas the day! Kodak and pocket camera, now so fiendish and universal, had then been the boon of boons.

The horrors of Daguerre, the ambrotype—and more often the tin-type—seized on the beauties and the brave, to hand them down to posterity in something *à la* Caskie.

Canvas had early been replaced by burlaps, domestic, or even tent cloth. Key painted Sumter on the first two and Washington used the last for "Latané." Tubes, brushes and all tools, as well as decent vehicles, were procurable only through the blockade. In the later days of the war I saw white drugs and castor oil used to prime a large canvas.

All this combined to make most pictures destructible and the lacking camera let them slide,

> "*Like the tenants that leave without warning*
> *Down the back entry of time.*"

Photos there were, but the secret of lifelikeness, and especially that of indestructibility, had not been whispered to expectancy. Had it been, what different idea had these pages been able to give of some who are missed altogether; of more who are done scant justice, even in the most skilful of modern reproduction.

THE BURIAL OF LATANÉ

MISSES PAGE WALLER, VIRGINIA PEGRAM, MATTIE PAUL, LIZZIE GILES, MATTIE WALLER, ANNIE GIBSON AND IMOGEN WARWICK

CHAPTER XXV

A VANISHING PICTURE

So important in history and in sentiment is the "Burial of Latané," so personal its interest and so singular its disappearance, that it demands a special history.

Washington was a Virginian by birth, claiming descent from the eldest stock of his name. He was a reticent fellow, of intensely nervous temperament, as is frequent with the art-instinct. In his case this was heightened by a lameness, apparently congenital, that slightly disfigured but in no sort disabled him. Those who knew him best in *ante-bellum* days at Washington never heard him allude to his lameness or its cause, nor did he seem to have closer relatives, although we understood that his mother was of the Dandridge family.

He had taste and facility, but was an erratic worker. Dusseldorf had been his *alma mater* and Leutze claimed him as an old pupil. He went to Richmond early in the war, after leaving several pictures at the capital, in the galleries of W. W. Corcoran, Mr. James McGuire and others. Well educated, polished and traveled, with refined tastes, fair tenor voice and fine address, despite his recurrent moodiness, Washington soon made foothold in the best Richmond society. Affable ordinarily, he made no close intimates, painting in West Virginia, about the Gauley section, and sometimes near the Potomac.

Then came the retreat from the Peninsula, the meteor campaign of the Valley, Seven Pines and the Seven Days' Fights. Between the last two came the inspiration for Washington's great picture.

The armies of Lee and McClellan lay before Richmond, like bloodhounds in leash, ready to spring at each other's throat. Only the tension of discipline kept apart the grapple, in which the tug-winning meant so much to the Blue—and all to the Gray.

McClellan waited, with his usual over-prudence, "for a more propitious moment to strike"; Lee, as his wont, waiting for McClellan.

Inaction, pregnant with wounds and horror and bloody death, lay supine between the armies. The sickly sun of early summer basked on the feverish hosts, eager to move but shackled by strategy. And in this siesta "Jeb" Stuart, chafing himself and feeling need of movement for his men and mounts, proposed to General Lee a circuit around the rear of the enemy.

The reconnaissance was to be in some force; was to gather information of outlying rear positions of the Federal and to round up such stock and supplies as went on hoof. The command was intrusted to Fitz Lee, with his own and Rooney (W. H. F.) Lee's brigades and with Captain William Latané, of the former, commanding the advance guard. The affair was successful in all regards. Quantities of stock were driven from the Federal herders, and only the mere show of opposition was made until the second morning. Then a hot skirmish in force took place; the Federals were driven back and the Confederates lost one man, Captain Latané. His younger brother, James, a preacher, and later bishop, took charge of the body and waited at the roadside while the ruck of pursuit of the bluecoats swept by. Then a corn cart loaded with sacks passed on its way to mill—the long inaction making the Hanover county folks almost forget that they were in flagrant war.

The cart belonged to Westwood, the family seat of Mrs. Catherine Brockenborough, that lay a few miles away on the main road of the Peninsula. It was speedily emptied and the sacks hidden in the brush. The body of the gallant young trooper was tenderly laid in the improvised hearse and the mourning brother and the faithful negro walked by it to the plantation. There the lady of the mansion was absolutely alone, save for the presence of a few trusted slaves.

The Peninsula, a narrow slip of land embraced by the Pamunkey and Chickahominy rivers, was the theatre of much stirring action during the war. It had just been made memorable by the retreat on Lee's army before Richmond, of John Bankhead Magruder's small corps, with which he had so brilliantly held off McClellan's overwhelming force at Yorktown, and in the slow and rear-guarded retreat. It was to live anew in picture and poetry and go in classics down the ages in the light of this "Pamunkey Raid" to the White House on that stream.

A fertile and beautiful tract, it was the seat of several important families; notable among its homesteads being those of Mrs. Brockenborough and her sister, Mrs. Willoughby Newton, mother of the former Bishop Newton, of Virginia. The latter, Summer Hill, lay on the main road, directly opposite Westwood. At the former place Mrs. Newton was entertaining her refugee nieces, the Misses Dabney, and her daughter-in-law, Mrs. William Newton. Two little children of the latter, Catherine and Lucy Newton, were there also, but there was no other white person on the place and the only men were old Uncle Aaron and a few faithful slaves.

Mrs. Brockenborough was the only white at Westwood.

Busied about her kitchen when the cart drove up, she sped to find the cause of its premature return. Young Latané told her the sad story and that he, perforce, must rejoin his command. He had given his horse to a wounded comrade and there was none to replace it. Roman as many Confederate matrons had proved themselves, the lady of Westwood recalled a steed hidden at a distant farm. She spared one of her men as a guide, comforted the stricken soldier with promise of proper burial for his dead, and sent him on to fight again for the Cause she loved.

This duty to the living done, she addressed herself to the sadder one before her. The slain man was prepared for burial, a simple coffin fashioned at the plantation carpenter-shop and the return of the messenger waited for. The negro came at last, but had been unable to reach the minister he had been bidden to summon beyond the Federal lines.

All day Mrs. Brockenborough waited; going at sunset to her sister and nieces across at Summer Hill. Next day still no parson came, only the rumor that he had been refused passage by the pickets.

Then, at sunset, the weeping women collected about the grave Old Aaron had dug, and Mrs. Newton, standing at its head, sent him to his eternal rest with the solemn ritual of the Episcopal Church. Never, perhaps, had its words seemed more solemn or more meaningful. The poet and the painter made equally vivid use of this scene. Thompson's verse has as much color as Washington's pigment:

> " *For woman's voice, in accents soft and low,*
> *Trembling with pity, touched with pathos, read*
> *Over his hallowed dust the ritual for the dead:*

> " *'Tis sown in weakness, it is raised in power'—*
> *Softly the promise floated on the air,*
> *While the low breathings of the sunset hour*

Came back responsive to the mourner's prayer.
Gently they laid him underneath the sod
And left him with his fame, his country, and his God!"

As a gentle woman's voice spoke the Promise, Mrs. Brockenborough and the two others acted as mourners, the pretty little children strewing flowers over the cavalry overcoat that palled the rough bier.

An old tree, a sapling then, marks the spot in the family burial ground at Summer Hill, where Latané, the sole victim of the raid around McClellan, was laid to rest. When the bloody tide of battle rolled the Northern Army back to its base, for seven consecutive and horrid days Summer Hill was seized for a Federal hospital. The ladies were relegated to the upper floor, and the field operating tables were set up on the lawn beneath the windows. Pitiful as grewsome it must have been to them to hear the groans of the wounded; the quick, stern order for removal of those who died beneath the knife.

Grim old Sherman had not then stamped it as an epigram, but those tried women felt in their hearts the ugly truth that "War is Hell!"

Among those present Mrs. Brockenborough lived until two years ago; an inmate of the Presbyterian Home for old ladies, at Richmond. She was far advanced in years, and had lost her sight entirely forty-one years ago. The two little girls, Catherine and Lucy Newton, are now Mrs. Walter Christian, of Richmond, and Mrs. St. Clair Brookes, of Washington.

John R. Thompson and William D. Washington almost simultaneously took up the theme, to its immortalizing and their own. "The Burial of Latané" was to live in poetry and in color. The poet wrote what Tennyson pronounced "the most classic poem of the Civil War." The painter limned a picture which, under less clouded skies and in more happy conditions of commercial art, had won him fame and fortune.

Singularly enough, this picture disappeared and no trace of it remains. At the peace, Washington took the canvas to England, hoping for a better price from some wealthy sympathizer there. Falling into financial straits before this was possible, he sold it to L. P. Bayne, a Southern banker and broker, of Washington and New York. Reliable Confederates saw the Latané in 1874.

Mr. Bayne died, and the picture disappeared. Nó trustworthy trace of it has since been made. Report was commonly accepted that it was later bought by a rich New Yorker, resold in Chicago and was destroyed in the great fire. The cow of Mrs. O'Leary kicked the bucket on October 8, 1871.

No one thing in my researches for these pages has caused the bootless correspondence and query of its disappearance, and I have been unable to find one fact later than 1874. Ten or twelve prints were made from the best negative procurable. The portraits were changed, and the photographs were destined to prove mementos of the artist's gratitude to his models. With his usual procrastination, he held them for some reason. One I secured, the others disappeared, but no one of the ladies ever received her copy. Mine was lost in some way, and no efforts of art dealers or of curio stores have later been able to recover a copy, even with the bait of considerable cash. The Nemesis of mystery seems to have followed all things in the later history of this fine and historic work. A steel engraving was made in 1868, and other copies later, I believe.

It was in the Pegram home that his final decision to paint it was reached and Miss Virginia Pegram volunteered to find the needed models. Their first meeting was beneath her roof. Ardent as earnest, these society girls entered heart and soul into the theme, lending their fair faces and forms to long and tedious posing during the heat of Southern summer, and trudging back and forth to his not too elegant studio through sun and storm.

The men, from time to time, "played many parts" and smoked many pipes. Myers, Randolph, McCarty and the writer were variously the negro, the corpse on the bier and occasionally the critics. The second rôle was less comfortable than the last. To lie prone for forty minutes under a heavy cavalry overcoat, on a rough cot and beneath a sun-heated tin roof was not inspiring, save with changed first syllable.

But at last the painting was done; was exhibited on Main street and created quite a furor.

Indeed, had Confederate pockets been fitted to the appreciation of the moment, the artist had grown suddenly rich at the hands of some early purchaser. Some of this was perhaps due to the beauty and popularity of

PAGE MC CARTY   WILLIAM B. MYERS
WILLIAM D. WASHINGTON

the models. Mrs. Newton was represented by Mrs. Leigh Page, eldest of the Waller sisters, and now the widow of a well-known lawyer and soldier. Miss Jennie Pegram, now Mrs. David McIntosh, of Baltimore (the figure in mourning), posed for Mrs. Brockenborough, the one nearest to the rapt reader of the ritual. One of the models corroborates my memory thus: "At the foot of the grave is Mattie Waller (Mrs. Ralph Cross Johnson, of Washington), Lizzie Giles (now Mrs. Sam Robinson, of Washington) leans on her shoulder, weeping. Between Jennie Pegram and Page is the demure figure of Mattie Paul, the only likeness in the group, I think." The little Newton girls of the original scene were substituted by little Imogen Warwick and Miss Annie Gibson, now living in New York.

For the reason that Southern men of means were using them for grim facts, rather than for sentiment, at that moment, the much praised picture found no purchaser. Gradually the incident became absorbed in newer and as striking ones and the painting became an old story. Washington painted many others possibly as good artistically. Of them the most important is "Jackson at Winchester," now owned by John Murphy, of Richmond. There is action and fine color in this, the likeness of the general being claimed as the best extant. There are many minor works of similar class and a number of portraits of noted men connected with the army and at Lexington and other points of his state.

After the war Washington disappeared from Richmond into a nowhere of his own, carrying the Latané with him. That he was in Europe is sure and there, as stated, it was sold. When he reappeared later and took the chair of fine arts at Lexington—founded there presumably for him by the banker, W. W. Corcoran, of Washington—the painter was reticent on all matters, and especially about this work. The mystery may never be solved, for Washington died at the school, and I have failed of all information thence as elsewhere.

CHAPTER XXVI

SOME HISTORY BUILDERS

ICI REPOSE M. A. LAURE VILLERÉ, *épouse du major* G. T. *Beauregard*, NEE LE 22 MAI, 1823, DECEDEE LE 21 MARS, 1850.

> *Esprit descendu du ciel, tu y es remonté:*
> *dors en paix, fille, épouse et mère chérie.*

IN the old country graveyard at Florissant, the plantation home of the Beauregard family in St. Bernard Parish, Louisiana, one may read this tender inscription on the stone that covers the grave of the beautiful daughter of a great colonial family, who was in this life the wife of a great Confederate general. Translated it reads: "Spirit from Heaven, thou hast returned; there sleep in peace, beloved daughter, wife and mother."

MRS. G. T. BEAUREGARD
(LAURE VILLERÉ)

This sequestered grave recalls the union of two great Creole families, the Villerés, of the old Magnolia plantations, and the Toutant de Beauregard, of which the maternal strain was the famous de Reggio.

How far back the Welsh Toutant family dates there is no record, though its position and leadership in Wales indicate a long line of its chiefs; the first of whom I find accurate historic detail is Tider the Young, who headed the last rebellion of Wales, before Edward First brought that province under the English crown 1281 A. D. Defeated and captured, Tider escaped and fled to France with a price upon his head. Still a youth in his teens, his prowess and fine person gained him service under Philip IV (the Fair). They gained him moreover, as wife, Mlle. de Lafayette, who was in the suite of the princess, the king's sister. Friction was hot between the two nations and Henry summoned Edward to France to acknowledge his suzerainty of the fortresses in Guienne. War was imminent, but was averted by Edward's proposal to marry Marguerite, which delayed alliance was consummated only in 1299. Tider went to England with his wife in the new queen's suite, but the king objected to his presence, as a tainted rebel; and the queen induced his sending to a charge in the continental possessions of England. There he prospered, as did his son, Marc. After the latter recovered his father's property at Saint Ange, influence got him a position under the English crown. The name of Tider was still odious to British ears, and Marc changed it to Toutant—from the old Gaelic—and that surname held for the Beauregard ancestors for three centuries. At the end of the sixteenth century the last male of the Toutant name died. His only daughter married Sieur de Beauregard, whence the family name of the American branch. When the "de" was dropped and replaced by a hyphen is not recorded; but the general used neither.

Jacques Toutant-Beauregard was the first to reach *La Louisiane* bringing a flotilla with supplies in de Bienville's governorship, and carrying back American timber. His success won him the cross of St. Louis from the *grand monarque*. He returned to Louisiana and married Magdalen Cartier. Of his three sons, Louis Toutant Beauregard married Victorine Ducros, daughter of a wealthy planter, of St. Bernard Parish. Of their three sons, the youngest, Jacques Toutant-Beauregard, married Héléne Judith de Reggio in 1798. Of their seven children, the third was Pierre Gustave Toutant-Beauregard, of Confederate fame.

Old as is his paternal ancestry, that of his mother is even more illustrious. He is of direct descent from the Dukes de Reggio. His great-grandfather, Chevalier Francois Marie de Reggio, cousin to the reigning Duke, had distinguished himself under his friend, Duc de Richelieu, at the siege of Bergen-apzoom; was given a commission and sent to Louisiana with his command by Louis XV. When the province went under Spanish rule this chevalier was made royal standard bearer, with other offices. He was close kinsman also to Marquis de Vaudureil, another colonial governor of Louisiana. Of his marriage to Mlle. Fleurian two sons were born, of whom the younger, Chevalier Louis Emanuel de Reggio, married Mlle. Judith Olivier de Vezin. Her daughter, Héléne Judith, was the mother of our general.

When eleven years old young P. G. T. Beauregard was taken to New York and placed under the charge of two veteran officers of Napoleon's army, Messieurs Peugnet. At sixteen years he entered West Point, graduating second in the class of '38, among forty-five members, and becoming lieutenant of engineers before he was of age.

At the academy he was quiet and studious, but watchful of his rights, courteous but determined in their maintaining and was quick-witted and a leader in sports and the riding school. He is credited with having kicked a football beyond cadet limits for the only time on record; and a much assigned witticism is pretty well conceded to him. The professor of engineering, quizzing the class, shot out at him the query:

"Cadet Beauregard, should the *trench cavalier* escape, what would you do?"

"Well, sir," was the instant reply, "I should vault on the

GENERAL G. T. BEAUREGARD

cheval de frise and put off after him!"

In 1847, Lieutenant Beauregard was in charge of engineer works at Tampico, having been with General Scott throughout the war and been twice wounded. Later he had other responsible posts; as from 1853 to 1860, when he was in charge of lake defenses of Louisiana and at the same time superintended the building of the custom house at New Orleans. On November twentieth of that year he was appointed superintendent of the West Point Academy and resigned his commission in the February of the next year. By the first of March he was in command of the Confederate army then organizing and was more spoken of for permanent commander-in-chief than anyone save General Braxton Bragg. He was later made one of the six full generals, and fought in the first and last battles of the war.

What this high-natured gentleman and true soldier did in war is familiar history. He and his young sons went earliest to the front, and from Sumter to surrender there was no important movement in which their name does not appear. The old name took on a new splendor that shone across seas. Two years after our war, another was imminent between the Danubian principalities and Roumania, and chief command of the latter's armies was offered Beauregard. That—and a similar one made two years later by the khedive of Egypt—he declined, to remain with his own people. He built two of her railroads; designed the great street railway system of New Orleans; and later, with General Early, supervised the Louisiana lottery.

The general was twice married; his first wife having been the woman acknowledged the most beautiful and the most charming of the belles of her day.

In widowerhood, years later, he wedded Mlle. Caroline Deslondes, one of the four beautiful and brilliant sisters of that great old Creole family. They were Henriette, Mrs. Adams; Mathilda, Mrs. Slidell; and Juliette, Mrs. Seixas. The second union was childless, Madame Caroline Beauregard having died while her husband was winning laurels on fresh fields after Bull Run. The name is all of descent from the Villeré line—the first alliance.

Marie Laure Villeré was a most typical Creole, of the early régime. She was daughter of Jules Villeré of the Magnolia plantations, and Perle Olivier, daughter of Colonel Charles Olivier. This Villeré family sent a representative to America with Iberville and de Bienville, in 1699: Etienne Roy de Villeré. His direct descendant was Governor J. Philip Villeré, who succeeded Governor Claiborne, in 1817.

This first marriage of General Beauregard left three children, two sons, and a daughter. The eldest, René Toutant Beauregard, was a mere boy when the war began, but went to the front as lieutenant of artillery, commanded his battery in the relief of Vicksburg, and surrendered as major

in Johnston's army after serving from Nashville to Atlanta in every previous battle. Now a judge in his native
state, he is the father of one son, named for his grandsire,
and in his father's profession. Major Beauregard married
Miss Alice Cenas: fourth daughter of M. Hilary Briton Cenas
and Miss Margaret Octavia Pierce, of Baltimore. Besides
the son, five daughters blessed the Beauregard-Cenas union:
Misses Marguerite, Laure, Alba (who is now Mrs. Henry
Leverich Richardson), Alice
and Hilda, the last two not
having entered society.

HILARY CENAS

Madame Beauregard's fam-
ily is one that has been high
placed and popular in the
social history of New
Orleans and Baltimore. The
children of Mr. Hilary Cenas
were seven sons, of whom
only one survives, and six
daughters: Heloise, Clarisse,
Anna Maria (now widow
of Mr. John Poitevent),
Alice (Mrs. Beauregard) and
Frances. The only living
brother is Mr. Louis Eugene
Cenas, who married Miss Lionide May, daughter of Captain Eugene May, of war fame.

Hilary Cenas, one of the elder brothers, was my boyhood
friend. He was sent to Georgetown College by his father,
in charge of Hon. Charles M. Conrad, Pierce's secretary of
the navy. He, the two young Conrads, Louis and Charlie,
were my neighbors and great chums. The tragic fate of
one of the last still sends a shiver through society, when
mentioned. Cenas, too, met a sad death, but one born out

of man's duty, well performed. He went into the Confederate Navy; and, as I have said elsewhere, was a favorite with men and women alike in Richmond. After the war, he returned to New Orleans, being then the head of his family. Ardent, fearless, and chivalrous, he was a foremost leader of his race against attempted carpet-bag domination. In the Jackson Square *émeute* he was shot in the foot; a wound that never healed and resulted in his widely lamented death in the spring of 1877. No truer type of Southern manhood was a sacrifice to the misnamed "peace."

The second brother, Henri Toutant Beauregard, was a young cadet at the South Carolina military academy and was detailed with his corps to guard the old fort. Growing to manhood after the war, he married Miss Antoinette Harney, of St. Louis, granddaughter of the famous old general, William S. Harney, of Florida fame. They have no children.

The general's only daughter, Laure Villeré Beauregard, reached womanhood while he was still in the zenith of his fame and in the vigor of green old age. Around her clustered the time-softened memories of the mother who had given her life for the girl's, and the deep love for the gentle and lovable nature that was wrapped up in him. So "Doucette," as he pet-named her, became his constant companion and idol, and the love he gave her was returned with interest. When, after refusing other offers, she married Colonel Charles A. Larendon, of South Carolina, in the early '80's father and daughter would not be separated. In the former's absence in active duty the infant had been taken by Madame Villeré, her grandmother, and partly reared at the old Magnolia plantation home.

The Nemesis of coincidence followed the last marriage. Mrs. Larendon gave her own life to bring her second daughter into the world, the first girl having died while very young.

The second was now to replace the lost ones of the past, and the whole hearts of her grandfather and father wrapped themselves in her. Happily the third Laure Beauregard—

LAURE BEAUREGARD LARENDON

who inevitably became "Doucette" also—was spared to their great love. Later Miss Larendon went to Paris, completing higher studies, and is now again at her father's home in New Orleans.

How the memory of Beauregard is conserved in the hearts of his compatriots may be indicated by a not new story. A group of Creoles were viewing the then new Lee statue, in New Orleans. One of them blew out a cloud of cigarette smoke, with the query:

"Lee? Who then ees this Lee?"

Another turned on him thoughtfully:

"Lee? Ah! yes, I know; I hear Beau'gar' speek well o' heem!"

No name has worked deeper into the broidery of history than Mason. Threads from it ramify through woof and warp—varying a bit in family color and twist—but in no tittle of rich and indurant family pride. There are at least three tall and sturdy trunks to the Mason family tree that reach far branches. These so intertwine as to puzzle all inexperts, and, to a degree, the families themselves. One of the oldest —and most prideful—of the living Masons wrote me a year ago: "In vain will the genealogist attempt to dispose traditions in any clear and comprehensible manner!"

Each branch claims to be "The Masons"; and so they are, for good blood and good wine lose nought by the dust of centuries and a few cobwebs; and *gourmets* have long wrangled as to whether the "crust" bettered, or weakened, the wine.

This gossip not being a biographical essay, nor yet a "Brett" only a few members of each noted family can find place in it, they, naturally, being the ones the writer recalls "for cause."

Colonel George Mason was an English officer and statesman of importance in the reign of the two kings Charles. After defeat in 1651 he embarked for America and settled in Virginia on a grant of land in Stafford, now Fairfax, county.

George Mason, of Gunston Hall, Stafford, was his direct descendant. He it was who wrote the Bill of Rights and the Constitution of Virginia, in 1776, and was in the assembly. In the next year he was elected to the continental congress, and had already gained the fame of one of the ablest debaters ever known in that state of orators. He was a member of the national convention that framed the United States Constitution, but he refused to sign that document and opposed it strongly and

GEORGE MASON, OF GUNSTON HALL

bitterly in the Virginia assembly. He declared and maintained that it "tended towards monarchy!" This original Mason was warmly admired and eulogized by

Jefferson, and the feeling between the two was real and mutual. George Mason, of Gunston, died in 1792. He left only one brother, Thomson Mason, of Raspberry Plantation, Loudon county. He had three notable sons, Stevens, John and Armistead, all having the Thomson name additional. Armistead was born in 1787, was Democratic senator from Virginia in 1815 and, four years later, was killed in a duel by his cousin, J. N. McCarty.

John Thomson Mason married Elizabeth Moir, and about 1812 moved to Lexington, Ky. He was the father of a great progeny that claim to be "the" Masons.

Of thirteen who reached adult age two lately survived. Miss Emily Virginia Mason, was living, past her fourscore and ten, at Washington; and Mrs. Laura Anne Chilton, widow of General Robert Chilton, still resides with her widowed daughter, Mrs. Peyton Wise, at Richmond. Only when this page had been put in type, Miss Emily passed away peacefully, in her ninety-fourth year. At the capital and through Virginia, the sorrow for her loss was genuine and universal; and it was echoed back from many a remote section where her strong, calm face had never been seen, but where her name was a household word. Others of this noted branch are seen elsewhere in passage through these pages.

James Murray Mason, a cousin of the Gunston Masons, was born in Fairfax county, in 1798. He was elected to congress in 1837 and was senator from 1847 and served fourteen years, during which he invented the "Fugitive Slave Law." He was an ultra for states' rights, a thorough Virginian in sentiment and habit, but blunt and outspoken in his public and private utterance, while nowise diplomatic. His selection, with John Slidell, to represent the Confederate cause at the most essential courts of Europe caused no small wonderment as to Mr. Davis's real belief in the possibility of recognition—not to speak of offensive and defensive alliance. Financial mismanagement was nowise condoned by diplomatic result; and the commander of the army was left to play "a lone hand," without drawing from the cards of his alleged "assisting" partners. Mr. Mason was essentially an old-timer, without experience in the modern chicane of diplomacy, and wholly wanting in that wily something that substituted for it in his more superficial colleague.

The Masons are allied to almost every notable family in Virginia, but most closely to the Lees. The elder of the two sons of Light Horse Harry, Admiral Sydney Smith Lee, married Anna Maria Mason, sister of Mrs. Samuel Cooper. Their six gallant sons, headed by " Fitz," will be met soon.

MRS. SYDNEY SMITH LEE
(ANNA MARIA MASON)

The head of the third house of Mason was a noted and very active American, albeit not directly descended from either of the others' progenitors.

John Y. Mason was born in Sussex county, in 1795, became secretary of the navy under President Tyler in 1844; attorney-general in 1845, and secretary of the navy in 1846, under the Polk administration. Later Mr. Mason was appointed minister to France by President Pierce; and died in Paris in 1859. Mr. Mason combined directness that seems to have inhered with the name he bore, with an astuteness that made him a more successful diplomat than his namesake and successor of that suave capital of intrigue.

There were four daughters of this family; three of whom are now living—Mrs. A. Archer Anderson, of Richmond; and Misses Susan and Saidie Mason, of Georgetown. The other daughter, Miss Emma Mason, was a brilliant and exceptionally handsome girl in war-day Richmond. She had much *chic*, and quite as much tact, being a prize to the beaux with brains, but a terror to the *gandins*. She married Mr. Barksdale; both are dead.

Still another branch, the Roy Masons, of Clieveland on the Rappahannock, were not direct descendants of George Mason, of Gunston; but were related by maternal line. One of the daughters of George Mason, 2d, married twice, her second husband being John Dinwiddie. Their daughter, Elizabeth, married General Fouke; and their daughter, or granddaughter, was the mother of Roy Mason, of Clieveland. Ten years ago this old home passed into possession of a collateral branch; the Masons of La Grange. It was burned while Miss Blount Mason was alone in the house, but she promptly rebuilt it.

James Murray Mason, of Clover Hill, near Fredericksburg, was direct descendant of James Roy Mason; and his son, Dr. Alex. Mason, was father of three daughters, of whom Mrs. Laura R. Webb, of Washington, is the only one left. Elizabeth, who married General E. P. Alexander, is dead; as is her sister, wife of that true gentleman and good soldier, my boyhood's mate and adult chum, Wade Hampton Gibbs, of Columbia, S. C. Three double first cousins followed the military bent. Monimia, Augusta, and Sue Mason married respectively, Generals Charles W. Field, Charles Collins and Dabney H. Maury; all West Pointers.

Blunt old General Harney remarked: "If there are any more Mason girls left the army will have to be enlarged!"

There *are* many more Masons left, but this chapter cannot be enlarged.

CHAPTER XXVII

No feet have left deeper imprint upon the historic soil of Virginia than those of the Wise family. In all public matters in their state, aggressive men of its two branches have cast strong lights and shadows upon the foreground of the national picture, and in war they acted out the motto of the Douglas.

The Wise name harks back in colonial history to 1635. In that year the first John Wise came over and took up lands. He married Hannah Scarbrough, sister to Sir Charles Scarbrough, court physician to Charles second; and to Col. Edmund Scarbrough, surveyor-general of the colonies.

The second John Wise, their son, married Matilda, daughter of Lieut-Col. John West, a cousin of Lord Delaware. Their son was the third John of the name; and he married Scarbrough Robinson, daughter of Col. Tully Robinson, a burgess and leading churchman; and of a very distinguished Virginia family.

Their son was the fourth John Wise; county lieutenant of Accomac and of Norfolk boroughs. He first married Elizabeth Cable; and his second wife was Margaret Douglas, daughter of Col. George Douglas, who was king's counsel and thirty-two years a burgess. Their son (of the second marriage) was the fifth John Wise. He also married twice; first Mary Henry, daughter of Judge James Henry; and second, Sarah Corbin Cropper. Her father was a Revolutionary major-general, having risen through every rank, under Morgan's command. He commanded at the battle of Mon-

mouth, while Morgan was in the South. John Marshall, the famed chief justice, was a lieutenant in the same regiment.

Their son, the sixth in direct descent—broke the continuity of baptism and was named Henry Alexander Wise.

A bold and clear-cut, if somewhat rugged figure stands out in the old congressman, minister to Brazil, governor and Confederate general. I shall never forget my first sight of him, in the smoky glare of wide-awakes, as he stood upon the gallery of an Avenue hotel and spoke to the surging, cheering Washington crowd. That was in 1855, when he was elected governor of Virginia, over the Know Nothing surge; and I can almost hear the yell that greeted his shouted: "Yes, I've got my foot upon the neck of Sam!" And he kept it there; as he did usually upon those of his opponents in a long, strenuous and generally successful career. Vigor, alacrity and tenacity were his attributes; and they were called upon by those who did not always "train with him." He was a member of the commission to adjust the boundary between Maryland and Virginia; and when Abraham Lincoln made that memorable visit to Richmond, close succeeding its surrender, Governor Wise was

HENRY A. WISE

the one man he sent to advise with him; and the veteran politician insisted on taking Hon. James Lyons with him.

The future governor was born in his father's house on the third of December, 1806. He was educated at Washington College, Pa., and afterward studied law. He married Ann Jennings, by whom he had four children; the second wife was Miss Sarah Sergeant, daughter of Hon. John Sergeant, of Philadelphia, by whom he had three children. He had no children by his third wife, who was Mary Lyons, of Richmond, Va. Three daughters and four sons reached maturity. The eldest daughter, Mary Wise, married Dr. A. Y. P. Garnett, of Washington; only one childless daughter remaining of a numerous family, save four children of a son, long dead, Henry Wise Garnett. The parents passed away years ago.

One of the daintiest memories of my Washington youth is the picture of the second sister, Miss Annie Wise. She married Frederick Plumer Hobson, of Goochland; and lived during the war's continuance on the farm twenty miles above Richmond. The next sister, Margaretta Ellen, whom everyone called "Nene," was a marked belle of Richmond war-time; her wit and pointed talk making the tall,

MRS. WILLIAM C. MAYO
(MARGARETTA WISE)

handsome blonde a centre of attraction to men who were not afraid of her—with cause. She married William C. Mayo, and survived him, residing in Richmond.

The eldest son, O. Jenning Wise was a remarkable man in every regard: a true cavalier, scholar, fighter, orator, and a duelist of note, from principle more than inclination. As a youth, he was noted in public affairs; became a politician and journalist from circumstance, and a soldier from choice. Killed at the head of his company in the desperate fight

at Roanoke Island, in February, 1862, his death was perhaps more lamented than that of any youth of that bloody year. The next brother, named for his father, was a minister, and a man of lovely character. He married Miss Hallie Haxall, and died in 1868, leaving no children to uphold the name. only one female grandchild remaining. Dr. Richard A. Wise, the third brother, was captain and brigade inspector on his father's staff. He married Miss Maria Daingerfield Peachy; and died while in congress, also leaving only one female descendant. Thus the perpetuation of the old

CAPTAIN JOHN S. WISE

name has fallen to the youngest son; a precocious and handsome boy when I met him at Richmond. This John Sergeant Wise, named for his maternal grandfather, was in the famous "fighting classes" of the Virginia Military Institute, that ran away to the battle of Newmarket and wrote the primer history of Southern truants in letters of blood.

John S. Wise was wounded at Newmarket, and his father

sent him to the country to recuperate and keep out of danger. How the sixteen-year-old did this, his own words to me in a private letter may best describe:

"I was sent, in October, '64, to southwest Virginia, to drill reserves; and got into a devil of a racket at Saltville two days after reaching there. Burbridge attacked the saltworks and we licked him. Then I was adjutant of the artillery defenses, from Richmond to Danville, under old Major Boggs. We had about one hundred heavy guns, at points along the line, and about one hundred men to fight them. We were a 'movable feast.' When the retreat began I was sent in from Clover Depot with despatches for General Lee, and got in and came out; delivering the last despatch he sent Mr. Davis."

After the war, John S. Wise graduated in law from the University of Virginia and practiced with his father, at Richmond. Being a Wise, he went into politics; and, aggressive and independent, he took his own head in the very thick of readjustment fights. He was elected congressman-at-large, on the Republican ticket in 1882, coincidently while his first cousin, George Douglas, was member from Democratic Richmond. He is now a successful practitioner in New York, having two chips of the old block in his office. He is also a vigorous writer of essay and fiction, and several of his books have won success. He is a strong and picturesque talker as well, and very popular in after-dinner efforts. About thirty-eight years ago he married Miss Evelyn Beverly, daughter of Colonel Hugh and Mrs. Nancy Hamilton Douglas, of Nashville.

This marriage perpetuates the old name, there being five sons and two daughters. The eldest is Hugh Douglas Wise, captain in the 9th Infantry. He married Miss Ida Hungerford, of Watertown, N. Y. The next brother, Henry Alexander Wise, is his father's partner in the law. He married Miss Henrietta Edwina Booth, of Virginia, and they have two children, a boy and a girl. John Sergeant Wise, Jr., is the third son, and also in the law firm.

Eva Douglas Wise, the next in age, married Lieutenant James T. Perrine Barney, of the 8th United States Cavalry, and their young son is named for his father. Jennings Cropper Wise married Miss Elizabeth Anderson, of Watertown, and their son renews the grandfather's name. The sixth of the family, Miss Margaretta Watmough Wise, is still unmarried, as is the youngest son, Byrd Douglas Wise.

The other branch of the Wise family were double cousins to these.

Tully R. Wise married his cousin, the sister of Henry A. Wise, and their children were seven notable sons, who made their mark upon the century past. John Henry, the 2d, still lives in California, where he was a merchant and collector of port under Cleveland. He is now past eighty. George Douglas, the third son, who was the Democratic congressman noted, was captain and inspector of Stevenson's division of Johnston's army. He is now living in Virginia though still a bachelor. The next, James M. Wise, was captain and ordnance officer of Wise's brigade. He married Miss Ann Dunlop, and left one son. Peyton, the next, married Miss Laura Chilton, daughter of General Robert Chilton, and died without issue. He was a good scholar, a good soldier and citizen, and well appreciated in his state. Frank, the next brother, married Miss Ellen Tompkins, daughter of Colonel C. Q. Tompkins. His widow survives with only one daughter. The youngest, Lewis Warrington, married Miss Mattie Allen. They are still alive and have no children.

John Wise, eldest son of Major John Wise and Mary Henry, and half brother to the governor—married Miss Harriet Wilkins. Their sons were Dr. John James Henry Wise and Capt. George Douglas Wise. The former died unmarried. George married Marietta Atkinson, daughter of Dr. Archibald Atkinson, of Smithfield, Isle of Wight. Killed at Petersburg, on his uncle's staff, he left but one child, Marietta, who never married.

Another direct branch of this notable family was that of John Cropper Wise, son of the fifth John by his second marriage and full brother of Governor Wise. He married Miss Anne Finney, of Accomac county, and became father of six sons and three daughters; the latter leaving no children. One son—John, who would have been the seventh of that name in direct line—died in his early youth.

Henry A., the next son, was at Roanoke Island, wounded and became professor captain of cadets at the V. M. I. as will be seen later. Louis, the third brother, was also at Newmarket, and wounded there. William Bowman, the next brother was wounded at Malvern Hill, and later lost a foot at Port Walthall. He died unmarried, last year.

Dr. John Cropper, the fifth brother, was in the United States Navy and medical director of the *Baltimore*, Captain Dyer's leader, in the battle of Manila bay. He married Miss Agnes Brooke, of Fauquier county. Heber, the youngest brother, is unmarried.

By the marriage of the governor's father, Major John Wise, to Miss Cropper, the family became identified with the Custis-Lees; by that of Nene Wise, with the Mayos; and by that of Henry A. Wise, Jr., with the Haxalls and Tripletts and by that of John Sergeant Wise to Miss Douglas, it was allied to the Carter, Byrd, Beverley, Bland, Hale, Kinkead and Hamilton families. In the last and present generations it is representative of almost every old family in the state.

Still another branch—more remote, but still very prominent one—is known as the "Craney Island Branch." Its head was Colonel John Wise, who married Miss Margaret Douglas, and his brother, Tully Robinson Wise, married her sister, Mathilda.

A son of the second couple became known as "Craney Island

MRS. HENRY A. WISE, JR.
(HALLIE HAXALL)

George." His name was George Douglas; and he inherited the Island estate from his great-grandfather, Colonel William Robinson. He married Miss Catherine Stewart, of Bowling Green; and their numerous children became known as the "Craney Island Wises." Their son, Captain George Stewart Wise, was a paymaster in the United States Navy. He married Eliza Stansberry, of Delaware; and had two sons: one George Douglas Stewart Wise, who married first Miss Laura May of Baltimore.

He was general in the United States Army, and his son was Admiral Fred May Wise of the navy. This family have a very large and scattered descent. The admiral's son is Major Fred May Wise, United States Marines.

Henry Augustus Wise, brother to Gen. Geo. Douglas Stewart Wise, was a commodore in the navy; and married the brilliant and popular daughter of Massachusett's "favorite son," Edward Everett. The pair were wholly in the swim during Miss Harriet Lane's reign; and the husband died in Genoa, leaving children who have married and scattered widely in North and South. One of the best known of the daughters is Mrs. Jacob D. Miller. Many "Craney Island" Wises still reside in the vicinity of Norfolk, notable among them, in this generation, being George Nelms Wise, of Newport News.

Intellect, culture, humor and conviction rarely centre in one man. They did in "V", as Captain Virginius Dabney was known to his intimates. He added in his make-up a tenderness almost feminine, and a loyalty that was quite that.

His life in New York was antithesis to Thompson's. Dabney fought fiercely with equals and against odds, and that he could not coerce surroundings never hinted to him the thought of changing these methods. So he lived and died a not unhappy if not triumphant man. His literary work in New York was hidden at its best, for that was in essays and critiques in unsigned papers and as reader for the great publishing houses.

Dabney's novels were *genre* pictures, but—and probably intentionally—far over the head of the general reader. "Don Miff" and "Gold That Did Not Glitter" had marked *succès d'éstime;* they were written less for the more material sort. His deeper impress on the New York of that day was his journalistic and critical work.

Born at Elmington, Gloucester county, in February, 1835, Virginius was named in honor of his state by that stern old Roman, his father. This Colonel Thomas Smith Gregory Dabney was about to leave the loved soil of his own birth and remove to Mississippi, where his new home at Dry Grove was made famous by his gifted daughter Susan (Mrs. Smedes). "A Southern Planter," her simple but elegant recital of old Southern home life, drew from Mr. Gladstone a letter of four autograph pages.

Colonel Dabney had one full uncle, Augustine Lee Dabney, and two half-uncles, George and Benjamin Dabney. These had descendants who, with his own sixteen children, made a house of at least Virginian if not biblical reach. The immediate descendants of whom Virginius was the head were Charles, Thomas, James, Charles, 2d, Edward, Sarah (now Mrs. J. R. Eggleston, of Raymond, wife of a gallant sailor "Reb" and head of her state's U. D. C.), Susan (Mrs. Smedes, of Gladstone Hall, Sewanee); Sophia (Mrs. Thurmond, also at Sewanee), Benjamin, Emmeline, Benjamin, 2d, Ida, Thomas S., so popular still in New Orleans; Lelia (living with Mrs Smedes) and Rosalie.

Eight of these have passed away and several of them have become noted in their chosen walks of work. They and their descendants have carried the Dabney name, and have made it respected, into every section of their country. They had blood-coadjutors in this in the children of the great-uncle, Augustine Lee Dabney, whose nine were Frederick Yeamans, Thomas Gregory, Marye, John Davis, Ann Robinson, Elizabeth, Martha Chamberlayne, Mary Smith and Letitia.

Respected and admired for great qualities by his friends and neighbors, Colonel Dabney was a man of iron mold and emphatically the head of his family, in the Roman sense. As indication that his word was law, one day he was crossing the hall with a large dose of castor oil for a sick child. Meeting a well one, he said briefly:

"Take that dose of medicine, sir—Well, Sambo?" He interrupted himself to hear the negro's message, then finished to the child: "—to your sick brother."

The abashed child gasped, "Why, papa, I took it myself!"

Virginius Dabney first married Miss Ellen Maria Heath, who died leaving one child, Richard Heath Dabney. His second wife was Anna Wilson Noland, and her children were Thomas Lloyd, Burr Noland, Susan Wilson, Virginius and Joseph Drexel, all of whom are still living except the last.

Richard Heath Dabney is the well-known professor of English and history of the University of Virginia, where his industry keeps full pace with his high attainments. He

also had been twice married, in 1888, to Miss Mary Amanda
Bentley and eleven years later to Miss Lily Heth Davis, by
whom he had two children.

Colonel Dabney's sister, Martha, married Dr. Lewis Chamberlayne and became the mother of several children, two
of them being noted figures in the Richmond war-time. Captain Hampden Chamberlayne and his sister Parke were a
great resource at the Mosaic Club. Miss Chamberlayne had,
too, that loyalty inherent in good blood, and hers strained
from the Hampdens and John Pym. After a courtship "en-
durin' ov de wah" she married rare George William Bagby,
the humorist, poet and editor of the *Southern Literary Messenger* elsewhere met. Widowed early, she reared a family
of sons and daughters who have been popular in their Richmond home and wherever else encountered. Miss Virginia
Bagby married Henry B. Taylor, Jr., of Louisa county; and
their family is of four children. Miss Parke married Charles
E. Bolling, of Richmond; the next sister, Martha, is Mrs.
George Gordon Battle, of North Carolina. She resides now
in New York City; and in Richmond lives Miss Ellen, the
unmarried sister. There are also four brothers: Prof. John
Hampden Chamberlain Bagby, of physical science, at Hamp-
den-Sidney college. Robert Coleman, the next brother is
in business, at Greenville, South Carolina; and Philip Haxall
Bagby is a lieutenant in the 6th United States Infantry.
George W. Bagby, Jr., is in the car service department of the
C. &. O. railway, at Richmond.

Direct antipodes to his predecessor, Thompson, in the *Messenger* chair, Bagby was a fluent and easy writer, with a unique
vein of humor. His "Mozis Addums" sketches were to a certain class of his state's life what Judge Longstreet's "Georgia
Scenes" were to his. He was a poet too, and his "Empty
Sleeve" became a camp classic.

"Ham" Chamberlayne had his sister's wit and humor and

was a great scholar, but eccentric and saturnine. He was a brave soldier and a true friend, a forceful, fluent writer, with a great future before him which the scythe of the grim Reaper cut off in its mid-promise.

The longevity of the men and women of the war has made possible many "reunions" of the Vets. and "campfires" of the G. A. R. But as the autumn of Time advances, the leaves fall faster—and more silently—in his forests.

In the five years of making this book, scores of its people have passed away; several after its pages were ready for press, as Miss Mason, Gen. S. D. Lee, Mrs. Hennie Hall Thompson, rare Joseph Bryan and well-loved Addie Deane Lyons.

This chapter was already printed, when another noted woman passed away. On the 23rd of March, Mrs. William Carrington Mayo—"Nene" Wise of happy memory—went to final sleep. She was true daughter of a great father and widow of a true and genial gentleman. Five children mourn their loss irreparable: Henry Wise Mayo, of New York; Mesdames William T. and St. Julien Oppenheimer, of Richmond; Mrs. Richard Parker Crenshaw, of Havana; and Mrs. James Brandt Latimer, of Chicago. She left but one brother, John S. Wise, of New York; youngest and last of the seven children of the great old governor. But there are hosts of close kin and old friends who send out heartborn sympathy to those who feel the All-wise hand so heavily.

CHAPTER XXVIII

OUR FOREIGN RELATIONS

EVERY empire must perforce have its "relations" with foreign ones to preserve that misty, but much discussed something—balance of power. The Southern Confederacy, claiming to be an empire within herself, was strictly kept in that position by the cordon of ships that sealed up her ports and the cordon of blue coats that defined her land borders all too distinctly.

She was literally an *imperium in imperio*. Yet she maintained one sort of "foreign relations" that in turn helped her to maintain her exceptional status for four unparalleled years of existence.

No history of the war would be complete without mention of the two regiments of the First Maryland, or the "Maryland Line," so linked with the memories of the A. N. V. They fought their way well and cheerily from Bull Run to Appomattox, forgetting home terrapin and jovial sociability in icebound camps and with scantiest rations. They gave the army noted generals and useful officers in staff and line.

Every Confederate reunion of today brings up new stories of sturdy, blunt and soldierly General Bradley T. Johnson, and of his brainy and helpful wife, Jane Claudia Saunders, daughter of Governor Saunders, of North Carolina—always a pair that made friends and held them by strength of nature that needed no adventitious aid from art. Their son, Bradley

Saunders Johnson, married Miss Ann Rutherford, of Goochland county, and they reside at Rock Castle.

Burly General Arnold Elzey and his faithful helpmate,
too, won hosts of friends; as evidenced by all Richmond's
sympathy in the old fighter's ugly wound that forbade
speech, even to the little remedial oath when his milk punch was
delayed.   Brilliant and dashing Snowden Andrews carried
for years the ghastly proof of his loyalty to conviction in the

THOMAS W. SYMINGTON

wound that tore his side
away and gave him pain
unspeakable.   But it carried
some balm in the warm
sympathy of all who knew
him and of thousands he had
never seen.

But the shell that took its
literal Shylock pound, cut off
besides the certain wreath
that was ready to encircle
his stars.   Three of those
came to Generals George H.
Steuart and John H. Winder,
and were worn usefully to
the ending; and lesser rank

sought the frank and manly "fellows from across" in meed
as full as it was well earned.

No parlor, mimic play-house, nor "starvation" in Dixie
was complete without the Marylanders.   They mixed the *ut-
ile cum dulce*, in rare good taste, many of them being "the
curled darlings of society."

Merest mention of that rare lot of gentlemen fighters de-
ploys across the field of memory a wealth of names and forms
and faces that only the stenograph might list.   Who of us
does not recall those splendid specimens of young man-

hood, the Symingtons, Stewart and Tom, fresh, vigorous and favorites with all women? The former is now a respected old citizen of Baltimore; but the other, ever recalled as the most vitally handsome fellow of his day, has long since left us. There, too, were the Brogdens, Harry and Arthur, if not the *Gemini*, then a well-groomed, courtly Hercules and a red blooded and high-toned Apollo. To this day Richmond and Baltimore repeat the quaint quips and quick sarcasms of the aptly named Lemmon boys; Captain George a perfect mental cocktail, for appetizing flavor with the dash of bitter, and Bill Lemmon, mixed in the same style with slightly variant proportions. Then "all the blood of all the Howards" offered to free flowing for principle, as had that of the sires of their race. The strain of the "Star Spangled Banner" came to the new flag when they and the Keys flocked to it. The Browns and Spences and Latrobes touched the left elbow with old-time comradeship of their houses; and the Carys and Skipwiths came home again to the seats of their sires. And when they came, one and all bore themselves as men who had a purpose and meant to do for it, cost what the doing might.

In the procession pass the forms of Curzon Hoffman, quaint Frank Ward and the beautiful, cameo face of Joseph B. Polk, General Winder's nephew and aide. Graceful, and gifted, he chose the stage as his "bread-bakery," soon after the peace; and his successes, first at Wallack's and Daly's in New York and later as a star in "Mixed Pickles" are widely known. The first commission signed by Jefferson Davis for the Maryland Line was that of one of these "foreigners."

This was at Montgomery, to First Lieutenant Theodore Oscar Chestney, of Washington City, who fought his way to his majority, survived the war and now commands columns of credits as cashier of the Central Georgia Bank of Macon, Georgia.

He is, moreover, the father of a large and interesting family, having married the daughter of that famous old naval hero, Captain Peter Ulmstead Murphy, familiarly known as "Pat Murphy," who commanded the Norfolk Navy Yard when the Virginians "borrowed it." His Chestney grandchildren are Kate, named for her mother who married the son of Major John F. Hanson, the journalist and Republican leader of Georgia; a second daughter, Miss Courtney, who married the grandson of Hon. William A. Graham, of North Carolina, secretary of the navy under Fillmore, and vice-presidential candidate on the Scott ticket; and a third daughter, who married Devries Davis, of the Southern Railway. The eldest son, Piercy Ulmstead, a civil engineer, is in the Macon post-office, and the second, Clement Clay Chestney, represents a great Macon firm in New York. The youngest, Brown Ruffin, has just finished his course at the Georgia Tech., at Atlanta.

But I must pause. I have omitted many? Verily, and of need; else had the list grown to *Leporello's* length, and names of all worth the record had been replica of the Maryland morning report.

Really but a part of Maryland, its name changed for cause, the District of Columbia could not keep its youth from fording the Potomac. There the north wind and the south wind blew the pollen of "rebellion" in to men's nostrils, and interest and old habit were alike impotent to keep the Washington and Georgetown boys at home. Many of these, like their brethren nearest North, are noted elsewhere in these pages; but one segment of them went South in a body, organized, drilled; and each became a picked man. The name of the National Rifles had long been famed as that of a veritable society corps. In its ranks were the flower of representative youth of the capital. Under Captain W. M. Shaffer, at the firing of the Sumter gun, it was a great peace company. The echo of that gun split it into two war companies. Obeying the command, "Fall in!" sundered by principle or prejudice, the men aligned in two platoons, facing each other with war in their eyes.

The Northern section held the armory, of course, the arms and the archives; the Southerners slung their knapsacks and marched South under Captain Shaffer, with Edmund H. Cummins and Charles H. Hill as his lieutenants. At first the company, holding to its old name, was attached to the Maryland Line ("Old Brad" Johnson) participating in the Bull Run overture and then put on advanced outpost duty at Munson's Hill. There Cummins succeeded to command, Hill rising to first lieutenant. But before the company had time to make another distinct

G. THOMAS COX,
CHARLES S. HILL AND E. D. H. CUMMINS

record the very quality of its membership almost broke it up. Shaffer was made a major on the staff. Cummins went to General Dabney Maury's staff on promotion to a captaincy and came out of the war with a record of admirable soldiership and stars on his collar. He was a splendid tactician and disciplinarian; of immense strength and agility and a trained athlete. He was my assistant in the National Drill and Encampment at Washington in 1886, and died in that city seven years ago. Charles Hill went into the engineer department on promotion so distinguishing himself as to draw the attention of Forrest to him, and he served on that great cavalryman's staff, taking his parole as a major.

George Thomas Cox was another National Rifleman who found promotion in the engineer department at Charleston, was sent to Mobile as a captain and settled there, married Miss Mollie Wilson, stepdaughter of Mrs. Augusta Evans Wilson, the celebrated authoress. His death followed hers after a few years. Their two sons, Ernest and George, are now heads of families. But again space restricts mention of many a clever fellow who did well what he left home and friends to do, and gained credit and often promotion for it. In the ranks of the Northern segment of the National Rifles were many true men who won name and fame in their line of duty. Notable among them was Renwick Smedberg, of whom I have spoken. That best of fellows and of dancers has won golden opinions in his new home near the Golden Gate. There he pets his grandchildren and fights earthquakes instead of "secesh"; making all too rare trips East to get a new leg from an appreciative government. In the ranks, too, were the Pyne brothers, Henry and Charles M., who lost his leg at first Bull Run and later went into the Church like his brilliant and wholly original father, Rev. Dr. Smith Pyne, so long rector of old St. John's.

I do not think that the lamented soldier and clubman, J. Henley Smith, was ever in the Rifles; or the Ratcliffe boys, with whom he rode long and hard and far with Mosby—and another, as will be told. Charley Forsythe was an old Rifle who, though a Michigan man, and protégé of Secretary Lewis Cass, went South and did good duty. His brother, L. Cass Forsythe, remained and later was in the Northern Regular Army.

The Northern segment of the Rifles was in command of Captain John R. Smead, who was killed at the second Bull

Run. The company was in active service in '61. Of its members was Alex. Shepherd, the later "Boss," and Captain "Billy" Moore, who was secretary to Andrew Johnson and later chief of police at the capital: a banker, and organizer of the present Washington Light Infantry.

A unique link between the states was Jackson's dashing aide, Henry Kyd Douglas, of Hagerstown.   Native Virginian, he was a Marylander from early manhood and his personal and professional gifts made him a marked man in the society and the law courts of Washington as well. Reckless yet reliable, he was trusted by his general, as shown in the latter's abrupt order: "Find Early and give him this!" The other general was "somewhere across the mountain," the night dark and the rain making roads fetlock deep; but Douglas rode seventy-six miles, killed or broke down three horses, found the general and brought his answer ere he slept.   After the war the tall, stately soldier was prominent in his profession and in Maryland politics. He was Governor Brown's adjutant-general for the state, long commanded one of its best regiments, and socially received special consideration in his own section and at the chief resorts of Northern fashion and elegance. He long fought his unconquerable foe, consumption, which carried him off four years ago. Of him, Charles King, soldier on the Federal side and romancer for both sides, wrote me: "Never did I know a man who more deserved the too-often used words, 'a soldier and a gentleman'!"

Superb John C. Breckinridge, statesman, soldier, and the choice of a great portion of his people for the first office in their gift, was the central figure around which grouped a galaxy of war-stars uneclipsed by the lights from any other state. The sons of the soil of Daniel Boone have ever been as brave and brainy as their best brethren, in the wars and in the councils that made and held together the federated states. Bright proof of this was that hero of three wars,

Albert Sidney Johnson, a West Pointer of the class of '26, Indian fighter and commander-in-chief of the Texan army and later the meteor of war in the Southern battle van.   When

the states parted, splitting asunder several of their units, much of the strongest brain and brawn of Kentucky ranged promptly under the Stars and Bars.   General Breckinridge brought with him a following of ardent and youthful fighters, and by his side stood Buckner and bold Morgan, Basil Duke and Preston, ready to lead them and their chosen comrades wherever danger lay. From first to last the peerless Kentucky chief proved his mettle and theirs, ringing true

GENERAL J. C. BRECKINRIDGE

at every touch of duty, vigilant and resourceful in cabinet as he was cool and brilliant in battle.   So the history and the romance of the war have been enriched and rubricated by the deeds of the boys from Bluegrass, and the legend-seeming ride of John Morgan had softer refrain in the new Tales of the Border than the blast of bugle and the clatter of answering hoof.

Genial and courtly General John B. Castleman, of Louisville, today has a wide and warm circle of friends all around the Union.   After the war he married a lady as notable among the young women of their state as he was among its younger "vets," Miss Barbee.   Their daughters have carried inherited graces of person and manner to social triumphs on both sides of the ocean.

Memory, unbidden, brings up another picture, ruddy, vivid

and bold. Frank, outspoken Colonel Tom Taylor was as good a soldier as ever buckled sabre. He was my messmate in the "nursery days" at Montgomery: restless for the front; and he commanded his Kentucky regiment with marked distinction. As a comrade from another state said of him: "Tom Taylor would have fought hell with one bucket of water!"

Harassed by spies and coerced by Federal garrisons already within her borders, the men of Missouri could not have made head against the protected Union sentiment, even as now stated, if it was really in the majority. But that did not deter the sons of "the River Empire" from carrying their principles to gunpowder expression. Even the shrewdness and vigilance which gave Captain Lyon his brigade, could not prevent the flower of its youth slipping through the net he spread about St. Louis. In the more open country there was scarce a let to Confederate manifestation, and the sympathizers with the South passed into her territory and joined her growing armies by scores and hundreds.

GENERAL STERLING PRICE

This gossipy recital must avoid historic semblance and need only remind one of the work done by steadfast General Sterling Price, so successful in battle and clever in raids. He was a Virginian who went early to Missouri and represented her in congress, before he was governor. He outlived the war but a few years. There were the Marmadukes; five brothers, all noted for work on land and sea and General John handling his brigade with fine record.

Missouri was remote; methods of the trans-Mississippi less picturesque than those of Virginian and middle Western armies; but the results upon both of them were helpful and effective to an extent hard to overestimate and in those results the Missourians had full share. In the social lights and shadows of the great war picture, however, they show less in the foreground grouping at first; and later the jealously guarded river prevented an immigration to the new capital of many an interesting and gentle non-combatant whose heart was as much with the Cause as though personal presence had accentuated it.

So, despite the distance of their red theatre, men walked its boards whose acting in the war drama thrills today, at mention of their names. General F. M. Cockrell, the bold senator from Missouri, now resident at Washington as member of the railroad commission, commanded the famed brigade named for him. Frequently too, in the last year of the war, he commanded the Missouri division, winning undying credit in both. Colonel Elijah Gates, now resident at St. Joseph, was the most undaunted and determined of soldiers. He was the Forrest of the trans-river fighters, lacking in education but brimming with the acumen of war. He came out of the press at Franklin with both arms shattered, holding the bridle with his teeth. With one arm left, he returned and fought to the surrender. This he did against hope, for he told a comrade after Shiloh that he had seen enough to satisfy him that the Cause was hopeless. The man to whom he spoke thus was Captain Albert C. Danner, who went in as a boy and served to the end as gallantly and steadily as any of the 6,000 in the Missouri brigade; that one of which General Maury writes, in his history, as "the finest body of soldiers that I had ever seen up to that time, or have ever seen since." And Captain Danner's record as a progressive citizen of Mobile squares with his war repute.

No men were better known with the Missouri Division than the Kennerly half dozen: brothers and cousins. Lewis Hancock, James and Sam were sons of Captain George Hancock Kennerly, of the old army. Herital trait and life in garrison fitted all three to win their father's grade, in the new one. All three are dead, though two outlived the war.

Capt. "Lew" Kennerly married Miss Mary, eldest daughter of Mr. and Mrs. C. K. Foote, of Mobile. Her next sister, Nellie, is widow of the late Richard H. Clarke; and their handsome and popular daughters, Helen, and Mary Morris, have recently become Mrs. Harry Smith, of New York, and Carl Seale, of Birmingham. Miss Sallie Foote married Mr. Charles J. Waller and is now a widow in Washington. All these sisters are brainy and clever women. Mrs. Kennerly's children are Sally (Mrs. Edward T. Herbert, of Cincinnati); Miss Alzire, and Messrs. Charles F. and Lewis Hancock Kennerly. The last is an artist, living with his mother and sisters, in Cincinnati; Charles, who married popular Miss Mary Fowler, is on engineer duty on Mobile harbor.

Captain Clark Kennerly, a first cousin, is still alive, in St. Louis. At eighty-five, he retains the elasticity of a man of fifty, in mind and body, being a vigorous walker and a fluent raconteur of valuable reminiscence. He married Florence, daughter of Mr. Augustus Brooks, long so popular in Mobile. Her next sister is today one of the best loved women, gentle, accomplished and selfless, in the city by the gulf. She is wife of the younger of the Irwin brothers, both of whom carry marks of service well performed. Col. Lee Fearn

Irwin made his best capture in Miss Mollie Brooks and he is prouder of their three married daughters and an unmarried son and daughter, than he would be of five presidential chairs. The youngest Brooks sister, Aline, is now Mrs. Ferd. Risque, of St. Louis, and mother of an adult family.

Captain Joseph Boyce, chairman of St. Louis reform council, stands high in that community. He was a gallant, chivalrous soldier "all through it." So was Captain Samuel Kennard, of the artillery, now one of the wealthiest merchants of St. Louis and a large owner in the Planters' Hotel. Captain "Hack" Wilkinson, another fighter whose valor belied his nickname, still lives and is doing well in Chillicothe. Charles B. Cleveland, of Marengo county, Ala., was a sterling and gallant fighter "through it all," and another, a present Mobilian, is Judge Robert L. Maupin. He had but one hand when the ball opened, but he raised a company of cavalry and did great work with it. Once captured, he was carried across the Ohio line, tried as a spy and condemned to hang. He passed the sentry by claiming to be the surgeon, "got" a blood horse and rode through the state of Kentucky—a hundred and ten miles in one night—and joined Morgan. This fact I celebrated in my romance, "John Holden, Unionist." Captain W. P. Barlow, "Old Bill" Duncan and others are gone: but their memories

"Smell sweet and blossom in the dust."

CHAPTER XXIX

WHOLLY different from that of their Western kith and kin— and, indeed, from that of any other state—was the case of the lithe and ever active Louisianians.

Those sinuous and picturesque fighters of the Franco-Latin races were ubiquitous in the army and in the merriment and, alas! be it said, in the deviltry of all the war-time.

Into the "Cradle of the Confederacy" glided soldiers and statesmen of the Pelican State, and the move to Richmond early made that city populous with those whose forms and faces might have seemed more congenial to Paris. With them to both cities, came languid belles, of olive complexion and piquant speech, that had made Tom Hood repeat of them: "*They* are the foreigners!"

Yet their hearts were American and their swords were Southern, let the glib tongues speak what accent they might.

Even in the glare of deeds from the famous Washington artillery, the Crescent Rifles and other *corps d'élite*, of English-speaking Louisiana, those of the Zouaves, the alert *Chasseurs-à-pieds* and the wild, looting Tigers of Major Bob Wheat who fell all too soon at first Manassas, show with steady and effective light. The last named made not a pious crew, but they fought.

The Zouaves battalion was commanded by two brothers, successively. The first was Lieutenant-Colonel Georges Auguste Gaston Coppens, who carried the corps to Pensacola and thence to the Peninsula. He was killed at the front on the great day of Sharpsburg, leaving a young wife, who had been Mademoiselle Bellocq, of New Orleans. He was succeeded by his brother, Marie Alfred Coppens, major of the battalion and its former adjutant. He was a gallant and capable soldier, survived the war and married Miss Pizzini, of Richmond. She survived him when he was drowned in Galveston bay, in 1868, while bathing. Both the Coppens were French to their finger-tips, as their own tongue had phrased it.   In face, form, military method and corps aspect they and their men might have been translated straight from an Algerian camp.

Agile, bronzed and muscular little fellows, with blue "bags" and gaiters, braided vests and scarlet jackets, surmounted by the dingy red fez, they—like their polyglot comrades of the Tigers—kept discipline on a dog-trot and subsisted on loot or nothing, with equal comfort. As fatalistic as Arabs, and perhaps as unreasoning, they fought as a matter of course and died with seeming carelessness. Their officers, as a rule, were courteous gentlemen, though language and tastes forbade the close comradeship their state's other soldiers held with those of the other "sisters in rebellion."

The men were a picturesque, reckless and ribald lot; some of them, apparently, needed killing—which they got, all of them needing soap, which they apparently did not get.

Wheat's early death in battle was the regret of the many friends he had before the war and those he made during his brief career in it.

The *Chasseurs-à-pieds* were a somewhat identical battalion, in language, usage, and outer appearance, though of probably better personnel and discipline. They were more thoroughly French, lacking the *Diego* element largely and with some American membership.

Major Henri St. Paul, their commander, was a veritable chevalier and "gentleman of France," whom I was proud to call my friend. He was scholar and linguist, lawyer and journalist, ultra as to personal honor and a good shot and perfect swordsman to defend his ideas on that score.

Adjutant John L. Rapier was then a tall, slender youth, but already a good soldier. Later he served in the Mobile forts and it was his pride that he had never surrendered, but escaped in an open boat. He went into newspaper work after the war, with St. Paul, who was then his father-in-law; finally becoming proprietor of the Mobile *Register*, and dying four years ago much honored and regretted. His next brother, Thomas G. Rapier, by strange coincidence never gave his surrender in. He was a boy midshipman with Mr. Davis's escort, at the capture; "borrowed" a mule and rode home to New Orleans with the parole he had written for himself. He has long been the head of the *Picayune* newspaper of that city.

Major St. Paul died twenty years ago, after giving up editing for law. Genuine sorrow followed his demise; deepest from those who knew him best. His ability and profession descended to his son, Judge John St. Paul, former state senator, of Louisiana.

Among the actual foreigners, who had served in European wars with distinction and added to it while they wore the gray, were several exceptional men. It was a privilege to meet the men who held the lives of thousands—the fate of the nation—in their hands; but even then the sympathies of all—and surely of the women—went out strongly to those foreign fighters who had concreted a sentiment into a sacrifice.

General Count Camille de Polignac was veteran of the staff in the French service and was chief of staff to General Beauregard. He was a typical modern Gaul; tall, thin and with grave face decorated with Napoleon beard, there was just a suspicion of La Mancha's knight in his mount. The rough humor of the soldiers often pelted him as he rode past: "Come out 'er them boots! We see yer mustache!"

Yet he was a great soldier, a knightly gentleman and a courtier, in field, camp and lady's bower. On one occasion, I heard Miss Pegram congratulate him on promotion to a brigadier, correcting herself to call him "Count." Simply as a child, he answered:

COL. HEROS VON BORCKE
(STUART'S CHIEF OF STAFF)

"No, Madame: God made me that; the other I made myself!"

De Polignac was often confounded with his cousin, Prince Emil de Polignac, who married the daughter of the plebeian banker, Meires. Asked why, he answered, "*Il faut bien dorer la pilule!*" (The pill must be gilded.) The fighting cousin got safely through our war in having serious wound of neither sort.

A German volunteer was as marked a man in the A. N. V. as was his French comrade. Colonel the Baron Heros von Borcke was formerly on the staff of the Prince of Prussia; but he asked leave, crossed to Dixie and became chief of staff to dashing "Jeb" Stuart. His given name was apposite; hero he was, if ever soldier won that title. He was wounded in the throat and they dared not operate. They told him that the heavy Minié ball must rest there, and should the cyst about it move, it would drop into the windpipe and strangle him.   The gallant foreign fighter lived his living death, rode gaily to the forefront of the charge and went as gaily into society.   When he died, years later, it was not the wound that took him off.   He was a man of grand physique; as tall as de Polignac but more muscular and with the stretch and chest of a prize-fighter.   He was not only a splendid tactician and organizer, but perfectly educated and thoroughly up in the literature and art of Europe, and he had the simplicity and gentleness of most cultivated Germans.   The two men wore swords that rivaled Colonel Skinner's famed blade, and both used them in personal combat almost as effectively as he had done.   But the German was more staid and introspective than the Gaul, of whose jests some odd ones survive.

Once he captured the officers of a cavalry regiment and their orderlies, single-handed and without a shot.   He was scouting alone; a favorite sport with him.

Clever, jolly and sympathetic Englishmen were frequent in the Confederacy, and sometimes very useful, but the fighting exceptions were rare.   A notable one was Captain Frank W. Dawson, of the Pegram artillery corps.   When the famous *Nashville* blockade runner was well out of British waters on her trial trip over, Captain Robert Pegram found a stowaway upon his ship.   A fresh-faced, intelligent youth, he said that he only wanted to fight for the South and was willing to work his passage to get the chance.   The captain demurred at enlisting a mere boy of another nation; but there was no help, the new ship was sailing precarious seas, and the stowaway landed at Wilmington, an utter stranger but a full-fledged Rebel.   He promptly enlisted in Willie Pegram's battalion of artillery as a private, rose rapidly and soon wore one gold bar on the red collar of his gray jacket.   Next he became corps ordnance officer, when Pegram was promoted and he surrendered as a captain, while awaiting promotion for gallantry on the field.   Cool, brave and reliable, Dawson was still a boyish looking, fresh-faced stripling when he gave, in his gurgling English voice and simple manner, the recital of his swimming aboard the *Nashville* and starving three days, to "dodge the British, you see."

How few of his listeners at the Mosaic Club dreamed of the tragic fate in store for him. He had adopted journalism and the noted Ben Wood, of New York, then reaching out for control of Southern newspapers, had bought the Charleston *Courier*. Dawson became its editor, in the business management of James Riordan, of Washington. Good soldier in war, he was proving himself good citizen of the reunited country of his adoption, when he was slain in private quarrel—protecting the good name of a woman. His martyrdom was mourned by a devoted wife and young family: singular reversal of the horrors of war and the blessings of peace.

Another Englishman and journalist—though much older and already notable at home—was long and popularly met in Richmond: Hon. Francis Lawley, son of Lord Wenlock. Mrs. Mattie Paul Myers writes me of him:

"You recall him as one of the handsomest and most agreeable men I ever knew," and her verdict is just. He was then correspondent of the London *Telegraph*, afterward its editor, and later on the *Times*, and also member of parliament. His letters from Richmond were bold and true, with strong Southern bias, but some prophecy in them.

Still another correspondent, and one equally widely known, in far different field, was Frank Vizitelly, of the London *Illustrated News*. He was equally clever with pen and brush, but a reckless, aimless sort of fellow, a boon companion, but forgetful of *Polonius'* sage advice as to a borrower and lender. A reminiscent friend recently asked me:

"Were you not at that memorable dinner, given by Gordon, Lord Cavendish and Vizitelly, which lasted from two o'clock until midnight, and was never paid for—by them?"

That was not one of my experiences with the artist, nor was it an exceptional event of the time. He was a daring fellow at other places than at dinner, as one of Mrs. Myers's letters proves:

"When I was in London last I saw in the crypt of St. Paul's Cathedral the name of Frank Vizitelly on a tablet of honor, as one of those who had died in the service of his country. I think he was killed in Egypt." The man had his faults, but good traits did much to balance them, and in the main he was, as his compatriots say, "not a half-bad fellow."

"Lord Cavendish," who swaggered largely in Richmond and imposed on some experienced society people, was a very different class of adventurer. He told very tough stories when he reappeared "from the front," and fought "the tiger" in reality. It turned out that he was an Irishman named Short, before he disappeared with loans from sundry dupes to whom he remained hopelessly absent-minded.

Colonel George Gordon, of the British army, was a real soldier who got into some trouble in England and came to cast his lot with the South. He was a big, soldierly looking man, with red whiskers, but with a sweet voice and beautiful manners. He was a constant visitor at the Pegrams', Mrs. Stanard's and other refined homes. He was a real fighter, however, despite his constant support to the noted corps that held the notorious gambling "club" near the Spotswood Hotel. But General "Jeb" Stuart knew a man when he saw one, and he put Gordon on staff duty and never expressed any regret for having done so.

Another Englishman with strong sympathy that did some practical work for the South was C. J. Cridland, consul at Norfolk when the war began, and later at Richmond, where he was a favored guest at the delightful home of Gustavus Myers. At that home Mr. Lawley resided during his stay in Richmond, host and guest being congenial friends and a most compensating coterie always collecting there. Cridland was a big man in a small body, and, during his Reconstruction days in Mobile—to which city he had been transferred—made many and lasting friends by his steady opposition to the rife aggressions and injustices practiced under the cloak of law.

Another consul, even more outspoken in his defense of human and not merely women's rights, was Albany de Grenier de Fonblanque, the British representative at New Orleans. This foreigner's love of fair play and his disgust of injustice by military power were expressed in no measured terms in his novels laid in the time of General Ben Butler's satrapy. He used such vigorous, as well as good, English as to give timely acceptance and lasting repute to his stories.

COL. JOSEPH ADOLPH CHALARON
(WASHINGTON ARTILLERY)

One connecting link between the Anglo-Saxon and the Gaul comes up unbidden when thinking of New Orleans. Colonel Jos. A. Chalaron, type of the best Franco-America youth, stands today the proof of the survival of the fittest and is regarded by old comrades and all citizens as the reincarnation of the old Confederate spirit.

The Chalarons come of warlike strains; several of their males having fought with renown under the first Napoleon; and a female ancestor present at his birth, having been made first *nourrice* to him who

"Born no king, made monarchs draw his car!"

Five Chalaron brothers entered the army; the last a mere stripling being forced to return to save the plantation from absolute devastation. Strangely enough not one was killed, though they were in the thick of every fight and bear scars of many a wound. Two died after the war; Antonio Jacques, the second born, who entered the famous Washington Artillery as a private and served through the war: and James, the fifth, the stripling above noted, who only consented to leave his battery on pledge that he might return and replace the first brother killed. The eldest, Joseph Adolph, who commanded the fifth company of the famed W. A., still lives as do the third, and fourth brothers: Stephen, who served in the second battery, and later in the ordnance department; and Henry, who fought under his brother in the fifth battery.

Randall, the poet, told me that Col. Jos. Chalaron said to him:

"I really seemed to bear a charmed life! Horses were killed under me; comrades fell all around me and many a one died in my arms; yet I am here, and spared, I hope, for usefulness in peace."

Mrs. Fanny Beers, in her "Memories" describes this useful young warrior, when he invaded Georgia to force supplies and medicines being sent to Bragg's army in its hideous retreat from Tennessee. Today, he is secretary of the Louisiana Historical Society, and superintendent of the Hall of Records, which embalms many precious memories of what the Confederacy gained from "Over Seas."

He is a courtly and interesting link between yesterday and today; and a mine of reminiscence.

Such were a few of the "foreigners"—as they were *not*,

in most cases—who helped to highlight the more sombre shadows of the war picture.

These come up automatically, but indubitably many more—like the Roman patricians at the funeral—are conspicuous by their absence.

CHAPTER XXX

BY LAND AND SEA

Meteor flashes of character, of action and of result show through the darkest days of Dixie in vivid gleams; not confined to one sphere of her life, but by land and sea, and in song.

Within the past two years, Georgians have reared in the grounds of their state capitol an equestrian bronze in which the soldier-statesman, John Brown Gordon, rides forth to the future, as the Cid. Need for the monument was scarcely great today, but the spontaneous act of a whole population is of sweet savor and its perfume will penetrate all history. Gordon was literally a "born soldier," although there was no inherited imposition upon him to urge arms as a calling. The son of Rev. Zachariah H. Gordon, he was born in Upson county, Georgia, June 6, 1832. From early youth he was an impulsive but clear-headed fellow, quick to decide and quite as quick to act, ready to take first place and, as he proved, wholly fitted to hold it. He graduated at the head of his class at the University of Georgia in 1852, read law in the office of his brother-in-law, Judge L. E. Bleckley and was admitted, but promptly gave up the idea of practice, to assist his father in coal mine interests that were growing valuable.

Gordon called his first company the Mountain Rifles, but one of the men declared: "Mountain hell! We're the Raccoon Roughs," and the baptism held for aye.

Originally meant for cavalry, the Roughs were dismounted before mounting by the dictum: "No more cavalry needed." Then, variously armed with sporting rifles, shotguns and rough pikes, but aflame with war spirit, Gordon tried on Milledgeville, then capital of Georgia, for enlistment. "Old Joe" Brown declined the proffer and the young captain made the wires hot, as he himself writes, with proffers to other governors. One of those, Moore of Alabama, accepted the

MAJOR-GENERAL JOHN B. GORDON

strangely named company and "we became one-twelfth of the Sixth Alabama, one of the largest regiments in the service." Gordon was early elected its major, then lieutenant-colonel and at the bloody Seven Pines commanded the regiment in Rhodes' brigade, with signal gallantry and ability that soon brought his wreath.

To Gordon's thinned command Lee left it to hold the centre against the assured impact of overwhelming numbers at Sharpsburg. How he held it, his simple narrative of the bare and bloody facts has told with a selfless simplicity that carries and clinches conviction. Through that trying day struck four times with painful and exhausting wounds, the true soldier acted out his great chief's motto and made duty the sublimest word and the panacea. Late in the day when Lee's aide dashed through the leaden hail to ask if he needed reinforcements, the blood streaming and powder-blackened hero pointed to his reeling, torn and still cheering line and answered: "Tell General Lee we are holding the centre!"

Next instant, he received the hideous wound in the face that stunned him, falling prone with his face in the cap that had drowned him in his own blood, save for the bullet holes through which its noble stream escaped.

Such was John Brown Gordon, captain of the Raccoon Roughs, self-made major-general and named, if not really commissioned, lieutenant-general of the Confederacy. Meet was it that his state and people reared his Bronze.

Two years after winning university honors, young Gordon married Miss Fanny Haralson. Loving, gentle and unflinching at trial, she was a fit helpmate for such a man and through every soul-harrowing test of the long war she was near him as counsellor, comrade and nurse. When she braved peril to fly to his side on Sharpsburg's night, she came to cheer, not moan and her kindred spirit welcomed her with the jest that must have agonized afresh his blood stiffened and shattered jaw.

"Mrs. Gordon, you have not a very handsome husband!"

She survives him at the old family home, "Sutherland," where their children were reared and where their father lived while twice governor and three times senator from his state. Of this union there were three children reaching adult age. Major Frank Gordon died only within two years of pneumonia, at Washington. His sisters are Frances, now Mrs. Burton Smith, and Caroline, Mrs. Orton Bishop Brown. There are two Smith children, the boy bearing his grandfather's name. Mrs. Brown's children are two boys and a girl.

Dignified and reserved in appearance, the general had strong magnetism, as proved by his frequent choice for high place, and by the devotion of the veterans. When fire destroyed Sutherland a decade gone, telegrams poured in from camps everywhere with offers to rebuild the home. Gordon promptly refused, saying the "Old boys are poorer than I am."

It has been noted that men of Northern birth or descent who gave allegiance to the Cause, wrought in it as steadfast and as effectually as did the longest lined of colonial, Huguenot or Creole fighters. General Cooper was from the further side of the Potomac, Colonel Ives was a New Yorker and many another illustrated this truth. Notable examples were two brothers, coming from Northern stock, though long resident in New Orleans: the Owen brothers, William Miller and Edward, of the famous Washington Artillery. The elder answered the last roll years ago, honored by his state and regretted by his comrades. The other still lives, typifying in his Northern home the loyalty of the Confederate soldier to the flag he fought for.

John Owen, their great grandfather, settled in Portland, Maine, about 1716. His son, John Owen, 2d, in 1745 served at Louisberg; and his grandson, Allison, was the father of Miller and Edward Owen. Philip Owen, a granduncle, was born at Brunswick, Maine, in 1756. He was a soldier in the Revolution, member of the general court of Massachusetts (Maine being still part of Massachusetts in 1812-13). He served at Ticonderoga and at the surrender of Burgoyne! and witnessed Andre's execution, his regiment being stationed at West Point on October 2d, 1780. Philip Owen, 3d, served in the War of 1812.

Judge William Miller, maternal grandfather to the Owen brothers, settled in Rapides Parish, in 1798. Four years later, he was made commissioner of the United States for the Spanish transfers of posts in Rapides. Dr. Meuillon was commissioner on Spain's part; and his daughter later became Judge Miller's wife. He was also appointed by Governor Claiborne, first United States judge in Rapides. In 1814, he raised a company and fought it under Jackson at the battle of New Orleans.

Both brothers were born in Cincinnati, being the only children of Allison Owen and Caroline Miller, old stock Ohioans. Business carried them to the South, where they became active and respected citizens and both entered the war at first call, in the famous Washington Artillery of their adopted city.

William Miller Owen, the elder, was its adjutant, distinguished himself by gallantry and was promoted to major. Then he became lieutenant-colonel of a Virginia battalion of artillery and had that rank when he surrendered with Lee. Immediately after that he returned to New Orleans and married, the year succeeding, Miss Carrie Zacharie, of the noted old Creole family. Gentle and loved by

COLONEL EDWARD OWEN
(NEW YORK CAMP U. C. V.)

all, she was pet-named "Happy Zacharie" by her girlhood friends. She survives him, as do their two sons, Allison and Pendleton Owen, all of New Orleans. Colonel Owen died fifteen years ago, after a useful public life, in which he did much to perfect the citizen soldiership of his state, and served capably as its adjutant-general.

Edward Owen went into the war as first sergeant of Battery A of this same battalion, was an efficient and marked soldier, was twice dangerously wounded and was promoted through intervening grades to captain of his original company ere Appomattox. He also returned to business pursuits in New Orleans and married there, in the year after the peace, Miss Hattie Bryan. After her death he removed to New York, where he has ever since been a conspicuous figure, not only in the "Southern colony," but in the business and political organizations of the city. He was first secretary of the Southern Society and chairman of executive committee of New York Camp, U. C. V., until his election as commander, which post he has held continuously for twelve years. This is one of the most notable in all the veteran ranks, both for numbers and distinguished personnel; and its annual dinners on Lee's birthday at the Waldorf-Astoria, have become very notable functions of the year.

This camp was organized in 1890, with these officers: Commander A. G. Dickinson; W. S. Keiley, adjutant; Joseph H. Parker, lieut.-commander; Edward Owen, paymaster and Stephen W. Jones, quartermaster. Succeeding commanders have been A. R. Chisolm, George C. Harrison, C. E. Thorburn and Edward Owen, reelected annually since 1898. The adjutants have been: Thomas L. Moore, Edwin Selvage and Clarence R. Hatton. The membership at organization was twenty-one; now it is three hundred and fifty.

A consistent Democrat, Colonel Owen was also a thorough business expert and his party early made him chief clerk of the commissioner's department of its city government, promoted him to its head for successive terms and when faction ousted him promptly selected him again for chief clerkship and actual management.

In 1874 the handsome and popular widower married Mrs. Adelaide B. Dick, of New York. There is one "fair daughter of my house and heart," Miss Mary Miller Owen.

The show occasions for the navy were few, but where they were given, the light on the waters shone bright, if not lurid. Foremost arises the familiar story of the "Viking

of the South." Admiral Raphael Semmes has written his
meteor-like record upon the history of his time in the pages
of many a nationality. Dubbed the "pirate" by the same
thoughtless catering to inflamed popular sentiment that
imprisoned Jefferson Davis, Semmes went to his grave be-
wailed by his own section and thoroughly respected by the
civilized world. And today the name of one of the oldest
and most ramified of American families takes added lustre
from having owned him as
one of its sons.

The several branches of
that family have helped to
people many a state and
have ever been noted for
brainy and loyal men, for
gracious, beautiful and accomplished women. Their
descendants are leaders in
the publicism and the schol-
arship of most of the large
cities today and at the time
of the war had already won
their way to prominence.
The sons and daughters of
Raphael Semmes, of George-

ADMIRAL RAPHAEL SEMMES
(TAKEN IN 1873)

town, have already been met in these pages. The "pirate" was
their cousin; and—as another reminder of the steadfast Northern strain—his wife was colonial and of the old stock that pio-
neered the West. Today their children prove their good blood,
in widely separated sections, shining in the forefront of professional and social life of the land with no uncertain gleam.

Admiral Semmes was the son of Richard Thompson Semmes
and Catherine Middleton and was born in Charles county,
Md., on September 27, 1809. He graduated at Annapolis

and entered the navy, which he left only to enter the Confederate service in 1861. He was one of three children, his brother having been Samuel Middleton Semmes. The young sailor married Miss Anne Elizabeth Spencer, of Cincinnati, her father being of English colonial stock and himself an early pioneer of the Ohio Reserve. He was captured by Indian hostiles and held captive nearly a year and ransomed only through the efforts of General Washington. This union bore six children, three sons and three daughters, most of whom are still illustrating the old name in the busy life of today. Spencer S. Semmes married the daughter of General Paul Semmes, of Gettysburg fame, and now resides in Arkansas. His family includes Spencer S., Jr., Paul J., Raphael, Oliver Middleton, Mary Anne, Frank, Kate, Electra, Myra, Lyman, Pruitt and Charles Middleton—a "baker's dozen," but all with the old leaven.

Oliver J., the second son, married Amante Gaines, daughter of Dr. Edmund Pendleton Gaines, and has three children: O. J., Jr., resident of Pensacola, Raphael and Amante, now Mrs. Percy Finley, of Memphis, and confessedly one of the most brilliant and original of that city's young matrons.

Raphael, the third son, married Miss Marion Adams and has five children, Raphael, Eunice, Aubrey, Richard and Marion. The father is well known to Memphis, Mobile and other cities as constructor and manager of electric rail systems, and is personally more like his father than either of the brothers.

In peace as in war the children of the "pirate" have borne themselves as worthy sons. Oliver was his father's partner in law and later was unanimous choice for judge of Mobile's criminal court, a post to which he has been re-elected for some thirty years.

The three daughters of the admiral are Mrs. Electra Semmes Colston, head of the female department of the Mobile public school system for a quarter century, and one of the most brilliant and cultured—as well as the best beloved and most altruistic—of women of her day. She is gentle and epigrammatic, a brilliant talker, and writer and the most loyal of friends; finds time for club work in women's best lines and is a social prize in public and private functions.

Her husband, Pendleton Colston, of Baltimore, died when their two sons were almost infants, the mother rearing them with care. Pendleton, who married Miss Esther Turner, of Bladen, died childless some years ago; his brother, Raphael Semmes Colston, married Miss Olive M. Tarrant, of Georgia, is a noted newspaper man and present city editor of the *Times-Democrat*.

MRS. CHARLES R. PALMER
(KATHRINA WRIGHT)

Kate Middleton Semmes the second daughter of the "viking," married General Luke E. Wright, when he was not dreaming of governorships, diplomacy or the war portfolio. She has long been a noted leader in the social world of Memphis and has illustrated American womanhood abroad, as able aide to her husband in three trying posts. The Wright family numbers five. The eldest sister, Anna, married John Watkins, after a brilliant belleship and is a factor in the Memphian society of today. Kathrina Middleton, the younger sister, married, at the American embassy at Tokio, Charles B. Palmer, now a banker in the Philippines. Eldrige, the eldest son, married Miss Minnie Pettus; Luke E., Jr., is a society bachelor, and Raphael Semmes recently wedded in the Philippines.

Anna Elizabeth Semmes, the third sister, was as popular as the others with the uniformed youths who thronged the Mobile home of the family in war-time. Soon thereafter she married Charles B. Bryan, another Memphian of note and has since been one of that city's most active and appreciated workers in all feminine progress. Her sisters of the Confederate Daughters have honored her with high office in their national council and Governor Patterson selected her as commissioner for the state to the Jamestown Exposition. There are two Bryan boys, Raphael Semmes, who married Miss Georgia Scott, and Charles Middleton, whose wife was Miss Bessie Smith. Thus it will be seen that Tennessee claims most of the admiral's direct descent, as she did much of his family, when B. J. Semmes and his brothers established in Memphis business. The latter is dead. He invested $80,000 in gold in Confederate cotton bonds and refused to sell them to the end. Another brother of Mrs. Ives, Dr. A. J. Semmes, of Savannah, was on Jackson's medical staff until he broke down in the Valley campaigns, when he took charge of Richmond hospitals. He married the daughter of Hon. C. M. Berrian, who was in Andrew Jackson's cabinet and later senator from Georgia. The surviving brother, "the baby of the family," is Captain Warfield Semmes, now a merchant of Memphis. He entered a Louisiana regiment while in his teens, was twice severely wounded and was promoted for gallantry and bears its honorable scars today.

A personality too marked in Richmond to miss mention was Commander John Taylor Wood, aide to the President and his nephew-in-law. He was elder son of Dr. Wood, United States Navy, who married a daughter of Zachary Taylor, older than the first Mrs. Davis. He promptly resigned, was given the same rank in the new navy and developed such traits of courage and mentality that Mr. Davis placed him on his personal staff.

But, as I have said, the naval service claimed others of the Davis family: the gallant young brothers of Mrs. Davis, Bennett and Jeff Davis Howell. Neither of them married, but both did good service on the *Alabama*. In the cemetery at Seattle stands a monument to the memory of the youngest, erected by the Masons to commemorate his death, which carried out the great Second Lesson. After the peace, Jeff Howell stuck to his seafaring, taking service on a Pacific coast liner and soon rising to its command. In a storm his ship and nearly all on board were lost. Captain Howell

JEFFERSON DAVIS HOWELL
(YOUNGEST BROTHER OF MRS. DAVIS)

was last to leave the wreck on an improvised raft, taking with him a woman and a child. She alone was saved, after days of hideous trial and privation, and she wrote his deathless eulogy in telling how he had given her the slender stock of food and water—starving and famishing ere he was swept away in his efforts to steer her frail refuge to safety.

Other staunch and true "seadogs" illustrated the salty side of Confederate endeavor, as the Barrons, father and son. The commodore we have already met. Loyal, sturdy, blunt Sam Barron, loved by man and woman equally for his heart of gold, was my friend in youth. He chafed under the cramp of circumstance, but sought any duty possible and did it well. After the war he married Miss Agnes Muse Smith, went into business and reared a family who now reside in Virginia with their mother. The eldest son died recently. Armistead W. and James S. Barron are still living. The latter captured a prize last year in the person of Miss Kate Massie Ryan of Norfolk. The daughters are Miss Sallie H. Barron, Mrs. Imogen W. Denny and Mrs. Agnes N. Segar.

LIEUT. SAMUEL BARRON

Barron's gentle and popular sister, so sought by the best of both sexes when in Richmond, became the wife of Captain Edward R. Baird, of General George Pickett's staff; she died twelve years ago, leaving ten children, who are still living.

Lieutenant-Commander John M. Brooke left the old navy to win fame in the new and to create an era in ordnance. Scientific, reticent and untiring, he perfected that famous gun which made toys of Federal frigates and jammed the turret of the "invulnerable" *Monitor*. I had the privilege of being at the test of this product of the Tredegar works: a banded, welded and laminated rifle, the first in the world to project a seven-inch shell. Indubitably this gun *was* a new era in warfare: the progenitor of the costlier—and far greater—bores of the recent past. Brooke was vindicated by experience.

Two of the naval "show prizes," rare as they were in the war lottery, fell to Admiral Franklin Buchanan. The first was in Hampton Roads, on a balmy morning, March 8th, with one so-called "ironclad"—the first and only effective one of the war, and with the Brooke gun—when he won the only naval victory of the war.

The ram *Virginia* was the razed U. S. frigate, *Merrimac*, gun-decked at water line; and turtled low with shell of railroad iron melted into 4-inch steel plates. Thus she had defence that a modern rifle-bolt had pierced as a hot needle would soft butter.

Her commander was Admiral Buchanan, with Catesby R. Jones second in command and Robert D. Minor, next. The "James river fleet" had been ordered down; consisting of four small wooden vessels: the flagship *Jamestown* of Commodore John R. Tucker; the *Yorktown*, Commander Ariel N. Barney: and the midgets of smallest class, *Raleigh* and *Beaufort*—saved by Captain Lynch from the debris of Roanoke Island. The entire flotilla carried only 27 guns, but Buchanan went out to attack an enemy out numbering him five fold and carrying 220 of the heaviest guns in the United States Navy!

On glided the strange low, brown monster—convoyed by the wooden toys—past the *Susquehanna*, the heaviest armed ship of the navy; on, straight for the *Cumberland* frigate: on, until her bow gun was in shortest pointblank range. Then the untried Brooke gun sent one shell at the frigate's stern. It ripped her open through gun decks, and tore away her bow. With colors flying and the men at quarters, the gallant ship shivered, lurched and went down by the bows: her dauntless captain, George Upshur Morris, ringing out the order, "Fire!" as her upper battery touched the water!

Never halting, the *Virginia* bore straight for the frigate *Congress*, nearer inshore; took her battery broadside like green pea pelting; and sent in one terrible, close range volley that literally riddled the huge ship. She hauled down her colors and Capt. Wm. R. Smith and Lieutenant Pendergrast, came off and surrendered the ship and themselves.

The entire fleet and shipping in the Roads, hauled away from the novel and invulnerable destroyer, taking shelter in speed and under the guns of Fortress Monroe. The *Monitor* warily held away; but daring combat next day, was cleverly stopped by one shot from the *Virginia*, that laid her helpless with a jammed turret. This ended the fight; a resultless one upon the end of the struggle, but a wondrous show of American pluck and manhood, on both sides.

As brilliant, and almost as solitary, a search for the Sangrael of victory, was Buchanan's fight with Farragut's great fleet, in Mobile bay, on the morning of August 6th. 1864. The Federal admiral on his *Hartford* flagship, steamed round the obstructions and past Fort Morgan, wholly untouched. He had four improved monitors, seven outclassing war steamers; carrying in all 199 guns and 2,700 men. Buchanan steamed down to defend the harbor, with the ill-constructed ram *Tennessee*: plated with railroad iron and still unfinished. The other "ships" were the wooden gunboats: *Morgan*, 6 guns, under Captain G. W. Harrison; the *Gaines*, 6 guns, Lieut.-Com'r. J. W. Bennett, and the *Selma* 4 guns, Lieut.-Com'r. Pat U. Murphy: in all 26 guns and 250 men. On the flagship, *Tennessee* the admiral had executive officer Commander J. D. Johnston, Lieut. Thos. L. Harrison and a picked staff. The fight was fierce and short: the vast preponderance of metal, men and speed making it hopeless from the first gun. But the wooden shells fought until splintered and sinking: and the flagship was surrendered by Johnston only after the admiral had been wounded and the stearing gear and gun carriages shot away.

In his blunt, short way, Farragut warmly congratulated Buchanan on the great fight he had put up; and he, as well as his officers, told their prisoners that they were amazed at the damage that had been inflicted upon their superior fleet. Yet, while "magnificent," this combat "was not war."

Strong indeed is the temptation to follow the white-winged flyers of the seas, loosened from the wrist of the struggling young nation hemmed in from contact by connivance of the selfish world-powers: to note the "derring do" of *Sumter* and *Shenandoah* and to roster the names of the men who followed Semmes if in a lesser orbit. But that would need a volume and the Fate's shears must needs clip the thread.

CHAPTER XXXI

"DIXIE" AND HER NEXT OF KIN

CONFEDERATE song would demand a separate volume, were attempt made to exemplify it. Temptation has arisen often, as these pages spun themselves, to do one or the other, and resistance to it has been difficult. But there are some singular errors about the more familiar specimens of the songs sung, which stalk among us with the restlessness—and the nebulousness—of Pompey's shade. "All Quiet Along the Potomac" has been as unsettled a moot for four decades as was "Beautiful Snow," or the letters of "Junius." Colonel Lamar Fontaine insists that *he* wrote it, at a Virginia outpost, while the North states day and date to prove that it was printed, prior to his contention, over the name of Mrs. Ethel Beers, in *Harper's Weekly*. Only when the deliverer of the aforetime blow to William Patterson comes up and confesses, will this momentous question ever down.

The origin of the first flag, and of the Confederate uniform, have been and still are claimed by as many discoverers as any modern patent. These I think I have stated correctly in early chapters, but there is widespread ignorance of the exact origin of two most popular Rebel ditties, one of which no less a critic than Mr. Lincoln declared "too good to be kept by the Rebels," and proceeded to Ben-butler it out of hand.

354

The esthetic musical critic will say that we should shame to adopt "Dixie" and "The Bonny Blue Flag" as *la Marseillaise* and the *Partant Pour le Syrie* of the Lost Cause. Of a truth, they were as ready inspirers, and perhaps as costly in the inspiration, to "t'other fellow."

I have been at pains to get the truth as to these two important songs: I have succeeded, beyond doubt. Mr. J. Tannenbaum is a veteran leader and minstrel manager and well known to the theatrical profession for a half-century. Of them he wrote me:

"There was only one Macarthy, and he wrote 'The Bonnie Blue Flag,' at Jackson, on the day Mississippi passed the ordinance of secession. He sang it first that night. Harry Macarthy was capable of inventing melodies, and he wrote other songs, among them, 'The Stars and Bars,' 'The Volunteer,' or 'It's my Country's Call,' 'Josephine Gay,' etc. I was his leader and manager and I harmonized and orchestrated all his songs at that time. Others claim to have written 'The Bonnie Blue Flag,' but they do not tell the truth. It was first published by Blackmar Brothers, of New Orleans, and some copies are still in existence to prove what I say. It ought to be known for all time that Harry Macarthy *is* the author.

"The 'Dan' you refer to is Dan Emmett, whom I knew well. He is the composer of 'Dixie,' which was sung by Bryant's minstrels, first as a 'walk-around,' which in those days finished a minstrel performance. He was noted for writing several 'walk-arounds,' among them 'High Daddy in the Morning,' 'We are all Surrounded!' etc. He died only a few years ago, his last appearance being with Field's minstrels, as an old man—an advertising card for Field. *He* wrote 'Dixie,' and this is established and no other has a right. This should not be misunderstood. He was a fine man, Dan Emmett."

A claim was recently made that "Dixie" was first written upon the walls of the old Mobile Theatre, on the sudden inspiration of Emmett. The leader then was "E. J. Arnold," now in his seventies, but still directing the orchestra of the Lyceum Theatre at Memphis.

In 1895 Mrs. Annie Chambers Ketchum, of Mississippi, claimed the authorship of "The Bonnie Blue Flag." The Southern press finally pushed that claim, and Mr. A. E. Blackmar wrote emphatically that his father had bought the original from the author and published words and music unchanged.

DANIEL DECATUR EMMETT

Emmett was the star of Birch and Backus, as endman. A similar and equally futile claim was made for Mobile as the cradle of "Dixie" but that was made vicariously. A traveling vaudeville manager wrote a long and circumstantial letter to the *Register*, giving the "facts" of the song having been written on the white wall of the old Mobile Theatre, by "Mr. E. J. Arnold." This was in 1860. The writer described the wild excitement and fervor of Dan Emmett, "great with Song"; and he stated that the curtain was about to rise and that Mr. Arnold had no paper. "Write it anywhere!" Emmett cried—"Write it on the wall!" And the aged orchestra leader, then and there, wrote his modern Danielscript.

Like Sir Lucius O'Trigger's quarrel, the story above is

"very pretty as it stands." The troubles with it are that there is no "E. J. Arnold" a leader anywhere: that the Mobile Theatre was burned in January, 1859, and no other was built until 1865. Moreover, Mr. Herman C. Arnold— now seventy-three years old and leader of the Memphis "Lyceum," writes me that he never told the story above quoted to anyone; that he never was at the Mobile Theatre, but at the New Montgomery Theatre, which opened with Wilkes Booth as star, in 1860. Mr. Arnold was leader of that theatre's orchestra; and he writes:

"Hearing Dan Emmett sing Dixie, I admired it very much and wrote the score for band and orchestra and I played it for the raising of the first three Confederate flags which were raised at the capitol at Montgomery and also at the inauguration of Jefferson Davis. It made such a sensation that it became the war tune of the South." And this settles the Mobile origin.

General E. P. Alexander—the gallant Confederate and cultured gentleman elsewhere noted as one of the lucky men who married the Misses Mason—now resides at South Island, South Carolina. On reading the Arnold romance, he wrote to me, deriding the claim. He says:

"I was married in April, 1860, ... and in June, or July, of that year returned to my post at West Point. Soon after, my wife and myself went down to New York, to see a play then running at Laura Keene's, called 'The Japanese Ambassador.' Those dignitaries were then in the city and the papers were full of all their doings. The play was evidently gotten up in a hurry; and one of Joe Jefferson's sons told me that his father was its author. In this extravaganza, some bogus ambassadors introduced by 'Brown, of Grace Church,' (when the real ambassadors were not able to attend), were called upon to sing a 'Japanese' song. A brother-in-law of mine was then in New York, George G.

Hall, son of Asbury Hall of Athens. He was the greatest
amateur violinist I ever heard. He knew more songs
than any man I ever knew. Hall told me about the play,
before taking me to hear it; and said that when the Japanese
song was called for, they 'played that old thing, Dixie!'
with an accent on the 'old!' So I went and heard 'Dixie,'
for the first time that night; but I believe it was already
in print, in an old sort of circus song-book, that I had had
as a boy, before I left Washington in 1853, to go to West
Point.

"However that may be, this one thing is certain: 'Dixie' was born from that play of 'The Japanese Ambassador.'
This was in the June, or July of 1860, before the election
of Lincoln in that November; and all the newsboys of
New York were whistling it within a week. On August 9th,
1860, I sailed for Colon; and, when we arrived ten days
later, 'Dixie' was there ahead of us and we found it had
preceded us to San Francisco, Portland and even to Washington Territory." Then, after scouting the Mobile story,
Gen. Alexander adds:

"I believe the song was a still older walk-around, and can
easily be found by anyone who will search old theatrical
song books and records of the time. The name 'Dixie' came
from a man named Dix, who owned many slaves on Man-
hattan Island and sold them to be taken South, just before
slavery was abolished. As the darkies are natural patron-
izers of every circus, their traditions and the name attached
to their place of habitation, has survived in the last line of
the chorus: 'In Dixie's lan' I take my stan, To live an' die
in Dixie!' "

Every word General Alexander writes is literally true; but
that more strongly corroborates Daniel Emmett's claim. I
myself base my belief upon his authorship of the song, on
a rainy Sunday of April, 1859, on personal knowledge of

himself; upon Mr. Tannenbaum's reliable letter; and upon a circumstantial statement written for me by Col. T. Allston Brown, author, manager and late dramatic editor of the *New York Clipper*. The Brown statement details the entire story; but I need only quote here what he tells of a restaurant party in the war-time:

"This is the origin of 'Dixie' and you can swear to it!

"I give it as received from Dan Emmett himself and from my own recollection. While I was dramatic editor of the *New York Clipper*, in 1861, Tom Kingsland, of Dodsworth's Band, was proprietor of a famous bar and lunch room in Broome street, much frequented by actors, newspaper men, minstrels, etc. D. T. Morgan, having come back from the army, in the winter, dropped in at Kingsland's.

"Sitting at the several tables and all, apparently, having a good time, were about twenty jovial fellows and among them, Dan Bryant. I was soon at a table with him, Nelse Seymour, Dan Emmett and others.

"Morgan told Emmett that, at night, he could hear the Confederate bands playing Dixie; and that they seemed to have adopted it down South, as their national air. Emmett replied warmly:

"'Yes: and if I had known to what use they were going to put my song, I will be damned if I'd have written it!'

"I asked him how he came by the idea. He tipped back in his chair, moved closer to my side and, speaking very low, said he supposed me too young to have heard a song which his mother (or grandmother) sang to him in his merry young days. He said it was called 'Come, Philander!' He was more than taken aback, when I told him that my mother had put me to sleep many times, with that same song. Then I repeated the first two lines to him: all I could remember:

'*Come, Philander, let's be marchin,*'
'*Every one for his true love sarchin!—*'

"'Yes: that's it!' cried Emmett. 'I based the first part of Dixieland upon that song of my childhood days.' He did not call it 'Dixie' but 'Dixieland.'

"While Emmett was with Bryant's Minstrels, one Saturday night in 1859, Bryant said to him: 'Dan, can't you get us up a walk-around? I need something new for Monday night.'

"At that time, all minstrel shows used to end up with a walk-around. Dan Emmett remained in the house all day Sunday; but by the afternoon, he had the words commencing: 'I wish I was in Dixie!'"

When Colonel Brown wrote the words above quoted, he had spread out before him the New York *Herald*, of Sunday,

CAPT. R. T. ("TRAV") DANIEL

April 3rd, 1859, with this advertisement: "Bryant's Minstrels !! Dixie's Land: another New Plantation Festival !!!!!"

It is strange indeed that, even in the South, during and after the war, there was so little real effort to fix definitely the origin of this and other popular songs and poems. They were accepted greedily by ear, when they hit the popular fancy: but it was rare that any man, or woman, who whistled, sang, or recited them, paused one instant to sift either their origin, or what of meaning they had.

I recall a lively talk, among members of the Mosaic Club,

when "Trav" Daniel and others were discussing this very "national air." Daniel was a star member of the unofficered club; a herital thinker, with much of his father's acumen, information and dry humor; and these he shared in common with his sisters, Augusta, Charlotte and Lizzie. He was very antithesis, in method, to his bubbling and impulsive brother-in-law, "Jimmie" Pegram.

At this distance, I cannot recall who were speaking of "Dixie," but I think Judge Ran Tucker, J. R. Thompson and Judge Daniel were among them. Trav made the point that a nation's song was its trademark and should be verified; but we were all too much in a hurry to stop and think in those days; and I have no recollection that "Dixie" ever came up as a contention thereafter, even in the Mosaic. It fitted into the time, was accepted as a Southern song, necessarily by a Southern man; and that was the end of it. Was it both, or either?

Daniel Decatur Emmett was born in Mt. Vernon, Ohio, in 1815, and was resident there in his eighty-seventh year. He died only four years ago.

One song, popular in both armies, and claimed by each long after the war, was "Tenting on the Old Camp Ground." It was undoubtedly of Northern birth.

The battle of Cedar Creek Hill bore many serious results, and some laughable ones, among them the loss of the Valley granary and meat-house, the over-done art, poetry and gush of Sheridan's ride, and Randolph's living line:

"*Where sadly pipes that* Early *bird that never caught the worm!*"

The night following this defeat, two members of a Vermont regiment composed and sang that song, which was later polished and published. Private Kittridge a New Hampshire boy, improvised the original words; Russell, a Green Mountaineer, composing the air as his comrade went on. Many still living can vouch for the truth of this statement, which has challenged dispute; among them being Captain W. A. Russell, now a resident of Berlin, Canada, the composer's brother.

Local rather than generic and with its frayed antiquity of musical setting, "My Maryland" is the nearest approach to a real anthem produced by the war. It was born out of occasion, and it grew to a national expression. In its springing from the smoking blood that dabbled the cobbles of Baltimore, at the first forcible tramp upon them of hostile feet, memory brings back that night of 1792 at Strasburg, when, with burning cheeks and blazing eyes, Rouget de Lisle wrote and chanted the words of *La Marseillaise*.

At Pointe Coupée, La., the young Maryland poet heard the echo of his stricken brothers' cries of anguish and defiance. He dipped his pen into his heart and "Maryland" sprang forth, full statured and full armed as did the mythologic brain-birth. The words caught the fevered spirit of the hour. In a month they were burning in the hearts of gathering clans.

Randall was my boy chum and college mate. He once wrote: "In our callow days Cooper De Leon and I made mud-pies and capped verses. . . . Today he is at home wherever pen and paper are to be found; and if they are in the vocative, a rusty nail and a white wall will do as well. . . . It will not do to wish that 'his shadow may never grow less', for it is not in the memory of man that he ever cast a shadow."

Neither of us had forgotten the dewy freshness of life's morning. Meeting at intervals only, we were the same old chums, as the shadows lengthened toward our sunset.

Randall was another of Northern descent who was Rebel to the core. His great-grandsire was a Pilgrim-bred, witch-hating Yankee, an elder in the church of Hate to dissent. What he was his poems tell. Born with the rare fire in him that only needed friction of a Cause to glow and incandesce, he met the need in the immortal one. He had written more graceful poems ere that, as "The Cameo Bracelet." That was when his somewhat errant fancy had made its throne at the feet of Miss Esther Jonas, of New Orleans.

Within his last year he recited those early strophes to their inspiration, now wife of Captain I. L. Lyons, with the third generation at her knee.

In years between, the poet's heart, beelike, had gathered honey where it listed. Rumor tells us that its one-time flower of flowers was the younger sister of Miss Augusta Evans, long since married and dead.

When the nominal peace came; Randall found his real one in marrying a lovely South Carolinian, Miss Hammond; and they had reared to usefulness five of their eight children. Two years

JAMES R. RANDALL
(AUTHOR OF "MY MARYLAND")

ago the youngest of these, scarce more than a bride, was taken from them. Another year, and the poet was taken from those she left.

Randall had written in the years since the war some strong poetry and much admirable correspondence and editorial. He had been editor of the Augusta *Constitutionalist* with

Colonel James Gardiner, and of the *Chronicle* with Senator
Patrick Walsh. He had worked with the Sage of Liberty
Hall upon his memoirs, and had held Washington positions
of trust. But, as the hart panteth after the water brooks,
the old journalist longed after the tripod. He went again
to the Crescent City of his early love, and edited the *Morning Star* and did telling correspondence for the *Columbian*.

In 1907, Randall was signally complimented by his native
state. She brought him from New Orleans to be her guest
of honor on "Maryland Day," at Jamestown Exposition;
then bore him back in triumph to his native Baltimore.
There he was feasted and hailed as the poet of the Cause,
honored though lost. Fair and noble Daughters of that
Cause demanded a complete edition of his poems; he was
whelmed in flowers, feasts and pretty speeches. Then he
went back to the old Augusta home, warmed with ambition
and cheered by the strong old love. He wrote me glowing
and hopeful note of it all. Before I could write congratu-
lations, the wires bore the news of his sudden death. Then
the tribute lately paid him in his old home swelled to a national pæan and the world heaped immortelles above the
grave of a people's poet.

Knowing my friend's lack of money-making habit, I
read with regret that Maryland promised a $25,000 statue;
Augusta a shaft and New Orleans another stone. Immediately, I sent appeals to the press and to those cities. I
felt that if we took care of the bread, the stone would take
care of itself. The appeal was universally endorsed: and
practically, in some quarters. Maryland, as a state, voted
his wife and daughter an annuity of $600 per year; and her
Daughters printed the poet's works in a handsome volume,
the *entire* proceeds from which go to his widow. A noble
matron of Nashville—an old friend of mine and of the Ran-

dalls—headed the Tennessee tribute with a hundred dollar check; and the U. D. C. division of Alabama sent its share. From distant and unexpected quarters, practical reminders came: and it was plain that the poet's song still echoed in the people's heart.

CHAPTER XXXII

THE PIOUS AND THE SPORTY

I HAVE written elsewhere that the early settlement of America had two impelling forces: greed and creed.

The Spaniards, in their thirst for acquisition of the Southern Gulf littoral, had only the first. It was the zeal of the Pilgrims that influenced their changing homes of generations for the frozen wastes of the far North, with their Indian hostiles. The French in *La Louisiane* and the English and Huguenot colonists of "the Virginia Plantation," perhaps doubled the motives, letting either predominate as occasion demanded.

As early as 1587, Peter Martyr dedicated his "History of the New World" to Walter Raleigh, and in another book on Florida, urged him "to prosecute the work for the only true motive, that induced the glory of God and the saving of the souls of the poor, misguided Infidels."

Whether because of this exhortation, or other cause, Sir Walter gave five hundred pounds the next year "for the propagation of Christianity in Virginia." This is of the piece with the claim of Bishop Meade, in his valuable book, that Smith and Sydney "were also for the glory of God and missionary spirit."

Richmond was a godly city when the first invasion by any government captured that capital. Yet, I think it is admitted that the surrender saw many a theory shattered and many a revered idol sprawled from its pedestal by un-usual, if not impious practices. Still, as in the described rush to the new national "Nursery," at Montgomery, that devil, dissipation, was of hue far less sable than that in which he has been swiftly, and quite as untenably, limned.

There were gross exaggerations of the gambling, the drinking and the debauchery of the leagured capital during those most bitter four years of blood and loss, trial and temptation.

With a promiscuous and unbridled population, largely untrained, crude and amen-able to the military law alone—while its civil sister slept—small indeed were the wonder had the slanders upon that point really been truths. And this is no afterthought. It was so agreed with Smith Lee, Fitz's next brother, after a round we made to inspect Richmond and compare the two cities, shortly after his voluntary withdrawal from the "Paris navy."

LIEUT. SYDNEY SMITH LEE, JR., C. S. N.

Practically every man in the South was in the army, and the pay of a soldier in the mid days of the war would not have bought a breakfast at the average Richmond restau-rant. Liquor, save as a medical ration, was almost wholly above reach, and tobacco, an absolute necessity with missed meals and physical and mental strain, was equally scarce and vile. Here was the temptation, when "the boys" came to Richmond, and luxuries as resistless as the green-sleeved Houris of Mohamet's heaven were thrust upon them, with added appeal to the greed latent in every soul. The wonder is not that so many yielded to the seductions of drink and cards, but that there were so many who did not.

When rations were reduced to the last limit in every camp, the faro banks of the capital spread great tables with peace-time meals sumptuously prepared, with liquors and even rare wines. These unaccustomed luxuries, underscored by really good cigars, were forced upon all comers, with no apparent care whether they gave promise of return in future losses. The sporting spider, in his seductive parlor, practiced—whether he had read it or not: "And he that hath not from him shall be taken even that which he hath." On the other hand, he did not hesitate to give before taking. These "hells" were not really open to all, unless introduced by an habitué; but the latter were numerous enough to give them a huge clientèle and to make them an evident feature on the face of the time. Men of all ranks and ages frequented them: some for greed alone, and more for that added to greediness. Their officials and dealers were usually recruited from Washington, and Baltimore, or from the popular "sports" of the Virginia watering-places, care being taken to select men "with a pull" from past acquaintance.

Strangely enough, with all this and much more of it in a minor key, there was little general drunkenness, and gambling, while wholly unpunished and even unchecked, was more the exception than the rule. The reasons for this were probably the same suggested at Montgomery: the absorption of men in great and continuous excitement and the outdoor life, on plain diet, that changed the physical man so quickly; and through him, the moral and mental one.

Private gambling, outside of the "corn-grain limit" of the camps, was confined to the hotels and private homes of the few that condoned. Club life, as such, was practically done away with in every Southern city. Poker, of course, was the popular game: it had always been, and is so, in that section as at the North. And that game divided the love of the more "game sports," with the "games of the house," faro and roulette. The house, however, treated its poker patrons with great consideration and liberality of food and drink, but they were no losers thereby, for the winner in the private game would often "drop his pile" at the bank, as though it burned holes in his pocket. The most notable of the Richmond hells was that of the Monteiro brothers, and the names of "Alf" and "Jim" grew familiar to even feminine ears. Great sums were won and lost at that house and, as the money slide went rapidly downward, fabulous-sounding sums were often quoted. Even when the Confederate bills were crisp and not much depreciated, I have known losses in an evening to run into five figures; but the cases were rare and the average one very small—whatever the will of the loser might have made them.

No habitué of the Richmond "hells"—and many a stiff-necked churchman of later days might "train with them"—but will recall Bill Burns and John Worsham. These men were chums from contact and professional pride; the former blunt, jovial and honest, the other refined, quiet and generous to a fault. Burns outlived the war and was later a marked figure on Pennsylvania avenue, on most days and almost all nights. But the "Storm and Stress" of the struggle finished his comrade, sometime ere its close.

I once wrote a novelette—"A Bayard of the Green Cloth"—and got much soft buffeting from the unco godly for making its hero a gambler. I had Johnnie Worsham in mind, no less than a well born Southern sport, while I wrote. Yet no real man who knew him will deny that the young faro dealer was the *preux chevalier* of gamesters: with a great heart, an open hand and graces of soul, not always inhered under a ruffled shirt. One blunt fighter—as true a man as ever drew breath, sword or cork—lately wrote me of him:

"Do I recall John Worsham? Well, I rather think I should. He fed us when all others failed us. He certainly was a high type of man."

This is homely praise? Perhaps: but it has all the verity of the mining camp obituary: "He done his durndest: angils kin do no more!"

Johnnie, as they all called him, was the soldier boy's best friend, even among the easy-going gambling fraternity. He served them the very best to be had, and he shared with them all he could get, when the pinch of starvation began. His death was regretted by the fighting lot.as that of a comrade.

His reckless mode of life was underlaid by a romance; and many a man-about-town, of that day, will vividly recall its handsome and magnetic heroine. They may also recall a narrow chested, tall placed house, near a popular hotel, which was the field of this romance. *Ay di me!* was that yesterday, or—the day before? Worsham's death let the feminine surroundings drift Westward: but those who recall the past of that episode, and then stare at the present, must confess that this world is a very small one indeed; and that, like Time, it has its "whirligig and brings in strange revenges!"

The hotels and restaurants of Richmond were fairly good at first and both battled bravely against fast increasing privation. They were one field of war dissipation, and tended to that reckless disregard of values which is typical of fighting soldiers; and which fell into utter contempt of the paper money as it grew less and less in value.

Morally, the tone of all ranks of society was wonderfully high. Civil laws, where not soundly asleep, were weak of execution from the army drain of men; and the provost substitute was more interested in guarding the body of the backslider than in mounting guard over his soul. The bars between the sexes were nominal; intercourse—under common sympathy in pride or sorrow for events in passage—was free and friendly, and, as before noted, the duenna was represented by X. Yet there was so little of open and brazen debauchery as to make it scarcely a consideration. Society guarded itself by habit and pride; its lower ranks, by absorption in an elevating and universal altruism. The Christianity of theory crystallized in the Christianity of practice.

From first to last the sporty did not predominate over the godly in the economics of the Confederacy The latter were in the ascendency at all times, and in Richmond there were churches in great numbers, presided over by able and earnest men, who made their mark upon the time. That the martial and religious spirit went hand in hand lacks no shining exemplars. Lee and Stonewall Jackson; the latter's brother-in-law, General D. H. Hill, Father Ryan, the brilliant and untiring poet-priest; Father Patterson, of Tennessee; Louisiana's Leonidas Polk, general and bishop; Pemberton, and Jefferson Davis himself, come up at the touch of suggestion. And what was true of the army was more discernible in those civil ranks of Dixie life, less diverted from active religion by over-activity of brain and body.

So, central and variously enough attended as to make them universally known then, the churches and pastors of Richmond will make a pleasantly reminiscent note. They were of all denominations, the actual list being this:

The Episcopal churches: St. Paul's, Rev. Charles Minnegerode, D. D., was General Lee's church and the scene of many historic weddings and funerals. Dr. Minnegerode was an intimate of President Davis, and visited him while in prison. St. James's was the church of Rev. Joshua Peterkin, D. D., another loved and popular preacher, and Dr. George Woodbridge held the pulpit of the Monumental. Grace church was Rev. Dr. Baker's, with a large congregation, and Christ church and St. Mark's were noted churches, though I cannot now place their rectors.

The Presbyterian churches were: First, Dr. T. V. Moore, and the Second was in charge of Rev. Moses D. Hoge, D. D., a most eminent preacher and very popular, especially with the soldiers. Dr. C. H. Read, was in charge of Grace street church, and Dr. R. R. Howison presided at the Third Presbyterian. All these had large transient congregations, when the war held great armies near the capital. The same was the case with the Methodist churches. The Centenary was Dr. Doggett's, and the Broad street was in charge of Dr. J. A. Duncan, later bishop of Virginia. The Clay street and Union Station churches were active and well attended, but I cannot trace their pastors. It is a trifle singular that it has proved easier to find a sergeant in one army than a captain in the other. Immersion in chronicle has let me fare better with the Baptist churches: The First, presided over by Dr. J. L. Burrows, the Second by Dr. D. Shaver. The Grace street Baptist was a centre of curiosity as well as of interest. Its pastor, Rev. J. B. Jeter, D. D., was one of the most marked figures of wartime Richmond. The pulpit of the Leigh street Baptist was filled by Dr. J. B. Soloman.

The solemnity of sacred things did not fully spike the batteries of the wicked wits. There were jokes—and sometimes jibes—at almost every black coat, however popular, and deservedly so. McCarty used to swear that he heard one pious sister confide to another, at the porch:

"I jes' do love to hear Brother Jeter!" and the other assented:

"Me, too, sister; he *do* preach *so* moanful!"

On one occasion a lovely and noble fellow in the fulminate works, was blown almost into shreds while fusing shells. Next Sunday his family's pastor explained in his notices: "Immediately after worship, beloved, we will hold service over the remains of our departed brother—*ahem!* I should have said, what remains of the remains."

St. Paul's was the church of fashion and the scene, as I noted, of many swell weddings. At these, in open church, the crush of the curious was always great. On one occasion its conduct was more picnicky than pious, flirtation raging with giggle and sigh, and jest passing from mouth to mouth. After one very large and fashionable wedding a wag pinned a penciled cartoon on the door of St. Paul's. It represented the pompous sexton, a noted character in town, standing at the portal and waving back some meek-faced worshipers who ask:

"But is this not the house of God?" and the janitor responds:

"Yes; but He isn't at home!"

Only to locate it justly, the familiar slip of the tongue made by Dr. Hoge may be pardoned repetition. When the war was nearly crushed to a close he prayed for General Breckinridge, then war secretary:

"And may his hand be so strengthened that his enemies may not trump over him!"

The Roman Church was ever sympathetic with the Cause, and its clergy and especially its Sisters of Charity and of Mercy did early, constant and indescribable labor for the bodies of the sick as well as for their souls. They wrought unceasingly, in the de Sales hospital on Brook avenue; in any other, where their white, unshaking hands found work to do—in Norfolk, Lynchburg and Charlottesville, as well as in all the wide stretch of havoc and misery that measured the Confederacy. One of these noble women has just passed the golden jubilee of her novitiate. Through the whole land the hearts of veterans went out in loving greeting to the meek and fearless war nurse, Sister Madeline O'Brien, in her Baltimore rest.

Rt. Rev. John McGill, war bishop of Richmond, was

RT. REV. RICHARD HOOKER WILMER
(WAR BISHOP OF MOBILE)

a stanch Rebel and a scorner of half-utterance. He did all that in him lay to promote the Cause and to heal those stricken by sickness, or sword, or—famine.

His cathedral pulpit was held by Revs. Robert H. Andrews, A. L. McMullen and John Hagan.

Rev. Leonard Mayer, O. S. B., preached at St. Mary's, and at St. Patrick's Rev. J. Teeling, D. D. These all did good work, they and the Jesuits—notably Fathers P. P. Kroes and P. Toale—carried piety and tending to Fortress Monroe, Fairfax and all the army lines.

Another bishop with warrior soul and unswerving loyalty to the Cause—and who was later Prelate of the Diocese of Humor in the American Church—was Rt. Rev. Richard Hooker Wilmer, war bishop of Mobile. Consecrated to that see in 1862, he forbade further use of the perfunctory prayer for the president of the United States. When the end came and General Thomas was in command, he sent for Bishop Wilmer and insisted that the prayer should be returned to its use in all the churches. The bishop refused flatly, pointing out that it would be as illogical as insincere. Then "Old Pap" declared he would close the Episcopal churches. Bishop Wilmer confessed that might gave the general power to do that, but no right to coerce his conscience; so the public worship ceased, and all services were held in private homes until the Washington government rescinded the Thomas order, and the dauntless churchman triumphed over the *inter arma* proverb.

Bishop Perry in his work on the "Bishops of the American Church," clearly shows that the action of the Alabama bishop was based on logic and law; and that its indorsement forced from the government was the step that marked forever the division of church and state in this Republic.

Some years later, when the guest of his daughter-in-law, Mrs. W. H. Wilmer, at Washington, he was walking at the then completing Thomas Circle. He asked the lady whose was the new equestrian statue. When she told him it was General Thomas, the clerical wit halted facing the figure, waved his hand and cried:

"I am glad to meet you again, sir; and I have all the advantage. Now, *you* cannot answer back!"

Only nine years ago, when in his eighty-fifth year, the stanch bishop died in Mobile. His daughter, Mrs. Minnie Wilmer Jones, wife of Colonel Harvey E. Jones, who left his leg in Virginia and is adjutant-general of Alabama Veterans, resides in Mobile, happy in her children and grandchildren. She is prominent in leadership in the Daughters of the Confederacy; and it was she who forced the passage of the resolution of Mrs. N. V. Randolph, of Virginia, praying the abolishment of the sponsor fad, and had it sent to General S. D. Lee, veteran commander-in-chief. Her brother, Dr. William Holland Wilmer, is the famous oculist of Washington, where he resides with his accomplished wife and three children, his eldest boy renewing the grand-paternal name.

Another Virginian—a man of war and a man of sport, and later a most famous man of God—was Thomas Underwood Dudley, Son of Thomas Underwood Dudley, the beloved city sergeant of *ante-bellum* Richmond, and his wife, Martha Maria Friend. Born in Richmond in 1837, young Dudley was classmate at the University of Virginia with Virginius Dabney and Dr. Wm. Porcher Du Bose. More notable men in different lines I do not recall, out of that character-breeding epoch. Dabney has already been seen at close range. Dean Du Bose was a born student and a preordained churchman; but he went into the war and got his first baptism of fire, ere going into the church to rise to the head of its writers and dean of one of its noted seminaries.

Dudley—"Tom," as every one called him—was a roundabout fellow, brimming with thought, wit, quick acquisitiveness of all worth knowing. He was a feature in college life; leading in all the fun and reckless jollity and—as Dr. Du Bose said in his memorial service—"not altogether out of its dissipations." As the same best authority added. "He was more of a boy, and more kinds of a boy, than anyone of his time."

All these three classmates went into the war: two of them Virginians and the other—as his name doubly proves—a Huguenot Carolinian. Dudley went in as private, but was promoted to quartermaster captain. Thus he lost that rapid promotion which his strong attributes would have forced from line service. Early after war, he entered the priesthood, under rather strange circumstances. For at college he had balanced between opinion and intent. He was of legal mental habit, not devotional, V. Dabney insisted.　Young Du Bose combated this with, the dictum that "Tom was born for the church!"

When the surrender was still green, and men were casting about what to do, a number of us youngsters decided to start, at least, with a rollicking visit to Baltimore. John Saunders had just moved there; Henley Smith was with us and his parents had a lovely home there; the clubs were sure to swing wide doors. So we went: Myers, Hampden Chamberlayne, Page McCar-ty, John R. Key, Innes Randolph, myself and Tom Dudley. Needless to recall what was done, eaten and imbibed in that round of gastronomy fit for Lucullus! The ancient town had indeed much caloric added to its time! We all roomed at "Guy's"—the old tavern: Dudley and Page McCarty being my roommates. One morning I was awakened at dawn by someone moving. Half-asleep, I asked: "Want iced water?"

"More than gold or precious stones," whispered Dudley. He added not to wake Page; he was dressed to

J. HENLEY SMITH
(OF MOSBY'S CAVALRY)

catch the Washington train, and take that day's Acquia Creek boat for Richmond. And he added: "Can't stand this pace: it means jim-jams, sure! I'm going home to law and corn pone!"

He went, and the next time I met him—at a family dinner

in Baltimore, years after, he wore clerical dress. The change possibly induced by Du Bose's insistence, was hastened by what I heard later. The story ran thus:

In those days the route from Washington to Richmond was mainly by boat and stage coach. Recognizing an old comrade in the tooler of the four-in-hand, the bishop-to-be clambered to the box seat and soon had the reins and was bowling merrily adown the pike. Then—whether from Baltimore on the nerves, or from sitting away from the brake—he picked up a big boulder, upset the coach and threw the insiders into a massed heap. They found their volunteer Phaeton with a fractured collar bone and ribs and left him at a wayside farm, with a country doctor who tied him immovable in starch bandages. Then, after days, the mail that had followed him to Baltimore—and several delayed telegrams—overtook the helpless man. These told him that his wife was desperately ill; and that he must hasten to Richmond, if he would see her alive. Sore in body and in conscience, the remorseful man took first conveyance and reached home. The old intent mastered him; and soon after his wife's death, he was admitted to the Episcopal ministry.

Ordained as deacon in June, 1867, he was placed at Harrisonburg. Next year he was ordained priest and made assistant to Dr. H. A. Wise, at Christ church, Baltimore; becoming rector of that important parish soon after. Then, April, 1875—less than a decade from his deaconite—and in his 38th year—he was consecrated bishop of the great diocese of Kentucky. His career in the church is too recent history to need note here. So is that as chancellor of the University of the South, to which he succeeded Bishop Gregg, of Texas, in June 1893.

Bishop Dudley was thrice married, his first wife having been Miss Fanny Cochran, of Loudon county, Va. She left four daughters: Catherine Noland, now Mrs. G. S. Richards, of New York; Martha Maria, now Mrs. James Kirkpatrick, of Collington, Md., Alice Harrison, now Mrs. William McDowell, of Lexington, Ky., and Fanny Cochran, the late Mrs. H. R. Woodward, of Middleburg, Va.

The second wife of the bishop was Miss Virginia Fisher Rowland, of Norfolk, Va. She had two sons, Thos. Underwood, Jr., of Middlesburg, and John Rowland Dudley, of Terminal, Cal., and Harriet Gardner Dudley, now Mrs. Tevis Goodloe, of Louisville, Ky.

The third Mrs. Dudley, who survives the bishop, was Miss Mary Elizabeth Aldrich, of New York. Her two children are Gertrude Wyman Dudley, now Mrs. H. S. Musson, of Louisville, and Aldrich Dudley of the same city.

Bishop Dudley's life was not only a great and busy one: it was resultful and efficacious. In it and the international respect and praise it won him, is ample room for pleasant contemplation to his numerous descendants of the second and third generations.

A still older church worked for the souls and bodies of its children.

Two Jewish synagogues were open all the war, in Richmond; the Portuguese, *Beth Shalome*, Rabbi George Jacobs, and the German, Bethahabah, Rabbi M. J. Michelbacher. And, outside of church charity proper, Jewish women wrought unceasingly in hospital and camp, nursing and feeding the needy; among them, well remembered Mrs. Abram Hutzler, Mrs. Abram Smith, Mrs. M. J. Michelbacher, the Misses Rachel Levey, Leonora Levy, now Mrs. Mayer Hart, of Norfolk; Bertha Myers, Clara Myers and Rosa Smith. To one and all, Jew and Gentile, hail!

Yet, after all—and with no irreverence and no disrespect to the cloth—the truest manifestation of real piety during the war gleamed out from the fetid and loathsome hospitals of camp and town.

CHAPTER XXXIII

HOSPITALS AND WOMEN'S WORK

IF religion be really charity wearing the mantle of heroism, then the noble women and the tireless men who tended
the wounded and the suffering wrought their own canon-
ization in the Unerring Sight. Nowhere on the globe have
war nurses worked more ceaselessly and more gently to
beneficent result; nowhere have they worked against such
tremendous odds of wearing strain, lacking appliances and
want of education and experience, in both the tender and
the tended.

The distant reaches of the trans-Mississippi, the long
suspense of Vicksburg, the ghastliness and horror of Bragg's
retreat; Richmond, Atlanta—every blood-hallowed section
of the fair South, wrote its undying epic of constancy, courage and self-sacrifice, on the white-washed walls of its
nearest hospital.

That matrons and mothers did such great deeds was heroic; that young and tender girls, nurtured as the darlings
of luxurious homes, stood with them, shoulder to shoulder, through all the war's length, was godlike!

There is no iota of exaggeration in the recitals of women's
work for those long, bitter yet resultful four years. Unhappily, it has been left too much to tradition when it
deserves graving upon bronze. Even its roughest recital is
a poem and its memory a sacrament; and, as in most other

things I attempt to describe, Richmond was the convex reflex of that highest manifestation of the Cause "In the land where we were dreaming."

Space permits but casual glimpse of the Richmond hospital trials; but by one all are seen. Nor will mention from memory seem invidious, for the grandchildren and one-time lovers of those dear old girls realize the literal truth that theirs was the beautiful charity that elects not in its giving of succor and of love, yet strives to hide from its left hand the benefactions of its right.

In a time when no sexagenarian was too feeble, no stripling too young, to answer to unceasing call for more men, every girl in Dixie stood ready to line up with the elder women and face the sickening or heartbreaking scenes that trod, swift and dizzying, in the red footprints of every battle. And not one record is extant that any single sister failed the mute call for aid from the lips of her gray-clad brother's wounds; that one turned inattentive ear to the message in the fleeting breath to those dear ones far away for whom—as well as for her—he died.

Through these pages, current note has been made of how the women, young and old, gentle and rough, began their sacrifices early for "the boys"; how the daintiest fingers fell to "scraping lint for the brave to bleed upon." But in those hope-sunnied days lint was an incident, as "French knots" were later, and wounds were the veriest shadow of a glib-spoken name. But as ideas fast indurated into hideous facts, the women of all degrees faced them with something deeper than bravery: higher and holier than calmness. Mrs. Mattie Myers wrote me photographic words of the young Fitz Lee, "When life was a jest, and war a pastime." But when the glamour dimmed and the jest was finding its echo from the Valley of Death, the lint-scraping girls had statured to veritable heroines—and never dreamed it.

Eyes that had brimmed over in early partings for the front, were tearless under duty's mandate in sight of hideous suffering and unaccustomed deaths; little hands that had known no rougher touch than that of a true love's lips, never trembled when holding the jetting artery, or soaking the blood-stiffened bandages from ghastly and loathsome wounds. And through all the strain and suspense and noisomeness, there were no mock heroics—no slightest tinge of self-illustration.

Elsewhere I have told how the young and brilliant belles of war-time would leave the hospital kitchen, or the more exacting ward, doff apron and cap to don what ball-dress the blockade had left them, or the tinsel and gewgaws of the mimic stage, again to work for the one Cause that was to them the Trinity of Love and Hope and Duty. To undying honor of the butterflies of that day's fashion, they never recalled their gaudy wings, nor longed for missing honey, when each and every one went back into the grub next morning.

Not for any ordinary pen is it to write the work of one tithe of the noble woman-helpers—to fix the shifting scenes of their wondrous drama of love and duty done. Yet I may record a few that crowd to memory, unbidden—resistless. One of their white-clad band has given her "Memories"; touching the Western and the Eastern war, as at Ringgold, Newnan, Buckner's and the heart-freezing wake of Bragg's retreat.

Mrs. Fanny A. Beers, of Louisiana, tells simply of her first duty at the sweet, fresh little "Soldier's Rest," on convenient Clay street, Richmond. Later, she was a refuge and ministering angel at Gainsville and Resaca, Ringgold and Atlanta: in the wake of Bragg's blood-stained retreat. There in charge were Mrs. Gwathmey, Mrs. Booker, Mrs. James Grant, with Misses Catherine Poitreaux and Susan Watkins, and not forgetting Mrs. Edmund Ruffin. Near this was a similar private refuge—would that they had half sufficed!—organized and managed by Mrs. Caroline Mayo. Great woman that she was, the flower of Virginia womanhood was quick to respond to her call. A little later, as the war began its first red steps toward quick-coming ghastliness, almost every great home in the city had its hospital-room, as described in Mrs. Louisa Haxall Harrison's letter, heretofore quoted. They were the nurseries of the famous and selfless nurses who made possible the tremendous work done in the vast and quick-overflowed museums of mangled manhood: as Chimborazo, Robinson's, Officer's hospital, the Georgia, Louisiana, Winder's, the Alabama and the Tompkins.

MRS. FANNIE A. BEERS

The story of the Alabama hospital at Richmond is luminous with the record of a woman who no less authority than General Joseph E. Johnston declared, "Was more useful to my army than a new brigade." Mrs. Hopkins had married before she wedded Judge Arthur F. Hopkins, of Mobile. At the first fighting, she offered her services to the state in its crude organizing; developed special fitness and was sent to Richmond, before Bull Run. There she organized and controlled that great house of mercy, all during the war, writing her biography indelibly on the heart of many a modest hero yet living—of many more that have been still for decades. Her memory lives, green and fragrant, in Virginia and in her home state.

Juliet Ann Opie was eldest daughter of Hon. Hierome Lindsay Opie, of Virginia, and was born in Jefferson county, Va., in 1816. She was in direct sixth descent from Helen Lindsay, daughter of Rev. David Lindsay, who died in Northumberland in 1667 and was only son of Sir Hierome Lindsay, of the Mount, Lord Lion King-at-Arms, of Scotland. In early youth Miss Opie married Capt. Alex. G. Gordon, U. S. N., and was early widowed. Later she married chief justice of Alabama, Arthur Francis Hopkins. She sold property in Alabama, Virginia and New York and gave nearly $200,000 to the Confederate cause. She was honored by vote of thanks of her state and her face was printed upon two of its bank bills. Not only untiring and self-sacrificing, she was twice wounded upon the field at Seven Pines, while lifting wounded men. She limped slightly from the last hurt, until her death at Washington in 1890, when she was followed to her grave at Arlington by Gray and Blue. Generals Joe Johnston, Joe Wheeler and Lieutenant-General Schofield, head of the United States Army, were among her mourners.

General Lee wrote to her, "You have done more for the South than all the women." Johnston has been quoted and, in a glowing letter Wheeler called her even more.

It is pleasantly coincidental that the daughter of the general who called Mrs. Hopkins "the Florence Nightingale of the South" was known to the soldiers of the Spanish war as "the Army Angel." Miss Annie Wheeler won unknowing, and worthily wore, that title by her beautiful work of love in the yellow fever hospitals in Cuba. Years before, General Joseph E. Johnston had written of Mrs. Hopkins as "The Angel of the South."

Her beautiful daughter, Juliet Opie, married old General Romeyn B. Ayres, while a young girl, and now resides at Laurel, Md. It was to her that the exceptional phrase of General Johnston was written. Her two young children sleep by her mother and General Ayres at Arlington.

The heights of Chimborazo had a great and busy hospital. Its brisk and brilliant matron was the Mrs. Phoebe Pember already spoken of. Hers was a will of steel, under a suave refinement, and her pretty, almost Creole accent covered the power to ring in *defi* on occasion. The friction of these attributes against bumptiousness, or young authority, made the hospital the field of many "fusses" and more fun.

Pretty and charming Mrs. Lucy Mason Webb has already been met on the mimic boards of charity work. She performed a heavier rôle, and that most success-

MRS. ARTHUR F. HOPKINS
(JULIET ANN OPIE)

fully, in her long engagement as matron in the Officer's hospital, under Doctors Charles Bell Gibson, A. Y. P. Garnett, Lafayette Guild and others. Her husband was killed in the collapse of the floor of the capitol at Richmond, and the universally loved widow devoted her best years to caring for suffering strangers, who yet were brothers.

One noble Alabama woman sleeps in the midst of the boys she loved and lived for in the "Soldiers' Rest" of Magnolia Cemetery at Mobile. Ann Toulmin Hunter was the mother of the soldiers, from the day the gray was donned. Unceasingly she worked for them in kitchen, camp and hospital, and when the first nameless dead of her state were collected and brought home—long preceding this era of pretty parks and pretty oratory—she never rested until name and roster had been recovered, in every case possible.

When she laid down for endless sleep her wish was carried out, and her rest is in the soldiers' last home.

A Georgia matron, whose war-time life and energies were devoted to the soldier, sick or well, left her high epitaph written in letters of love, upon the monument she reared to their honor. The widow of Dr. John Carter of Augusta, had been a belle and beauty as Miss Martha Milledge Flournoy. Her married life had passed in society: and her widowhood, prior to the war had changed her mode of life but little. But when the call came, Mrs. Carter threw all her exceptional strength of character into work for the boys. She helped the men at the front with forwarded food, clothing and delicacies; aided the Georgia hospitals in Virginia with contributions and personally tended the sick and wounded and buried the dead, when the grasp of active war held her own state. Mrs. Carter's memory is still green with the veterans; and she has made theirs immortal by her *post-bellum* energy and influence. She it was who organized and for many years was president of the Ladies' Memorial Association; and her zeal and judgment made possible that stately monument to the Confederate dead, of which Augustans of today are justly proud.

Mrs. Carter's death brought universal regret, social and civic, in the home city she had served so well. Of her children but two survive, but the third and fourth generations cherish her memory. Major Mason Carter, 5th U. S. Infantry (retired) is now at San Diego, Cal. He went through the Civil War; and I latest recall him and his gifted and gracious wife, when he was detailed as tactical head of the

Sewanee cadets and the pair were marked factors in the cultured circles of the mountain. His sister, Sophia Flournoy Carter Johnson, resides at the university; and she is credited with being the brightest and most helpful of the many handsome widows there, who tea and talk and help the needy. Her mother's tact and energy have descended on her and her experience and dramatic tact make her the younger "set's" leader. In her picturesque home is her daughter, Miss Florine Johnson; but the three sons are scattered. Flournoy Carter Johnson resides in New Orleans; a skilled chemist. He married Miss Julienne Sneed, a Memphis belle and popular in all three of her homes; being frank as intellectual and a delightful musician. Two sturdy and pretty boys complete that family.

Sebastian King Johnson is still a bachelor, residing in Columbus, Ohio; but his youngest brother sets him good example. Bertram Page Johnson is first lieutenant in the 20th U. S. Infantry, stationed at the Presidio, Monterey, Cal. He married Miss Augusta Ford Hill, of Helena, Mont.

The children of Dr. and Mrs. John Carter who died were: Captain Milburn Carter, killed on the Confederate side at Missionary Ridge; Dr. Flournoy Carter, who served as surgeon of Rhett's battery; and Barron Carter, U. S. ensign, who served as aide to Commodore Tatnall.

Miss Emily Virginia Mason has already appeared in this narration *en doyenne* of her family. Past her ninety-fourth birthday, she had still a wonderful greenery of heart and strength of character and vivacity of mind. She lately wrote me with her own hand and retained her quaint and pretty humor. I recall her at eighty-four years of age arranging to chaperone a party of young girls on an extensive tour of Europe.

The combination of attributes noted made her a leader in the great work of the hospitals, all during the war. No roster of its immortal matrons would be complete without her name. She was almost ubiquitous at the Greenbrier White, Norfolk, Charlottesville and Lynchburg, and was chief matron of the Winder hospital at Richmond, to the very close. With her worked the only other daughters of John Thomson Mason who reached womanhood, Mrs.

Catherine Armistead Rowland (whose daughter, Kate Mason Rowland, late lived with Miss Mason at Washington) and Mrs. Laura Ann Thomson Chilton, now of Richmond.

The work of Miss Mason has been recorded often in print, notably in the *Atlantic Monthly* and in Mrs. Davis's book, and she was herself a forceful and piquant writer, whose pen has been much in demand.

Only in the February of this year, the brave, loyal and gentle nature of this venerable lady of another day

EMILY VIRGINIA MASON IN HER 92D YEAR

yielded to a sudden stroke of paralysis. She never rallied and, on the 17th of that month—when this page was ready for the press—she passed into her better life, painlessly and almost imperceptibly. About her bedside were the few still left of those nearest and dearest to her; but the thousands who knew her name, yet had never seen her face, sent to them a true and deep sympathy that was heartborn and a balm. Baltimore, Washington, and all Virginia will mourn for "Miss Emily"; but the general regret has no limits of section. All who knew of her even, feel that a vital link between the past and the present has been broken.

No memory of woman's work in trying days is without an echo of another Virginian, who labored beside her, almost as early and in the same rich field of Charity and Love. The name of Miss Sallie Tompkins,—sister of Col. Christopher Q. Tompkins and "Aunt Sallie" as she was known to those near her—glows freshly today in the heart of many a brave fellow who is still here, only through her ministrations at the Tompkins Hospital at Richmond, of which she was the head and soul. Original, old fashioned and tireless in well doing, she was as simple as a child and as resolute as a veteran. She is living as these lines are written, I think, near the capital in which her work was done; but she is very old. She bears the unique distinction of being the only woman commissioned as captain in the Confederate Army.

From the group of noble women who wrought and sacrificed most in the war, Mrs. Henri Weber stands out clearly.

Margaret Isabella Walker was the eldest daughter of Hon. Carleton Walker, collector of the port of Wilmington in 1812, and of Caroline Mallet; and was born in 1824, at Fayetteville, in that state. Her twin brother was Dr. John Mosely Walker, long since dead. The girl was most carefully educated by an accomplished father, in her home state and at the Barhamville Institute, Columbia, S. C. While she was still a girl, he failed by heavy endorsements for a friend, then governor of his state; and the daughter began that career as a teacher, in which she attained such fame. When her family moved to Tennessee she taught at Columbia, and later in Nashville. There she met Professor Henrich David Christian Frederich Weber, a notable teacher of that day. A warm attachment was followed by a marriage in 1852; and the pair settled in Nashville and taught together until the war began. But the husband was a Unionist by principle and education; and moreover, he had interests in the Northwest. He went to Cincinnati, as a base; and his wife remained for the moment with her kinsfolk in Tennessee, all her sympathies, education and instincts being warmly pro Southern. Then the expected "short war" waxed longer and more bitter; Donelson fell and Nashville; and communication was wholly cut off between the pair. Mrs. Weber, with her two little sons, fled to the home of her sister, Mrs. Adams, at Lafayette, Ala. There she struggled on alone, until the neighbors lost all means of paying for tuition; hearing only at rare intervals, any word from her husband. Meantime she never wearied of caring for the well men at the front, or nursing the sick and wounded, or sister-like, soothing the last hour of suffering here and speeding the fleeting soul. Her record as a nurse and comforter is no less white because never blared abroad. It was graved deep on the hearts of her protégés.

Then came what was misnamed Peace. The madman's pistol had murdered the infant conciliation and the leaders of the Cause were corralled by blind rage and driven into prison pens. The eyes of all the world—the patience of civilization—were strained to one reeking and unwholesome casemate at Fortress Monroe. And, just then, Professor Weber's influential friends secured conduct through the lines for his wife. He sent her passports and funds to reach him at Cincinnati, by way of Roanoke Island and Norfolk. At the former, she was robbed by the guard and she landed at Fort Monroe penniless and unable to communicate with her husband. But she learned, for the first time, of the treatment of "the prisoner of state" and of his shackling by Stanton's order, at the servile hands of that general, whose service had taught him that obedience to hint of superior was the best soldiership.

Burning with indignant shame, Mrs. Weber forgot self, husband, her recent destitution. For the time, she trans-

figured insulted Southern womanhood. She had ticket
for herself and the boys to Washington and Baltimore.
Thence she hastened to Washington and the White House.
She had known the statesman *sartor* at home; and he received her courteously. But that trimmer to the wind
of expediency and the moment was just then adamant.
Her plea for justice—even for release of the man she knew
to be innocent—moved Mr. Johnson no tittle. He scoffed
at the idea of any interference with "Stanton's justice;"
and, convinced that there was no more power to move him,
Mrs. Weber gave rein to her disgust and there, in the White
House, lashed his accidency with verbal knouts. When
she finally reached her husband and related the episode,
he cried:

"What have you done, wife? We have been separated
for four years and tomorrow we shall be sent together to
the penitentiary!"

But no such finale came. Andy Johnson was either too
busy and baited, or too jealous of his surroundings, ever
to vent personal malignity upon the helpless ones in his
clutch. Years after, he met Mrs. Weber, without recalling
the incident in any way.

A few years after the war, Professer Weber died; and his
widow—after completing the careful education of her children—continued to teach at Nashville and added up, in all,
forty years of service to the youth of that city. No marvel
then, that when she died in Nashville, two years ago, the
day of her funeral was made a memorial one by the mayor:
all schools being closed and the teachers and pupils following
the flower hidden casket to Mount Olivet.

Mrs. Weber had two sons: John Walker Weber and Henri
Carleton Weber; both cultured and experienced instruct-
ors for years. The elder died after long and useful management of the Sewanee grammar school under Bishop

Quintard and Dr. Hodgson. Professor Carleton Weber is now superintendent of the schools of Nashville, his native city. She had also two step-children, Mary E. Weber, now Mrs. F. E. Farrar, and Frederich E. Weber. She also adopted a daughter, Eva Theodora, now Mrs. Lyman Syms, of Jeffersonville, Ind.

John Weber, Mrs. Weber's elder son, left four children:

MRS. L. M. WILSON
(AUGUSTA EVANS IN 1867)

Caro Carleton Weber—now Mrs. Marvin Sneed, of Calvert, Tex., and the mother of two children, Marvin and John W. Sneed:—Margaret Isabella Weber, John Walker Weber and Lee Ellis Weber, all residing in Nashville.

The children of Carleton Weber are six: Beulah Beaumont Weber, Louise Weber, Margaret Isabella Weber, Sarah Carleton Weber, Dorothy Weber and Henri Carleton Weber; all of Nashville.

It is notable that this remarkable woman began teaching at the age of eighteen, and lived to be eighty-six. She married in 1852, and when eighty-two years old wrote her reminiscences: after having always been a fluent and popular writer of poems and sketches. She was a stately, elegant personality: a delightful *raconteuse;* and the summer society of Sewanee looked to her as its head.

Another Alabama girl, who later reached more general fame, was a wise and willing worker in the hospitals and camps near her home. Augusta Evans Wilson, one of the most successful women authors of America, was then a tall, young brunette, with much promise and even more altruism. Her father's home was close to the Summerville camp and the writer-to-be spent all of her time in its kitchen and at the bedsides of the sick. Even that early they required little forcing to take her "compositions." In her age and fame perhaps more valued than the many tokens and souvenirs, sent her from the noted far and near, are the rough rings, bracelets and baskets, cut from buttons and fruit seeds by her convalescents, as only possible expression of the love and reverence they bore her.

These are but few of the many whose names escape me, as they worked for love, and not renown. All honor to the few still left! Equal meed to those who wait the final bugle that will rename their "unknown dead."

CHAPTER XXXIV

THE CRUSH OF THE " 'CONDA"

THERE is ever a reason given when one side to a contest is defeated. If I were asked the most active cause in the Confederate collapse I should say: The blockade whipped us. It crushed the early hope and strangled the laboring breath of the moribund desperation of a hemmed-in few, resisting many, peering into black hopelessness, across the line of bristling bayonets in front and a cordon of armored and armed ships behind their only egress and ingress.

Aptly did camp slang name the blockade the " 'Conda." It was the crush of the " 'Conda" that squeezed us to death.

At first flush of war the masses of the South really believed that one Southerner " could whip a half-dozen Yankees and not half try."

This feeling was shared, at first, by many an earnest fighter, who won the best results after he had learned that one to two was easier odds and one to one more sure. It is plain that deathless John Brown Gordon felt this when he took the " Racoon Roughs" to Atlanta armed only with pikes. Gallant Barney Bee believed it at cost of a priceless life when he cried to Jackson: "They are driving us, sir!" Many another, in yellow sash as in unmarked butternut— urged by dearest and best loved little heroes in homespun at home—believed it, until too late.

Calm Lee, astute Stephens, inspired Jackson, swinging old Longstreet—tough Jubal Early—Jefferson Davis himself—never trusted in the fallacy, preproved by their knowledge of a common people, rent asunder by beliefs and interests that *seemed* to mean life to each segment. But facing the fact discouraged none of the thinkers.

No one of the leaders of the South ever feared the foe in front; all of them cast nervous glances over their shoulders at the blockade behind them. Decades ago I smoked my post-prandial cigar, at Atlanta, with a division commander, who had won first spurs in Florida and had worn them worthily in all subsequent wars—General William S. Walker.

"General," I casually Sir Oracled—"the blockade whipped us."

He shifted the brief stump of his leg across his crutch; blew one blue ring through another, ere he answered slowly: "Well, that . . . and the fact that the mothers of the South did not bear all male children!"

As the war wore on the blockade became a serious problem, and ere its close a hideous one, in the straining clutch for the very means of life. The gradual drain of resources had habituated even the wealthier classes to plain fare and little of that; but when the whole carrying power of the one poor railroad—ill equipped and constantly threatened by cavalry raids—was overtaxed by dire demand of the army at Petersburg, privation grinned out of most costly cupboards. And even had there been the transport for it there was no product in the land capable of supporting the army and the people, in any sort of needful comfort. Only in portions of the trans-Mississippi were supplies of meat and corn quite adequate to the demand; but the entire cis-river Confederacy starved and fought.

As the struggle drew to its close, thoughtful men saw that

we were dying in gasps under the crushing folds of the "'Conda." We were not permitted to fight it out to the bitter end and die, but to waste and shrink in an exhausted receiver, that had no pinhole of hope nor refreshment piercing to its vacuum.

Yet, there was neither despondency nor pessimism among the thinkers of the older set. If felt, it was hidden, or whispered only in cabinet, or council of leaders. The young and the gay held cheer in their hearts, whatever they may have had upon the board. The gloom brought to Richmond's kitchens by the blockade never was allowed ascent to her parlors.

It has been shown how the women and girls sustained the ardor of the men; sharing with them to the very last every dainty now growing rarer daily—even denying themselves necessaries of life to "give to the boys." It has been shown, too, that out of this very sharing of what each had, grew the most unique assemblies, or balls, ever known in the land. This mutuality of moral support was the origin of those exceptional "starvation parties" which lasted to the very eve of the *Dies Iræ*. They were the wraiths and *manes* of aforetime splendors in every point, save two: the old time hospitality and the genuine enjoyment. In a pretty long society experience, I recall no dances where higher courtliness and real refinement shone than in these impromptus of the butternut beaux and calico-clad belles of the middle '60's.

The toilettes? Well, there were some few who held to the remnants of glories, when the larders were not even restaurants for ants. The recent letter of a brilliant woman recalls this, in quotation of "a great get-up" at a very swell wedding reception:

> "*Let me whisper: this dress, that I now wear for thee,*
> *Was a curtain of old, in Philadelphee!*"

The over-pious and the pessimistic shook sad heads at the recurrent starvations: "It was dancing on the grave's edge!" But the girls and the gay ones laughed reply:

"These poor boys have little enough of fun and frolic; and it is little enough to give them all they ask."

In the "mire-truce" of winter, or when they slipped in on duty, *that* was always a dance.

The beaux came from every state and every arm of service. The navy men were always popular, for "Annapolis dancing" as well as better things. What girl of that day forgets Walter Butt, Hilary Cenas, the Lee boys, or Henry Marmaduke?

There was quite a flutter when the last named was transferred from Mobile station to Richmond. He was an original with nomadic turn that has clung to him, even in the old bachelorhood he is now passing at Washington, in congenial and altruistic work for friends of old. Henry Hungerford

LIEUT H. H. MARMADUKE, C. S. N.

Marmaduke was the fifth of the six Marmaduke brothers: all in service save one too young. These were Colonel Vincent Marmaduke who fought his Missouri regiment from start to finish. He first married Miss Spence, of Tennessee, who left two daughters: Mrs. Dr. Harrison and Mrs. Robert Cary, of Kansas City. His later marriage to Mrs. Ames, of Missouri, brought no children. He and she are both dead.

General John S. Marmaduke won high repute in the

Western army and was governor of Missouri after peace. He died a bachelor.

The third Marmaduke, Meredith Miles, married Miss Harvey, of Missouri, and had several children. They moved to Florida, where their many descendants are well known, as well as in other states to which they have scattered.

Darwin W. Marmaduke first married Miss Sappington, of Missouri, who died without children; but the second wife has three. She was Miss Mary Crawford, daughter of Colonel James Crawford, of Mobile. The children are James Crawford Marmaduke, of Seattle; Zemula, Mrs. George C. Pope, of Iowa; and Mrs. Henry Ames, of St. Louis.

The fifth brother we have seen; and the youngest, Leslie Marmaduke, now lives in St. Louis. He also married one of the Crawford sisters (Zemula), the third being now Mrs. Wm. M. Mastin, of Mobile. Leslie Marmaduke has two unmarried daughters.

But while there was penury at the capital there was often luxury at the port. The blockaded towns, especially Wilmington, had opportunities for things they had never dreamed of before. When families in Richmond, who were on easy terms with *truite à la Tartare*, recognized Strasbourg pie as a friend and sipped burgundy familiarly, were living entirely on cornmeal, rice and slim-side bacon, I was sent to Wilmington for a blockader's cargo of ammunition. Capua and Corinth rolled into one had not seemed more like fairy-land.

The ordnance cargo had not managed to elude the lazy, hulking double-enders guarding the Cape Fair; but a trader steamer had slipped in from Nassau with perishable cargo, in part. At the blockade headquarters I dined on Southdown mutton, brought over on ice, fresh fish, tropical fruits and even oysters. The men themselves took them all as a matter of course, but I fear that my own appetite and won-

derment must have startled my really hospitable hosts.
I had been to the ports before on similar missions, but then
the privation inland and at the border had not made the
contrast so glaring. All the ports had more or less comfort,
but Wilmington was the veritable city of Lucullus on the
Confederate map.

Around that city, too, centred most of the stirring incident and romance of "runnin' th' Bloc." That little river
was the feeder, in great part, of the cannon that spoke to
Pope, McClellan and Joe Hooker—even to Grant for a time—
and bade them "Stand back!" It was the hope of the sur-
geons and eager hospital matrons, for medicines and appliances that the smaller "Potomac Ferry" could not furnish.
It was, too, the grave of more than one adventurous fellow
and of one beautiful woman, whose fate was stranger than
that of Absalom. It was down that river, too, that handsome and ill-fated Frank Du Barry floated to his death,
and was buried in the sea, with a sail winding-sheet and a
32-pound shot at his feet.

The last time I saw "Jimmy" Clark was forty-four years
ago; the day that Lee evacuated Petersburg. He had been my
boyhood friend in Washington and my partner in more than
one round of the cosy parlors, or the glittering gambling dens
of Richmond, when he came back from Camp Chase, in
February, 1865. On the morning of Lee's retreat, Clark
was watching the shell-ignited tobacco warehouses, with
the pretty Lucas sisters, as his parole kept him from better
duty. Capt. Frank Markoe galloped up and told him he
was to take Miss Mary Lee back home on a train that would
bring in Field's division. In his late letter to me, Clark says:

"I landed Miss Mary safely, at Mrs. Lee's, Grace street,
about two A. M. next day; and left Richmond before day-
light, up the canal for the Valley. I did not see any of the
boys, if indeed any of them were left in Richmond."

James Louis Clark was the son of Major Michael M. Clark, U. S. A.; and though born in barracks, was my chum at the Rugby Academy, at Washington; now Hotel Hamilton, on K and 14th streets. His lovely mother was Miss Anne Matthews Johnson, of Frederick county, Md., and the other children were: Duncan Clinch Clark, who married Miss Chrissie Haywood; Jula Lee Clark, John Mackay Clark, Thomas Johnson Clark, who married Miss Elizabeth Magruder; Annie Johnson Clark, who married Joseph Rieman; and Charles Michael Clark. The married ones all reside in Baltimore. "Jimmy" came South as quartermaster of the First Maryland, resigned to go on Stuart's staff and then commanded Troop F, of (Harry Gilmore's) Maryland cavalry battalion. He was a popular fellow in Washington and later in Richmond with both sexes. After the war he disappeared in the then Wild West. He was district attorney for the Leadville district and is now at his mine in Colorado, 135 miles from a railroad. Last June I wrote a syndicate sketch of Jefferson Davis. In faraway Columbine, Clark picked up a copy of the Savannah *News*, saw my name on the article and sent a tracer letter to that city. Since we have corresponded and recently he wrote me of a Richmond breakfast that defied the blockade and was remarkable in its collection of notables of that day. It is worthy of reproduction also, as showing Gen. Jos. E. Johnston's estimate of Gen. R. E. Lee. It was at the time when General Johnson was ordered to command the Western army, on recovery from his wound at Seven Pines; and when the relative merits of Lee and Johnson were much discussed. Clark writes that he was in Richmond, having resigned from the First Maryland and not having yet joined Gen. J. E. B. Stuart as volunteer aide. He adds:

"Gen. Johnston's first act had been to appoint Major Alfred Barbour, who had been his chief quartermaster at

Manassas, to the same position in the Western army; and Major Blue Moore, who had been first assistant, to his old post. A week or so before the general went West, a breakfast was given by Majors Barbour and Moore, at Old Tom Griffin's, on Main street. Rumor said the breakfast was to honor the reconciliation between Senator Henry S. Foote and Hon. Wm. M. Yancey, who had been estranged after long intimacy; and both these great men were enthusiastic partisans of Gen. Johnston.

"Major Barbour presided at head of the table; Senator Foote at his right and Gov. Milledge T. Bonham of South Carolina, next. Then came Gen. Gustavus W. Smith and next, Major John Daniel, of the Richmond *Examiner*, with his arm in a sling from the wound received while acting as Johnson's aide, at the time both were shot down. Next sat Gen. Johnston, on the left of Major Blue Moore, who held the foot of the table. On Major Moore's right, I sat: next me, John Bonne Cary and next, his brother, Wilson M. Cary, who was going West, with Major Moore. On his right was Gen. John B. Floyd, late Buchanan's secretary of war; and finally, Mr. Yancey, on Major Barbour's left. And "The breakfast was one such as old Tom Griffin alone could prepare, though I recall nothing of a *menu*, rare in those days. Being a youngster, I was all attention to the talk.

"Gen. Johnston, as usual, was taciturn; still suffering much from his unhealed wound. But Mr. Yancey and Mr. Foote were the life of the party, while others, of course, contributed their mite to its success. Mr. Daniel—the most brilliant editor the South had—was a close second to Gen. Joe Johnston for taciturnity. Gen. Bonham sang several sweet little love songs; but the head of the table virtually had the whole innings: Yancey and Foote vieing in brilliancy. Suddenly, Mr. Foote said:

"'Gentlemen, what do you think? Some time ago, Mr. Yancey characterized me as an old duffer!' Then, turning to Mr. Yancey, 'Now, Yancey, you know I was married a little over a year ago. You are to come and take breakfast with us tomorrow; and we will show you as fine and bouncing a boy of three months, to disprove your epithet!'

"And, amid great laughter, Mr Yancey agreed to adopt the breakfast and the boy!

"The breakfast lasted from ten to twelve o'clock; and then Mr. Yancey said to Old Tom Griffin: 'Bring fresh glasses and fill bumpers of champagne.'

"When this was done, Mr. Yancey arose and said: 'This toast is to be drunk standing,' and he looked straight at Gen. Johnston, who kept his seat, when all the rest arose; 'Gentlemen, let us drink to the health of the only man who can save the Confederacy—General Joseph E. Johnston!'

"The glasses were emptied with enthusiasm amid great applause. The general had not yet touched his glass. Now he took it up and said gravely: 'Mr. Yancey, the man you describe is now in the field, in the person of General Robert E. Lee. I will drink to his health!'

"Mr. Yancey's reply came like a flash: 'I can only reply to you, sir, as the speaker of the house of burgesses did to Gen. Washington:—"Your modesty is only equalled by your valor!"' Then the breakfast was over."

The Wolf had early begun his permanent siesta upon the doormat. The dire straits for food and shelter, succeeding the battles around Richmond caused the government to endorse and encourage the hegira started by the fears of the floating feminine population. Georgia and North Carolina were the favorite refuges in their inland towns, like Charlotte, Salisbury, Milledgeville and La Grange. At the last, my mother and sisters were measurably comfortable, later in the war. While not wholly immune from raids, the little places gave families easier access to Richmond and to earlier news, thus living in less anxiety and at cheaper rate. So, refugee life became a distinct war system and some of the coteries in the disused factories and school buildings were of cultivated women and exceptionally bright young girls. They were as free from men as the latter day watering-places; but convalescent young heroes and droppers-in returning from brief fur-loughs prevented utter stagnation of sentiment. Especial prizes were men notable in society for marked traits, as "Jim Frazer, the handsomest man in the army:" so written down in a delicate but faded handwriting. Sometimes flirtation ran its length; and more than one engagement "for three years or the war," became a reality before it matured. One special case attracted much comment then and is still recalled.

CAPTAIN JAMES FRAZER

Mr. I. I. Jones, a prosperous merchant of Mobile, discounted Jepthah of old and, in the language of the green cloth, "went him five better." A man of sense, as well as of taste, he educated his sextette of daughters under his own eye and kept it jealously upon them. They had singular unanimity of beauty; all being gifted with the peculiar charms of form and face and voice that mark the highbred Hebrew maiden. Sarah, the eldest, is now Mrs. Louis L. Morrison, of New York, and has a notable family· Mr. L. L. Morrison, Jr., being a prominent lawyer of that city. The second, Julia, married Mr. J. K. Cobin, of the same city. Their daughter, Miss Rosalind, a brilliant and most sought musician, is now Mrs. Ransom Wright, of Augusta, Ga., and the only son, Mr. I. Jones Cobin, coincidently wedded the most noted and popular of Mobile musicians, Miss Julia McPhillips. They now reside in Brooklyn.

The third of the Jones sisters, Adelaide, married and died long since, as did her children; and the fourth, Emily, became wife of a famous rabbi of New Orleans, Rev. James K. Gutheim. She was prime mover in the great Touro Infirmary, of that city. Her funeral, a few years after that, was participated in by clergy of all denominations; over ten thousand people of all classes and van-loads of floral devices, making it a sort of mortuary carnival. The fifth sister, Bertha Jones, married Major Thomas P. Brown, one of the most popular and prominent of Mobile's merchants. There, still reside two of their fourteen children: Mr. T. P. Brown, Jr., who married Miss Winnie Forbes; and Bertha, wife of Mr. A. E. Reynolds; while Mr. Colden Brown is a merchant of Hong Kong.

When a girl in her teens, the youngest of the Jones sisters was heroine of a romance at La Grange. Miss Esther was perfect type of petite brunette in face and figure; her midnight hair still in long plaits. She soon became *the* toast with youthful heroes, straying into that almost Adamless Eden. There were other notable women there, too; Mrs. Phillips, of Ship Island; the families of Senators Sparrow, of Louisiana, and Ben Hill, of Georgia; Mrs. Clay, Misses Emily and Esmeralda Boyle, the poetess, and many another.

The pretty stranger, though young, was already affianced to dashing Garland Webb, a troop captain from Kentucky. He was at the front, but his younger brother, John Webb, chanced in La Grange and set up protectorate over his sister-to-be. At a soirée in honor of her, one of those trifles that made the sum of life, with the hot bloods of that day, fell out between Webb and Captain J. S. Barrett.

Next morning saw the whole town wending its way to a suburban field. All women were on tiptoe of excitement, except the innocent cause of the affair of honor. But when she "Saw his body, borne by her on a shutter," Miss Jones shrieked, flew to the telegraph office, and wired her sire to come. He arrived promptly; meeting at the station arriving Captain Webb, who came to nurse his brother, or—bury him! Happily, no need for that last ceremony, so Yew and tears were replaced by orange blossoms and smiles. The beautiful *casus belli* became Mrs. Esther Webb. All the "colony" assisted at the pretty, if sudden, function: Misses Hennie Hill and Fannie Sparrow were bridesmaids. But the sequel was an early funeral at New Orleans; and the girl-widow went to her father. She was much sought by army beaux; but it was several years before she married Mr. Clifton Moses, of South Carolina. Again widowed, she devoted her life to rearing her two lovely daughters. Only one of them, named for her father, now survives, to be the stay and comfort of her mother's advancing years.

Mrs. Phillips, the Boyle sisters and many another of the La Grange refugees have passed the shadowy border. Miss Hennie Hill married, many years ago, Mr. Edgar Thompson, of Atlanta. Only in mid-February of this year she died in that city. She was the only daughter of the great senator; but his two sons still illustrate the famous name in the state for which he did so much: Ben H. as chief justice of her court of appeals; and Charles S. Hill, solicitor of the superior court of Fulton county. So, the orator-statesman's name will be kept in its present green life by his descendants of the third generation.

Miss Fannie Sparrow, the bridesmaid named here, was

the youngest of the three daughters of Senator Edward Sparrow. The eldest was Anna, who married Mr. Decker, of New Jersey and had several children; one of them now being wife of Hon. C. S. Wyly, of Lake Providence, La. The next sister, Kate, when widow of George Sanderson of Natchez, married George Foster. Her two daughters are Mrs. Joseph H. Kent, of Roanoke, Va., and Mrs. J. M. Tompkins, of Lake Providence.

Miss Fannie, the bridesmaid, married Captain A. M. Ashbridge, and went to reside in Pau, France, during the war, but returned to the Lake Providence neighborhood. One of her daughters is now Mrs. C. A. Voelker, wife of the prominent planter of the same parish.

How many names recur in these pages to recall the line of the old song:

"Some at the bridal and some at the tomb!"

CHAPTER XXXV

FEW habitués of Washington, in winters preceding the war, have forgotten "the beautiful Greenhows." Mrs. Rosalie Greenhow was still handsome and young-looking, although one of her daughters, Miss Florence, was a confessed belle and the easy peer in good looks of her famous cousin and rival, Miss Adèle Cutts. The second sister, Miss Gertrude, was also a charming girl; and the then baby of the family was little Rosa, her mother's idol.

The beautiful eldest sister married Lieutenant Treadwell W. Moore, of the regular army. Of course she remained North, love being more masterful than section, and her son, Captain Treadwell W. Moore, is now with his infantry command in the West.

The father became a general and died in 1876; the mother died at Narragansett Pier in 1892, and four years later Captain Moore married Flora Green, daughter of General C. L. Cooper, U. S. A. They have no children.

Mrs. Greenhow was the sister of Mrs. J. Madison Cutts. Their daughters divided capital belleship until Miss Adèle Cutts became the wife of Senator Stephen A. Douglas. Later she married a noted army man, Captain Williams; and their daughters have since been popular factors of Washington sociality.

Mrs. Greenhow was a famous beauty, and as Rose

O'Neill gained the sobriquet of "the Wild Rose." She married Mr. Greenhow of the state department, and at his death was still a young and elegant woman. Southern enthusiast she was, and when the war came offered her aid to Mr. Davis and did useful and delicate secret service. Once she collected a large sum of money abroad, changed it into gold and went to Nassau, to take a blockade-runner into Wilmington. Safely passing the fleet in Cape Fear river, she was landing in a small boat when her footing missed, and she went to the bottom. The gold, belted about her waist, drowned her before the sailors could reach her. In her arms, all the voyage, she had carried her beautiful little girl, Rose, scarce more than an infant. The child was saved, educated partly abroad, and returned to America in the early '70's. She went upon the stage in New York, was induced to leave it by friends; and later married an army officer. During Mrs. Cleveland's time at the White House, she was a noted beauty at the capital and a protégée of that tasteful and charming "first lady." Miss Gertrude Greenhow died unmarried in the South, late in the war or shortly after it.

The story of poor Du Barry was an equally pathetic one. Of fine old Maryland stock, splendid physique, and much personal magnetism, he had left a marine commission behind to come South from conviction. The second year of the war saw him a captain of ordnance at Mobile. It was gossiped in Washington society that he had left the love of his life behind him, in the keeping of a pretty woman with a "signer's" name; but he was suddenly married in the Gulf City, in her very fresh widowhood, to Mrs. Willie Chandler. This lady, whom I first knew as Miss Carrie Holbrook, of New York, had a peculiar sway over men from her early girlhood. Scarcely accounted beautiful, she could have given "handicap" to any prize beauty after the first half hour. Chandler's early death left her with two children, Holbrook, who died before reaching full manhood, and Florence—the unhappy Mrs. Maybrick, whose case has so moved the sympathetic on both sides of the ocean. The Du Barry nuptials followed the burial of his predecessor swiftly enough to cause an equal amount of gossip. Within the year I had urgent letters to try and have him sent abroad, as the doctors said a sea voyage was the sole hope for some mysterious malady that was rapidly ending him. Influence and his old memory with the Davis and Mallory families soon got him orders to purchase ammunition abroad. I met him on arrival at Richmond, shocked to see but a wreck of the brilliant fellow. I was *en route*, as it chanced, to Wilmington, convoyed the party to that port and held the later Mrs. Maybrick on my lap much of the tedious and trying trip. They boarded the slim speedy

MADAME VON RORQUE
(CARRIE HOLBROOK)

blockader; she ran swiftly through the lubberly watchers at the river's mouth and the next day was safe at sea. That afternoon the gallant tar in command of the runner was startled by the news that Du Barry had died very suddenly. The·again widowed wife insisted upon his immediate burial, at sea; declaring that his emphatic wish. The last of the society favorite was slid from a plank into the Atlantic, to stand upright in its depths until it gives up all its secrets at the Judgment day. Mrs. Du Barry went abroad and was married more than once again. She was last the Baroness von Rorque and resided in Germany, where her last husband has wealth and rank. Madame was unhappily in evidence at the lamentable trial of her unfortunate daughter, the two appearing wholly bound up in each other. Since Mrs. Maybrick's reappearance in America, I believe her mother has returned also, for permanent residence.

Of the once wonderful little magnetizer of our sex, a veteran warrior and society man wrote me very lately, from the Pacific coast:

"And speaking of old Washington days, I was again reminded of Frank Du Barry in reading the other day of Mrs. Maybrick. That took me back to Frank and further back to the Holbrook house, in 14th street, New York; and I again almost see the face of Carrie Holbrook in front of me! She was a wonderful dancer, as you recall; and I knew her very well. After Frank's death she married some Englishman, I think.''

I think the lady made several marriages, after that with Willie Chandler, when she had recently shone in Baltimore and Washington circles She met her first husband while in Mobile, to visit her uncle, Rev. Jos. H. Ingraham, the polygon divine who wrote the "Prince of the House of David," the "Pillar of Fire," and some far different romances. That marriage connected Miss Holbrook with some of the oldest families in the South.

Gradually—then more rapidly, fatally—the stricture of the "Conda" tightened about its predestined prey. Better naval workshops, unlimited cash or equivalent credit abroad and the navies of the world to draw from at will, strengthened the coil and closed every port hermetically, save Wilmington. But that port was literally the key to the Confederate situation; its lungs and heart combined So the brain of the nation fostered it with every food and stimulant that poverty and depletion could command. Reponse quick and earnest came; but the vitality that feeds upon itself must at last succumb. Captures and shipwreck reduced the blockade vessels that could not be replaced, and the reckless, daring officers of the risky service, finding themselves without ships, began to drift into other fields. My last visit to the port, to carry a cargo of shells to Richmond, was sad contrast to the first one I described here. The town was listless and dull, the river front deserted, and the blockade managers moody from suspenseful watch for the now rare incomers. These brought no more luxuries, the dire need for shot and shell and arms relegating them to simply army transports. They were received gravely and their cargoes rushed to the front as fast as one badly equipped road—constantly raided and frequently cut— could compass that result.

HON. EDWIN DE LEON
(C. S. COMMISSIONER ABROAD)

Meantime, the fall of New Orleans had closed the small incoming at the Passes and had sealed the river.

My brother and his wife ran into New Orleans in one of the last of the low, swift steamers that eluded the fleet assembling for ascent to the city.

Tiring of diplomatic mission in Europe, which he felt could avail nothing, he took *congé* and sailed for Bermuda, to run the blockade and join the army. He had married while in Egypt, but his wife had never been on this side. Now she insisted on sharing the peril of his venture, even urging him to take the very first vessel. This chanced to be an old one for New Orleans. The trip was safely made but at the Passes the runner was sighted and closely chased by several gunboats. My sister was, of course, the only woman aboard, and while shells were passing over the craft she learned for the first time that its entire cargo was composed of shells and powder. The runner was struck twice, but landed her two passengers safely at the Crescent City, whence they proceeded direct to Richmond.

After the fall of New Orleans, and later of Vicksburg, the re-inspired North redoubled the numbers and the vigilance of its land-bordered blockade. Especially was this the case along the Potomac, infraction of that coil of the "Conda" having theretofore been a pastime with adventurous men and earnest, helpful women.

Of these, some were the tenderest darlings of home and society, but they braved the roughness of camp and the long, icy rides to the river—often through hostile lines that caused hiding by day and progress only at night—to what was known as the "Potomac Ferry." Strangely enough, the ferryman was often an old Maryland "plantation hand," more loyal to "ole mar's" than to the Bluecoats fighting for his freedom—as they thought.

Both Misses Hetty and Constance Cary crossed the river more than once, bringing back rare drugs for the sick and information as valued for the generals. Sometimes a despatch or a plan of a marching raid was curled in the soft tresses of a Baltimore woman, sent through as "rebellious," on the flag of truce boat.

"Jeb" Stuart, Fitz Lee, Pierce Young—and others for aught I know—intrusted some women with permanent passes through their lines, to come and go at will. But there was another class, seeking notoriety, gain—or something else—more than the good of the Cause, and the flare from their overadvertised flambeaux has obscured the quieter light of some better—and far more useful—women volunteers.

We have met Miss Chestney before, in soubrette parts" and as a tyrannous 'teener. She was the friend and trusted adjutant of Mrs. Randolph, in all entertainments for charitable ends. She was a native Washingtonian and sister of Major Oscar Chestney, named lately.

In the late '50's Carusi's dancing school was the Mecca of the gilded squads of the national capital. There, was met a petite and blonde beauty, who danced like a sylph and had a tact and a wit all unknown to the average of the "best society" of mythologic date.

Every function, social or dramatic, in Richmond, knew Miss Chestney; every fellow with good taste admired her, but her pose was that of a reticent "Victory" and her triumphs—save the blockade and stage ones—were never discussed. Today, as the widow of Hon. George H. Butler, this lady is familiar to the cultured and diplomatic circles of the capital. She is the replica of Ninon de L'Enclos, physically, for none meeting her as strangers could believe that this belle of the '60's had ever known the war save by report.

Elsewhere I have mentioned Ratcliffe and Henley Smith of Mosby's corps. The latter has late gone to answer "*Adsum!*" when his name was called from the great roll. A gallant, generous, cultivated gentleman he was, descended from a line of such, his father having been Hon. J. Bayard H. Smith, of Washington and Baltimore. Both were lawyers and both, as the grandfather had been, treasurers of the Washington monument association; the first of the three having been one of the founders of the old *National Intel-*

ligencer. Henley Smith, in his late 'teens, was at Princeton, when the echo of the Sumter gun came to him. He ran away, joined Mosby and served through the war with wounds and credit, but never sought the promotion that wealth and influence would have added to commendation. After the war he settled in Washington, marrying and spending the leisure of wealth in study and travel abroad, and elegant, but unostentatious hospitality in his Dupont Cir-

MRS. GEORGE H. BUTLER
(JOSEPHINE CHESTNEY)

cle home. He died suddenly at Florence while on a Continental tour, leaving his widow to bemoan his passing away in a strange land and without warning. In 1867 Henley Smith married Miss Rebecca Young, daughter of McClintock Young, of Frederick county, Md., who had passed most of her girlhood in Baltimore; and much of their married life was spent in that city. The union was childless.

In his last letter to me Smith described a ride he and Ratcliffe took with Miss Chestney when she crossed the Potomac in 1865 to get medicine and clothing. She made the trip alone, after her escorts were forced to leave her, returning successful and remaining South for the rest of the war.

The river blockade was broken often, to advantage of the hospitals and the larders of Richmond, often to the bringing of important cipher despatches that gave warning of coming raids or advance in force. It was the "underground

mail" too that told the "foreign" fighters of the loved ones
at home. Nor was it without its humors and its comic
episodes. Randolph, the ever-ready, has embalmed one
of its meaner advantagings in a clever parody beginning:

> *We rowed across the Potomac,*
> *Maryland!*
> *We put up cash and then rowed back,*
> *Maryland!*
> *We're loaded deep with hats and shoes,*
> *Or medicines the rich can use—*
> *At prices that just beat the Jews!*
> *Maryland, my Maryland!*

There is neither need nor space to touch upon the dry
and familiar details of the naval composition of the Confederacy. The glamour and romance, in great part, and
pretty nearly all of the usefulness of the sea side of the picture, hang about the dashing and reckless work of the wooden
flyers. But obdurate circumstances forced the rest from
resultful sequence into mere episodes—brilliant, immortal,
but null.

So it was with the outside attempts of the gallant, experienced and eager naval men, chafing at inaction or uncongenial duty and crushed in by the bulky folds of the "'Conda."

The hoped-for building of iron-clad gunboats—the dear
ambition of hopeful and able Secretary Mallory—was cut
off in infancy by closer-drawn land blockade giving quicker
ingress to cavalry raiders. Building in sequestered rivers,
many of them had to be destroyed to save capture. A
saucy speech there anent was made to the secretary by Miss
Maggie Howell. Invited to inspection and lunch aboard
a new ironclad, in the James, near "Rocketts," full praise
was given by all. As we left the side the genial host said:
"Well, ladies, I have shown you everything about them."

"Everything but one," Miss Howell replied demurely, and to the secretary's surprised stare, she added: "The place where you blow them up?"

The story of the greased money-slide—*facilis descensus,* indeed—had been told too often to re-detail. Hanging at slight discount from gold for nearly the whole first year, Confederate bonds and currency alike began a drop as sudden and as shocking as a broken elevator in a sky-scraper. Ten, twenty, a hundred for one, was the quick-coming ratio. In the last year of the confessedly hopeless struggle, twelve and fifteen hundred dollars in notes was often given for one gold dollar. The last pair of riding boots I bought cost eighteen hundred dollars, but they would have been a rare bargain, at the exchange rate, in any Northern city.

It is related that General Lee was first recipient of the ever-quoted differentiation of past and present, by an old woman neighbor of his. In Richmond one day he met the good dame, with a large basket and a small purse to which she clung with eager grip. Ever pleasant, even when oppressed with cares, the great leader said:

"You must think it is Christmas, from the size of your basket?"

"No, indeed," she retorted sadly. "Time was when I carried my cash to market in this purse and brought the provender home in the basket. Now I have to tote the notes in the basket and I can just bring the marketing back in the purse!"

There was deep truth under this exaggeration and its parent was the blockade. Had the ports been open, or forceable, had the steel line along the border been penetrable, had the state and treasury departments listened to reason and urgence, in putting the cotton of the South abroad, *in time*, as a basis of credit, there might not have been a chance for the Cause in which all fought and suffered and starved alike, but the fighting had then been done without the backward glance that showed starvation in the home of the loved ones far away; misery and suffering in the unsupplied homes of the torn, and fevered effigies of man, left by the dire crush of the "'Conda."

CHAPTER XXXVI

IN FAME'S OWN HALL

SOME rare names shine out of History's page, as though created for its illumination.

GENERAL ROBERT E. LEE

These stand examplars for all time. Fame takes their wearers by the hand, with Justice and Truth on either side, to pedestal them in her own "Hall."

Before one niche in Fame's own hall, every comer seems to hear, as in whispers from remoter past, his own father's words of another, who stood first in war and peace, first still more in the hearts of his countrymen.

The war between the states from its origin in deep-rooted prejudices and its growth to red maturity, in an era of strong men, on both sides of the historic river, threw to the surface of bubbling events more than one who was to hold thenceforward the eye of the world.

Of them, one rises today whenever that war is named: a man calm, noble and potent beyond his peers. In mid-rush of interest, ambition and self-seeking, this grand form elicits admiration, respect and affection in the hearts of all "conditions of men"—and women. No life I can recall is more truly epitomized in the lines penned by his state's truest poetess, on the death of one of his bravest lieutenants, Turner Ashby:

> "*Bold as the Lion-Heart, dauntless and brave;*
> *Knightly as knightliest Bayard could crave:*
> *Sweet, with all Sydney's grace—*
> *Tender as Hampden's face—*
> *Who, who shall fill the space,*
> *Void by his grave?*"

Young people, without exception, loved Lee. He was their friend in word and in deed, even when the stress of action, or the shadow of desolation bore upon him.

His gentleness to the young and his knightly thought for women are pointed by one simplest act, best told in the simple words written me by Mrs. Harrison, of Baltimore —"little" Louisa T. Haxall at the time of Appomattox:

"I was away from Richmond when the girls were

MILDRED LEE
(YOUNGEST DAUGHTER OF GEN. LEE)

asking for buttons and stars from General Lee's coat, after the surrender and he was at home on Franklin street. On my return, I was visiting his daughter Mildred, and the general asked if I would go with him into his little office. Out of one of the little old trunks he had carried through the war, he took a button and a star which he said he had saved for me, thinking I would care to have them.

"You may be sure I did. The button I have, set in gold in Geneva, Switzerland. The star I keep, unset.

"A while later, my father heard that 'the mess' at General Lee's home had had no meat for some days—and no money to buy it—so he sent some hams in my name, knowing that then they would not be refused; and other things from our farm helped in their menu for many months."

Robert Edward Lee was facile, if modest, the centre of every group into which he came, whether cabinet, council, conference of military leaders, highest social functions, or giddy throngs of youth.

Descended from historic stock, "their names, familiar in your mouths as household words," the brilliant acumen and oratory of Richard Henry Lee and of his cousin, Henry Lee, were almost forgotten in the calm, impelling presence of the man to whom his fellows, no less than his inferiors, looked up with a confidence and hope that touched upon idolatry.

When the war was over and the "solitude" made in the South was called "Peace," the wrath of an incensed and policy-goaded North halted hatred and suspicion at the threshold of one Southern leader. The breath of most venomous rumor never once sullied the mirror-surface record of this Virginian. Mrs. Clay, incidentally and with no thought of praise, or word of wonderment, notes that when the Johnson junta summoned Lee, as witness, in 1866, all men of all parties paid him deference that was silent homage.

When the gratitude, love and admiration of his own people reared an equestrian bronze to their great soldier, at their once capital, even his old foes forgot for a time that "the war is not yet over." They, too, paid the tribute to the man that they had denied to the leader.

Decades later, when his centennial came, a world bared its head in deference and respect for worth that knew no narrow bounds, but permeated the greatness of a time. Then some who had weighed that side of his career—statesmen from every quarter of this and other countries, scholars and poets with the world's ear, even the universal press—

all paused in mid-rush of ambition, greed and self-seeking, to lay their tributes of bay and oak and laurel on that one man's grave.

Then, voices long discordant joined in strange, new unison; chanting one pæan to greatness too white to be denied its purity. Then, even that most strenuous denouncer of the past and dead "rebellion,"—he who had once at least over-stepped the further bound of unforgiving zeal, in his vig-

MAJ.-GEN. W. H. F. ("ROONEY") LEE

orous mode of speech—these, one and all, spoke the name of Lee in deference that neared to love. And in love is found all highest and purest tribute to this rare nature. His tallest and fairest monument rises from the hearts of his people—self-erected, sempiternal.

The twice-told tale of "Lee to the rear" was one proof irrefutable of this love. Even in death and disaster his simple words were held as priceless guerdon and fadeless epitaph.

When dainty but knightly Lord Page King rode through

the hail of Fredericksburg and died with Lee's message to his own general upon his lips, the former spoke three words that stand with the family record *ære perennius*: "Poor, brave boy!"

When the boy cannoneer laid his meteor career at the feet of Glory and fell,

"Hushed in the alabaster arms of Death,"

his name was linked to immortality in three words of Lee: "The gallant Pelham!"

Only short months ago I dared essay "The Living Lee," for his centennial. Then the reckless, contumacious boy-fighter who had carried General Lee's last despatch safely to Mr. Davis wrote me of the verses and added: "God! what a privilege to have lived in his time and known him."

Lord Bulwer, following "Cinq Mars," made the greatest, if the craftiest, cardinal of France, himself a soldier, boast that his secret to control of men, of a kingdom and almost of a world, was "Justice!"

What was the talisman of Lee, the magnet that drew to him all hearts of men? It was something higher than Justice: Truth, in its highest meaning of loyalty, constancy and faith; truth unswerving, to country, to race and to his Maker!

This ingrained truth permeated every fibre of the man, dominated every act of his life. It shone through his early boyhood at Alexandria, where his father had carried him, at four years of age, for schooling; in his still earlier days, when orphaned at eleven years and he bore it, clear and radiating, through his West Point life. He was a "model cadet" and pointed to as example for his classmates. That Mentor-trait made him the "gentleman subaltern" in the day of frontier-duty recklessness; the trusted and favorite staff-captain of Scott in Mexico; the efficient and praised superintendent of his *alma mater*; and through them all, the patriot citizen.

Even criticism now concedes that he loved his country even as he loved his state. His own words tell that when he longingly erased the "U. S." from the sword, still stainless. Who may doubt his real patriotism after reading the heart-break in that letter to his wife that hid, for her sake, some of the struggle, suspense and anguish of his decision, made wholly for truth's sake.

I have classed General Lee as a "Union man"; that class of fighters who struck for conviction, but ever without hate. He, loving the mother-state more, loved her mother none the less.

*Who held the olive high above
    the sword,
But "Duty" read as God's
    sublimest word!*

He could have been nothing else. His name, lineage and dearest ties and interests were all too inextricably

MRS. ROBERT E. LEE
(MARY RANDOLPH CUSTIS)

mixed with the Union not to bring a sigh with every blow against it that Duty struck.

Defeated, though not disarmed,* through the just sense of the victor, he was at heart and in *post-bellum* precept, a Union man in the real and better sense. He had no confession of error to make, no forgiveness to crave. Loving one part as nobly as he had proved, he could never have hated the whole,

*General Lee's sword was never offered to General Grant as currently stated. It was, therefore, never returned.

even when falsely dominated and misdirected; even when his fair state was relegated to "District One!"

Another Mexican veteran who carried his captaincy to a major-generalcy, in the '60's, was also a "Union man." William S. Walker was a stripling lieutenant at Chapultepec. He was the first Bluecoat over the castle wall, and with hand upon the halyards to run down the captured flag, heard the voice of his captain behind him. The young Bayard turned, saluted and asked his senior to do him that honor. When he was a major-general with one leg, at Atlanta, a decade ago, it was my privilege to meet him often and to hear some novel facts about two wars. One of his stories proves that General Lee's quiet vein of humor was not obscured by the smoke of battle and that he perhaps knew the never spoken prejudice of the ultra secession element.

At one closely contested battle Walker bore a message from his corps commander to General Lee. At the moment of its delivery one of that corps brigades, commanded by a gallant fellow who had carried his convention for secession, but could not hold his men against overwhelming odds, fell back in disorder.

Not taking down the field-glass, through which he watched this check, the general said quietly to Walker:

"Order General—— to put in ——'s division. Major, it seems to be left to us 'Union men' to win this battle!"

Personal beauty is the least of all attributes to be considered when speaking of the truly great, yet General Lee won admiration at a casual glance.

Mrs. Chesnut records at length her impressions on first seeing him. She was driving with Mrs. Preston and two other ladies, when President Davis rode by, mounted on a superb Arab stallion, sent him through the blockade by my brother. Mr. Davis was an exceptionally fine horseman. The white stallion was of straight descent from the mares of the Prophet

and my brother had to smuggle him out of Egypt. Yet the
dear old Carolina chronicler frankly states that the magnificent man on another white horse, afterward so famous as his
pet, Traveler, attracted all the curiosity of the feminine
quartet. Mrs. Chesnut distinctly records him as "the
handsomest man I had ever met."

By odd coincidence another Carolinian, of the other sex
and far wider experience of men, used these identical words
of their subject, about the same time. In his "Secret History of Confederate Diplomacy," Edwin De Leon describes
an interview that has not gone into history. When he ran
the blockade, he was closeted with Mr. Davis discussing the
foreign situation. General Lee entered hurriedly, with a
telegram.

"Addressing Mr. Davis he said: 'I have some news from
Savannah, Mr. President.'

"Mr. Davis looked up quickly, a shade of anxiety on his
face, as he replied: 'I hope it is good news?' General Lee
calmly replied, 'I regret to say that it is not. Fort Pulaski
is taken.' A flush of vexation passed over the worn face of
the President. 'Should this have been, General? You
know that fort. You examined its defenses a short time since.'

" 'In my judgment it was impregnable,' answered General
Lee, and then went on to state what those defenses were;
adding with his unvarying fairness: 'Our information, as yet,
is too scanty to permit us to judge of the merits of the case.
This only is certain: the fort has surrendered.'

"What struck me most in this interview," Mr. De Leon
says, "was the manner in which these two leaders took the
reverse; the unshaken fortitude—the almost Indian stoicism
—displayed by General Lee and the absence of all petulant
complaint on the part of the President. It was a lesson in
self-command and dignity, for both doubtless felt more than
they cared to show to one another.

"At that time General Lee—unworn by the anxieties and privations which afterwards aged him in appearance—was, I think, one of the handsomest men I have ever seen. His face was closely shaven, and a small, dark moustache shaded the upper lip. Both in face and form he looked a young man, while his stately figure, carried with military erectness, induced all who passed him by to turn and look again."

AGNES LEE
(THIRD DAUGHTER OF GEN. LEE)

In my first book upon the war-time, "Four Years in Rebel Capitals" (printed in 1867), I told of the return of stanch Major Tom Brander to his desolated home city. Then came the most touching scene of the war's ending: the love and veneration of his neighbors for Robert Lee.

"Next morning a small group of horsemen appeared on the further side of the pontoon. By some strange intuition it was known that General Lee was among them and a crowd gathered all along the route he must take, silent and bareheaded. There was no excitement appearing—no cheering, but as the great chief passed, a deep, loving murmur—far deeper than either—rose from the very hearts of the crowd. Taking off his hat and merely bowing his head, the man great in adversity passed silently to his own door. It closed upon him and his people had seen him for the last time in his war harness."

When next they saw him leave that quiet home, it was as the calm, simple citizen of Virginia—the plain man of duty.

Uncouth indeed were the hand that would draw the curtain from what had been the strain and struggle and heartbreak of that brief interval—the travail and the trial preceding self-conquest. The minor physical trials have been naively told in Louisa Haxall's words: the strain on brain and soul had made *them* as nothing.

But the stainless sword that the magnanimous victor never asked for was sheathed forever. The Arthur of modern war had hung *Excalibur* upon the walls of History.

It is now accepted truth that this man might have led the armies of the Union; might have fought at the forefront for the flag that lineage, habit and logic all had made so clear to him. General Scott, ever his warm and outspoken admirer, had recommended him for the leadership of the forces that were massing to "save the Union."

Quite recently the G. A. R. posts of Washington grew restive at the "treason" that permits plain statement of an historical fact, by a Virginia woman, to be conned in the public schools of the capital. Our "comrades across" need have borrowed no trouble. Robert Lee had refused the substance forced into his hand by the most potent power at the war's opening. The fact remains; its tenuous shadow through time need never have disquieted.

Close after the peace, overtures were made to General Lee to take command of the armies of Roumania, against the Danubian principalities. He declined the proffer, on principle, as he had the urgence from Scott. Then the offer, as seen, was made to Beauregard.

Potent French influences behind Maximilian urged appointment to marshalship in the army of Mexico upon the defeated Confederate chief. He never paused to consider the suggestion, nor a similar one from the khedive of Egypt, ready for the formal making, had my brother been able to give the least hope for its acceptance.

When Lee sheathed the sword honored at Appomattox,

GENS. R. E. AND G. W. C. LEE

it was forever. Thenceforward the sublimest word, "Duty," was to be read—Peace. When he gave his parole, it was not lisped in the letter to be violated in the spirit. He was "not made of such slight elements!"

The man of war had become the Virginia citizen of peace, pledged to labor to her rehabilitation through the right and the reason in him even as he had preferred to do before the trial by fire.

In his conduct of the university that now bears his name, twinned with the other "First in Peace," he wrought

for the upbuilding of his state, and through her, of a re-perfected Union. In both his eldest son succeeded him.

The pungent paragraphist and caustic satirist, Donn Piatt, has partly listed for us, in his "Men Who Saved the Union," such bright exemplars as Lincoln, of Kentucky; Stanton, of North Carolina, and Thomas, a Virginian.

James R. Randall suggests another Virginian, Farragut, who perhaps did as much in his watery way as any of the trio, toward the brilliant "wreckage." The list *may* not be expanded from the trans-Potomac, but there were unnamed and unnoted workers in the South, saving and recementing the recent shattered segment by their work to save the relegated "Districts."

> *"Keen was the smart, but keener far to feel*
> *He plumed the pinion that impelled the steel."*

Foremost among such rebuilders was Robert Lee.

No need have such men of statue or of eulogy; of pæan or of poem. They grave their own stories deep upon time. Tardy Truth at last erects their forms in Fame's own Hall!

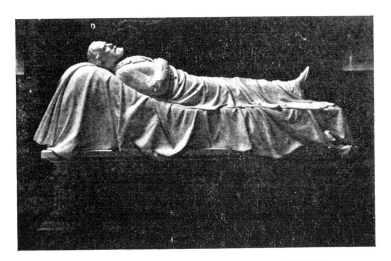

STATUE OVER THE TOMB OF GENERAL LEE AT LEXINGTON
(BY VALENTINE)

CHAPTER XXXVII

THE proverbial veracity of good blood has found· fresh proof in that of the Lees, since far beyond "the Conquest." There were Lees, or Lias, or Leighs, in Normandy, harking back to the followers of Rollo and, possibly, in the van of that rough Viking. Launcelot Lee came over with the conquering William, and fought valiantly at Hastings. Sir Lionel Lee was in the Crusades as a favorite knight of doughty Richard the Lion Heart, displaying such prowess at the storming of Acre as to win later the earldom of Litchfield, with broad acres which he named "Ditchley."

The progenitor of the Virginia Lees was Richard Lee, of Shropshire, England, who came over in 1641, under the protection of his friend, Sir William Berkeley, governor and favorite under the first Charles.

Richard Lee sat down on the broad acres in York county, ceded him by the crown, building his manor near Green Spring, the Berkeley home. He became a noted man in the colony, having many grants of new lands and many offices of honor and profit under Berkeley and succeeding governors; was burgess, justice, secretary of state and member of the king's council, at different times. In physique he was imposing and handsome; in character, dignified, generous and loyal to friends, traits he has sent shining down time through his descendants. He and his sons

owned many plantations in the Northern Neck of what is
now the state, as "Stratford," "Ditchley," "Lee Hall,"
"Langley," and "Coton," all named from the old English
seats of the family.

At his death, in 1663, he was succeeded by his son Richard,
2d, and in his issue, the family branched into three distinct
divisions. These were the Stratford line of Richard, 3d;
the Ditchley one headed by Hancock Lee, and the Cobb's
Hall branch by the young-
est son of the second Richard, Charles Lee. Details of
this earlier family, interesting
as they are, must give place
to later connections. Richard
Lee, 2d, married in 1674,
Letitia Corbin, whom he survived with their six sons and
one daughter, Anne, who
married Colonel William Fitzhugh. In her will she left
"to my son Henry, my grandfather Corbin's wedding ring,"
the grandson being the
grandsire of the Confederate
chief.

ADMIRAL SYDNEY SMITH LEE
(SON OF "LIGHT HORSE HARRY")

Of the six sons of this Richard Lee, those directly connected with this reminder are Thomas and Henry, the fifth
and sixth. The former was prominent in all matters of the
commonwealth and noted in its Indian difficulties. He
was princely in his entertaining at Stratford, and was known
to chronicle as President Lee. He married Hannah, daughter of Colonel Philip Ludwell, as his second wife, after the
death of the first spouse, the celebrated Lady Berkeley.
Thomas Lee was acting governor of the colony for con-

siderable time and the king sent him royal commission as governor, the first ever written in the name of a native Virginian. His death, in 1750, occurred before the tardy ship

CAPTAIN R. E. LEE, JR.
(YOUNGEST SON OF GEN. R. E. LEE)

mail delivered the parchment. He left six sons unsurpassed in the history of Virginia—the great "band of brothers, intrepid and unchangeable," of whom President John Adams wrote. These were Thomas Ludwell Lee, Richard Henry Lee, Francis Lightfoot Lee, William Lee, Philip Ludwell Lee, and Arthur Lee. The brilliant granduncles of Robert Edward Lee, were all men of high parts, admirable culture and of preeminence in the stirring antecedents of Revolution. When the Westmoreland Declaration against the Stamp Act was signed in 1765, four of their names were found upon it. Two of the brothers signed the Declaration of Independence, Richard Henry and Francis Lightfoot Lee. Both of the Virginia signers were born in the same room at Stratford wherein the Confederate general first saw the light, seventy-five years later.

Allurement to dwell upon the splendid achievements of this branch of the family must needs be curtailed; space hastens me to that of the second son of the second Richard Lee, who was the great-grandfather of our general. He was appointed by Governor Spottswood to succeed his father as naval officer of the Potomac; but he took no other office and little active part in public affairs. He married Mary

Bland, daughter of Theodoric Bland, of Westover, thus allying the Lees to the Randolph and Tucker families.

They had three sons, all of whom were in the colonial house of burgesses. The eldest of these, Henry Lee, was also county lieutenant of Westmoreland, up to and during the Revolution. What brings him closest to our interest today is that he was grandfather to "The Living Lee," his son, Henry, third successive to the name, having been "Light Horse Harry," of Washington's army. His elder brother, Charles Lee, was Washington's attorney-general.

Young Henry was a brilliant and distinguished student at Princeton. Graduating early, he changed the usual foreign tour of well-bred youth of that day for a company of militia at the battle of Lexington, commanding it with such dash as to win instant note as a soldier. He was quickly promoted to major and lieutenant-colonel, in command of "Lee's Legion" of light cavalry, from which he took his sobriquet. He won the respect and love of Washington and a place in military history scarcely second to that of his son. Congress voted him its thanks, and presented him a special medal for detailed achievements.

ANNE CARTER LEE AND
MARY CUSTIS LEE
(ONLY GRANDDAUGHTERS OF GEN. LEE)

General Harry Lee married his cousin Mathilda, daughter of Philip Ludwell Lee, thereby becoming the owner of the Stratford estate, shortly after the surrender of Cornwallis.

He was three years governor of Virginia and her representative in congress. On the death of Washington he spoke
that eulogy of him which has become immortal, little dreaming that his own youngest born would have it fitted to him
so closely thereafter.

By his marriage with his cousin, Henry Lee had four chil-

ROBERT CARTER LEE
(YOUNGEST SON OF ADMIRAL LEE)

dren, and by his second, with
Anne Hill Carter, six children. Seven of these were
sons, of whom four reached
adult age; these were Henry, Charles, Sydney Smith
and Robert Edward Lee.
This youngest son was elev-
en years old when his
father died in Georgia, in
1818, at the home of his old
commander, General Greene.

It were more than twice-
told tale to any reader to
trace the record of Robert
Lee. Going to West Point
in 1825, he graduated in
'29, second in a class of
forty-three, entered the
Engineers and two years later married Mary Randolph,
daughter of George Washington Parke Custis, of Arlington.

This union was a model one, bringing tender sympathy
and high incentive to the soldier's early life, that never
flagged in the zenith of his fame, or when trial, suspense
and loss unspeakable whelmed his country and his home
in desolation.

The pair had seven children, George Washington Custis, Mary Custis, William Henry Fitzhugh, Anne, Agnes,

Robert Edward, Jr., and Mildred. Only the eldest sister, Miss Lee, is living, and spends most of her leisure time abroad.

Miss Anne Carter Lee died in 1862 and was buried at White Sulphur Springs, in North Carolina. There her grave is lovingly tended by a woman's association formed for that work of love. Her sister, Agnes Lee, followed her eight years after the surrender. She sleeps beside her mother, at Lexington. Miss Mildred Lee was the youngest of the family. She was the "Baby girl," growing up during the war, and was her father's pet, if he had one, in his great and even love for his children. She was the idol of the household as well as of the veteran organizations, on the rare occasions when she came into their contact. She died only in March, 1905, followed by the universal sorrow of the South and a wide sympathy from the North.

All the Lee men and boys, the general's three sons and six nephews, went early into the Confederate service and stayed in it to its ending. All of them did active and good service, and three won the rank of major-general, not because of their name, but from the merit and manhood in them. Of them all, only four are now living. General Custis Lee and Captain R. E. Lee, Jr., the general's sons, and two of his nephews, John Mason Lee and Daniel Murray Lee. The first is the present head of the Virginia Lees, a cultured and courteous gentleman, who resides at Ravensworth, Burke Station. He never married and is a great sufferer from rheumatic gout, which prevented his retaining the presidency of Washington-Lee University, to which he was unanimously chosen as successor to his father; and which unfits him for active use of many of his high attributes and exceptional accomplishments. He graduated with distinction from West Point, in 1854, about the time that "Little Joe" Wheeler entered the academy.

General Custis Lee went early into the Confederate service, rising to command of his division through service in the field and especially good work in the planning of the defenses of Richmond, as well as in command around that city.

William Henry Fitzhugh Lee, the next brother, was

called "Rooney" by their father and the army, and even history has adopted the name, to distinguish between him and his first cousin, of the same name, abbreviated to Fitz. He was educated at Harvard, but appointed to a lieutenancy in the army, at the express request of General Winfield S. Scott, who ever held the father in high esteem. Later, young Lee left the army and became a planter at the White House on the old Custis estate, where George Washington changed the pretty widow's name to his own.

MRS. W. H. F. LEE
(MARY TABB BOLLING)
R. E. LEE, JR.   DR. BOLLING LEE

At the outbreak of the Civil War, "Rooney" Lee entered the army as a captain, rose grade by grade, and surrendered as a major-general. That grade he won at the age of twenty-seven, through distinguished and resultful command of cavalry when opposed by some of the best Federals.

He was later elected to congress three times, and was twice married. His first wife was Miss Charlotte Wickham, cousin of General Wickham. She died in 1863, after losing her two young children. Three years later, the widower married that belle and beauty of later war-time, Miss

Mary Tabb Bolling, who survives him, with two sons, Colonel R. E. Lee, 3d, and Dr. Bolling Lee. These are the only grandsons of General Lee: already proving "ensample of fair name" through which their gentle mother will live in history as a modern Cornelia.

Robert E. Lee, Jr., was but a youth in 1861. He promptly put on a private's jacket in the Rockbridge battery of the Stonewall Brigade, and won his captaincy on the cavalry staff, under "'Rooney" Lee, "Jeb" Stuart and others. He was twice married, first to Miss Charlotte Haxall, who died childless, and later to Miss Anne Carter, daughter of Colonel Carter, of the University of Virginia. Today, with two daughters, Mary Custis and Anne Carter Lee they reside at Romancoke, near West Point.

The third son of "Light Horse Harry" and Ann Hill Carter—next older than Robert—was Captain Sydney Smith Lee, of the old navy. He could have been an admiral had not the impulse of race carried him across the Potomac. There he was promptly accorded his former rank, did good work and became the trusted adviser of Secretary Mallory from his thorough familiarity with the men of his old service. He became admiral when the law created that grade. He married Anna Maria Mason, of the Gunston branch, and strangely enough in Virginian duplication of names, the sister of Mrs. Samuel Cooper, Sarah Maria Mason.

Fitz Lee was the eldest of their six children, all sons. A graduate of West Point, he was a dashing dragoon in the old service; familiar beyond need of reminder in the new one; consul-general to Havana, and so retained by the adverse party for his war knowledge; governor of his state, its desired candidate for senator and later brigadier-general in the regular army. Fitz Lee's later record and his death, with the universal grief it brought, are too recent to rehearse.

He married Miss Ellen Bernard Fowle, daughter of William Fowle, of Alexandria, and she survives him with a family of five, three daughters and two sons. Miss Ellen Lee married Captain Rhea, of the Seventh United States Cavalry; her next sister, Anne, married Lieutenant Lewis Brown, and the youngest, Virginia, lately married Lieutenant John

CAPTAIN HENRY CARTER LEE
C. S. CAVALRY
(4TH SON OF ADMIRAL LEE)

Carter Montgomery, all of the same regiment. The eldest son, Captain Fitzhugh Lee, is in the Seventh Cavalry, and was attached to the presidential staff at Washington, and George Mason Lee is a lieutenant in the same regiment.

Sydney Smith Lee, the brother next to Fitz, was a lieutenant in the Confederate Navy. He was first in the Drewry's Bluff batteries, and thence was sent abroad to await the building of the foreign cruisers. Tiring of inaction in what he and Sam Barron called "The Paris Navy," he was recalled and served on coast defense duty and in the small inland-built ironclads, of brief life. He never married, though he survived the surrender and was as popular with the gentler sex as with his own. He died in 1887.

Major John Mason Lee, elder of the two surviving sons of the admiral, now resides in Stratford county. He made good record in the cavalry of the A. N. V., winning his rank;

and after the war married Miss Nora Bankhead, daughter of Dr. Bankhead, of that neighborhood. There are five children of this union: Miss Nannie Mason Lee, Mrs. Linwood Antrim (Dorothea Lee) of Richmond; Mrs. C. P. Cardwell (Bessie Lee), of Hanover; John M. Lee, Jr., and Bankhead Lee.

Henry Carter Lee, next brother to John Mason, also served in the cavalry and gained his captaincy. He married Miss Sallie B. Johnston, and resided in Richmond, dying there two decades ago. They had three sons and one daughter: Johnston and Smith, now of Richmond; Willie, now living in New York, and Miss Nannie Mason Lee, of Richmond.

No youngster was better nor more pleasantly known in war-time Richmond than Dan Murray Lee, the next youngest son of the admiral. He entered the C. S. N. at its formation, as a midshipman, and came out of it web-footed as it were; passed-middie and staff captain. He was on the *Merrimac* of famous memory: later at Drewry's Bluff, on the *Chickamauga*, and in the *Chicora* and other vessels in the long defense of Charleston; at the capture of Plymouth and Fort Fisher and

CAPT. DANIEL MURRAY LEE
(5TH SON OF ADMIRAL LEE)

later in the batteries around Richmond. He was captured at Sailor's Creek, escaped and joined his brother Fitz and acted on his staff, with rank of captain. Was at

Appomattox, but escaped and only surrendered a week later, at Farmville. Thirty-two years ago he married Miss Nannie Ficklen, whose mother was Miss Fitzhugh, of

MRS. DANIEL MURRAY LEE
(NANNIE FICKLEN)

Chatham, who married Mr. Ficklen, of Falmouth.

Dan Lee now resides at Highland Home, near Fredericksburg, on a model stock farm. The pair have six children; two girls, Misses Edmo Corbin and Mary Custis Lee: D. M. Lee, Jr., J. B. F. Lee, Sydney Smith Lee and H. F. Lee. The eldest lives in California; the second on his Mexican ranch; the third is lieutenant in the United States Marine Corps in Cuba and the last is at the V. M. I., Lexington.

The youngest of the six brothers was a mere boy all during the war, but went in and saw service during its last year. This was Robert Carter Lee, now dead many years. He never married.

Such is the roster of the Lee family in war and peace, and there is no need to emphasize its place "in the hearts of its countrymen."

CHAPTER XXXVIII

JACKSON was gone: the Valley was unguarded, and its wastes were the open back door to the capital. There was dire need of men to check the secure invader. Then young boys sprang to the rescue.

General Scott Shipp, the lieutenant-colonel, commandant of the Virginia Military Institute, at Lexington, was called upon by Breckinridge. Not one boy flinched. Shipp led every one big enough to "tote" a musket, fought them against Sigel's artillery until he was shot down, and even then the youngsters stayed in under Captain Henry A. Wise until the fight was won; capturing the Union battery and many prisoners. They went in a battalion of 470, in four companies commanded by Collier Harrison Minge, of Alabama, Company A; C. W. Shafer, of Virginia, Company B; S. S. Shriver, of Virginia, Company C, and B. A. Colonna, of Virginia, Company D. They left eight dead upon the field, and forty-four wounded. The former roll of honor reads: W. H. McDowell, of North Carolina; S. F. Atwell, W. H. Cabell, J. B. Stanard, F. G. Jefferson, H. T. Jones, C. G. Crockett, and J. C. Wheelright, all of Virginia.

Captain Minge was given the post of honor in command of the artillery section and—as a comrade writes me—"bore himself very gallantly." Colonna, "Old Duck," was at hand-to-hand; hammering a gunner over the head with his cadet dress sword. Shriver also was conspicuous for dash and coolness. The color-bearer was complimented for vim and pluck, and the sergeant-major, Woodbridge, coolly took

GENERAL SCOTT SHIPP, V. M. I.

his place forty paces beyond the line, to form on, as though on dress parade. "Little General" C. C. Randolph, who had been Stonewall's courier, and was sent to the V. M. I. "because he was no larger than a broiling chicken," was fearfully wounded, and it is a wonder he ever recovered. He is now the Rev. Charles Randolph, of Evington, Va. First Sergeant Erskine Ross, of "A," was distinguished for gallantry. He is now United States circuit judge in California, and Color-Bearer Oliver Perry Evans also became a San Francisco judge. First Sergeant A. Pizzini, Jr., was specially noted for "grit," as was peach-cheeked "Coonie" Ricketts, the envied pet of the petticoats. Winder Garrett, of Williamsburg, ran his bayonet through a gunner in the charge that took the battery, and he and Charlie Faulkner captured twenty-two big Germans, barricaded in an icehouse. Cadet Levi Welsh, of "B," made a great mark for daring, and Patrick Henry, of Tennessee, won his spurs through all the fight. Grim and gallant Professor-Captain Henry A. Wise always commended the bearing of Edmund Berkeley, Bob Brockenborough, Preston Cocke and Pem Thomson. All were Valley boys, except Cocke, who was from the James River Valley, but of the old Preston blood.

That a number of Alabama boys were in, I chanced to know. H. Walker Garrow, a fine fellow, later loved in Mobile, was one. Another letter, equally unsuspecting of publication, from Minge, says:

"The cadet corps' little stunt at Newmarket seems to have crept into history as a marginal note. This 'seed-corn battalion,' as President Davis styled it, when he heard of the slaughter of the innocents, has been tenderly handled by all the recorders. It was without question a most beautiful and touching illustration of Lee's grand maxim, 'Duty is the noblest word in the language.' And then the book closes.

"There are no specific records left and no specific deeds. Hunter, in his campaign of desolation up the Valley, destroyed the institute and its records, June 11th, 1864. The rosters were obtainable only from the memories of those officers whose duty it was to call the company rolls. These were collected and revised with care, until I think all who participated in the battle were enrolled in the four companies. I had been honored with the first captaincy and helped to

CAPT. COLLIER H. MINGE
(COMMANDING BATTERY)

return that roster. Other cadet officers did the same for their several companies and the result is in the possession of the institute. It is inscribed on four tablets on sides of the base of a memorial standing at the entrance to Jackson's memorial hall. I would not trust myself to call over that company roll again at the age of sixty-two.

"Sir Moses Ezekiel—'Zeek,' of tender memory—was one of the boys."

After the war Minge went into the cotton business in Mobile, thence removing it to Shreveport. Now he is the prosperous, if portly, head of houses in Shreveport, New Orleans and Texas towns, with a summer home at Mississippi City. He married Miss Eva, daughter of the noted and popular Colonel A. J. Ingersoll, of Mobile's halcyon days. Their family of adult boys and girls is the pride of the most youthful grandmother in her section. Collier H., Jr., married Miss Theo Vance; uniting Revolutionary blood of South Carolina and Virginia. Ethel Ingersoll married Mr. Richard Montague Walford, an English gentleman in the cotton business. Miss Ingersoll Minge, the second daughter, was recently queen of New Orleans carnival; the third Miss Jeannie Dixey, like her, refuses to leave the paternal roof.

I have noted already that Gaylord B. Clark was at the V. M. I., Newmarket. He was sent early from his native Mobile to Lexington as a pupil to General Pendleton; entered the institute and was a sergeant in the "cornseeds." How he bore himself is told in a late letter from a comrade: "He was the man who made everybody laugh, under hottest fire. He grabbed the tall sugar-loaf hat of some Yankee officer, placed it on his head, put one foot on a dead artillery horse, folded his arms and struck an attitude. Then he coolly asked whether he did not look like Napoleon Bonaparte."

He became a noted lawyer in Alabama and a power in her publicism. He married a brilliant belle of *post-bellum* Mobile —Miss Lettice Smith, whose father was Colonel Robert

White Smith, a prominent merchant and a cavalry commander in the war. On her mother's side she is of the Virginia Hunters. Mrs. Clark is a still youthful and popular society woman, with two children: Gaylord, who took his degree in his father's profession at the University of Virginia, and Lettice Lee Clark, one of the most popular young women of far Southern and Virginian society.

Another son of Francis B. Clark, his namesake and next to Gaylord, graduated at the V. M. I., before entering the law and becoming his brother's partner. He left two sons, Francis B. Clark, Jr., of Texas, and Rev. Willis G. Clark, of Montgomery. The military strain of the family blood inheres in General Louis V. Clark, of the Alabama National Guard. His cadet company won the first prize at the interstate drill mentioned, and he was later on headquarters staff at Washington and

GAYLORD B. CLARK
(CADET AT NEWMARKET)

Chicago encampments. The other living brothers are J. Shepherd Clark and Burnet L. Clark, editors and owners of *El Comercio*, the Spanish trade journal of New York. Mrs. Burnet L. Clark, as Miss Armantine Oliver, was one of the most beautiful and charming belles of the after-war Mobile. She retains both traits in her New York home, and has loaned them to her fair young daughter, Miss Pauline. The youngest of the six sons of Francis B. Clark except Louis, is Le Vert Clark, now of Detroit. He was in the Mobile law firm, but married Miss Parke, of the Michigan metropolis, and removed there.   Gaylord Clark had but one sister, Miss Nellie, who married Norman Brooks and resided in New York until widowed.   Now she lives with her father and brother, in Birmingham, while her only son, Russell Sage Brooks, completes his university career.

When my brilliant, yet astute, friend, Henry W. Grady, told the North of the "New South," he knew the efficacy of a rallying cry as well as did the inventors of " Old Hickory" and "Tippecanoe and Tyler, too!" as well as did Colonel Bryan when he inverted the "Crown of Thorns" and amalgamized the "Cross of Gold."

Grady knew that there was—and could be no "New South."   He knew that it was the same old South, bracing her every sinew and girding up her loins for a fresh struggle with the conditions of day-after-tomorrow, out of the methods of day-before-yesterday.   He knew, thinker that he was, that the habits and traditions of three centuries could no more be whistled down the wind by a word than they could be uprooted by the sword, and what he knew then exists today.

The North and the South alike cherish their memories, the bitter through proper loyalty, the sweet through love.

The United Confederate Veterans were organized for two objects: to preserve the sweet and bitter memories with equal care: higher still, to aid the disabled, the suffering and the needy of those who had thrilled them with the Rebel yell indescribable, and had won worthily the right to wear "the true cross of honor."

The U. C. V. organized first on June 10, 1889, at New Orleans, unanimously choosing John B. Gordon commander-in-chief, with Clement A. Evans as his first adjutant-general.   Never during Gordon's life would "the boys" hear another name offered for their leader.   Only his death brought his successor in Lieutenant-General Stephen D. Lee.

Just before the reunion of 1898, this true knight and gentle souled paladin was suddenly stricken with fatal illness. Not the death of Gordon even, was so truly and universally lamented. Honest and chivalrous, he was indeed loyal and true, equally to his country and his friends. A mighty sob went up from the hearts of Dixie,—echoing back from many a Northern voice—for his requiem. He was succeeded by General Clement A. Evans: a good soldier and churchman and a disciplinarian.

At organization the camps of the Vets numbered only a few score. Today they number over 1,500, covering every state and territory in the Union. Yet this was not the first commemorative body, by many years. Already separate bodies of old soldiers had existed in Mobile, Richmond, New Orleans, Charleston and Chattanooga. Each of these claims seniority, but certain it is that the "R. E. Lee Association" celebrated the nineteenth of January, 1867, at Mobile, and remained a growing society when it merged into Raphael Semmes Camp, No. 11, U. C. V., in 1890.

What the Veterans have done for perpetuation of facts and records has been seen of all men, and honored by their old fighting opponents. With them fraternization has been frequent, notably at Atlanta, Boston and New Orleans. Both have verified General Damas, of Bulwer's play: "It is astonishing how much I like a man after I have fought with him!"

There may be exceptional cases of sectional rabies, but there is no generation *stegomyia maligniati* to sting it to epidemic on the people who wore the blue or doffed the gray. The exceptional Dammerses prove the rule of mutual respect and recognition of the men who had bought their knowledge of each other with their blood.

I chanced to be managing secretary of perhaps the first important encampment at which the Blue and the Gray went under tents together, at Mobile, in 1885. Then General C. S. Bentley brought down the "Northwestern Brigade," of Iowa, Illinois, Michigan, Minnesota, Wisconsin and Ohio, under General H. H. Wright, of the First Iowa.

Two years later I held the same position at the National Drill and Encampment around the Washington Monument. There General C. C. Augur, U. S. A., was in command, with H. Kyd Douglas, of Stonewall Jackson's staff, adjutant-general; Fitz Lee, then governor of Virginia, with a brigade, and officers of all grades from the old soldiers of North and South.

At both these encampments the picked flower of citizen soldiery—at the latter to the number of 12,500 on the morning report—embraced men who had been through the war and bore its scars. At both absolute harmony and good-fellowship reigned, and no single case of ill-feeling, taunt or bitterness developed. Similar instances were the Atlanta Exposition and the G. A. R. reunion at Boston in 1904.

The organization of the Daughters began at Nashville in 1894, when only three chapters convened and elected their founder, Mrs. M. C. Goodlett, of that city, president-general. There are now *eleven hundred and fifteen* chapters, embracing almost all the states, with many of their most representative women, to an aggregate membership computed at nearly 60,000. The present heads are Mrs. Cornelia Branch Stone, of Texas, president-general; Mrs. A. H. Voorhies, of San Francisco and Mrs. D. A. S. Vaught, of New Orleans, vice-presidents-general; Mrs. A. L. Dowdell, of Alabama, and Mrs. A. W. Rapley, of St. Louis, recording and corresponding secretaries. Mrs. L. E. Williams, Kentucky, is treasurer-general. In the interim the presidents-general have been Mesdames John C. Brown (Nashville), Fitzhugh Lee (Alexandria), Kate Cabell Currie (Dallas), Edwin G. Weed (Jacksonville), James A. Rounsaville (Rome, Georgia) and A. T. Smythe (Charleston).

As with the Veterans, each state is organized under its own head and the object of all is the care of the sick and aged, preservation of cemeteries and aid to the soldiers' homes, in most of the states.

Of similar sentimental birth came the United Sons of Veterans a decade later. What real need there is for their existence was found in a nucleus for a memorial order, when all the Vets have passed away.

Still, the idea took with the young men of the South- ern states, and the three or four camps of their beginning now number hundreds in an aggregate of many thou- sands. This picturesque, well-uniformed and some- times eloquent body has added largely to the glitter and the giddiness of the annual reunions of the "old boys."

The first commander, chosen at the Richmond organizing, was, J. E. B Stuart, of Newport News.

Rt. REV. THOMAS FRANK GAILOR
(BISHOP OF TENNESSEE)

The present officers in chief are: John W. Apperson, general commanding, and N. B. Forrest, Jr., adjutant-general, both of Memphis, Tenn., re-elected at the last convention.

Bishop Thomas Frank Gailor, the brilliant and stalwart prelate of Tennessee, whose father died on the Field of Perry- ville, was urged in consecutive years to accept the command- in-chief. This carries with it the rank major-general. He declined, saying that a bishop should not hold military rank except for war-need. Urged next year he said he could accept only on two conditions, that there should be unanimous choice and that the military features of the organization should be entirely abrogated. Only thus, he felt, could the real usefulness of the Sons be best assured.

Gradually the need that had bred the organizations seemed fulfilled, the novelty of the reunions began to wane and the parades had to seek, in their function as crowd-drawers to entertaining cities, the addition of beauty and youth in what many declared to be too many sponsors and too much display. What had been a grave event, with something in it of sacredness, fell into a society function that hid the original intent almost wholly from view. Naturally, some "old fogies" of the parent order grew restive under a change that obscured their light. What they had introduced as a pretty and appropriate innovation threatened to grow equally overbalancing and costly.

There is no blame to the Old Boys. They are not what someone called Tom Ochiltree, "a war cocktail," but the straight war distillation, and the longer they are kept out of wood the purer the spirit.

So it made the judicious grieve when they thought they saw these venerable *patres non conscripti* relegated to the rear, behind the young alignment of brilliant and fresh Sons and even of dainty and daintily sashed Daughters.

At the Atlanta reunion, where "Little Joe" Wheeler, fresh from Cuba, rode at Gordon's right hand the cynosure of all eyes, a grim old Vet left a note at his hotel for any old comrades who called on him:

"Gone home; found too little Vet and a d——sight too much Sponsor and Son!"

The memory-born novelty may wane, the reunion may die of old age, but the memory that bore both will live when the last old Reb is headstoned, when the sponsors' sashes have mildewed with time, and the "Generals" epaulettes are black with the tarnish of forgetfulness and cheap gilt.

The recent death of a very noted and widely mourned Daughter of the Confederacy calls up vivid memories of her famous husband. General Edmund Kirby Smith, son of Joseph Lee Smith and Frances Kirby, was born at St. Augustine in 1824. Their old home is now the library of the old city, by his donation. He graduated at West Point in 1845, seeing first service in the Mexican War. Later he was assigned as professor at the academy. He was a major when he joined the South and was made brigadier-general. Wounded at Bull Run, he was nursed at Richmond by Cassie Selden, the brave and gifted daughter of Armistead Selden and Caroline Hare, of Lynchburg. The result was the marriage that made her "the Bride of the Confederacy." Made lieutenant-general in 1862, General Smith was assigned to the trans-Mississippi Department the next

GEN. EDMUND KIRBY SMITH
(COMMANDING TRANS-MISSISSIPPI
DEPARTMENT)

year and in 1864 was made one of the six full generals. His command was the last to lay down arms, many of its officers crossing to Mexico to avoid surrender.

General Smith went to Cuba and his wife to Washington, where his old comrade, Grant, arranged for his return. He was president of the Altantic & Pacific Telegraph Company until 1868, when he became chancellor of the University of

Nashville. In 1875 he accepted the chair of mathematics at Sewanee, University of the South, which he held until his death in 1893.

The young wife had followed her husband through the war, sharing his dangers and privations in "the 'cross river kingdom." Their home at Sewanee became a centre of hospitality and Mrs Kirby-Smith never forgot the old soldiers of that mountain region. Each year she gave a garden party to the Vets of the three counties, and they mourn her death as a sister's. She was a woman of dominant character and practical sense and her voice was listened to in the councils of the Daughters. Her eleven children were reared—and several of them, and the twelve grandchildren, born at Sewanee. They all survive her and are: Caroline Selden (Mrs. W. S. Crolly, of New York); Fannie (Mrs. Wade, of Los Angeles), with two children; Edmund Kirby-Smith, now of Mexico, who married Virginia Dellez, and has four children; Lydia (Mrs. Roland Hale) with two children; Nina (Mrs. Randolph Buck, of Indianapolis), with two children; Elizabeth and Josephine Kirby-Smith; Dr. Reynold Marvin Kirby-Smith, who married Miss Thomson, of Atlanta, and has two children; William Selden and Ephraim, both mining in Mexico; and Dr. J. Lee Kirby-Smith, a bachelor, in New York.

Very recently Ephraim, youngest of the eleven children, married Mary Carroll Brooks, daughter of Preston S. Brooks, of Sewanee, and granddaughter of the famous Congressman Preston S. Brooks, of South Carolina. Distinguished in Pierce Butler's Palmetto regiment, in Mexico, he was representing his state in the lower house, when Charles Sumner spoke words in the senate insulting to the aged and infirm Senator Pickens Butler, a kinsman of Brooks. Next day, the latter made a *cause célèbre* by caning the Massachusetts man in his seat in the senate, just ere that august body was called to order.

Again the to-be-expected has happened. Just closing this page, the printer heard echo of wedding chimes from far Sewanee mountain. In mid-March, Miss Josephine Kirby-Smith, the youngest of the six sisters, became Mrs. Roades Fayerweather, at new St. Luke's chapel, donated to the university by the late Mrs. Telfair Hodgson, as memorial to her husband and daughter.

The newly wedded pair will reside in Baltimore, leaving Miss Elizabeth Kirby-Smith at the old home: the only unmarried sister—for the present.

CHAPTER XXXIX

"The past is past; what's done is done for aye!"

HAUPTMANN, the great German, was as much philosopher as poet when he wrote that line of "The Sunken Bell."

Every brew, when pure, leaves aftermath. When Fate is the brewer the aftermath is often bitter. That of the Lost Cause, sweet and bitter commingled, is ours; nor would we change it for any less of either, not permeated with the sacred savor of memory.

Seismic convulsion had torn and tumbled a great national structure. Upon its supposed ruins Hope, Valor and Ambition essayed the rearing of a new one that in turn toppled and crumbled into dust.

The new design was too nearly like the old. It fell, even as Babel, because it essayed a too great height, builded too fast, and the conglomerate foundation could not concrete.

Across the debris of a people's hopes and struggles, through the still luminous dust from their downfall, bright and noble forms pass in long procession, fadeless and ever new; and each Confederate *Banquo*

"Bears a glass that shows me many more."

Some have essayed their work of "resurrection" and have found vending for their cadavers of reputation, exposed to the dull scalpel of controversy. Not always was this for the sake of history or of truth.

454

What was really done can never be undone to the satisfaction of any. Attempts to undo it are ever futile; worse, they are fecund of Dead Sea fruit, dry and acrid to the taste, even when happily seedless.

The war is over, despite the natural soreness of old wounds under friction, or an occasional bitter afterthought. The pact between the generals had made this truth an earlier one by four decades, had Lincoln lived. Still, it is now ten years since belief in our having one common country sent "Little Joe" Wheeler from his legislative seat to one in the discarded saddle: sent one of the oldest of the Lees back to the flag under which he had first fought.

The reasons for failure are always as numerous as the reasons for war. They are equally as unprovable. A great Confederate, when asked why we lost the battle of Gettysburg, replied: "Stonewall Jackson died too soon."

LIEUT.-GEN. JOSEPH WHEELER

That was epigram, not proof. So Reconstruction may be summed up: Abraham Lincoln died too early.

But for the madman Booth's pistol, that jarred apart the closing wound of war-born hatred, there had been no bitter aftermath. That one reverberation in the Washington opera box swelled into the vaporous vastity of the Geni's cloud in Arabian Nights' tale. Out of it strode that Afrite of hate, horror and long-lived rancor; the evil spirit that blighted the seeds sowed by Lee and Grant—Johnston and Sherman.

At that vibration the promised fruits of humanity, homogeneity, nationality, were scattered to the wind for a time.

Upon the horrors, injustice and grotesque illegality of Reconstruction this is no place to dwell. These demand an ampler page and have been treated in history, essay and symposium by abler pens than mine. Yet their more potent material rests behind. Yet, applying the wisdom of Talleyrand to Reconstruction, it stands forth more glaring than a crime: as the most egregious error ever perpetrated upon policy by politics. Were it not pitiable it would be laughable.

That fallacious makeshift abruptly cut off the fine nose of national wealth, to spite the Southern face; procured a few lewd votes, that its political lechery could not use, and essayed the elevation to equality of an unliftable race by amendment petards that now uncomfortably hoist their inventors higher than their would-be victims.

The Macaulay of politico-economics, when he comes to stand upon the ruins of this rotten bridge across momentary expediency, will record it as the silliest error in all the annals of government by enactment.

The government of a victorious and firmly placed party studiously proclaimed what its own second-thought found it vital to very existence to disprove after offering rewards for the heads of palpably innocent men. Hatred was smeared over political venality in slimy distortion; while a purposely inflamed political sense, with dilated nostrils, sniffed up its savor.

Had the madman's pistol missed fire that fateful night in the theatre the martyred president had lived greater still in history. He would have confirmed the cartels between his generals and ours at Appomattox and Atlanta.

There would have been no Reconstruction; and the nascent respect of the one section for the other had never been strangled in its cradle by the puny Hercules of hate.

Natural instinct and paying interdependence would have written Mr. Lincoln's word, "Union," at the head of the page. He could then have well afforded to let the tricksters of politics "write whatever you please under it!"

Direct issue, too, of Reconstruction was that lynching—equally bugabooed, too, by purpose or imagination—which was a fine art, with hideous cause as *motif* in the South, and has been transplanted, without the cause, into a tough trade in the North.

Honesty, policy, and common sense have long since cremated the very bones of Reconstruction; and the process has killed even their loathsome odor.

But all the aftermath of unrest and rancor was not confined to one side of the Potomac.

No trial where the witnesses have all been "discharged by death," could bring any verdict that would stand the test of posterity. Criticism is one thing; narration of new facts—legitimate progeny of history—another.

The better afterthought of the South had settled down into calm acceptance of the inevitable. It was trying honestly the "let-well-enough-alone" philosophy. It indubitably was regretful, where not shocked, by the exhumation and exhibition in the gossip morgue of the "unsent message" to congress of Mr. Davis, giving his reasons for refusal to obey the popular wish to replace Johnston in command before Atlanta. *Cui bono?* was the universal query when the print appeared. That paper could have *proved* nothing, even had Mr. Davis sent it in to the Richmond congress. It could only have added, then, to the bitterness of the Davis and Johnston partisans in that body, and to the widespread dissatisfaction upon the quarrel, in the army. Even at that

time, it could have settled no one fact to the satisfaction of
any doubter on either side, for the reason that—like General
Johnston's later retort—it was merely the one man's differentiation of himself and another man.

No one who comprehends the character and motives of
Mr. Davis doubts for an instant that he must have had cogent
reasons for withholding an important state paper that had
cost labor, thought and midnight oil. That reason *must*
have been one of two; the inefficacy of the paper to convince,
or his own belief that its utterance would indurate a pair of
prejudices that were fast growing into opposed hatreds. For
the "unsent message" added no tittle to the truth of history.
It gave no scintilla of proof for the correctness of its writer's
estimate of the man whom General Hood himself, William J.
Hardee and Alexander P. Stuart joined in a telegram to have
retained in command—whom General Lee immediately
called back to the post denied him, when he became commander-in-chief.

More unhappy still was the publication of the legacy letter,
written by Mrs. Davis to her old friend, Judge Allen Kimbrough, of Mississippi, to exculpate herself from aspersion
of disloyalty to section and principle, because she had found
it practical, or needful, to live at the North. But if that
letter was needless, tactless and ill-timed was the forcing of
that letter by Mrs. Kimbrough upon the unwilling assemblage
of the Daughters, at Gulfport, in 1906.

No honest thinker could ever have condoned the dis-
crediting of the wife of the dead president for selecting her
own residence. Brave and brawny men have done the same,
in hundreds of cases, leaving home, friends and traditional
surroundings for the openly avowed purpose of gain. Criticism
never has assailed them, and there was less cause for the
singling out of a bereaved—and somewhat neglected—woman
for venomed, if misdirected, shafts. But what the few said,

the many never heard, nor, hearing, had believed, until the needless post-mortem defence raised futile whispers to a roar and set up a skeleton in the united feminine closet.

Sectional pride is the proper thing: sectional prejudice is the silly one. Looking back across a clear calm retrospect, may we not see in the latter one active motor of the Civil War? Then glance at the social and business positions of the "Southern colony" in New York today: note her now old Southern Society, of which an early secretary was a Virginian Randolph.

Prejudice is of long life, albeit confined to no particular habitat. Only yesterday, veterans and cadets from Georgia flocked to the escort for the Taft inauguration; aides from other Southern states rode down the line and Alabamians received the all-states guests at the night's ball. But, only day before yesterday, General Rufus Rhodes was assailed by ultra Southern

LIEUT. WILTON RANDOLPH

scribes, for invoking God's blessing upon Mr. Taft, when he went to invite him to his home-city (quite a proper "grace before meat"); and for editorial intimation that the people's choice of the big president was preferable to raising a flag of tattered and torn platitudes, on a nickel plate staff, above the White House.

The day before that, Dr. Hannis Taylor, of Washington, was soundly basted in some Southern presses, for writing in the *North American Review* that "the Solid South was a national calamity" but Mr. Taylor was only borrowing of Scripture, in stating that the house—however strongly based must fall, if divided against itself.

It is nearly two decades since I was even more widely berated for my article in that same *Review*—"The Weakness of Mr. Davis's Strength"—which showed that he failed of attempt to do, in his own proper person, what those he had gathered about him could not accomplish. All of which recalls the wisdom of the negro preacher, who answered brother Jasper, of Richmond:

"Ya-as,m' breddren, de science folk hab proobe de sun *do* stan' still an' de wurl' hit do moobe. Doan' yer be like de sun. Git er Moobe onter yer! Ef de wurl' do moobe, den dem az doan' moobe too, ez dead sho' ter fall offen hit!"

I have noted Don Piatt's clever differentiation of "Men Who Saved the Union." It may be pertinent in this aftermath of great events to glance at some of the men who *made* the Union, before it grew to need of the saving process. He who is accepted as "Father of his Country," was a Virginian. A neighbor of his was author of the Declaration of Independence; Richard Henry Lee offered the resolutions that produced it, and two of those six brothers of that name were signers. Madison was main framer of the Constitution, and its accepted expounder was another Virginian, John Marshall.

In one of his meaty and reminiscent addresses, Honorable Champ Clark, of Missouri, took for his theme cognate facts, seemingly forgotten by many bookmakers and most bookreaders. He reminded his hearers that it was Governor Patrick Henry who sent George Rogers Clark, "the Hannibal of the West," to acquire the great Northwest Territory; that Jefferson and Polk gave the Union its splendid trans-Mississippi purchase and that Monroe brought the Floridas under the flag. Mr. Clark also took up eminent Southerners who had illustrated American genius and discovery, showing that they were neglected and often ignored by Northern book-makers and cyclopedists. He instanced the famous William Rufus King, of Alabama, congressman, senator, diplomat, who died as vice-president; Dr. Crawford W. Long, of Athens, Ga., who invented chloroform, while the credit is given Dr. Samuel Guthrie, of New York. The former's state has chosen his figure for Statuary Hall, as one of its two representatives.

Mr. Clark notes that Robert Toombs and Charles Sumner were contemporary senators, and that Northern cyclopedists give the latter three or four columns and the Georgian about a quarter column. Lincoln gets five or six columns; Jefferson Davis, one.

The reminiscent congressman ever has his facts well in hand. He ought to have added that Matthew F. Maury made the Atlantic cable a possibility by his deep sea soundings and that Professor Robert Ellett, of South Carolina University, gave the basis of dynamite, the great destructive, and of collodion, the best reconstructive, by perfecting guncotton. Gorrie, of Florida, first made artificial ice; and his state will make his statue one of her two in the capital at Washington.

It was Duncan N. Ingraham, a South Carolina captain, of the "St. Louis," in the harbor of Smyrna, who first carried the Monroe Doctrine to the deck of an Austrian warship, and brought Martin Costza away, safely wrapped up in it.

These are some few things the men of the South did to make the Union. And her women have "done things" too. Which more aided the women of the country and its moral tone, Harriet Beecher Stowe, or Augusta Evans Wilson?

Verily, my one-legged philosopher, General Walker, might have added to the losses of the South in her mothers not bearing all male children, the patent one that her authors did not write all the histories.

One theme most pregnant, and cognate with the after-math of the great struggle, I perforce leave untouched. Its mere mention brings up so many innate and collateral facts—so many persons of historic interest—that it would overstep all possible boundaries of space in this narration. Attempt to condense the origin and effects of the diplomacy of the Confederacy—its promises and errors and their results; and its twin failure, finance—were hopeless; and I have

been forced to leave it to a wider, and a separate field. From Georgia's pioneer commissioner, Thomas Butler King, through the Yost-Mann-Yancey experiment, to the Mason-Slidell *fiasco*, the story intertwists European and American history of that day so closely that no singled threads of either could be made distinct.

So, for the moment, I have left diplomacy and finance where they placed themselves —in *nubibus!* Yet this is a legitimate theme for History; not being the story of the

LIEUT. S. S. LEE, 3D.
(U. S. MARINE CORPS)

calamities of individuals, but of a great nation—conceived, nascent, possible of self-existence. Nor is this the place to discuss whether the last had been a universal blessing, or a local curse.

Verily, the war *is* over, save in a few hearts that beat only for prejudice or profit; or in the still tender ones of some "dear old girls," who *feel* when they would reason: who cannot be—whom none would have—"reconstructed."

Joe Wheeler sleeps at Arlington, with the *derring do* of both armies twinned upon his monument. His comrade both in the blue and the gray was laid to rest under the national flag, amid pæans from the North:

> *He sleeps; but over ev'ry re-fought field,*
> *Mem'ry shall wake Fitz Lee to ride again!*

And his sons and the husbands of all his daughters wear sabres with U. S. on their blades; while his youngest nephew wears the blue today in Cuba.

Only recently, in sturdy Tennessee, the veteran fighters of the Confederacy marched to the music "of the Union," as escort to the president of *their* country, and that stalwart statesman—little condoning of what he deems "rebellion"—told them he felt their action the highest honor done him during his tour.

When the thirteen tattered ensigns of the Maryland regiments were lately placed, as trophies of her glory, at Annapolis, United States officers in the escort bared their heads; their pupils—the flowers of descent from fighters on both sides—shouted in unison to the strains of "Dixie" by the government band.

Recently, the son of the hero who ignored Lee's sword, with his noted comrades, revisited the National park at the precedent Occidental Port Arthur and struck hands with the old generals and the young "unreconstructed" governors of the South. And Frederick Dent Grant had already told us that the greatest Fourth of July of his boyhood was when, as a lad of thirteen, he went with his father for conference with General Pemberton at Vicksburg. And he added: "Our men were no sooner inside the lines than the armies began to fraternize . . . . I saw our men taking bread from their haversacks and giving it to the enemy they had so recently been starving out."

Later still, the ranking officer of the Union, General Bell, chief-of-staff, presented to the Virginia Military Institute, a silken replica of their Newmarket battle flag, burned in the Hunter raid of 1864. It was received, in words as soldierly and as glowing as his own, by Hon. John S. Wise, of the New York bar: himself a cadet veteran, wounded at "the corn-seed battle."

And, as last seal of peace, President Roosevelt—who once branded Jefferson Davis and his men in gray as "traitors" yielded to the plea of Mrs. Cornelia Branch Stone and her Daughters of the South, and replaced the name of the Confederate chief upon Cabin John bridge. And the order was issued by his secretary of war, the veteran Luke E. Wright—of Tennessee!

And so the aftermath of war is fruity with memories, wafting northward or southward across the Potomac. So should it be: so will it be as long as true men honor the brave and true.

The old rhyme tells us that the knights of eld are dust and their good swords corroded in the dews of time. But the knights of the Southland live; their forms sealed in bronze and marble, their memories vivid and ever-present in the hearts of all.

Sighs in each breeze the dirge's tender tone,
Shrilling anon to clarion pœan loud;
Telling of loss and travail, once thine own.
That make old foes of common kinship proud.

Arch o'er their sleep the Laurel and the Yew—
The Oak that triumph crowned, old Rome to glee.
Wreathed by Love's hand above the Gray or Blue,
Their leaflets touch to Immortality!

Women in America

FROM COLONIAL TIMES TO THE 20TH CENTURY

An Arno Press Collection

Andrews, John B. and W. D. P. Bliss. **History of Women in Trade Unions** (*Report on Conditions of Woman and Child Wage-Earners in the United States,* Vol. X; 61st Congress, 2nd Session, Senate Document No. 645). 1911

Anthony, Susan B. **An Account of the Proceedings on the Trial of Susan B. Anthony, on the Charge of Illegal Voting at the Presidential Election in November, 1872,** and on the Trial of Beverly W. Jones, Edwin T. Marsh and William B. Hall, the Inspectors of Election by Whom her Vote was Received. 1874

The Autobiography of a Happy Woman. 1915

Ayer, Harriet Hubbard. **Harriet Hubbard Ayer's Book:** A Complete and Authentic Treatise on the Laws of Health and Beauty. 1902

Barrett, Kate Waller. **Some Practical Suggestions on the Conduct of a Rescue Home.** *Including* **Life of Dr. Kate Waller Barrett** (Reprinted from *Fifty Years' Work With Girls* by Otto Wilson). [1903]

Bates, Mrs. D. B. **Incidents on Land and Water;** Or, Four Years on the Pacific Coast. 1858

Blumenthal, Walter Hart. **Women Camp Followers of the American Revolution.** 1952

Boothe, Viva B., editor. **Women in the Modern World** (*The Annals of the American Academy of Political and Social Science,* Vol. CXLIII, May 1929). 1929

Bowne, Eliza Southgate. **A Girl's Life Eighty Years Ago:** Selections from the Letters of Eliza Southgate Bowne. 1888

Brooks, Geraldine. **Dames and Daughters of Colonial Days.** 1900

Carola Woerishoffer: Her Life and Work. 1912

Clement, J[esse], editor. **Noble Deeds of American Women;** With Biographical Sketches of Some of the More Prominent. 1851

Crow, Martha Foote. **The American Country Girl.** 1915

De Leon, T[homas] C. **Belles, Beaux and Brains of the 60's.** 1909

de Wolfe, Elsie (Lady Mendl). **After All.** 1935

Dix, Dorothy (Elizabeth Meriwether Gilmer). **How to Win and Hold a Husband.** 1939

Donovan, Frances R. **The Saleslady.** 1929

Donovan, Frances R. **The Schoolma'am.** 1938

Donovan, Frances R. **The Woman Who Waits.** 1920

Eagle, Mary Kavanaugh Oldham, editor. **The Congress of Women,** Held in the Woman's Building, World's Columbian Exposition, Chicago, U.S.A., 1893. 1894

Ellet, Elizabeth F. **The Eminent and Heroic Women of America.** 1873

Ellis, Anne. **The Life of an Ordinary Woman.** 1929

[Farrar, Eliza W. R.] **The Young Lady's Friend.** By a Lady. 1836

Filene, Catherine, editor. **Careers for Women.** 1920

Finley, Ruth E. **The Lady of Godey's:** Sarah Josepha Hale. 1931 **Fragments of Autobiography.** 1974

Frost, John. **Pioneer Mothers of the West;** Or, Daring and Heroic Deeds of American Women. 1869

[Gilman], Charlotte Perkins Stetson. **In This Our World.** 1899

Goldberg, Jacob A. and Rosamond W. Goldberg. **Girls on the City Streets:** A Study of 1400 Cases of Rape. 1935

Grace H. Dodge: Her Life and Work. 1974

Greenbie, Marjorie Barstow. **My Dear Lady:** The Story of Anna Ella Carroll, the "Great Unrecognized Member of Lincoln's Cabinet." 1940

Hourwich, Andria Taylor and Gladys L. Palmer, editors. **I Am a Woman Worker:** A Scrapbook of Autobiographies. 1936

Howe, M[ark] A. De Wolfe. **Memories of a Hostess:** A Chronicle of Friendships Drawn Chiefly from the Diaries of Mrs. James T. Fields. 1922

Irwin, Inez Haynes. **Angels and Amazons:** A Hundred Years of American Women. 1934

Laughlin, Clara E. **The Work-a-Day Girl:** A Study of Some Present-Day Conditions. 1913

Lewis, Dio. **Our Girls.** 1871

Liberating the Home. 1974

Livermore, Mary A. **The Story of My Life;** Or, The Sunshine and Shadow of Seventy Years . . . To Which is Added Six of Her Most Popular Lectures. 1899

Lives to Remember. 1974

Lobsenz, Johanna. **The Older Woman in Industry.** 1929

MacLean, Annie Marion. **Wage-Earning Women.** 1910

Meginness, John F. **Biography of Frances Slocum, the Lost Sister of Wyoming:** A Complete Narrative of her Captivity of Wanderings Among the Indians. 1891

Nathan, Maud. **Once Upon a Time and Today.** 1933

[Packard, Elizabeth Parsons Ware]. **Great Disclosure of Spiritual Wickedness!!** In High Places. With an Appeal to the Government to Protect the Inalienable Rights of Married Women. 1865

Parsons, Alice Beal. **Woman's Dilemma.** 1926

Parton, James, et al. **Eminent Women of the Age:** Being Narratives of the Lives and Deeds of the Most Prominent Women of the Present Generation. 1869

Paton, Lucy Allen. **Elizabeth Cary Agassiz:** A Biography. 1919

Rayne, M[artha] L[ouise]. **What Can a Woman Do;** Or, Her Position in the Business and Literary World. 1893

Richmond, Mary E. and Fred S. Hall. **A Study of Nine Hundred and Eighty-Five Widows Known to Certain Charity Organization Societies in 1910.** 1913

Ross, Ishbel. **Ladies of the Press:** The Story of Women in Journalism by an Insider. 1936

Sex and Equality. 1974

Snyder, Charles McCool. **Dr. Mary Walker:** The Little Lady in Pants. 1962

Stow, Mrs. J. W. **Probate Confiscation:** Unjust Laws Which Govern Woman. 1878

Sumner, Helen L. **History of Women in Industry in the United**

States (*Report on Conditions of Woman and Child Wage-Earners in the United States,* Vol. IX; 61st Congress, 2nd Session, Senate Document No. 645). 1910

[Vorse, Mary H.] **Autobiography of an Elderly Woman.** 1911

Washburn, Charles. **Come into My Parlor:** A Biography of the Aristocratic Everleigh Sisters of Chicago. 1936

Women of Lowell. 1974

Woolson, Abba Gould. **Dress-Reform:** A Series of Lectures Delivered in Boston on Dress as it Affects the Health of Women. 1874

Working Girls of Cincinnati. 1974